HER STORY

SECOND EDITION

WOMEN IN CHRISTIAN TRADITION

BARBARA J. MacHAFFIE

FORTRESS PRESS / MINNEAPOLIS

HER STORY
Women in Christian Tradition
Second Edition

Scripture quotations are from the New Revised Standard Version Bible, copyright © 1989 by the Division of Christian Education of the National Council of the Churches of Christ in the USA and used by permission.

Additional acknowledgments are on pages 345–46.

Cover art: Vigee-LeBrun, Louise Elizabeth (1755–1842). Mme. Mole-Raymond (1759–1833), actress with the company of the Comedie italienne in Paris. 1786. Louvre, Paris, France. Photo © Erich Lessing/Art Resource, N.Y. Used by permission.
Cover design: Diana Running
Author photo: Jo McCulty © Marietta College. Used by permission.
Frontispiece: Photo © Art Resource, N.Y. Used by permission.
Interior design: Zan Ceeley, Trio Bookworks

Additional materials for further study of *Her Story* are available at www.herstorytext.com.

Library of Congress Cataloging-in-Publication Data

MacHaffie, Barbara J.
  Her story : women in Christian tradition / Barbara J. MacHaffie.—2nd ed.
    p. cm.
  Includes bibliographical references and index.
  ISBN 0-8006-3826-3 (pbk : alk. paper)
  1. Women in Christianity—History. 2. Women in Christianity—United States—History.
I. Title.
  BV639.W7M24 2006
  270.082—dc22

2005032802

The paper used in this publication meets the minimum requirements of American National Standard for Information Sciences—Permanence of Paper for Printed Library Materials, ANSI Z329.48-1984.

Manufactured in the U.S.A.

10   09   08   3   4   5   6   7   8   9   10

HER STORY

SECOND EDITION

Elizabeth Cady Stanton (1815–1902) and Susan Brownell Anthony (1820–1906), reformers.
Photograph, gelatin silver print, c.1870. Photographer: Sarony, Napoleon (1821–1896).
Location: National Portrait Gallery, Smithsonian Institution, Washington, D.C., U.S.A.
Photo: © Art Resource, N.Y. Used by permission.

To

Fraser Glen MacHaffie

Beverly Ann Zink-Sawyer

Ruth Patterson

and

in memory of my mother

Eleanor Katherine Gohrs Zink

CONTENTS

6. NINETEENTH-CENTURY PREACHERS AND SCHOLARS 195

7. AMERICAN WOMEN IN CATHOLICISM AND SECTARIANISM 233

INTRODUCTION TO THE
SECOND EDITION

Books surveying the history of Christianity have been traditionally "his stories"—describing the flaws and celebrating the achievements of great theologians, eloquent preachers, and powerful administrators. *Her Story* makes one contribution toward redressing the balance by illuminating in broad terms the forgotten history of over half of the Christian community. This survey brings historical knowledge and debates about women in the Christian past before a wide audience of students and members of communities of faith by asking probing questions: What roles did women play in leadership structures, in religious ceremonies, and in the creation of a theological tradition? What roles did they find for themselves outside "official" institutional churches or the formalities of worship? How were females and the feminine (characteristics assigned by cultural traditions to women) regarded in devotional and theological writing?

Her Story first appeared in 1986 and depended upon feminist historical and theological scholarship that was still in its early stages. Published several years later, the accompanying text, *Readings in Her Story*, used primary sources to illustrate and expand upon the conclusions of the first book. Both of the books covered biblical history, the early church, the western medieval past, and the Protestant Reformation. To make the contents of these surveys more manageable in size, the last five chapters of each text focused on women in the context of American religion.

Her Story and *Readings in Her Story* have been influenced and shaped by the way scholarship on women and religion had evolved by the early 1980s. The books depend upon historians who collected facts about women in Christian history both as individuals and as a group in an effort to make known what was previously unknown or ignored. They also reflect a new approach to the past that frankly recognizes that Christian tradition and the biblical text have often served to support patriarchy and functioned to oppress and degrade women. Rather than claiming that the Christian past and the Bible should be discarded, however, *Her Story* and *Readings in Her Story* go on to support Eleanor McLaughlin's statement that "Christian faith and institutions have been at certain times and under certain conditions radically supportive of women and informed by women's experience."[1] Finding evidence to support this latter claim has led in some unexpected directions. Readers are taken outside the culturally dominant Catholic and Protestant groups to movements such as Shakerism and Gnosticism. They are also forced to consider the personal expressions of faith found in letters, diaries, and devotional writings alongside of theological works and sermons on which Christian history has traditionally depended.

In preparing material to accompany a CD-ROM edition of the original texts in 2002, it became apparent that a massive amount of significant new scholarship on the topics covered in them had appeared and needed to be incorporated. A new edition of *Her Story*, therefore, was begun in 2003. While the general contours of this historical landscape remain the same across the two editions, many of the details of that landscape have been filled in and refined. What is different about this second edition? The readings from primary sources are now combined with the main text into one book. It also incorporates new directions in interpreting existing historical data. Women in the early church, for example, were able to claim power and opportunities for themselves in the first decades of Christian history only to see that power eroded. The first edition of *Her Story* examines reasons for this; the new edition provides an even fuller explanation by taking into account, for example, Karen Torjesen's argument that the honor/shame code of the ancient world and the building of Christian basilicas are relevant here. The second edition also qualifies some of the claims originally made in the early years of feminist historical studies. Thus, Jesus and the Gospels are no longer seen as radical exceptions to the views of the entire Jewish establishment on women, but rather representative of a strand of Judaism that was more open to women.

This new edition also includes some new topics such as the status of Mormon women and the emergence of womanist theology. And it offers more nuanced and developed interpretations of events and personalities (such as the Reformation advocate Argula von Grumbach) that are given brief attention in the first edition. Finally, this new text attempts to clarify material in the first edition in light of over fifteen years of classroom use.

As with all brief surveys of long periods of history, this one has inevitably omitted material that some readers may have wished to explore. In the post-Reformation period the focus is on the United States. The history of women in modern European Christianity is both well developed and important, and this text can only suggest that it be examined through such tools as Dale Johnson's *Women and Religion in Britain and Ireland*.[2] This new edition also does not include a separate chapter on women and the Bible and does not attempt to explore the history of women in ancient Israel. Rather, it is interested in how the Bible has been interpreted throughout Christian history to oppress women and to empower them. As part of this interpretive history, *Her Story* considers the principles of feminist biblical interpretation and applies some of them to the New Testament as a way to more fully understand the situation of women in the early church. The spotlight, therefore, is always on women in the Christian tradition; and the Bible, like that tradition, is examined as both a source of patriarchy and liberation.

In an effort to make the history accessible and effective for use by colleges, seminaries, and church study groups, this edition has some additional new features. The bibliography has been updated; it is by no means exhaustive but does contain many newer books, essays, and articles that have informed the writing of the second edition. A Web site has been developed to provide access to questions for discussion, additional primary source readings, a glossary, Web links to aid in further study, and a research guide for writing in the history of women and Christian tradition. The Web site name is www.herstorytext.com.

As mentioned, a number of selected primary source readings illustrating important themes have been included directly after each chapter of *Her Story*. In these readings you will encounter the voices of men and women who argue persuasively with words of reason and beauty, who shout angrily with words of protest and condemnation, and who even question the way we use words. Here you will recover some of the voices of women who have been silent for so long. I have often chosen readings that are discussed directly in the main text, while other readings have been authored by men and women similarly highlighted. All the additional readings illustrate important themes and issues in the story of women in Christian history and serve to remind readers that the tradition has both patriarchal and feminist threads running through it. Readers might find it helpful to consult the entire text from which these excerpts have been taken in order to understand fully the development of important arguments.

I owe an enormous debt of gratitude to many people who have made both editions of *Her Story* and the publication of accompanying readings possible. Marietta College, where I have taught since 1983, offered computer facilities for the first edition, grant money (with help from the Lilly Foundation) for the original collection of readings, and, most recently, a sabbatical year and a research award to enable me to write a second edition. In particular, the staff of Dawes Library at the College has never tired of securing interlibrary loans and tracking down obscure journal articles. The original publications were made possible by the work of Phyllis Zoerckler; this new edition was only brought to a successful completion with the help of Mary Zimmer, Susan Dyer, Paula Lewis, and student Brandon Donelson-Sims. Kate Skrebutenas, dear friend and reference librarian at Princeton Theological Seminary, made my weeks there happy and productive ones, and Union Theological Seminary in Richmond welcomed me on campus for four weeks of research during my sabbatical year. I continue to enjoy working with the editorial staff at Fortress Press; names have changed but their enthusiasm for these books has not. In the early 1980s Thelma McGill-Cobbler saw the first text through publication. Michael West supported and improved the 1992 book of readings, the CD-ROM, and this second edition, and Zan Ceeley is a new but much valued editorial partner. I have over the years continued to be grateful to Martin E. Marty, Robert T. Handy, Freda Gardner, Elizabeth Howell Verdesi, Kathleen Cannon, and Carolyn DeSwarte Gifford for their work on the original manuscript of *Her Story*. I have tried in this new edition to incorporate some of their suggestions that could not be accommodated in the 1986 text. One thing that has not changed over the past twenty years is the affection and appreciation I have for the three people to whom *Her Story* is dedicated.

HER STORY

SECOND EDITION

Orante figure. Early Christian fresco.
Location: Catacomb of the Giordani, Rome, Italy.
Photo: Scala / Art Resource, N.Y. Used by permission.

Chapter 1

WOMEN AND THE
EARLY CHURCHES

THE CHALLENGE OF
EARLY CHRISTIAN HISTORY

Anyone who wishes to study the status of women in the first six centuries of Christian history is faced with a challenging task. During this period, the church spread beyond Judaism and Palestine into the vast expanse of Greco-Roman culture. It was both persecuted and elevated to a position of eminence, all the while struggling to come to terms with the intellectual movements of the ancient world. Beliefs and practices varied greatly from place to place and century to century. There was no clearly defined and universally accepted tradition passed directly from Jesus to a body of faithful leaders. Recent scholarship points instead to a struggle within the church over many issues, including roles for women.[1] At the same time, our sources of information for this period are scarce and often fragmentary and ambiguous. Yet the early years of Christianity are vital to the status of women, for they established attitudes and practices that still continue in the Christian community.

Biblical scholars and theologians make some important suggestions for those who want to explore the history of women in the early church.[2] They remind us that our sources of information have been written and interpreted by men, often with unfortunate results. We have overlooked, for example, the information in the New Testament on the work of women and instead assumed that the church was a "man's church." We have forgotten that most sources tell us only what men thought about women. We have assumed also that the categories such as "apostle" and "prophet" only include men unless women are specifically mentioned. We should instead remember that what we know about the activities of women probably only represents the tip of the iceberg. It is likely that women participated in the early development of the church to a much greater extent than our sources imply.

Learning about the history of women during this period has been aided by several new historical strategies beyond that of simply reading early Christian texts with suspicion. Scholars have been looking increasingly at archaeology, art (specifically mosaics and frescoes), and inscriptions to provide material about women. They are also looking more carefully at the Jewish, Greek, and Roman contexts in which Christian women lived in an attempt to discern where their experiences may have conformed to these cultures and where they deviated.

Both Greco-Roman and Jewish cultures present a far more complex picture of women than was previously assumed by scholars. Greco-Roman culture was dominated by an honor/shame ideology in which men were rewarded for public effort and achievement while women were to guard their "shame" or chastity by remaining obedient and secluded.[3] Yet Roman women appeared freely in a variety of public places as well as managed their households. It was not unusual for wealthy women to be patrons of clubs, and both Greek and Roman women were accepted as priestesses and prophetesses.

In the first century, Judaism—so central to the development of Christianity—also reveals diverse perspectives on women and a wide range of practices. The dominant model of a virtuous woman was one who remained at home and obeyed her husband, a theme reflected in the book of Esther, for example. Women were not required to fulfill most religious obligations apart from dietary and sexual laws and the lighting of Sabbath candles. Although we get only a glimpse of first-century Judaism from later rabbinic literature, strong continuities concerning attitudes toward women are present across the centuries. Many rabbis regarded women as socially and religiously inferior to men, and some even expressed contempt for them. Not only were men cautioned against speaking to women in public, but also women were not permitted to be witnesses in a court of law, nor were they to be counted in a quorum necessary for the formation of a synagogue congregation. At the temple in Jerusalem, they were to be restricted to an outer court; in the synagogues, they were to be seated separately and were not permitted to read aloud or to assume any public position. Perhaps most significant, they were not permitted to study the scriptures. One rabbi vigorously made this point when he wrote, "Rather should the words of the Torah be burned than to be entrusted to a woman."[4]

Yet there was disagreement among the rabbis themselves on some of these points. A minority argued that women should indeed study the Torah and that both women and men be permitted to initiate divorce proceedings. And of course the day-to-day reality of women's lives often challenged official teaching. Women and men were forced, for example, to relate and communicate in public places simply to keep society functioning. Indeed, inscriptions from synagogues in various parts of the Roman Empire give women leadership titles such as "mother" and "elder." Bernadette J. Brooten concludes that these titles were more than honorific; they reveal that women had liturgical, teaching, judicial, and financial responsibilities.[5] Both Jewish and Greco-Roman culture, therefore, reinforced the silencing and subordination of women but at the same time made it possible for Christianity to accept active women members and powerful women leaders.[6]

THE PROMINENCE OF WOMEN IN THE EARLIEST CHURCHES

In light of the Jewish practice that defined a synagogue congregation by the number of circumcised males present, the fact that early Christian communities had inclusive membership was unusual. We have clear evidence, however, that women were included as full members of early Christian communities. For example, Saul (before his conversion) sets out to arrest both men and women who had adopted the new faith of Christianity (Acts 8:3; 9:2). Another passage in Acts (17:11-12) claims that in Beroea, a Macedonian city, both men and women "received the word with all eagerness, examining the Scriptures daily to see if these things were so." Also, Luke's Gospel, which is a rich source of material on Jesus' teachings about women and his ministry to them, contains evidence that it was shaped by a social context in which large numbers of women were interested in and responding to the Christian message.[7] Some historians argue that women were in the majority in the early Christian congregations; they use comments made by ancient writers who ridicule Christianity as woman's religion and inventories of women's clothing found at early Christian sites as evidence.[8] Historians also suggest that this large female membership resulted from the variety of significant roles offered women, as well as the fact that the early church banned infanticide. While these new roles were shaped by and similar to what women were doing in Jewish and Greco-Roman cultures, the Christian community offered them to a broader range of women and in a more radical form, as we shall see.

What can we learn about the lives and ministries of these early Christian women? While direct evidence is limited and women's ministries are not well defined, we do have hints at what was happening from a variety of early Christian documents. Historians generally agree that women had a decisive part in the creation of the church and played a more prominent role in the first generation of Christianity than they did in later centuries.[9] One reason for this was the flexible and informal organization of the church. There appeared to be no division between ministers and lay people; leadership was shared among members. Every member, male and female, was regarded as having certain gifts from the Holy Spirit that could be used in the service of the community. Some of these gifts were given to members who had been appointed in a formal way by the community to do a variety of tasks. Others were given directly and indiscriminately by the Holy Spirit and were simply recognized by the community. But even more important than church organization was the way in which the Gospel tradition and the Gospels themselves, along with the writing of Paul, could be interpreted as moving women beyond silence and subordination.

Jesus and the Gospels

A significant number of female characters appear in the Gospels and a significant amount of text is devoted to their stories. They do, in fact, take on theological significance as they reveal Jesus' identity and mission and model the nature of true discipleship. The Gospel writers also present Jesus as someone who questions all social structures including the honor/shame ideology of the ancient world.

Discipleship in the New Testament breaks down barriers of gender, class, race, and culture; and so women, while rarely called "disciples," are described as those who follow and serve Jesus. Luke names specific women along with an unidentified group who travel with Jesus, and the latter are also mentioned in Mark and Matthew (Luke 8:1-3). Their "service" may have been domestic, but it is also possible that the Gospel writers may have been using an early Christian term involving proclamation.[10] In all of the Gospels, most women are portrayed as effective disciples. They are models of a spirit-filled life in Luke and they are "good seed" that bear fruit in Mark. The Samaritan woman in John shows more faith than Nicodemus (John 3:1-21), and Mark compares the female disciples favorably to the male followers who abandon Jesus (Mark 14:32-50 and 15:40).

As effective disciples, women in the Gospel tradition fill the role of apostle in some instances because they convey important messages about Jesus to others. The Samaritan woman recognizes Jesus as a prophet who discerns her life situation (perhaps a series of levirate marriages), but she then grasps his messianic identity and obeys the command to tell her neighbors. Mary Magdalene, likewise, assumes an apostolic role not only in conveying the message that Jesus had risen from the dead, but also by verifying her claim in describing Jesus' appearance to her. Some scholars suggest that Mary's example may have been the foundation for female power and leadership in the early church. The Christian community, with no basis in Gospel fact, later identified Mary as a penitent whore, possibly to diminish her influence.[11]

In his teachings and his actions, Jesus turns established social structures upside down: the kingdom of God values service, humility, and faith rather than political and religious power. "Family" means those who are loyal to Jesus and includes those on the margins of society. It is within this context that Jesus challenges the gender rules of his culture. A woman is was hemorrhaging appears unaccompanied in a crowd (Matt. 9:18-26; Mark 5:24-34; Luke 8:40-56). She not only touches Jesus, a strange man, but she extends her impurity to him. Yet Jesus both heals and commends her for her faith. In a similar violation of cultural norms, Jesus speaks to the woman at the well and takes a drink from her (John 4:1-42). She is a Samaritan, a group hated by the Jews, and a female, but Jesus still engages her in significant theological conversation. And although scholars disagree on the best interpretation of the story of Mary and Martha (Luke 10:38-42), Jesus does seem willing to teach a woman seated at his feet much as male students surrounded a rabbi.

While much in the Gospel tradition could be used to support the full participation of women in the Christian community, there is also some ambivalence in the material. Jesus does not appoint a woman to his group of twelve intimate disciples, and he does not make any statements on male/female equality. His teachings on divorce could be seen as forcing women to stay in abusive marriages or to endure years of isolation with no chance to remarry. Usually unnamed and rarely spoken to, the women of Luke especially are relegated to the passive roles of listening and pondering. Luke has been very influential in the creation of a Christian tradition that does not affirm female leadership but relegates women to the margins of the community.[12]

The Writings of the Apostle Paul

Aside from the creation stories, the writings of the apostle Paul have been cited most frequently in discussions about the status of women in the Christian community. A controversial figure on the question of women, Paul has been condemned as the eternal enemy of women and has been celebrated as the only consistent spokesperson for the liberation of women in the New Testament. The truth may lie somewhere in between.

Paul was probably not the author of certain passages often cited in support of the view that he degraded women. It is likely that these passages (Col. 3:18; Eph. 5:21-33; Titus 2:3-5; 1 Tim. 2:8-15 and 5:3-16) originated at a later time and reflected changes in the environment of the early Christian community as well as its organizational structure. In the eyes of many contemporary interpreters, the material that does come from Paul himself reflects a marked ambivalence toward women. He was a man in conflict. On the one hand, Paul knew the transforming power of the gospel and clearly recognized that relationships in the human community would be altered dramatically as a result. On the other hand, certain features of his Greco-Roman and Jewish backgrounds intruded upon his belief that women and men should be full participants in the churches. Keep in mind, too, that his letters were occasional pieces to specific mission situations and not intended to present a systematic position.[13] By the end of the second century, therefore, such diverse writers as the author of 1 Timothy (who counseled women to be silent and submissive) and the *Acts of Paul and Thecla* (in which Thecla preached, traveled, and made independent decisions) could claim Paul as an authority.

Paul's recognition of the radical difference that life in Christ makes to people is summed up in Galatians 3:28, probably inspired by a statement used in early Christian baptisms. The Jewish male of Paul's day was expected to thank God daily that he was not a Gentile, a slave, or a woman. The man of Greek culture used a similar formula to express the same sentiments, and this text may have been an attempt to parallel and contradict these expressions. In the Christian community, these natural and social barriers broke down. The values, roles, and customs of the world were replaced by a new reality. But what did these words really mean in terms of gender relations? They were given diverse interpretations as Christianity developed. Some said they refer to equality in the heavenly kingdom of God. Another interpretation said that male and female differences disappeared for the female ascetics who had given up reproduction and taken on male personality traits.[14] Still others believed it was important to see that this new order of existence applied not only to a person's relationship with God but also to the actual life of the congregation. Paul in fact indicates that conditions expected in the future kingdom are in some ways already realized in the community of believers, and he warmly greets and commends women workers in the churches.

First Corinthians 7:1-40 is a lengthy discussion on the subject of marriage. Clues in the text indicate that women in the congregation had adopted a variety of lifestyles, including celibacy and church membership (both with and without their husbands). There is considerable disagreement over the meaning of this passage for their status, but scholars argue that Paul seems to be on uncomfortable ground here. His comments on the marriage relationship are unusual in light of his own Jewish and Hellenistic background as well as the cultural situation in which he is writing. Marriage, as he describes it, shows a surprising degree of mutuality between husband and wife. There are six passages in I Corinthians 7 (3-4, 10-11, 12-13, 14, 16, 32-33) that suggest reciprocal or equal responsibilities in the relationship. He claims, for example, that "the wife does not have authority over her own body, but the husband does; likewise the husband does not have authority over his own body, but the wife does." This is a remarkable statement for a man writing in the first century, although Elizabeth Castelli cautions us to ask whether men and women experience this text in the same way. Often physically weaker than men, women who surrender their bodies are much more vulnerable to abuse.[15]

In this passage, Paul also plants a seed that has the effect of reinforcing a new social alternative for women. He presents celibacy as a way of living because he believes the end of time to be near. Women can choose not to marry and raise children. Later on, the church shaped Paul's ideas on the renunciation of marriage into a lifestyle that was often liberating for women. Women were eventually given a vocational status in which they are not only independent but also accepted as equals by their male coworkers.

The ambivalent attitudes Paul held about women become even more obvious in I Cor. 11:2-16. He clearly assumed in verse 5 that women can be vehicles of God's spirit. They, like men, can pray and prophesy in the congregation, and by prophesying, Paul meant intelligible preaching and teaching that built up the faith of the church. The prophets at Corinth seemed to hold rank and power. In this passage, however, Paul also launches into a "bad-tempered tirade" in which traditional honor/shame conventions take over.[16] This passage appears within a long section on the proper way to conduct worship. It seems that Paul was concerned with curbing the abuses and stopping the chaos in the Corinthian church. Antoinette Clark Wire argues that the old established families, which originally made up the Corinthian congregation, were joined by individuals who brought with them an ecstatic and participatory form of worship.[17] People were praying, singing, and prophesying all at once; they were speaking in tongues without interpreters and women were carrying out these activities without head coverings. Paul reacts by insisting that women cover their heads while praying or prophesying in order to maintain decency and order.

In the process of defending his position, Paul explicitly argues for the subordination of women to men. The head covering was necessary because it symbolized the subjection of the female. God was the head of Christ, Christ the head of the male, and the male the head of the female. Paul turns to rabbinic Judaism to defend his position in verses 8 and 9. Woman was made from man and in his image, according to Genesis 2. Also, she was made *for* man, to exist as his helper. It is interesting that he does not use the argument of I Timothy that states that women are subordinate because they are morally inferior to men. He then supplements this theological defense with an appeal in verse 13 to what was proper or customary in his social setting. Paul suddenly interrupts himself in verses 11 and 12 with a comment that seems to undermine his argument. He is unable to keep himself from making a qualifying remark, showing the deep impact that the transforming power of the gospel had on him. These verses express a degree of mutual support between male and female that is more compatible with Gal. 3:28. The general lines of Paul's argument in I Corinthians 11 follow the presuppositions of his culture; by inserting these two verses, however, he points to a new set of assumptions operating in the body of Christ.

Wire draws our attention to another important passage, I Cor. 14:33b-36. This text commands that women keep silent in the churches. Scholars disagree over whether in fact Paul wrote these verses since they could have been added later to the original letter. Some believe Paul is quoting his enemies in order to refute them, while others argue that Paul is objecting to disruptive speech. Wolfgang Stegemann claims that while women who carried out religious rituals could be accepted in Paul's culture, they could not engage in theological debate, which, he argues, Paul objects to here.[18] It is also possible that Paul is silencing the disorderly female prophets we read about in chapter 11. What is most significant about all these approaches is that the text can be read as not undermining Paul's egalitarianism.

MINISTRIES OF WOMEN
IN THE EARLY CHURCHES

Evangelists and House Church Leaders

Women were clearly involved in the spread of Christianity and in the establishment of new congregations, which met in private houses. In Romans 16, Paul refers to women who have been his coworkers in the evangelization of the Hellenistic world and commends Mary, Tryphaena, Tryphosa, and Persis for having "labored hard" in the Lord. In the same chapter, he pays tribute to the outstanding missionary work, including teaching doctrine to Apollo, of Priscilla (or Prisca) and her husband Aquila. Priscilla's significance may be highlighted by the fact that she is mentioned before her husband in four out of six references, a literary device to suggest importance. Some biblical scholars believe that Priscilla's role in teaching doctrine is reported without comment because it was not an unusual role for women.[19] In Phil. 4:2, Euodia and Syntyche are described as women who have worked or "struggled" side by side with Paul. To emphasize their importance, Paul mentions them in the body of the letter rather than the salutation. There is no indication in these passages that women were subordinate to or dependent upon Paul.

House churches were crucial to the success of the early mission efforts because they provided support and sustenance to the growing Christian congregations. They were the places in which the Lord's Supper was celebrated and the gospel preached. It is recorded that women provided the facilities for some groups, especially if the women were wealthy and prominent members of the community. Acts 16:14, for example, mentions Lydia, a successful businesswoman who offered her house to the Christian church. She is baptized along with her household, which she appears to have ruled. Although many interpreters of the New Testament in the past have translated the name in Col. 4:14 as the male name "Nymphas," it is generally agreed that the verse correctly reads, "Nympha and the church in her house." The house of Mary, the mother of John Mark , was also used in this way (Acts 12:12).

Households in the ancient world were places in which women taught, disciplined family members and servants, and managed material resources. If wealthy, women also frequently presided over groups of visitors under their patronage. Managing the household required the same qualities as serving the community, including humility, sobriety, and a sense of order. Although we cannot be sure of the role women played in the worship and administration of house churches, leadership roles would not have been surprising.[20] The churches conceived of themselves as households of God. In the New Testament, women are not only described as the patronesses of house churches but also as their leaders. The letter to Philemon greets Apphia "our sister," who, together with Philemon and Archippus, was a leader of the house church at Colossae. Also, in 1 Thess. 5:12 Paul commands the church to give respect and recognition to the laborers and coworkers who "have charge of you in the Lord." In other places he uses these identical descriptive phrases to refer to his female colleagues. He believed that the authority of Euodia and Syntyche (Philippians 4), who worked with him at Philippi, was so great that their dissension would do serious damage to the community.

Leadership Roles beyond House Churches

Phoebe appears to have been a prominent woman in the early church. Paul calls her both *diakonos* and a *prostasis* in Romans 16, titles that have been misinterpreted traditionally. *Diakonos*, although grammatically masculine, is usually translated as "deaconess," implying that Phoebe only did the subservient and female-oriented tasks of the deaconess in later Christian history. Yet when Paul uses this word in other contexts, he is referring to individuals who preach and teach as official congregational leaders. Furthermore, *prostasis* is usually translated as "helper" but in the literature of the first century, the word commonly indicates a leader, president, or superintendent. The word means "to rule or manage" when used as a verb. Biblical scholars, however, have also suggested that *prostasis* may mean "patroness," a way to indicate that Phoebe, in Roman tradition, offered money and protection to congregations and acquired prestige in return. It is likely that Phoebe not only held great authority in Cenchreae but also was widely respected throughout the Christian community.

Another female leader of the early church is probably revealed in Rom. 16:7. Here, Andronicus and Junia are commended for their outstanding work in spreading the gospel. Again, translators in the past, finding it inconceivable that a woman would be called "apostle," used the male name "Junias." Junia, however, was a common female name in the first century, and church leaders as late as the medieval period had no problem accepting the female form. Gospel accounts of the risen Jesus also reveal that women could fulfill the requirements for the role of apostle. In their direct confrontation with the risen Jesus, women receive a commission from him to preach the gospel.[21]

Female Prophets

Some ministries in which women were clearly involved continued long after female teaching and sacramental functions were officially discouraged. Women, for example, filled the role of prophet in the early churches. Prophets were not formally ordained or appointed by the congregations; rather, their authority was based on their reception of immediate revelation and inspiration from the Holy Spirit. Such revelation involved the clarification of texts, instruction in Christian living, and the discernment of God's will for individuals and communities. In this way, women contributed to the construction of early Christian teaching. In some instances, it seems that they presided over the life and worship of individual congregations. The *Didache*, a manual of church order from the second century, claims that the traveling prophets filled a role of great importance, some celebrating the Lord's Supper. The four daughters of Philip were prophets (Acts 21:9) who ministered first in Caesarea and then moved to Hierapolis in Asia Minor. The female prophet from Thyatira in Rev. 2:20 is also portrayed as holding great power in the community.

Montanus and two women, Priscilla and Maxima, led a religious movement that developed at the end of the second century. The Montanists, as their followers came to be called, enthusiastically proclaimed the Christian message, believing themselves to be channels for divine truth. They thus continued the tradition that God speaks through believers other than church officials. There is evidence in the Montanist movement that women were given access to leadership positions, although women were bishops and presbyters only in Montanist groups that split from the main movement. Women such as Priscilla, whose oracles were collected and circulated in writing, were held in great honor as "prophetesses."

What lay behind this openness to women at a time when subordination was becoming a Christian norm? The Montanists believed that since Eve was the first to eat of the tree of knowledge, women were more likely than men to be recipients of divine wisdom and revelation. They also did not discriminate on the basis of sex because of Paul's statement that "in Christ, there is neither male nor female." As happened in subsequent centuries, their emphasis on the direct inspiration of the Holy Spirit invalidated gender distinctions. But perhaps most important, Montanists believed the end of the world was near, allowing for a radical disruption of the status quo.

Sacramental Ministries

It is not clear whether women functioned as presbyters or priests in the early churches and whether they baptized people and celebrated the Lord's Supper, although there are strong suggestions that they did. There are fragments of information from archaeological discoveries that suggest a wide role for women in these early years; no inscription or painting, however, is unambiguous. Some Greek-language tombstones that refer to women as presbyters have been located, although it is not certain whether these women were presbyters in Jewish or Christian congregations. Also, one fresco from a Roman catacomb appears to depict a group of women jointly celebrating the Lord's Supper, probably during a catacomb vigil to mark the anniversary of the death of a Christian friend. These figures are all characterized by upswept hair, slender necks, sloping shoulders, and a hint of earrings. The figure actually breaking the bread is clothed in distinctively female dress. Another third-century Roman fresco from the Priscilla catacombs in Rome called "The Veiling" has been interpreted traditionally as a wedding ceremony. A prominent woman holding a scroll, a seated bishop touching her shoulder, and a young man in the background holding a veil in shades not typical of wedding colors suggest, however, that this is the ordination of a presbyter.

Many groups that advocate the ordination of women to the priesthood also point to a mosaic in the Roman church of Santa Praxedis. The mosaic shows Mary and two female saints along with a woman identified as Bishop Theodora. Some scholars indicate that her coif shows she is not married and is, therefore, neither the wife nor the mother of Bishop Theodo. Rather, she is a bishop in her own right.

The vehemence and frequency with which the sacramental functions of women are denounced also suggest that these activities may have been going on in some places. By the end of the second century, the writings of theologians and pastors as well as books of discipline and church order repeatedly condemn such activities. The need for repetition may bear witness to the continuing failure of such commands. Manuals such as the *Didascalia Apostolorum* (a book of church order from Syria, written between 200 and 250 C.E.) and *Apostolic Church Order* (a document regulating church practices from Egypt, written around 300 C.E.) prohibit women from baptizing or conducting the Lord's Supper. The general message was that women could not exercise authority over men and could not speak at the church's public gatherings. Although some leaders permitted women to instruct other women in private and their husbands at home, others forbade women even to write about their faith because this was similar to teaching. Similar sentiments are seen, finally, in a letter sent by Pope Gelasius to the bishops of southern Italy and Sicily, an area strongly influenced by Byzantine culture and perhaps Montanism and Gnosticism. In one of the papal decrees in the letter the pope condemns female priests who were officiating at sacred altars.

CREATING A PATRIARCHAL CHURCH

As the church grew and became more structured, it gradually underwent a process of "patriarchalization" in which women were excluded from positions of leadership and authority. Historian Virginia Burrus writes that it is difficult to point to one clearly defined moment of downfall.[22] The process, however, had started by the end of the first century and by the fifth century hostility toward prominent women had circumscribed their activities. They were restricted to ascetic communities and the clearly subordinate diaconate. This change was caused by a complex set of factors, and one of the most significant was the emergence of patriarchal texts that were accepted as authoritative by more and more congregations.

A strong protest against the leadership of women in the early churches is registered in several passages of the New Testament (Col. 3:18; Eph. 5:21-33; Titus 2:3-5; 1 Tim. 2:8-15; and 5:3–16). These passages were probably written between 80 and 125 C.E. Although this is a matter of scholarly conjecture, the arguments for a later dating are persuasive.[23] The texts do not describe the status of women in all the churches but instead reflect an unsettled state of affairs and try to impose upon the Christian communities the patriarchal standards of the ancient world. This approach eventually prevailed in the Christian churches but not without difficulty. Throughout the early centuries, church authorities, as we have seen, continued to rule against the leadership of women, an indication that women persisted in assuming authoritative roles in some places.

The passages listed in the paragraph above come from a school or tradition of writers influenced by Paul, although the style and vocabulary are different from what appear to be the genuine works of the apostle. The outlook or perspective of these chapters tends to preserve the more traditional patriarchal dimension of Paul's writing. The dominant images of women are submissive wife and mother. Women are commanded to be subject to their husbands in Col. 3:18 and Eph. 5:22. Obedience to the husband as God's chosen authority is a message to be passed on from older women to younger ones in Titus 2:5. The relationship between the head and the body is used as an analogy both for the relationship of Christ to the church and the husband to the wife. This analogy has had lasting implications for women in the Christian tradition. Men were identified with the spirit and mind while women were associated with that which is sensual, earthy, and related to physical needs and desires. Men were instructed to love their wives, but, as one biblical scholar puts it, Christians were simply exchanging "pagan patriarchy" for a "love patriarchy."[24]

These letters also provide a theological rationale for the subordination of female to male that goes beyond what Paul suggests in I Corinthians II. The first and second letters to Timothy attribute this status to the fact that woman was created after man and that she was easily deceived by the devil. Second Timothy 3:6 reflects this by declaring that false beliefs may be spread by weak women throughout the community. First Timothy suggests that women may compensate for this transgression through obedience in marriage and childbearing. The option of celibacy to work for the kingdom of God is not presented.

Appropriate behavior for women in the churches, the "households of God," is also prescribed. First Timothy 2 prohibits women from speaking or teaching and from exercising any kind of authority in the congregations. Questions on religious matters were to be discussed at home under the guidance of a wise husband. The bishop is defined carefully as "the husband of one wife" and is to be judged by his success in exercising patriarchal authority over his own household. Thus, the leadership of the Christian churches is defined as male. The restrictions placed on women in these sources eventually came to be the normal pattern for the Christian community.

What were the reasons behind the curtailment of female leadership in the latter part of the first century that is reflected in these texts? By the time the letters discussed in this section were composed, the churches had begun to realize that the end of the world was not upon them. Instead, they had to prepare for a long stay in the world, which, for most congregations, also meant coming to terms with the Greco-Roman culture around them. That culture was often hostile to Christianity, charging it with secret cannibalism and disloyalty to the Roman emperor and imposing harsh penalties upon its supporters. The dominant culture was also experiencing turmoil over women's roles. It was a culture, as we have already observed, dominated by an honor/ shame ideology in which virtuous men pursued honor and success in the public sphere while virtuous women protected their "shame" or chastity by being discreet, subordinate, and secluded. In reality, however, Greco-Roman women were doing such things as traveling and controlling their own property. The early Christians may have wished to draw as little attention to themselves as possible in this hostile and insecure environment. They adopted and even surpassed traditional cultural views on appropriate behavior for women and in so doing began to stifle female leadership in the churches.[25]

In addition to the emergence of authoritative patriarchal texts, other factors served to erode female ministry. A less frequently articulated but nevertheless real concern of early churchmen was the fear that menstruating women would somehow pollute the worship services and sacraments of the church. Ancient cultures regarded menstruating women with fear and suspicion. We can only speculate on reasons for this. The monthly cycle may have linked women with cosmic forces because it resembled the cycle of the moon. Blood was almost universally regarded as a mysterious, awe-full life force—yet women bled and did not die. Whatever the reasons, menstruation was seen as giving women power and this power was believed to be evil and destructive ultimately. Among people who believed that the whole cosmos could be upset if nature intruded into human culture, women were viewed as a source of foul contamination. And so menstrual blood was thought to rust iron and sour new wine. It was even feared that sexual intercourse with a menstruating woman would cause castration. Women were often isolated from the community each month and rigid controls were placed on them.

These attitudes passed into Judaism, Greco-Roman culture, and eventually into Christianity, although they did compete with beliefs that only the soul could be unclean and that the secretions of the body were ordained by God. Whether Christian women initially obeyed Jewish purity laws is not clear, but by the third century the church was increasingly turning to the Old Testament for guidance. One early Christian bishop, Dionysius the Great, urged that restrictions be placed on menstruating women. Subsequent church councils repeated his view that "impure persons" should not be allowed near the altar. In some places, this prohibition was extended to say that menstruating women should not even enter a church. During the seventh century, for example, one archbishop of Canterbury proclaimed that "women shall not in the time of impurity enter into a church, or communicate."[26] Women may not have seen these restrictions as unreasonable because the purity tradition in ancient cultures was such a strong one.[27]

Finally, women were probably eased out of certain ministries as the church underwent organizational changes, particularly as the church found growing favor with the governing elite of the Roman Empire. In the early decades of church history, the concept of ministry included a variety of tasks and included all the members of the community. The Holy Spirit, who acted through the community but was not bound by it, gave the gifts needed to fulfill these distinctive services. By the fourth century, however, a gradual shift in the church's understanding of ministry and in its organizational structure had started to occur. The church became more hierarchical. A superior ministry, which included teaching and sacramental functions, began to emerge over and above an inferior laity. The church took as its organizational model the civil service of the Roman Empire. More and more power was vested in the offices of bishop and presbyter or priest, and those who filled them were selected by other members in positions of power. Because of its bias against placing women in positions of authority and superiority, it was impossible for the Christian community to select women as bishops and presbyters.[28]

Furthermore, once the church acquired legal status, it began to build basilicas as places for public worship. The basilica in Roman culture had political meaning as places where public officials presided; they were different architecturally from the pagan temples that the church sought to avoid. Prominent women would have been presiding in public and political space, a violation of Roman gender ideology.[29]

A new look at the documentary and material evidence shows that women had a variety of roles and were surprisingly important in the earliest Christian communities. Their position, however, eroded fairly quickly for many different reasons after this flurry of participation in ministries that were open to both men and women. Women were shunted into the special "orders" of widow, deaconess, and virgin as male leaders struggled to gain the upper hand.[30]

WIDOWS

One role for women that is dealt with extensively in early Christian literature is that of widow. Originally widows were simply the worthy recipients of charity from churches, provided that they were known for their righteous lives and completely without other resources. They were enrolled or registered throughout the early centuries of church history as eligible for donations along with orphans, although whether they belonged to a structured organization is not clear.

By the third century, however, widows also began to appear in many places as members of a special "order" to which they were appointed. To qualify for this special appointment, a woman generally had to be over sixty years old (fifty in some places) and married only once. She was obligated to live a life of complete chastity. She was not ordained but simply appointed or "named," often in a simple public ritual. Her main task was that of prayer for the whole church and for her benefactors. Behind this task was the ancient belief that God heard the prayers of the widowed and oppressed. The widow was thought to be particularly effective in praying for the sick and was sometimes encouraged to lay hands on the sick. Frequent fasting became an additional obligation accompanying prayer in some places. The widow exercised no liturgical ministry, although Tertullian and the *Testamentum Domini Nostri Jesu Christi* (a Syrian work from the second half of the fifth century) argued that widows were entitled to special seating in the church.

Powerful leaders within the early church were never comfortable with the widows, who were recognized as legally independent and who often had both wealth and life experience. Through church orders appealing to the authority of the apostles, these leaders often tried to place the widows under the control of bishops and bring an end to some of their activities. The "good widows" were meek, silent, and stayed at home—fixed, like the "altar of God"; they taught only very simple things in private and did not baptize. The "bad widows" ignored their duty to guard their sexual reputations by going out, seeking donations, and having the arrogance to teach theology. The example of Jesus—since he was not baptized by his mother and did not commission women to teach—was cited repeatedly. Eventually, the order of widows was absorbed into the much more highly controlled positions of deaconess and virgin.

Female Deacons

By the end of the first century, male deacons were a recognized part of church structure. They cared for the needy, prepared new converts for baptism, read the Scriptures in worship, and distributed the Lord's Supper. As assistants to the bishop and under his authority, male deacons were set apart to serve (*diakonein*) the community. Evidence for the existence of female deacons in the earliest congregations, however, is ambiguous. First Timothy 3:11 may refer to both men and women when it gives instructions for the appropriate behavior of deacons. Also, a letter written by Pliny, the governor of Bithynia, claims that he tortured two young Christian women who were called *ministrae*, or ministers, in their community. If women were deacons in the earliest years of Christian history, their duties are not clear. They may have been identical to those of the male deacons.

By the end of the third century, however, female deacons, or "deaconesses," filled a special role in many places in the early Christian world, a role dramatically different from the one they may have occupied earlier. Both manuscript evidence and inscriptions coming from the Eastern churches in places such as Jerusalem, Syria, Greece, and Asia Minor give a clear record of the existence and nature of this ministry. At first women were appointed by the bishop from the entire congregation, although as time passed they were required to be virgins or widows. Their main tasks were aimed at keeping the church from harmful scandal in a hostile culture. The women deacons visited sick women in their homes and anointed women at the time of their baptism. They also received baptized women when they emerged from the water. In all of these situations, the church feared that male deacons might be exposed to nude or semi-clothed females. Some early Christian literature attributed additional duties to the women deacons. They were to distribute charity to poor women, find seats for women in church, and act as intermediaries between women and the male clergy. Sometimes they were even charged with the responsibility of teaching recently baptized women about Christian life.

What happened to this office is a reflection of the church's general impulse toward segregating men and women, and the rationale for this is evident in the ordination prayer for deaconesses.[31] In many places, between the third and sixth centuries women deacons were regarded as part of the clergy, and they were ordained to their office. The procedure for this ritual in the church orders follows that for the male deacons. The *Apostolic Constitutions*, for example, contains the following prayer for the ordination of a woman to the office of deacon: "O Eternal God, . . . the Creator of man and of woman, who replenished with the Spirit Miriam, and Deborah, and Anna and Huldah . . .

do Thou now also look down upon this Thy servant who is to be ordained to the office of a deaconess, and grant her Thy Holy Spirit."[32] But unlike that for deacons, the prayer for deaconesses also asks that God deliver the woman from filthiness of the flesh and spirit and reminds the congregation that God did not shun being born of a woman.[33]

Despite the fact that these women were ordained to a clerical office, they occupied a subordinate and circumscribed position. They were excluded from some of the tasks the male deacons performed and did not assist, for example, at the Lord's Supper. In some of the church orders, they were specifically forbidden to carry out activities reserved for the bishops, presbyters, and male deacons. At the baptismal ceremony, they were barred from pronouncing the baptismal formula.

WOMEN OUTSIDE THE ORTHODOX MAINSTREAM

Gnosticism

The status of women in groups that deviated from what became mainstream, orthodox Christianity is very important to us because women may have been given some public responsibilities. One of these movements, Gnosticism, has been especially interesting to scholars, although it was not as much a religious movement as a cluster of movements that had certain beliefs in common. Gnosticism drew upon a multitude of religious and philosophical ideas circulating at the end of the first century. The Gnostics generally believed that a supreme God, who could not be known, differed from the spirit that created the material world. Creation was the result of either malice or disobedience toward the supreme God, and the material world that resulted was evil. In the turmoil of creation, however, sparks of divinity from the supreme God were imprisoned in certain human beings. A redeemer had been sent to release these imprisoned sparks by giving people special knowledge (*gnosis*) of the existence of the supreme God and the true origins of the world.

Gnosticism had a profound impact upon the interpretation given to the life and work of Jesus in many places. The gnostic Christians argued that Jesus was the redeemer who had been sent to pass on this special knowledge necessary for salvation to his apostles. They backed up their ideas by appealing to certain parts of the New Testament as well as to special books that they believed to contain material handed down by the apostles.

The exact role played by women in the gnostic groups is uncertain. There are indications in some texts that women may have been prominent in the communities and regarded in an authoritative light, functioning in some circles as prophets, teachers, priests, and even bishops. Karen King suggests that Gnostic rejection of the body created a community in which leadership was based on spiritual achievement and open to women along with men.[34] In the *Gospel of Mary,* for example, Mary Magdalene is given a special revelation by Jesus and is urged to teach it to the other disciples. In a later gnostic book, *Pistis Sophia,* Mary is also given an important role, as Jesus' words imply: "But Mary Magdalene and John, the maiden, will surpass all my disciples. . . . They will be on my right hand and on my left and I am they and they are I."[35] In both of these gnostic texts, the patriarchal trend of the early church, which would become dominant, is represented in the words of Peter, who rebukes Mary for her brashness and doubts the legitimacy of her message. This practical equality may have been based on gnostic descriptions of God as containing masculine and feminine dimensions, although these references lack clarity and were limited to certain groups within Gnosticism. Some systems, however, reinforced patriarchy by claiming that the female represented decay and mutability.

Orthodox Responses

A strong school of thought in the early church opposed gnostic Christianity. This opposing tradition came to be regarded as the orthodox, or "catholic," tradition while the other groups were denounced as heretical. In the case of Gnosticism, orthodox Christians were certainly offended by the ideas that the created world was evil and that Jesus was not truly human. Yet we must at least consider the possibility that orthodox Christianity, which had already succumbed to its male-dominated cultural environment, excluded and persecuted the Gnostics partly because of the varied roles they gave to women. Scholars suggest that later forms of Montanism were also labeled heretical in part because of female leadership. Church leaders justified this by looking back at the founding mothers of Montanism and describing them as false prophets, being possessed by demons, and as sexually adventurous—typical

consequences when women were not submissive and domestic.[36] The orthodox church used the threat of heresy to curtail female activity even further,
making the struggle against deviance another factor in nudging the church
toward patriarchy.[37]

Patristic Attitudes toward Women

Attitudes toward women in the Christian tradition even in the twenty-
first century have been shaped in no small way by a number of theological
writers who lived in the first six centuries of Christian history. The influence wielded by these men is reflected in their designation as the "fathers of
the church." They had a variety of vocations and lived in many geographic
locations throughout the Greco-Roman world. For example, Clement of
Alexandria was a teacher, Jerome was a biblical scholar and secretary to Pope
Damasus I, and Augustine was bishop of the North African city of Hippo.
The church fathers included prominent figures in the church hierarchy as
well as in the monastic communities.

The life, death, and resurrection of Jesus was central to their work, but
the church fathers had to convey and explain the message of the Gospels
in terms that would be compatible with the thought patterns of the Greco-
Roman world. There was a strong tendency in this culture to divide reality
into two opposing or contradictory spheres, the sphere of mind and spirit
and the sphere of the body, or flesh. The mind and spirit were identified
with that which was good or virtuous while the flesh was represented as that
which had to be overcome or conquered. Sometimes this line of thought condemned the body and the material world as hopelessly evil and corrupt, and
it deeply influenced the growth of the ascetic spirit within the churches (see
chapter 2).

This dualistic approach to the world, as it was called, had an influence on
the way in which women were regarded. Women were identified traditionally
with the body while the mind was seen as essentially masculine. The result
was an association of the female with the flesh, the material world, and the
drive to satisfy physical desires and, therefore, with that which was evil. This
association was of course largely due to women's role in childbirth as well as
menstruation.

The church fathers certainly made statements that degraded women and the feminine. Such ideas have been picked up and quoted at length by people in the Christian community who have tried to keep women silent and subordinate. Yet these theologians could not ignore the Christian doctrine of the goodness of creation, the blessing of God on married life, and the equality between male and female that Paul proclaims. The works of the church fathers relevant to women, therefore, are not only numerous but also complex, but we can suggest some of the major ideas that emerge on the nature of women, virginity, and married life.

Women Prone to Sin

One prominent belief of the church fathers is that women are responsible for sin in the world. Many turn to the Genesis story to support this, although some of the writers, such as Tertullian and Ambrose, sometimes describe the first sin as a joint responsibility. The fathers also see women as a continuing source of sin in the world since they seduce men away from the lofty heights of mind and spirit to the base concern for physical satisfaction and pleasure.

As a potential source of sin and danger to the spiritual well-being of the community, women were therefore to be kept subordinate in church and society. While some of these theologians regarded subordination as the penalty for Eve's sin, Augustine taught that woman was created as inferior to man. He argued that woman was created with a mind and spirit that were weak and readily overcome by strong physical passion. Even in the Garden of Eden therefore the male was to rule, govern, and teach.

The church fathers do make it clear that men and women are equally redeemed by baptism in Christ, however. In terms of their souls before God, gender was irrelevant. Even for Christian women, however, spiritual equality could have no counterpart in the concrete life of family, church, and nation. Although Christian women might have interior purity, they were still bound to the flesh, which could seduce and succumb to physical pleasure.

Both men and women are advised to adopt a lifestyle of chastity and modesty in a number of these treatises, but the instructions for women are particularly lengthy and explicit. The behavior of the Christian woman is meant to contrast sharply with the behavior of women in the urban centers of the decaying Roman Empire. The Christian woman is to stop using makeup (the work of the devil) and avoid wearing jewelry. She is to wear a veil to signify her subjection and not to appear in silk dresses, which would show the shape of her body. She is to seclude herself at home and be careful not to visit the public baths.

Marriage and Sexuality

None of the church fathers condemns married life as evil and against the will of God, although Jerome comes close to doing this in a strong plea for the virgin life. Married life is treated generally with delicacy and sensitivity. Some of the fathers stress that husband and wife should live in a relationship of love and trust. They encourage marriage partners to serve each other and to fulfill their mutual responsibilities. They contrast the Christian marriage to that of the non-Christian marriage, in which passion rules the domineering husband and the lusty wife.

There is a strong tendency in these works, however, to see sexual union as tainted with sin. Some of the fathers claim that God's original creation consisted of a single spiritual being who had no sexual characteristics, while others believe that male and female characteristics were part of the perfect creation but were not to result in sexual union. This union became a reality only after sin entered the world. Augustine argued that sexual union did take place in paradise but without lust and under the complete control of the male will and mind. After the Fall, however, lust took over and not only passed on original sin to the offspring but tarnished the relationship between man and woman as well.

The Virgin Life

Augustine and the earlier writer Clement of Alexandria both approved of sexual intercourse to produce children. The union, however, should be the product of the will and not the passions. More commonly, Christians were urged to avoid marriage and sexual intercourse entirely. The life of virginity was celebrated as infinitely preferable to all other marital states. The virgin was regarded as possessing the most important "charism," or gift from the Holy Spirit. Mothers were urged to dedicate their daughters to the chaste life. Jerome even taught that the only possible justification for sexual union was the production of more virgins: from coitus came virgins just as from thorns came roses and from shells came pearls.

Some of the church fathers suggest practical reasons for choosing the virgin life. Tertullian claims that it freed men and women to be martyrs. Other writers argue that the monastic life offered women protection in a brutal society. Jerome, in his effort to advocate chastity, gives lurid descriptions of married life to deter young men and women. He asks men why they would want to get involved with the perpetual whining and nagging of a wife, and he describes to women the discomforts of pregnancy and the pain of childbirth.

Aside from these practical reasons, many of the church fathers provided theological support for their celebration of the virgin life. Both men and women who chose this life of physical denial anticipated or had a "head start" on the life that awaited them in the kingdom of God. Christians in the kingdom would be given spiritual bodies like those of the angels, without sexual characteristics. For some of the writers, virgins were also concrete examples of God's original creation that would be restored in the future kingdom. By erasing their sexuality, male or female, they already participated to some extent in a new order of reality.

In the writings of the church fathers, virginity became the one channel in the Christian community through which women could acquire some measure of practical equality with men and some kind of official standing within the church. The price a woman paid was dear; she was to obliterate her "femaleness" (see chapter 2). She did this by denying her childbearing ability, by fasting to eliminate her menstrual cycle, and by making herself as unattractive as possible. The equality baptism brought to women in the earliest decades of the church's history was restored in part in the virgin life. The church fathers along with many other men speak highly of the learning and dedication of these women. Jerome, for example, praises the biblical scholarship of a group of virgins from the Roman aristocracy as well as their rigor in denying themselves physical pleasures. Women in this life could be allowed some measure of authority and freedom because they no longer represented the powerful lower nature that could lure men away from the virtuous life of mind and spirit. Yet while they were admired and celebrated, even ascetic women were feared; the solution eventually was to require that they be strictly cloistered behind convent walls.

WRITERS, POETS, AND PILGRIMS

Although the works of the church fathers dominate the written records of the early church, there are several religious works written by women in the first centuries of Christian history. While later female writers generally came from religious orders or monastic communities, some of these early women were married and all were from the upper classes of Roman society. The content and style of their works varied, but all made some contribution to knowledge of the Christian faith. Examples of this can be seen in Proba's *Cento* and Egeria's manuscript describing her trip to the Holy Land as well as Perpetua's story.[38]

Martyrdom and the Witness of Perpetua

The early Christian communities were subjected to periods of persecution during the first centuries of their existence, and women formed a significant portion of those who were martyred. Were their experiences different from those of men? Conflicts between women and Roman authorities over religion were certainly intensified by their refusal to conform to the expectation that they submit to male rule. Women aroused strong emotions—anger, pity, and sometimes remorse—as they defied men and appeared in public in alien space normally reserved for male combat such as the Roman Colosseum.

One such period of persecution occurred in Carthage from 202 to 203 c.e. Christians who refused to worship the gods of the Roman Empire were singled out for punishment. Saturus, a Christian teacher, and five of his newly baptized pupils were arrested. Among them was Perpetua, the daughter of a wealthy civil servant, and her slave girl, Felicitas. Educationally as well as economically privileged, Perpetua left a remarkable written record of the experience of martyrdom in the early church.[39] Her work was later given an introduction and conclusion by an editor and circulated for many years among congregations. It represents the earliest known piece of Christian literature written by a woman. This work allows us to glimpse not only her understanding of Christianity but also her view of the society in which she lived and her role among the other Christian prisoners.

Perpetua's story is about a woman's spiritual awakening that moved her beyond given social and religious definitions.[40] Freed from the law of the

Romans and the expectations of her culture by God, who was the highest authority for a Christian, she was able to forge a new identity. She transcends her roles as daughter and mother in favor of a new family of confessing Christians; she then moves beyond her status as a new Christian to assume spiritual leadership—and challenges her culture's definition of female character.

Perpetua rejects the domestic norms to which she is expected to conform in two important ways. She disregards the pleas of her aged father, who constantly visits her in prison and urges her to compromise her beliefs. She also gives up her newborn son, whom she has been nursing in prison, to her father, thus relinquishing her responsibilities as a mother rather than give in to the Roman authorities. In both of these instances, her family ties are not broken lightly but with great sadness and suffering. She describes her appearance before the governor, Hilarion, in the following words: "Hilarion . . . said, 'Have pity on your father's grey head; have pity on your infant son; offer sacrifice for the emperors' welfare.' But I answered, 'I will not.' Hilarion asked, 'Are you a Christian?' And I answered, 'I am a Christian.' And when my father persisted in his attempts to dissuade me, Hilarion ordered him thrown out and he was beaten with a rod. My father's injury hurt me as much as if I myself had been beaten."[41]

Martyrdom also disrupted the church's steady march toward the subordination of women, creating a set of circumstances in which the egalitarian conditions of the early church reasserted themselves.[42] Certainly the community around Perpetua in prison reflects some of the egalitarianism connected with the earliest Christians. Perpetua emerges as a figure of authority who has been claimed by the Holy Spirit. She takes on a prophetic role, for example, in communicating God's will to her companions. "My brother said to me, 'Dear sister, you already have such a great reputation in that you could ask for a vision indicating whether you will be condemned or freed.' Since I knew that I could speak with the Lord, whose great favors I had already experienced, I confidently promised to do so."[43] She experiences a series of prophetic visions, which assure her friends that a new and far better life awaited them after death and that they would be victorious over their fears and their persecutors. In her visions as well as in that of Saturus, Perpetua is also raised to a position of spiritual authority even over the male clergy, who were emerging as a powerful force in the church, by settling a dispute among them. And it is her prayer of intercession that wins a place in paradise for her deceased brother.

During her days in prison, Perpetua also transcends her identity as a woman by assuming both masculine and feminine characteristics. She is called the "true spouse of Christ" and the "darling of God" on the day of her martyrdom. She is described as sister, mother, and daughter, and she acts with gentleness, tenderness, and maternal compassion. But she is also a leader and intercessor who is strong and courageous, all traits that her culture associated with men. She chides the jailers for their inhumanity, slyly arguing that it would reflect well on them if the martyrs stayed in good physical condition since they would appear in the arena on Caesar's birthday. She shows herself clearly in charge when she guides the hand and sword of her executioner. In one of her visions of her coming battle with the forces of evil, she sees herself as a man who is stripped of his clothing and rubbed with oil for combat. This image of the "manly woman," common in the ancient world, would be used by Christians for centuries to speak of women who had overcome their weak female bodies and characters by spiritual development. Yet in this same vision she sees herself as the peaceful daughter who is given the branch of victory, representing the Christian who is freed from society's expectations of women and men.

Although Perpetua's story may have been preserved and edited by Montanists to illustrate the ongoing work of the Holy Spirit, it was soon used more widely for purposes of instruction and inspiration. Excerpts from her story were read as part of the official liturgy in many places. The anniversary of her death became the occasion for special celebrations; a basilica was dedicated to her in Carthage; and Augustine, the Bishop of Hippo, preached several sermons in her honor. Gradually, however, the memory of Perpetua faded in the Christian tradition. This was partly due to the prominence of earlier martyrs who were leading bishops, but it may also have been caused by the growing power of the male clergy who considered the writings of a woman inadequate and improper for official church use. Martyrdom represented an extraordinary opportunity to challenge the status quo and deviate from prescribed roles; when circumstances were less chaotic, women found few chances for authority outside the ascetic community.

Proba's Cento

Proba was a matron of the prominent and wealthy Anicii family. She probably became a convert to Christianity sometime in her adult life. Like other women of the Roman privileged classes, she had a great deal of leisure time and she used some of it for the study of classical culture and for writing. Her *Cento* was probably written sometime around 351 C.E.

Cento was a popular form of poetry in the Greco-Roman world. The author of a cento borrowed lines and half-lines from the works of a master poet such as Virgil or Homer and arranged them to suit his or her own purposes. Although this appears like plagiarism to us, it was considered to be a high form of praise for the master poet. Proba rearranged parts of Virgil's works on secular subjects in order to tell biblical stories. The first part describes the history of Israel up to the giving of the Law. Then Proba jumps to the life of Jesus, using the verse of Virgil to describe events such as the slaughter of the firstborn in Egypt, the storm on the lake, and the Last Supper.

Although her *Cento* does remain faithful to orthodox views on Jesus, Proba omits large portions of the gospel story in her effort to patch Virgil together and ends up with an adaptation that many scholars see as absurd and forced. Her work, which required a prodigious memory and literary skill, was not given a favorable reception by church authorities in Rome; however, it continued to be used as a textbook for centuries. Education in the classics continued to be a requirement for professional and social success, and the *Cento* provided what was needed: Christianized access to Virgil.

Proba's *Cento* is also significant because it represents a challenge to the exclusion of women from the creation of a Christian theological tradition. In her own way, Proba was attempting to do what the church fathers were doing: interpret Jesus for the Greco-Roman world in familiar thought patterns. Many Roman citizens found the language of the Bible clumsy and were often suspicious and hostile toward Christianity. Proba's *Cento* sought to bridge this gap.

Egeria's Pilgrimage to the Holy Land

A literary work of an entirely different kind from the pen of a woman was discovered at the end of the nineteenth century in the library of an Italian monastery. The manuscript describes a pilgrimage made to the Holy Land, probably in the early fifth century. Scholars believe that the account was written by Egeria.

The only information we have about Egeria must be inferred from her manuscript itself. In it there is evidence that she was a wealthy woman: she was on the pilgrimage for several years, she traveled with an extensive entourage, and she was given preferential treatment in many places by those in authority. The Bishop of Edessa greets her as one who has come from the remote end of the earth, possibly a reference to her home in Gaul or Spain. While she is not as learned in the classics and Latin as aristocratic women, she reveals herself to be well read in the Scriptures. She frequently discussed the Bible with her hosts and often tried to interpret her travels in light of biblical stories. She bombards the Bishop of Carrae, who was "very learned in Scripture," with a whole series of questions about the geographic movements of Abraham's family including "where the well was from which Saint Jacob gave water to the sheep which were herded by Rachel the daughter of Laban the Syrian."[44] It is probable that Egeria belonged to a group of virgin women who were bound together by strong ties of affection, who studied the Bible together, and who had some liturgical responsibilities. She frequently refers to her readers as "ladies," "my venerable sisters," and "my light." They were not members of a religious or monastic order, and there is no hint in Egeria's account that she lived a life of poverty.

The account itself is really a travel diary describing a pilgrimage that lasted a long period of time. The first half of the manuscript relates her stay in Jerusalem, tours to Egypt, the Sinai Peninsula, and Transjordan, and her homebound journey to Constantinople. The second part gives a detailed account of the forms of worship used in the foremost Jerusalem church. Egeria's work is not simply a catalogue of places but provides insights into local practices, people, and traditions, which are often missing in most travel diaries. Her work is of great value because of the information it provides on early Christian worship and architecture in the age of Constantinian church building, as well as the condition of the biblical sites in the fifth century. But her diaries had theological significance as well. Believing that she was called by God to her travels, Egeria enlivens and confirms the truth of the Bible for herself and her community.

During her pilgrimage, Egeria stops at the shrine of Saint Thecla near Selucium. Thecla was celebrated in the early church as a missionary who had been converted by Paul and commissioned by him to teach. In the *Acts of Paul and Thecla* (in circulation by the end of the second century), she breaks off her engagement and, in the face of violent family opposition, adopts the virgin life. She is presented as a woman of enormous power and zeal, as is clear by her victory over attempted rape and execution by fire and beast. Although commissioned by Paul, her direct relationship with God is symbolized by her self-baptism. While Thecla herself may be legendary, scholars now suggest that the story reflects the teaching and sacramental ministries of some early Christian women. It may have even been created and preserved by them.[45] Yet the later church celebrated her for her willingness to die rather than compromise her virginity. As female leadership was curtailed in the early churches and the roles of widow and deaconess disappeared, the virgin life became an important source of female power and male approval. In medieval Christianity, the "good woman" was a virgin while all other women were associated by nature with the powers of darkness.

Readings for Chapter 1

1.1 CHRISTIAN WIDOWS

This selection comes from a collection of church laws, the Apostolic Constitutions, *compiled in Syria around 380 C.E. In addition to incorporating the* Didascalia Apostolorum, *the legislation covers matters such as liturgical procedures, fasts and feasts, schism, heresy, and Christian burial. It also describes the duties of members of the Christian community. Women, when widowed, were entitled to the support of the church if they were sober, chaste, pious, and the wives of only one husband. They were not to discuss doctrine lest they misconstrue it. The church, in fact, was not to allow any woman to teach. Such teaching, the document argues, would be contrary to the example set by Jesus and the biblical injunction that women be subject to men. Widows, furthermore, were to remain within the confines of their homes to pray for the church.*

Source: "Concerning Christian Widows." In *The Work Claiming to Be the Constitutions of the Holy Apostles, including the Canons,* translated by Irah Chase, 81–83. New York: D. Appleton, 1848.

That the widows are to be very careful of their deportment.

Let every widow be meek, quiet, gentle, sincere, free from anger; not talkative, not clamorous, not hasty of speech, not given to evil-speaking, not captious, not double-tongued, not a busy-body. If she see or hear any thing that is not right, let her be as one that doth not see, and as one that doth not hear; and let the widow mind nothing but to pray for those that give, and for the whole church; and when she is asked any thing by any one, let her not easily answer, except questions concerning faith, and righteousness, and hope in God; remitting to the rulers those that desire to be instructed in the doctrines of godliness. Let her answer only so as may tend to subvert the error of polytheism, and demonstrate the doctrine concerning the monarchy of God. But of the remaining doctrines, let her not answer any thing rashly, lest, by saying any thing unlearnedly, she should cause the Word to be blasphemed. For the Lord hath taught us, that the Word is like *a grain of mustard seed,* which is of a fiery nature; and, if any one useth it unskilfully, he will find it bitter. For in the mystical points we ought not to be rash, but cautious. For the Lord exhorteth us, saying, *Cast not your pearls before swine, lest they trample them with their feet, and turn again and rend you.* For unbelievers, when they hear the doctrine concerning Christ not explained as it ought to be, but defectively, and especially that concerning his incarnation or his passion, will rather reject it with scorn, and laugh at it as false, than praise God for it. And so the aged women will be guilty of rashness, and of causing blasphemy, and will inherit a woe. For, saith he, *Woe to him by whom my name is blasphemed among the Gentiles.*

That women ought not to teach, because it is unseemly; and what women followed our Lord.

We do not permit our *women to teach in the church,* but only to pray, and to hear those that teach. For our Master and Lord, Jesus Christ himself, when he sent us, the twelve, to make disciples of the people and of the nations, did nowhere send out women to preach, although he did not want such; for there were with us the mother of our Lord, and his sisters; also Mary Magdalen; and Mary, the mother of James; and Martha and Mary, the sisters of Lazarus; Salome, and certain others. For, had it been necessary for women to teach, he himself would have first commanded these also to instruct the people with us. For if *the head of the wife be the man,* it is not reasonable that the rest of the body should govern the head.

Let the widow, therefore, own herself to be the *altar of God,* and let her sit in her house, and not enter into the houses of the faithful, under any pretense, to receive any thing; for the altar of God never runneth about, but is fixed in one place. Let, therefore, the virgin and the widow be such as do not run about, or gad to the houses of those who are alien from the faith. For such as these are gadders and impudent; they do not make their feet to rest in one place, because they are not widows, but purses ready to receive, triflers, evil speakers, counsellors of strife, without shame, impudent; who, being such, are not worthy of him that called them. For they do not come to the common resting place of the congregation on the Lord's day, as those that are watchful. But they either slumber, or trifle, or allure men, or beg, or ensnare others, bringing them to the evil one; not suffering them to be watchful in the Lord; but taking care that they go out as vain as they came in, because they do not hear the Word of the Lord either taught or read. For of such as these the prophet Isaiah saith, *Hearing ye shall hear, and shall not understand; and seeing ye shall see, and not perceive; for the heart of this people is waxen gross.*

1.2 THE MARTYRDOM OF PERPETUA

One of Christianity's oldest and most descriptive accounts of martyrdom is in large part written by a woman. The author, Vibia Perpetua, daughter of a wealthy Carthaginian family, was arrested along with five friends in 202 or 203 C.E. at the direction of Septimus Severus. The account of her imprisonment and visions was supplemented and verified by fellow martyr Saturus and later given an introduction and conclusion. In these sections from Perpetua's story, she makes clear her willingness to defy the norms of family, society, and state although she does so with regret. They also illustrate the androgynous character of the story, presenting Perpetua both as daughter and combatant, nurturer and rebel.

Source: "The Martyrdom of Saints Perpetua and Felicitas." In *The Acts of the Christian Martyrs,* introduction, texts, and translations by Herbert Musurillo, 109–19. Oxford: Clarendon Press, 1972.

While we were still under arrest (she said) my father out of love for me was trying to persuade me and shake my resolution. "Father," said I, "do you see this vase here, for example, or waterpot or whatever?"

"Yes, I do," said he.

And I told him: "Could it be called by any other name than what it is?"

And he said: "No."

"Well, so too I cannot be called anything other than what I am, a Christian."

At this my father was so angered by the word "Christian" that he moved towards me as though he would pluck my eyes out. But he left it at that and departed, vanquished along with his diabolical arguments.

For a few days afterwards I gave thanks to the Lord that I was separated from my father, and I was comforted by his absence. During these few days I was baptized, and I was inspired by the Spirit not to ask for any other favor after the water but simply the perseverance of the flesh. A few days later we were lodged in the prison; and I was terrified, as I had never before been in such a dark hole. What a difficult time it was! With the crowd the heat was stifling; then there was the extortion of the soldiers; and to crown all, I was tortured with worry for my baby there.

Then Tertius and Pomponius, those blessed deacons who tried to take care of us, bribed the soldiers to allow us to go to a better part of the prison to refresh ourselves for a few hours. Everyone then left that dungeon and shifted for himself. I nursed my baby, who was faint from hunger. In my anxiety I spoke to my mother about the child, I tried to comfort my brother, and I gave the child in their charge. I was in pain because I saw them suffering out of pity for me. These were the trials I had to endure for many days. Then I got permission for my baby to stay with me in prison. At once I recovered my health, relieved as I was of my worry and anxiety over the child. My prison had suddenly become a palace, so that I wanted to be there rather than anywhere else. . . .

A few days later there was a rumor that we were going to be given a hearing. My father also arrived from the city, worn with worry, and he came to see me with the idea of persuading me.

"Daughter," he said, "have pity on my grey head—have pity on me your father, if I deserve to be called your father, if I have favored you above all your brothers, if I have raised you to reach this prime of your life. Do not abandon me to be the reproach of men. Think of your brothers, think of your mother and your aunt, think of your child, who will not be able to live once you are gone. Give up your pride! You will destroy all of us! None of us will ever be able to speak freely again if anything happens to you."

This was the way my father spoke out of love for me, kissing my hands and throwing himself down before me. With tears in his eyes he no longer addressed me as his daughter but as a woman. I was sorry for my father's sake, because he alone of all my kin would be unhappy to see me suffer.

I tried to comfort him saying: "It will all happen in the prisoner's dock as God wills; for you may be sure that we are not left to ourselves but are all in his power."

And he left me in great sorrow.

One day while we were eating breakfast we were suddenly hurried off for a hearing. We arrived at the forum, and straight away the story went about the neighborhood near the forum and a huge crowd gathered. We walked up to the prisoner's dock. All the others when questioned admitted their guilt. Then, when it came my turn, my father appeared with my son, dragged me from the step, and said: "Perform the sacrifice—have pity on your baby!"

Hilarianus the governor, who had received his judicial powers as the successor of the late proconsul Minucius Timinianus, said to me: "Have pity on your father's grey head; have pity on your infant son. Offer the sacrifice for the welfare of the emperors."

"I will not," I retorted.

"Are you a Christian?" said Hilarianus.

And I said: "Yes, I am."

When my father persisted in trying to dissuade me, Hilarianus ordered him to be thrown to the ground and beaten with a rod. I felt sorry for father, just as if I myself had been beaten. I felt sorry for his pathetic old age.

Then Hilarianus passed sentence on all of us: we were condemned to the beasts, and we returned to prison in high spirits. But my baby had got used to being nursed at the breast and to staying with me in prison. So I sent the deacon Pomponius straight away to my father to ask for the baby. But father refused to give him over. But as God willed, the baby had no further desire for the breast, nor did I suffer any inflammation; and so I was relieved of any anxiety for my child and of any discomfort in my breasts. . . .

The day before we were to fight with the beasts I saw the following vision. Pomponius the deacon came to the prison gates and began to knock violently. I went out and opened the gate for him. He was dressed in an unbelted white tunic, wearing elaborate sandals. And he said to me: "Perpetua, come; we are waiting for you."

Then he took my hand and we began to walk through rough and broken country. At last we came to the amphitheater out of breath, and he led me into the center of the arena.

Then he told me: "Do not be afraid. I am here, struggling with you." Then he left.

I looked at the enormous crowd who watched in astonishment. I was surprised that no beasts were let loose on me; for I knew that I was condemned to die by the beasts. Then out came an Egyptian against me, of vicious appearance, together with his seconds, to fight with me. There also came up to me some handsome young men to be my seconds and assistants.

My clothes were stripped off, and suddenly I was a man. My seconds began to rub me down with oil (as they are wont to do before a contest). Then I saw the Egyptian on the other side rolling in the dust. Next there came forth a man of marvellous stature, such that he rose above the top of the amphitheater. He was clad in a beltless purple tunic with two stripes (one on either side) running down the middle of his chest. He wore sandals that were wondrously made of gold and silver, and he carried a wand like an athletic trainer and a green branch on which there were golden apples.

And he asked for silence and said: "If this Egyptian defeats her he will slay her with the sword. But if she defeats him, she will receive this branch." Then he withdrew.

We drew close to one another and began to let our fists fly. My opponent tried to get hold of my feet, but I kept striking him in the face with the heels of my feet. Then I was raised up into the air and I began to pummel him without as it were touching the ground. Then when I noticed there was a lull, I put my two hands together linking the fingers of one hand with those of the other and thus I got hold of his head. He fell flat on his face and I stepped on his head.

The crowd began to shout and my assistants started to sing psalms. Then

I walked up to the trainer and took the branch. He kissed me and said to me: "Peace be with you, my daughter!" I began to walk in triumph towards the Gate of Life. Then I awoke. I realized that it was not with wild animals that I would fight but with the Devil, but I knew that I would win the victory. So much for what I did up until the eve of the contest. About what happened at the contest itself, let him write of it who will.

1.3 ADORNING WOMEN

One of the thirty-eight surviving treatises written by Tertullian (c. 160–220), a presbyter in Carthage, deals with appropriate apparel for women. Probably written in 202, the text reflects Tertullian's hatred of North African, non-Christian culture and his growing interest in the puritanical and uncompromising lifestyle of Montanism. It has been both applauded and denounced as an indictment of women, although the writer does urge modesty on men and never questions women's equal access to grace. Tertullian's purpose is to persuade Christian women to abandon elaborate dress, ornaments, and cosmetics. He reasons that the sex that brought sin into the world should wear humble garb and renounce the skills of adornment that were taught by the angels of darkness. He also reminds women that such attire tempts men and betrays impure impulses within their own souls.

Source: Tertullian. "On the Apparel of Women." Translated by S. Thelwall. In *Ante-Nicene Fathers: Translations of the Writings of the Fathers down to* A.D. *325,* edited by Alexander Roberts and James Donaldson. Volume 4:14–15, 18–21, 25. Buffalo: Christian Literature Publishing, 1885.

If there dwelt upon earth a faith as great as is the reward of faith which is expected in the heavens, no one of you at all, best beloved sisters, from the time that she had first "known the Lord," and learned (the truth) concerning her own (that is, woman's) condition, would have desired too gladsome (not to say too ostentatious) a style of dress; so as not rather to go about in humble garb, and rather to affect meanness of appearance, walking about as Eve mourning and repentant, in order that by every garb of penitence she might the more fully expiate that which she derives from Eve,—the ignominy, I mean, of the first sin, and the odium (attaching to her as the cause) of human perdition. "In pains and in anxieties dost thou bear (children), woman; and toward thine husband (is) thy inclination, and he lords it over thee." And do you not know that you are (each) an Eve? The sentence of God on this sex of yours lives in this age: the guilt must of necessity live too. *You* are the devil's gateway: *you* are the unsealer of that (forbidden) tree: *you* are the first deserter of the divine law: *you* are she who persuaded him whom the devil was not valiant enough to attack. *You* destroyed so easily God's image, man. On account of *your* desert—that is, death—even the Son of God had to die. And do you think about adorning yourself over and above your tunics of skins? Come, now; if from the beginning of the world the

Milesians sheared sheep, and the Serians spun trees, and the Tyrians dyed, and the Phrygians embroidered with the needle, and the Babylonians with the loom, and pearls gleamed, and onyxstones flashed; if gold itself also had already issued, with the cupidity (which accompanies it), from the ground; if the mirror, too, already had license to lie so largely, Eve, expelled from paradise, (Eve) already dead, would also have coveted *these* things, I imagine! No more, then, ought she *now* to crave, or be acquainted with (if she desires to live again), what, when she *was* living, she had neither had nor known. Accordingly these things are all the baggage of woman in her condemned and dead state, instituted as if to swell the pomp of her funeral. . . .

For they, withal, who instituted them are assigned, under condemnation, to the penalty of death,—those angels, to wit, who rushed from heaven on the daughters of men; so that this ignominy also attaches to woman. For when to an age much more ignorant (than ours) they had disclosed certain well-concealed material substances, and several not well-revealed scientific arts—if it is true that they had laid bare the operations of metallurgy, and had divulged the natural properties of herbs, and had promulgated the powers of enchantments, and had traced out every curious art, even to the interpretation of the stars—they conferred properly and as it were peculiarly upon women that instrumental mean of womanly ostentation, the radiances of jewels wherewith necklaces are variegated, and the circlets of gold wherewith the arms are compressed, and the medicaments of orchil with which wools are colored, and that black powder itself wherewith the eyelids and eyelashes are made prominent. What is the quality of these things may be declared meantime, even at this point, from the quality and condition of their teachers: in that sinners could never have either shown or supplied anything conducive to integrity, unlawful lovers anything conducive to chastity, renegade spirits anything conducive to the fear of God. If (these things) are to be called *teachings*, ill masters must of necessity have taught ill; if *as wages of lust*, there is nothing base of which the wages are honorable. But why was it of so much importance to show these things as well as to confer them? Was it that women, without material causes of splendor, and without ingenious contrivances of grace, could not please *men*, who, while still unadorned, and uncouth, and—so to say—crude and rude, had moved (the mind of) *angels*? or was it that the lovers would appear sordid and—through gratuitous use—contumelious, if they had conferred no (compensating) gift on the women who had been enticed into connubial connection with them? But these questions admit of no calculation. Women who possessed angels (as husbands) could desire nothing more; they had, forsooth, made a grand match! Assuredly they who, of course, did sometimes think whence they had fallen, and, after the heated impulses of their lusts,

looked up toward heaven, thus requited that very excellence of women, natural beauty, as (having proved) a cause of evil, in order that their good fortune might profit them nothing; but that, being turned from simplicity and sincerity, they, together with (the angels) themselves, might become offensive to God. Sure they were that all ostentation, and ambition, and love of pleasing by carnal means, was *displeasing* to God. And these are the angels whom we are destined to judge: these are the angels whom in baptism we renounce: these, of course, are the reasons why they have deserved to be judged by man. What business, then, have their *things* with their *judges?* What commerce have they who are to condemn with them who are to be condemned? The same, I take it, as Christ has with Belial. With what consistency do we mount that (future) judgment-seat to pronounce sentence against those whose gifts we (now) seek after? For you too, (women as you are,) have the self-same angelic nature promised as your reward, the self-same sex as men: the self-same advancement to the dignity of judging, does (the Lord) promise you. Unless, then, we begin even here to *pre*-judge, by pre-condemning their *things*, which we are hereafter to condemn in *themselves*, *they* will rather judge and condemn *us*. . . .

Handmaids of the living God, my fellow-servants and sisters, the right which I enjoy with you—I, the most meanest in that right of fellow-servant-ship and brotherhood—emboldens me to address to you a discourse, not, of course, of affection, but paving the way for affection in the cause of your salvation. That salvation—and not (the salvation) of women only, but likewise of men—consists in the exhibition principally of modesty. For since, by the introduction into an appropriation (in) us of the Holy Spirit, we are all "the temple of God." Modesty is the sacristan and priestess of that temple, who is to suffer nothing unclean or profane to be introduced (into it), for fear that the God who inhabits it should be offended, and quite forsake the polluted abode. But on the present occasion we (are to speak) not about modesty, for the enjoining and exacting of which the divine precepts which press (upon us) on every side are sufficient; but about the matters which pertain to it, that is, the manner in which it behoves you to walk. For most women (which very thing I trust God may permit me, with a view, of course, to my own personal censure, to censure in all), either from simple ignorance or else from dissimulation, have the hardihood so to walk as if modesty consisted only in the (bare) integrity of the flesh, and in turning away from (actual) fornication; and there were no need for anything extrinsic to boot—in the matter (I mean) of the arrangement of dress and ornament, the studied graces of form and brilliance:—wearing in their gait the self-same appearance as the women of the nations, from whom the sense of *true* modesty is absent, because in those who know not God, the Guardian and

Master of truth, there is *nothing* true. For if any modesty can be believed (to exist) in Gentiles, it is plain that it must be imperfect and undisciplined to such a degree that, although it be actively tenacious of itself in the *mind* up to a certain point, it yet allows itself to relax into licentious extravagances of attire; just in accordance with Gentile perversity, in craving after that of which it carefully shuns the effect. How many a one, in short, is there who does not earnestly desire even to look pleasing to strangers? who does not on that very account take care to have herself painted out, and denies that she has (ever) been an object of (carnal) appetite? And yet, granting that even this is a practice familiar to Gentile modesty—(namely,) not actually to *commit* the sin, but still to be *willing* to do so; or even not to be *willing*, yet still not *quite* to refuse—what wonder? For all things which are not God's are perverse. Let those women therefore look to it, who, by not holding fast the *whole* good, easily mingle with evil even what they do hold fast. Necessary it is that *you* turn aside from them, as in all other things, so also in your gait; since you ought to be "perfect, as (is) your Father who is in the heavens. . . ."

You must know that in the eye of perfect, that is, Christian, modesty, (carnal) desire of one's self (on the part of others) is not only not to be desired, but even execrated, by you: first, because the study of making personal grace (which we know to be naturally the inviter of lust) a mean of pleasing does not spring from a sound conscience: why therefore excite toward yourself that evil (passion)? why invite (that) to which you profess yourself a stranger? secondly, because we ought not to open a way to temptations, which, by their instancy, sometimes achieve (a wickedness) which God expels from them who are His; (or,) at all events, put the spirit into a thorough tumult by (presenting) a stumbling-block (to it). We ought indeed to walk so holily, and with so entire substantiality of faith, as to be confident and secure in regard of our own conscience, *desiring* that that (gift) may abide in us to the end, yet not *presuming* (that it will). For he who presumes feels less apprehension; he who feels less apprehension takes less precaution; he who takes less precaution runs more risk. Fear is the foundation of salvation; presumption is an impediment to fear. More useful, then, is it to apprehend that we may possibly fail, than to presume that we cannot; for apprehending will lead us to fear, fearing to caution, and caution to salvation. On the other hand, if we presume, there will be neither fear nor caution to save us. He who acts securely, and not at the same time warily, possesses no safe and firm security; whereas he who is wary will be truly able to be secure. For His own servants, may the Lord by His mercy take care that to *them* it may be lawful even to *presume* on His goodness! But why are we a (source of) danger to our neighbor? why do we import concupiscence into our neighbor? which concupiscence, if God, in "amplifying the law," do not

dissociate in (the way of) penalty from the actual commission of fornication, I know not whether He allows impunity to him who has been the cause of perdition to some other. For that other, as soon as he has felt concupiscence after your beauty, and has mentally already committed (the deed) which his concupiscence pointed to, perishes; and you have been made the sword which destroys him: so that, albeit you be free from the (actual) crime, you are not free from the odium (attaching to it); as, when a robbery has been committed on some man's estate, the (actual) crime indeed will not be laid to the owner's charge, while yet the domain is branded with ignominy, (and) the owner himself aspersed with the infamy. Are we to paint ourselves out that our neighbors may perish? Where, then, is (the command), "Thou shalt love thy neighbor as thyself"? "Care not merely about your own (things), but (about your) neighbor's"? No enunciation of the Holy Spirit ought to be (confined) to the subject immediately in hand merely, and not applied and carried out with a view to *every* occasion to which its application is useful. Since, therefore, both our own interest and that of others is implicated in the studious pursuit of most perilous (outward) comeliness, it is time for you to know that not merely must the pageantry of fictitious and elaborate beauty be rejected by you; but that of even natural grace must be obliterated by concealment and negligence, as equally dangerous to the glances of (the beholder's) eyes. For, albeit comeliness is not to be *censured*, as being a bodily happiness, as being an additional outlay of the divine plastic art, as being a kind of goodly garment of the soul; yet it is to be *feared*, just on account of the injuriousness and violence of suitors: which (injuriousness and violence) even the father of the faith, Abraham, greatly feared in regard of his own wife's grace; and Isaac, by falsely representing Rebecca as his sister, purchased safety by insult! . . .

These suggestions are not made to you, of course, to be developed into an entire crudity and wildness of appearance; nor are we seeking to persuade you of the good of squalor and slovenliness; but of the limit and norm and just measure of cultivation of the person. There must be no overstepping of that line to which simple and sufficient refinements limit their desires—that line which is pleasing to God. For they who rub their skin with medicaments, stain their cheeks with rouge, make their eyes prominent with antimony, sin against HIM. To them, I suppose, the plastic skill of God is displeasing! In their own persons, I suppose, they convict, they censure, the Artificer of all things! For censure they do when they amend, when they add to, (His work;) taking these their additions, of course, from the adversary artificer. That adversary artificer is the devil. For who would show the way to change the *body*, but he who by wickedness transfigured man's *spirit*? He it is, undoubtedly who adapted ingenious devices of this kind; that in your persons it may be

apparent that you, in a certain sense, do violence to God. Whatever is *born* is the work of God. Whatever, then, is *plastered on* (that), is the devil's work. To superinduce on a divine work Satan's ingenuities, how criminal is it! Our servants borrow nothing from our personal enemies: soldiers eagerly desire nothing from the foes of their own general; for, to demand for (your own) use anything from the adversary of Him in whose hand you are, is a transgression. Shall a Christian be assisted in anything by that evil one? (If he do,) I know not whether this name (of "Christian") will continue (to belong) to him; for he will be his in whose lore he eagerly desires to be instructed. But how alien from *your* schoolings and professions are (these things)! How unworthy the Christian name, to wear a fictitious face, (you,) on whom simplicity in every form is enjoined!—to lie in your appearance, (you,) to whom (lying) with the tongue is not lawful!—to seek after what is another's, (you,) to whom is delivered (the precept of) abstinence from what is another's!—to practise adultery in your mien, (you,) who make modesty your study! Think, blessed (sisters), how will you keep God's precepts if you shall not keep in your own persons His lineaments? . . .

Perhaps some (woman) will say: "To me it is not necessary to be approved by men; for I do not require the testimony of men: God is the inspector of the heart." (That) we all know; provided, however, we remember what the same (God) has said through the apostle:

"Let your probity appear before men." For what purpose, except that malice may have no access at all to you, or that you may be an example and testimony to the evil? Else, what is (that): "Let your works shine"? Why, moreover, does the Lord call us the light of the world; why has He compared us to a city built upon a mountain; if we do not shine in (the midst of) darkness, and stand eminent amid them who are sunk down? If you hide your lamp beneath a bushel, you must necessarily be left quite in darkness, and be run against by many. The things which make us luminaries of the world are these—our good works. What is *good*, moreover, provided it be true and full, loves not darkness: it joys in being seen, and exults over the very pointings which are made at it. To Christian modesty it is not enough to *be* so, but to *seem* so too. For so great ought its plenitude to be, that it may flow out from the mind to the garb, and burst out from the conscience to the outward appearance; so that even from the outside it may gaze, as it were, upon its own furniture,—(a furniture) such as to be suited to retain faith as its inmate perpetually. For such delicacies as tend by their softness and effeminacy to unman the manliness of faith are to be discarded. Otherwise, I know not whether the wrist that has been wont to be surrounded with the palmleaf-like bracelet will endure till it grow into the numb hardness of its own chain. I know not whether the leg that has rejoiced in the anklet will suffer itself to be squeezed into the gyve! I fear

the neck, beset with pearl and emerald nooses, will give no room to the broadsword! Wherefore, blessed (sisters), let us meditate on hardships, and we shall not feel them; let us abandon luxuries, and we shall not regret them. Let us stand ready to endure every violence, having nothing which we may fear to leave behind. It is these things which are the bonds which retard our hope. Let us cast away earthly ornaments if we desire heavenly. Love not gold; in which (one substance) are branded all the sins of the people of Israel. You ought to *hate* what ruined your fathers; what was adored by them who were forsaking God. Even *then* (we find) gold is food for the fire. But Christians always, and now more than ever, pass their times not in gold but in iron: the stoles of martyrdom are (now) preparing: the angels who are to carry us are (now) being awaited! Do you go forth (to meet them) already arrayed in the cosmetics and ornaments of prophets and apostles; drawing your whiteness from simplicity, your ruddy hue from modesty; painting your eyes with bashfulness, and your mouth with silence; implanting in your ears the words of God; fitting on your necks the yoke of Christ. Submit your head to your husbands, and you will be enough adorned. Busy your hands with spinning; keep your feet at home; and you will "please" better than (by arraying yourselves) in gold. Clothe yourselves with the silk of uprightness, the fine linen holiness, the purple of modesty. Thus painted, you will have God as your Lover!

1.4 EGERIA IN THE HOLY LAND

This text is part of an account of a pilgrimage to various sacred sites in and around the holy land, to which is added a description of the liturgy used in Jerusalem. It was probably written by Egeria, a wealthy woman of high social status, sometime between 404 and 417 and addressed to a group of learned and devout women serving the church where she lived. She does not simply list the places she visits but enhances her account with details such as the quality of King Agbar's portrait and the customs linked with the feast day of Saint Helpidius. She reveals that she is well read in Scripture and worthy of the hospitality of great bishops and monks.

Source: "The Pilgrimage of Egeria." In *A Lost Tradition: Women Writers of the Early Church,* edited by Patricia Wilson-Kastner et al., 102–3, 105–7. Lanham, Md.: University Press of America, 1981.

And so again making my way through several rest-stations, I came to the city whose name we find in Scripture, Batanis, which is a city even today. The church, with a holy bishop who is both a monk and confessor, has several martyria. The city contains multitudes of people, for an army with its tribune is based here.

Setting out from there, we arrived in the name of Christ our God at Edessa. When we had arrived there, we immediately went to the church and martyrium of Saint Thomas. Thus having prayed according to our custom, and having done all these things we habitually do in holy places, we also read there some things about Saint Thomas. The church there is large and very beautiful and newly built, and truly worthy to be a house of God. Because there were so many things there which I wanted to see, I had to stay there three days. So I saw many martyria and also holy monks, some living by the martyria and others having their dwellings far from the city in secluded places.

Then the holy bishop of the city, a truly religious monk and confessor, having hospitably received me, told me: "Because I see, daughter, that you have taken such a great work upon yourself, because of your piety coming even from the ends of the earth to these places, we will show you whatever you want, whatever it would please Christians to see." First giving thanks to God, I then asked him to be so kind as to do as he had offered. He first led me to the palace of King Agbar, and showed me there a large portrait of him, quite like him, they say, and as lustrous as if it were made of pearls. Looking at Agbar face to face, he seems to be truly a wise and honorable man. Then the holy bishop said to me: "Here is King Agbar, who before he saw the Lord believed in him as truly the Son of God." Next to that portrait was one also made of marble, said to be his son Magnus, whose countenance was also gracious. . . .

Having passed three days there, I had to go all the way to Carrae, as they now call it [Charra = Haran]. But in

Scripture it is called Charra where Saint Abraham lived, as it is written in Genesis that the Lord said to Abraham, "Go from your land and from the house of your father and go into Haran," and so forth [Gen. 12:1]. When I reached there, that is, Charra, I went immediately to the church which is within the city itself. I soon saw the bishop of the place, a truly holy man of God, himself a monk and confessor, who kindly offered to show us all the places we wished. Then he led us immediately to the church outside the city which is on the site where Saint Abraham's house was, a church made from its stones and on its foundations, as the holy bishop told us. When we had come into that church he prayed and read a passage from the book of Genesis, sang a psalm, and the bishop having said another prayer and blessed us, we went outside. He then kindly agreed to lead us to the well from which Saint Rebecca carried water. The holy bishop told us: "Here is the well from which Saint Rebecca gave water to the camels of the servant of Abraham, Eleazar" [Gen. 24:15-20]. He consented to show us everything.

The church, which, as I said, ladies, venerable sisters, is outside the city, where once was the house of Abraham, now has there a martyrium to a certain holy monk called Helpidius. It was our good fortune to arrive there the day before the martyr's day of Saint Helpidius, nine days before the kalends of May [April 23]. On this day from everywhere within the borders of Mesopotamia all the monks come to Haran, even the great monks who dwell in solitude and are called aescetics, both for that feast which is very highly celebrated here, and for the memory of Saint Abraham, whose house was where the church now is in which is laid the body of the holy martyr. It was more than we had hoped to see these truly holy men of God, the Mesopotamian monks, whose reputation and life are heard of afar. I never thought that I would be able to see them, not because it would be impossible for God to grant this to me, because he has deigned to grant everything, but because I had heard that they did not come down from their dwellings except on the Pasch and on this day, and because these are the sort who do marvelous works. And I did not even know on what day was the martyr's feast, as I said. Thus, God willing, the day arrived for which I had not dared hope when we had come. We stayed there two days, for the martyr's feast and for seeing all the holy men who graciously agreed to receive me and speak with me, even though I did not deserve it. Immediately after the martyr's feast they are not to be seen there, because soon after nightfall they seek the desert and each of them goes to the cell where he lives. In this city, apart from a few clerics and holy monks, I found not a single Christian, for all are pagans. Just as we reverence the place where Saint Abraham first dwelt, honoring his memory, so also the pagans greatly reverence a place about a mile outside the city, where are tombs of Nahor and Bethuel [Gen. 29:24].

Because the bishop of the city is very learned in Scripture, I asked him, "I beg you, my Lord, tell me something I would like to know about." He replied, "Ask what you will, daughter, and I will tell you if I know." "I know through Scripture that Saint Abraham with his father Terah and Sarah his wife and Lot his brother's son came into this place, but I have not read that either Nahor or Bethuel traveled here [Gen. II:31]. I know that only the servant of Abraham afterwards came to Charra to seek Rebecca, daughter of Bethuel son of Nahor, for Isaac, the son of his master Abraham." "Truly, daughter, it is written as you have said in Genesis, that Saint Abraham came here with his family; the Canonical Scriptures do not say at what time Nahor with his family and Bethuel arrived here [Gen. II:31]. But clearly at sometime afterward they must have come here, for their tombs are about a mile from the city. For Scripture testifies truly that the servant of Saint Abraham came here to receive Saint Rebecca, and again that Saint Jacob came here that he might take the daughters of Laban the Syrian" [Gen. 24:28].

Then I asked him where the well was from which Saint Jacob gave water to the sheep which were herded by Rachel the daughter of Laban the Syrian [Gen. II:28]. The bishop told me: "Within about six miles of here is a place next to a village which then was the land of Laban the Syrian; when you wish to go there we will go with you and show it

to you, for there are many holy monks and aescetics, as well as a holy church in that place." I also asked the holy bishop where was the place where first Terah and his family lived among the Chaldeeans. Then the holy bishop responded: "The place of which you speak is from here ten days journey into Persia. From here Nisibis is five days, and from there to Ur, the city of the Chaldeeans, is five more days. But now there is no access for Romans there, because the Persians hold the whole territory. Particularly this part which is on the Roman borders of Persia and Chaldee is called Syria Orientalis." He kindly told me many other things, as had also many other holy bishops and monks, always about the Scriptures and the deeds of holy men, of monks, that is; if they were dead, of the marvels they had done, if they are still in the body, of what is done daily by those called aescetics [2 Cor. 12:3]. For I do not wish your affection to think that the monks have any other stories than those of the divine Scriptures and the deeds of the great monks.

1.5 THE ACTS OF PAUL AND THECLA

This reading comes from the apocryphal Acts of Paul and Thecla, *written sometime near the end of the second century and set in the towns of southern Asia Minor. In the story, Paul arrives at Iconium and preaches that men and women cannot hope for resurrection from the dead unless they abstain from sexual relations. A wealthy virgin, Thecla, watches from a nearby window and is captivated by Paul's message. She breaks off her engagement to Thamyris and dedicates herself to perpetual virginity. The wrath of both family and local Roman authorities ensue, Paul is driven from the city, and Thecla is condemned to death by burning. A miraculous storm douses the flames, however, and Thecla sets out to find Paul and travel to Antioch with him. Paul welcomes her but refuses to baptize her. The text below takes up the story as Thecla is attacked in the street by the amorous Alexander. She is eventually commissioned to teach and even baptizes herself, but these privileges are linked to the virgin life and "becoming like a man."*

Source: "The Acts of Paul and Thecla." In *The Apocryphal New Testament*, translated by Montague Rhodes James, 277–81. Oxford: Clarendon Press, 1924.

[26]And Paul sent away Onesiphorus with all his house unto Iconium, and so took Thecla and entered into Antioch: and as they entered in, a certain Syriarch, Alexander by name, saw Thecla and was enamoured of her, and would have bribed (flattered) Paul with money and gifts. But Paul said: I know not the woman of whom thou speakest, neither is she mine. But as he was of great power, he himself embraced her in the highway; and she endured it not, but sought after Paul and cried out bitterly, saying: Force not the stranger, force not the handmaid of God. I am of the first of the Iconians, and because I would not marry Thamyris, I am cast out of the city. And she caught at Alexander and rent his cloak and took the wreath from his head and made him a mocking-stock.

[27]But he alike loving her and being ashamed of what had befallen him, brought her before the governor; and when she confessed that she had done this, he condemned her to the beasts. But the women were greatly amazed and cried out at the judgement seat: An evil judgement, an impious judgement! And Thecla asked of the governor that she might remain a virgin until she should fight the beasts; and a certain rich queen, Tryphaena by name, whose daughter had died, took her into her keeping, and had her for a consolation. . . .

[31]And the governor sent soldiers to fetch Thecla: and Tryphaena left her not, but herself took her hand and led her up, saying: I did bring my daughter Falconilla unto the sepulchre; but thee, Thecla, do I bring to fight the beasts. And Thecla wept bitterly and groaned unto the Lord, saying: Lord God in whom I believe, with whom I have taken refuge, that savedst me from the fire, reward thou Tryphaena who hath pity on thy handmaid, and hath kept me pure.

[32]There was therefore a tumult, and a voice of the beasts, and shouting of the people, and of the women which sat together, some saying: Bring in the sacrilegious one! and the women saying: Away with the city for this unlawful deed! away with all us, thou proconsul! it is a bitter sight, an evil judgement!

[33]But Thecla, being taken out of the hand of Tryphaena, was stripped and a girdle put upon her, and was cast into

the stadium: and lions and bears were set against her. And a fierce lioness running to her lay down at her feet, and the press of women cried aloud. And a bear ran upon her; but the lioness ran and met him, and tore the bear in sunder. And again a lion, trained against men, which was Alexander's, ran upon her, and the lioness wrestled with him and was slain along with him. And the women bewailed yet more, seeing that the lioness also that succoured her was dead.

³⁴Then did they put in many beasts, while she stood and stretched out her hands and prayed. And when she had ended her prayer, she turned and saw a great tank full of water, and said: Now is it time that I should wash myself. And she cast herself in, saying: In the name of Jesus Christ do I baptize myself on the last day. And all the women seeing it and all the people wept, saying: Cast not thyself into the water: so that even the governor wept that so great beauty should be devoured by seals. So, then, she cast herself into the water in the name of Jesus Christ; and the seals, seeing the light of a flash of fire, floated dead on the top of the water. And there was about her a cloud of fire, so that neither did the beasts touch her, nor was she seen to be naked.

³⁵Now the women, when other more fearful beasts were put in, shrieked aloud, and some cast leaves, and other nard, others cassia, and some balsam, so that there was a multitude of odours; and all the beasts that were struck thereby were

held as it were in sleep and touched her not; so that Alexander said to the governor: I have some bulls exceeding fearful, let us bind the criminal to them. And the governor frowning, allowed it, saying: Do that thou wilt. And they bound her by the feet between the bulls, and put hot irons under their bellies that they might be the more enraged and kill her. They then leaped forward; but the flame that burned about her, burned through the ropes, and she was as one not bound.

³⁶But Tryphaena, standing by the arena, fainted at the entry, so that her handmaids said: The queen Tryphaena is dead! And the governor stopped the games and all the city was frightened, and Alexander falling at the governor's feet said: Have mercy on me and on the city, and let the condemned go, lest the city perish with her; for if Caesar hear this, perchance he will destroy us and the city, because his kinswoman the queen Tryphaena hath died at the entry.

³⁷And the governor called Thecla from among the beasts, and said to her: Who art thou? And what hast thou about thee that not one of the beasts hath touched thee? But she said: I am the handmaid of the living God; and what I have about me—it is that I have believed on that his Son in whom God is well pleased; for whose sake not one of the beasts hath touched me. For he alone is the goal (*or* way) of salvation and the substance of life immortal; for unto them that are tossed about he is a

refuge, unto the oppressed relief, unto the despairing shelter, and in a word, whosoever believeth not on him, shall not live, but die everlastingly.

³⁸And when the governor heard this, he commanded garments to be brought and said: Put on these garments. And she said: He that clad me when I was naked among the beasts, the same in the day of judgment will clothe me with salvation. And she took the garments and put them on. And the governor forthwith issued out an act, saying: I release unto you Thecla the godly the servant of God. And all the women cried out with a loud voice and as with one mouth gave praise to God, saying: One is the God who hath preserved Thecla: so that with their voice all the city shook.

³⁹And Tryphaena, when she was told the good tidings, met her with much people and embraced Thecla and said: Now do I believe that the dead are raised up: now do I believe that my child liveth: come within, and I will make thee heir of all my substance. Thecla therefore went in with her and rested in her house eight days, teaching her the word of God, so that the more part of the maid-servants also believed, and there was great joy in the house.

⁴⁰But Thecla yearned after Paul and sought him, sending about in all places; and it was told her that he was at Myra. And she took young men and maids, and girded herself, and sewed her mantle into a cloak after the fashion of a man, and departed into Myra, and found Paul speaking the word of God, and went to him. But when he saw her and the people that were with her was amazed, thinking in himself: Hath some other temptation come upon her? But she perceived it, and said to him: I have received the washing, O Paul; for he that hath worked together with thee in the Gospel hath worked with me also unto my baptizing.

⁴¹And Paul took her by the hand and brought her into the house of Hermias, and heard all things from her; so that Paul marveled much, and they that heard were confirmed, and prayed for Tryphaena. And Thecla arose and said to Paul: I go unto Iconium. And Paul said: Go and teach the word of God. Now Tryphaena *had* sent her much apparel and gold, so that she left *of it* with Paul for the ministry of the poor.

Chapter 2

VIRGIN AND WITCH: WOMEN IN MEDIEVAL CHRISTIANITY

The images of women that emerge in medieval literature were shaped to a large extent by a few literate monks, bishops, and noblemen. In both secular and church writings, images of women oscillate between two extreme positions—which historians have described as "the pit and the throne"—that ignore the humanity, complexity, and individuality of women. On the one hand, women are denounced in strong terms as wicked and inferior. This virulent misogyny (a hatred and distrust of women) reached its peak in the witch hunt that swept across Europe from the fifteenth to the eighteenth centuries. On the other hand, women are praised, idealized, and adored in the symbol of the Virgin Mary and as the courtly lady in the popular tales of chivalry.

Many medieval theologians repeated some of the main ideas about women found in the church fathers. Thomas Aquinas, a thirteenth-century scholar whose influence is still evident today, claimed that woman was created as subordinate and inferior to man. Not only was she second in the order of creation, but she was also endowed with less intellectual capability and, consequently, less ability to make right moral decisions. Reviving ideas from ancient Greek biology, Aquinas argued that male sperm provided the original form and active energy of a human being and would normally produce another male. Women were therefore misbegotten humans, thus necessitating the establishment of gender roles, according to Aquinas. Men in this world must rule over women because men were more perfect and intelligent. Aquinas also strengthened the tie between women and the world of the flesh. Women were created as helpers in the work of generation, passively providing the matter that was activated by the male seed.

This overwhelming sense of female inferiority permeated not only theology but popular culture as well. The widespread vices of women were constantly stressed; stories about adulterous wives far outnumbered those of unfaithful husbands. The monastic literature frequently portrayed women as talking too much, causing discord, loving gold, being disloyal, and being sexually insatiable. A companion theme was the need to keep women under control in church and society to keep them from spreading sin. Books of "wikked wives" detailed all the women of the Bible and history who had led men astray. Literature addressed to young women urged them to honor and obey their husbands, even when their husbands were evil. Church law specifically permitted wife beating as a way to control female corruption and disobedience.

A few positive attitudes toward women did find their way into medieval theology. Aquinas and others stressed that, although inferior, women had been given the important task of procreation by God. Some theologians also insisted that men and women have rational souls and that in the future kingdom of God, male and female would be "equivalent." The institution of marriage itself was also given a slightly more positive character. Marriage was increasingly described as a sacrament, which conferred God's grace upon those bound in it. Virginity, however, was still applauded as the best lifestyle for women since it dissociated them from sexuality and therefore from evil.

THE LIFE OF VIRGINITY AND CHASTITY

The Growth of Asceticism

By the end of the third century, a growing number of Christians were adopting a lifestyle of asceticism. They denied themselves physical pleasures such as eating and warmth, doing only what was necessary to stay alive. They practiced voluntary poverty and complete abstinence from sexual relations. This "exercise" of self-discipline (from which the word "asceticism" comes) was seen as good preparation and eventually as a substitution for martyrdom, as well as a way to a more holy or perfect life in the eyes of God. Less time and resources spent on the preparation of food and on personal appearance meant more time and resources for prayer, worship, and acts of charity. Some Christians also believed that the kingdom of God and the end of time would be brought nearer if the followers of Jesus practiced self-denial.

Christian ascetics looked to the biblical tradition to justify their lifestyle. The Old Testament does recommend periods of fasting and sexual abstinence, but overall it applauds the goodness of the created world and married life. In the examples and teachings of Jesus and Paul, however, the ascetics believed that they found strong support. Jesus told his disciples that they must deny themselves and follow him. His life was one of a poor nomad who had no possessions and who lived a life of complete chastity. Paul frequently spoke of the need to quell the passions of the flesh. He endured nakedness and cold for the gospel and, above all, he counseled that celibacy was preferable to marriage. Christian asceticism gained further impetus from prevalent philosophies in Greco-Roman culture. Some of these philosophies not only advised the avoidance of physical pleasure, but they also expressed contempt for the material world as evil, which went far beyond biblical teachings. Bodily needs and desires had to be conquered because they were obstacles to spiritual growth.

Domestic and Monastic Asceticism

Many women as well as men adopted the ascetic way of life in the Christian community. Abstinence from sexual relations was the defining characteristic and only later was invariably accompanied by giving up personal wealth. Originally the word "virginity" covered a variety of lifestyles. Some virgins were widows who vowed to live in perfect chastity and self-denial for the remainder of their lives. Other virgins were married women who persuaded their husbands to relinquish sexual relations and live together in chastity. Still others were young unmarried women who lived lives of *integritas* or complete virginity. These unmarried women are occasionally mentioned in writings from the second century, but it was not until the following century that they were recognized as a special order within the community. These quint-essential ascetics were regarded as special symbols for the union of Christ with the church and called the "brides" or "spouses" of Christ. By the fourth century, intact virginity was praised extravagantly as a life leading to salvation and sainthood.[1] Some church leaders encouraged women to flee, mutilate their bodies (such as the women of Coldingham Priory in Scotland who cut off their noses and upper lips to repel Danish invaders), and even commit suicide, all of which served as evidence that their wills remained chaste in the face of rape. By the same token, women who willfully compromised their virginity would be turned away from Christ's bridal chamber and suffer unspeakable humiliation. They were guilty of adultery in civil and church law, and in some places put to death.

The living arrangements of consecrated women throughout the early and medieval periods of Christian history were diverse. Women remained in their own homes, became partners in "spiritual marriages," took up residence in the desert, and later became members of monastic communities.

Domestic Asceticism. Many women chose to live the life of chastity in their own homes. This was a particularly attractive option for wealthy women who could remain in seclusion on their estates and gather around them female friends, relatives, and servants of a similar spirit. Early Christian pastors and theologians were concerned with the problems the "virgins of the world" faced. They dispensed advice on the kind of company these women should keep, the clothes they should wear in order to avoid attention, and the strategy they should use in dealing with family pressure to marry. Women with property faced subtle and sometimes violent attempts to persuade them to abandon their vows and prevent family wealth from passing into the hands of the church. Of course, their seclusion often had to be compromised from time to time as they conducted business, went into marketplaces, or attended church.

The Spiritual Marriage. Another lifestyle chosen by women was the "spiritual marriage" in which a man and a woman committed to a life of chastity together, sharing the same house and sometimes the same bed. The couple engaged in an intimate but not sexual relationship. There are many condemnations of this practice in the writings of early bishops and theologians, and many church councils forbid it right through the Middle Ages. The assumption, of course, was that men and women could not cohabit and at the same time be faithful to their vows of chastity. But another concern was that women were initiating these relationships; they were not being properly submissive and the men who cooperated were emasculating themselves by, for example, shopping for their partners.[2] Yet these spiritual marriages met a need for women who did not live near a monastery and who were not wealthy in their own right. They could, in this arrangement, depend on a man of similar ideals for a livelihood and protection. Also, the *Agapetae* (the name given to consecrated virgins who depended on lay men for support) seemed to share a deep and often intellectual friendship with their male partners, which Greco Roman culture believed to be impossible between men and women. They raised for the Christian community the possibility of relationships between men and women that are other than sexual and yet intimate and compassionate.

Another form of spiritual marriage that lasted well beyond the medieval period was the chaste cohabitation of a man and woman in an otherwise typical marriage. One of the most celebrated examples was the marriage of the Roman aristocrats Cecilia and Valerian. Dyan Elliott sees these arrangements as possible ways in which women asserted their independence and undermined their husbands' authority; spiritual marriages were frequently initiated by wives and precluded the supreme act of submission—sexual intercourse.[3]

The Monastic Community. The ancient historian Palladius records that there were some twenty thousand women living in poverty, chastity, and solitude in the desert surrounding Egypt. Historians do not know how accurate his numbers are, but they do know that women were an important presence in the desert and received a constant stream of visitors seeking spiritual wisdom. In the case of both desert and domestic asceticism, women may have seen communal possibilities for ascetic living earlier than men did.[4] Such possibilities were given structured expression by Pachomius in the early fourth century. From this time on, monasteries for men and women proliferated throughout the eastern part of the Roman Empire as the history of asceticism became "a growing story of rules and formal houses."[5] What began as a disorganized impulse grew into the highly organized tradition of monastic life.

Some communities of women shared a roof with a male community, others were separate but close to male monasteries, and some existed on their own.

Women typically lived under the authority of a superior or leader and according to certain regulations of lifestyle set out in the monastic "rule." One such rule was developed by Pachomius for men and women who lived in two monastic communities in Egypt; it illustrates the daily life and responsibilities of some four hundred women. They spent most of their time in household tasks and in a routine of worship, prayer, and Scripture study. These contemplative tasks, which had been done by the widows in the churches, were gradually taken over by the monastic communities. The women were kept away from men, apart from a priest who celebrated the sacraments, and they were expected to remain enclosed ("cloistered") in the buildings for the rest of their lives. Material goods were shipped back and forth in baskets across a river that separated the male and female communities. All of these features of the Egyptian communities became standard in ascetic life in western Europe.

By the fifth century, monasticism appeared in the western part of the Roman Empire. The first communities of women there lived under a variety of rules, such as the one written by Caesarius, Bishop of Arles, until the rule of Saint Benedict grew in popularity and was imposed by Charlemagne throughout his empire. Women spent time in study, prayer, and household tasks. Their lives were shaped in large part by their abbesses, the female superiors of the communities. And although all of the early communities separated women from the world, there were numerous opportunities for women to become involved in mission work and even politics. These opportunities diminished, however, as the church underwent a period of reform and revival in the eleventh and twelfth centuries. A concern for the authority of the pope and bishops coupled with an exaggerated fear of the temptations all women represented to celibate men were at the heart of the reform. The freedom the abbesses initially had was curtailed, and the church began to enforce the strict enclosure of women. "Double" monasteries for men and women were closed.

Important changes occurred again in the twelfth through fourteenth centuries as new types of ascetic communities emerged. These communities were in response to a desire on the part of lay people to recover the lifestyle and faith of the apostles. A large number of women were attracted, but their enthusiasm was discouraged, often because of the church's view of the nature and role of women. The Cistercians (an order established in France in the eleventh century that revived a strict obedience to the monastic rule of Saint Benedict) believed that the female sex was not capable of obeying the austere rules and attaining the level of perfection demanded by the order. The Dominicans and Franciscans both had a tradition of encouraging the spirituality of women but soon began to repel any attempts by women to open convents under their rules and ministered to by their members. Economic reasons were sometimes given: the men would have to support these new groups of women financially since they frequently came from the lower classes of society and were without wealthy patrons. The argument that close association with women was dangerous to the spiritual well-being of the monks, however, was more evident. As one official document from a new religious order (the Premonstratensians) claimed, "The poisons of vipers and dragons are healthier and less harmful for men than familiarity with women."[6]

Some of the new orders that emphasized the public preaching of the gospel, such as that at Fontevrault in France, did welcome women as members but opened convents for them that prevented them from having any contact with the outside world. Obviously, this strategy excluded women from evangelical preaching, which was one of the main activities of the order. There was a growing insistence in the medieval church that women leading the virgin life be locked securely away behind cloistered walls. This opinion was based on the belief that women would easily give in to sexual temptation and would compromise those men with whom they came into contact. Cloistering had long been recommended in some places, but in 1298 Pope Boniface VIII tried to impose it upon the whole church in his constitution *Periculoso*. Strict rules were laid down regarding the conversations a monastic woman could have with outsiders as well as the occasions on which she could leave the convent. The Catholic Church tried to enforce this general policy well into the twentieth century.

In some instances, those women who wished to pursue a life of poverty and active mission but who could not find a place in the new or established religious orders joined the Beguines. The Beguines were autonomous groups of women that emerged mainly in urban areas of Germany, northern France, and the Low Countries. The women involved did not take irrevocable vows but did adopt a chaste and simple style of living, often supporting themselves by working in the textile industry. Some lived at home while in other areas, Beguine convents, a cluster of buildings, were set up near hospitals. The women ministered to the poor and sick but, despite their good works, the church regarded them with suspicion: here were unmarried women who were not cloistered and who devised their own rules. Their informality placed them outside the disciplinary structures of the institution, and their emphasis on righteous living and a personal relationship to Christ associated them with movements that the church was trying to eliminate.

The Recluses. Women could also choose to become recluses or anchorites, living in a small cell close to a monastery or, by the twelfth century, attached to the wall of a city church. Frequently, after a mass for the dead was said for the recluse to signal her death to the world, she was enclosed in the cell for the duration of her life. She typically had a window open to the outside world and one looking into the church to enable her to hear Mass. The recluse gave up her freedom to go place to place in order to develop a higher freedom, spending time in prayer and reading and using the solitude to take part in the work of salvation.[7] But recluses were also highly revered by the people who lived around them as women who had been touched by the prophetic spirit. They gave advice, settled disputes, foretold events, and even pronounced on the fate of the dead.

Power and Autonomy in the Ascetic Life

In practical terms, communal life gave women physical protection both from the risks of childbearing and from the risks of living alone in a society that became increasingly unstable and dangerous as the rule of Rome disintegrated. But the ascetic life also offered women opportunities for choice, freedom, and participation from which they were excluded in church and society. It is impossible to know what motivated individual women to take up the ascetic life. A love for Christ, the coercion of family, and a fear of social disorder were no doubt common reasons. But they may have also been attracted by the chance to break through the barriers of tradition and overcome female subjection.

Crossing Boundaries. Especially during the early centuries of Christian history, the ascetic life gave women freedom to travel. The rules that disapproved of women making journeys on their own changed for those who went on pilgrimages in the name of religious devotion. Melania the Younger, for example, traveled throughout Italy, North Africa, Egypt, and Palestine. The Holy Land was a favorite destination. Wherever these ascetic women traveled, they were greeted with honor and gifts. Some women who headed convents attended church synods and traveled to inspect their estates; others took part in the extensive efforts to Christianize the Germanic tribes that invaded the western half of the Roman Empire. They carried on the tradition of celibate women preaching, teaching, and evangelizing, which seems to be reflected in early church texts such as the *Acts of Paul and Thecla*.

Ascetic women held positions of authority in an informal manner. By virtue of their holiness and personal piety, women were treated frequently with respect and deference by the whole community, including men of high standing among the clergy. Eleanor McLaughlin has described these women as being "empowered" by their holiness.[8] This power was often believed to take concrete form in the ability to perform miracles, or, as one historian describes it, the power to restore and integrate the natural order.[9] Lioba, an eighth-century English ascetic, is recorded as having calmed a storm and healed the sick in her community. She was honored by bishops, nobles, princes, and even the emperor Charlemagne.

Power stemming from a holy life also took shape in the ability to acquire great learning, which also attracted men of authority within the church. The ascetic life gave women the opportunity to study and rewarded them for intellectual achievement. Although he argues that women have a greater need to read the Bible because of their sin, Jerome was a passionate defender of the right of women to engage in challenging biblical scholarship. For him, the writer of a text and the reader of a text were united at a level that transcended the limitations of the female body and nature.[10] Melania the Younger acquired a formidable theological education, debated doctrine, and taught an array of men and women including the emperor Theodosius. Marcella became an expert on the Bible in Rome and aided the clergy with their dilemmas of translation and interpretation. Lioba was skilled in classical philosophy, theology, and canon law. This erudition gave her an almost mystical authority and prompted the bishop Boniface to seek her help in bringing order to the missionary churches in Germany. Such women, however, were counseled to show self-effacement and to appear as pupils even when they were teaching.[11]

Asceticism also allowed for friendships between men and women that would otherwise have been difficult to realize in Greco-Roman culture, where friendship could only exist between equals. Both Jerome and John Chrysostom are best known for the large circles of women they counted as friends. These women could be treated as equals because they had become "like men" by controlling their sexuality, eliminating their reproductive functions, and cultivating traits such as courage and rationality.

The Abbesses. Monasteries for women were also headed by women, giving them an opportunity to exercise authority and leadership within the institutional sphere of the Christian community. The list of women in this capacity begins with individuals such as Paula, the associate of Jerome, and the sister of Augustine, and continues throughout Christian history. The medieval abbesses, however, most clearly illustrate the temporal (relating to the affairs of this world) as well as spiritual power that the monastic life offered to women.

The abbess usually headed a group of women living the monastic life, although in countries such as England and northern France, they sometimes headed double monasteries of men and women. In many places in early medieval Europe, they enjoyed the same powers and privileges as abbots, bishops, and noblemen. They sat in parliaments, attended church councils, signed official church decrees, and oversaw the affairs of the clergy and lay people who lived on the often vast lands owned by the abbey. The word "ordination" is sometimes used to describe the consecration of an abbess. Although she was not given the power to administer the sacraments, she was given the same signs of high office that a bishop received. These included a ring, mitre (a special headdress worn by bishops and abbots), and crozier (a staff resembling a shepherd's crook carried by bishops and abbots as a symbol of office). In addition to offering spiritual guidance, some abbesses heard the confessions of those in their charge and, despite the wrath of the church hierarchy, even administered penance and granted absolution for sins. The power of the abbesses began to decline, however, as early as the ninth century: their ordination became instead a blessing, they gradually came under the authority of local bishops, and the church eventually dissolved double orders.

A Chance to Choose. Finally, and perhaps most significantly, the ascetic life gave women an opportunity to exercise free choice and a basis for rejecting the demand that they marry and bear children for the sake of the patriarchal clan. The decision to lead a chaste life was an autonomous one in a society that left little up to the preferences of women. Although not all families objected to such a decision, many women experienced family pressures to conform to tradition since both their reproductive potential and their money would otherwise be withdrawn from the use of the ruling class.[12] Many women protested by appealing to the authority of God. Popular poetry in fact spoke of the convent as a refuge from the hardships of married life. In medieval France, for example, Saint Burgundofara hid in a basilica when her father wanted to betroth her. When Saint Maxellinda insisted on keeping her vow of chastity even after her marriage, her husband tried to rape and abduct her and eventually murdered her. The experiences of Christina of Markyate provide one of the fullest accounts of a woman's protest and initiative.

Christina, the daughter of an English nobleman, was born at the end of the eleventh century. An account of her life describes her marriage to Burthred despite the fact that she had made a vow to be a virgin when she was thirteen. She refused to consummate the marriage, which was forced on her by her parents. She escaped several plots by her husband and family to lure her into the marriage bed. Once, when Burthred and his drunken friends invaded her bedroom, she avoided them by hanging by her fingertips between the bed curtains and the wall. Although Christina initially had the support of the bishop, even he began to pressure her into relenting after receiving a bribe from Christina's father. She eventually escaped from her home disguised as a boy and took up the life of a hermit. Within the medieval Christian community, she became recognized as a woman of power and authority that extended far beyond the confines of her cell.

Food was also a way in which women exercised choice since it provided them with a means to control and manipulate their environments. Caroline Bynum points out that stories of holy women have "insistent and complex food motifs," and these stories, more often than those about men, involve extreme fasting as a central part of spirituality.[13] Women identified a resource in their lives over which they had direct control, which could be renounced voluntarily in the cause of Christ. They fasted to make menstruation cease and to avoid the sexual urges that they believed food stimulated, thus transcending their femaleness. They avoided unwanted marriages or pressured families to become more devout by self-starvation. They also challenged the control of male clergy by receiving the Eucharist in visions directly from Jesus himself.[14]

Ambiguous Space. While the life of chastity, fasting, and austerity presented new opportunities for power and participation, it did not always have an overall positive effect on the status of women. The monastic community, in fact, represents a somewhat ambiguous space for women.[15] It did not, for example, open up the offices of priest and bishop to women; women continued to be controlled and dominated by men and had to rely on male priests for a wide variety of services including the sacraments. The ascetic tradition also suffered from the deeply rooted tendency of the churches to value the writings and lives of the male ascetics above the lives and works of female ascetics. As various reform movements throughout the history of the church became increasingly successful at imposing cloistering on women, women often lost their opportunities for mobility and equitable relationships with male colleagues.

Eleanor McLaughlin, along with many other scholars, suggests that there was a profound difference between the experiences of men and women who entered religious orders.[16] While men were expected to deny themselves sexual experiences, they retained their masculine nature, which society associated with courage, rationality, and self-discipline and therefore with spiritual advancement. Women, however, were expected to erase their female natures, which were determined by the functions of procreation and the demands of the flesh. They were encouraged to become "like men" in their anticipation of the kingdom of God. In the stories of female ascetics, a concrete sign of this change in nature was wearing the clothes of a man or making every effort to erase the features of the female body (such as cutting hair). It also meant developing intellect, rationality, loyalty, and courage. Furthermore, women who endured death and engaged in self-mutilation to protect their virginity became praiseworthy role models. The celebration of the virgin life tended to degrade women who were not prepared to erase their femaleness and who continued to be wives and mothers. Finally, we are left to ponder whether the monastic ideals intensified rather than broke with tradition. The monastic life may have, in many cases, hindered the self-development and independence of women and instead reinforced traits of passiveness and dependence.

Medieval Mariology

In contrast to the image of woman as evil seductress, the church as well as medieval society also placed woman on a pedestal as a paragon of virtue and piety. The idealized woman, however, was not a sexual creature. In secular tales of courtly love and chivalry, this image comes across forcefully. In these stories, a beautiful and pure woman is adored by a male lover (not her husband), who in turn is inspired to perform great acts of heroism for his lady. There is no sexual encounter, only spiritual love. Such a woman stood in a superior position and encouraged morality, patience, and humility in her chivalrous lover. The church, of course, had its counterpart to the lady of courtly love in the figure of the Virgin Mary. Especially in the twelfth and thirteenth centuries, the mother of Jesus commanded great devotion and adoration and inspired holy living in many Christians. She was honored in liturgies, churches were dedicated to her, and thousands of pilgrims each year journeyed to churches that displayed her relics. This exuberant devotion to Mary and medieval beliefs associated with her did not appear overnight but evolved slowly as each age saw Mary anew in terms of its own needs and values.

Evolution of an Image

The New Testament provides very little information on Mary in contrast to the rich body of story and theology that had accumulated around her by the medieval period. The earliest biblical reference, Gal. 4:4, does not mention Mary directly, but only states that Jesus was born of a woman. Acts 1:14 places her in the community of Christians, but the Gospel references describe her relationship to Jesus as ambiguous and peculiar. In some passages, the relationship appears to be tinged with hostility (Mark 3:31-35; John 2:1-11). Only in John's Gospel (19:25-27) does Mary play a role in the last events of Jesus' life.

Luke and Matthew both include Mary in their accounts of the birth of Jesus, but only Luke makes her the center of the drama. Both accounts reveal Mary as an ordinary Palestinian woman who is obedient to the will of God. Both accounts also identify Mary as a virgin at the time of Jesus' birth, and they imply that his conception was miraculous. Scholars disagree about the source of this idea, which was well established in Christian circles by the time the Gospels were written. It may have come from the Greek version of the Book of Isaiah, which prophesied that "a virgin will conceive and bear a son." Or it may have been borrowed from Greco-Roman culture, which ascribed virgin births to its great heroes and leaders to illustrate their divine origins. In any case, for the early church the virgin birth was probably used to show that Jesus was chosen by God and that he shared both a divine and human nature. It was more a statement about Jesus than about Mary. There is no conclusive biblical evidence that Mary remained a virgin for the duration of her life. That question would be posed by a later age.

In the second century, a cluster of theological ideas and stories about Mary began to grow. Mary's nature and role became the object of intellectual speculation and Mary herself became the focal point of popular devotion.[17] This "cult" of the Virgin Mary was fully developed by the twelfth century. Mary was the Christian counterpart of the romantic lady in medieval tales of chivalry. The cult of Mary was influenced by a number of things: biblical imagery that portrayed Israel as the bride of God and the church as the bride of Christ, pre-Christian goddess worship, and the theological debates over the nature of Jesus.

The virginity of Mary quickly emerged as an essential feature of theology and popular piety. This was especially true as the ascetic lifestyle became more popular. As sexuality became associated with sin, it was necessary to remove sexual relations from the origins of Jesus as the sinless Son of God. Those who supported the virgin life also used Mary to show that God had placed a seal of approval on chastity.

Virginity was extended from the conception of Jesus to his birth and to Mary's entire life as Christian theology developed. Mary became the perpetual virgin who gave birth to a child without having the seal of her womb, or hymen, broken and who remained a virgin until her death. These ideas were spread by an early Christian book, the *Book of James*, which includes many stories about the birth, childhood, and adult life of Mary. Joseph, for example, is portrayed as a widower to explain the existence of the brothers of Jesus in the New Testament.

Apart from virginity, one of the earliest images associated with Mary was that of the New Eve. Mary, it was said, reversed what Eve had done. Eve had broken God's commandments and passed sin and death on to her offspring. Mary, however, was obedient to God and brought redemption to the world through the birth of Jesus. She was the spiritual mother of Christians who were participants in God's new creation. Mary also represented the whole church or community of believers in her obedience and faith. Both as the New Eve and as the symbol for the church, or bride of Christ, Mary took her place in art and literature as the spouse and consort of Jesus who reigned in heaven.

Historians believe that when Christianity became the official religion of the Roman Empire in the fourth century, it was profoundly affected by the beliefs and customs of pre-Christian religions that had been practiced by the new converts. Many of these ancient religions worshiped a mother goddess who was the source of all life and the one from whom the earth, all living creatures, and even the gods themselves derived their being. This goddess devotion may have been transferred to Mary with the coming of Christianity. In particular, it may be the source of the image of Mary as the Mother of God. This image was reinforced by a strong theological view that said that the divine and human natures of Jesus were intermingled such that it was possible to speak of Mary as the mother of God (God-bearer) and not merely as the mother of the Christ. Mary is still regarded in some agricultural communities as the source of fertility for land and people and the source of good fortune and good weather.

After the first few centuries of Christian history, it became increasingly common to see Jesus as a terrifying judge who was far removed from humanity in his heavenly domain. He was concerned more with punishment for sin rather than with mercy and love. Mary therefore began to assume the role of mediator, speaking on behalf of Christians before God. It was believed that since she had been a human mother she would not turn away even the most wicked child. She would plead for grace on behalf of all who came to her and God and Jesus would hear her petitions. As a mediator of grace, Mary became an adored figure in the religious life of ordinary people. They flocked to her shrines, built chapels in her honor, and celebrated the special events in her life with festivals and processions.

Although they did not become official doctrines of the Catholic Church until the modern era, two important theological ideas about Mary had emerged by the twelfth century. One was that Mary had been taken up bodily or "assumed" into heaven at the time of her death. She existed, just like God the Father and the Son, in a heavenly realm where she could mediate for believers on earth. This doctrine of the assumption nurtured the image of Mary as the queen of heaven who reigned over the hosts of heaven at the right hand of Christ. Medieval art is resplendent with scenes of the Virgin with crown and jewels, displaying the signs of royal office. The other idea about Mary evolved eventually into the doctrine of her immaculate conception. The church believed that although Mary was fully human and the product of sexual relations that passed on original sin, God had cleansed her from this sin at the moment of her conception. God also preserved her from any additional sin during her lifetime. In this way she provided a pure, sinless womb for Jesus.

Mary and the Status of Women

What significance has Mary had for the status of women in the Christian community?[18] It is possible to dismiss Mary as an image not useful and even harmful to modern women, an image created by celibate men to keep women in their place. According to Marina Warner, there is a definite correlation between the popularity of Mary and the low status of women in past and contemporary cultures.[19] Mary has reinforced the idea that the virgin, or chaste, life is most pleasing in the eyes of God. This belief, as we have already seen, has had both a liberating and oppressive effect on women. Women as virgins did gain a measure of freedom and equality with men but only by learning to loathe their sexuality and female natures. Scholars also observe that although Mary was a woman, the circumstances of her life could not be duplicated by ordinary women. The birth of Jesus was without pain, marriage was without the sexual union of two bodies, and death did not mean the decay of her flesh. After her death, Mary took on the role of queen with the exceptional honor and luxury that implied. Even when a parallel and more human vision of Mary developed in popular literature, it simply reinforced traditional ideas about women. In these popular stories, Mary polishes the ornaments in the temple, becomes hysterical at the crucifixion, and is softhearted rather than logical when dealing with sinful human beings. She, therefore, deserves to be venerated because she was submissive and obedient. Recently visions and messages believed by many faithful Catholics to come from Mary have also been used to condemn abortion and feminism.

What Mary represents is much more complex. The Mary of the New Testament offers a model of discipleship and even female preaching as she announces her good news to Elizabeth in the Magnificat. She does not show self-abasement but, rather, argues with an archangel and declares that she will be called blessed. And she clearly illustrates God's concern for the poor and oppressed.[20] Elizabeth Johnson argues that Mary could become an important resource in revising our doctrines of God to include qualities such as mercy, warmth, and intimacy. She is a powerful representation of aspects of the divine forgotten in the Church's emphasis on Father, Son, and Holy Spirit.[21]

WOMAN AS WITCH

The Witch Hunt

The general consensus among historians is that between one hundred and two hundred thousand people were prosecuted in what has become known as the European witch hunt. No one factor can explain the witch hunt, which lasted roughly from 1450 to 1750 and eventually touched the American colonies. Toward the end of the fifteenth century in Europe, a coherent theory of witchcraft took shape in the minds of church authorities, government officials, and ordinary people. At the heart of this image was the widespread belief that witches were people who had made pacts with the Devil. They promised to worship the Devil, be his sexual partner, and renounce the Christian faith. These ideas were rooted in certain theological developments that had been appearing in academic writing since the twelfth century. The Devil became a figure of enormous power and status, the controller of an army of demons that infested the earth. The Devil made pacts, held large gatherings called Sabbats, and left marks on the bodies of his devotees. He gave them the ability to fly through the air to attend Sabbats, where they worshiped the Devil, ate the bodies and drank the blood of children (mimicking the Christian Eucharist), and indulged their sexual appetites. At these orgies as well as at home, it was said that the witches surrounded themselves with small animals or "familiars," which were really demons in disguise.

It was believed that, in exchange for this devotion, witches gained magical powers to inflict harm on their neighbors and aid Satan's kingdom.

Witches were said to cause crop failure, illness, and even death. Particularly, it was believed that they had special powers over the procreation of children through their abilities to cause impotence, infertility, and miscarriage. The practice of magic for evil ends was bad enough; it was transformed into heresy when devotion to Satan replaced devotion to God. Thus, witchcraft became a crime of heinous proportions, and the churches, both Catholic and Protestant, looked to the civil authorities to eliminate it through torture and execution.

Historians generally agree that this picture of the witch existed only in the minds and writings of people and never in reality.[22] Throughout the Middle Ages, some village people did practice popular magic and healing, and fragments of Greek and Roman religious practices persisted in medieval Europe. These activities, however, were a far cry from the full-blown image of the witch as it emerged in Christian history. The image of the witch was a product of folklore, ancient non-Christian religious traditions, and medieval Christian theology. People were accused of worshiping the Devil and acquiring supernatural powers. They confessed—under torture—and thus a body of evidence accumulated that the church could use to crusade against witchcraft as a danger to the faith and the social order.

In addition to the growth of demonology and a coherent theory of witchcraft, social, political, and legal conditions of the fifteenth and sixteenth centuries also contributed to the witch hunt. The tragic effects of wars, famines, and plagues made the power of evil very real to people. Religious upheaval and a shift from the traditional manor economy to commerce added to the sense of despair. Finally, the church, by the fourteenth century, had in place a body of traveling investigators and judges (called the Inquisition) to expose theological error.

The Association of Women with Witchcraft

Upon examining those individuals who were imprisoned and executed as witches, it becomes clear that women were much more frequently persecuted than men.[23] Although numbers vary from place to place, in general the ratio of those convicted and executed was four women to every one man. Certainly in the popular imagination, the image of the witch was—and continues to be—female. Even our Halloween decorations and contemporary dictionary definitions reinforce the long-held belief that a witch is "a woman practicing usually black witchcraft."[24]

As with the causes of the witch hunt, there is no single explanation for why women were more frequently persecuted than men. The witch hunt emerged in a period of violent sentiment against women as evil instruments of the devil. They were therefore likely candidates for devil worship and pacts with the Prince of Darkness. The *Malleus Malleficarum* ("Hammer of Witches") was published in 1486 by two German churchmen as a guidebook for those who wished to rid the Christian world of witchcraft. Although other works echoed many of the ideas of the *Malleus,* it was the most popular publication of this kind. It specifically asserted that witchcraft was more likely to be found among women and it went on to give detailed reasons why this was so. (1) Women were by nature feebleminded and easily swayed by false doctrines. (2) Women were also morally weak and particularly inclined toward deceit and revenge; and therefore, they would not only be adept at keeping their activities secret but would seize any opportunity to cause harm to those around them. (3) The Christian faith of women was weak, and they would easily renounce Christianity and have few qualms about stamping or excreting on the crucifix. (4) Above all, the *Malleus* insisted that women had insatiable lust that caused them to submit willingly to the sexual advances of the Devil. They had, it was believed, "more pleasure and delight" with the incubus or demon who came to them in the night than with any mortal man. The identification of witch as woman was reinforced, of course, by the popular belief that the Devil, as a divine power, had to be male when he assumed a human form. These ideas were embraced and widely shared by the officials— clergy and judges—who carried out the hunt. Because of both Catholic and Protestant concern for the religious education of believers, however, these beliefs gradually filtered down to lay men and women as well.[25]

A hatred of women alone, however, cannot explain the targets of the witch hunt because not all women were accused and prosecuted. Some scholars suggest that Protestant leaders used accusations of witchcraft to rid communities of rebellious women who refused to conform to the ideal of obedient wife, an important foundation for godly families and societies.[26] Others suggest that factors operating at the local community level may help us understand the circumstances that often gave rise to initial accusations of witchcraft. Accusations were most often made against older women, usually widowed or unmarried and/or poor.[27] Why were such women the targets of the hostility of their neighbors? In many medieval communities, it was the older woman who knew and passed on the folklore traditions regarding healing, abortions, food preparation, and contraception. She was also the one to preside over births and prepare corpses for burial. She knew how to prepare herbal medicines and how to use charms and spells to fight evil. When something went inexplicably wrong—food spoiling or a baby dying—black magic seemed an inescapable conclusion.

The old woman living alone was vulnerable in other kinds of ways. Loneliness and poverty may have given her a reputation for being marginal or odd. The curses she might have muttered when she fought with her neighbors or was refused their help were interpreted by her neighbors as spells and the summoning of evil spirits. In some ways, she may have made her neighbors, who were becoming increasingly concerned about their rights as individuals, feel guilty about their neglect of communal values and in turn take out their guilt on her. Also, she had few legal powers with which to defend herself against the machinery of church and state. Finally, theologians taught that the Devil physically marked his women and gave them special "teats" from which the demons could nurse: when exposed, the moles and growths common to an aging body sealed the fate of many helpless women.

Medieval Women Challenge and Protest

At all socioeconomic levels of society, women performed vital services and were often recognized for their contributions in everyday life. These circumstances alone challenged the official view of women as mentally and physically incompetent and as morally defective. Aristocratic women, for example, took full responsibility for running their husbands' estates while they were away at war or imprisoned. Humanist education, which advocated the renewal of European society and culture based on the study of ancient Roman and Greek texts, gradually was extended to middle-class women to prepare them for maintaining family property and fortunes through letters, conversation, and competent household management. Women in the middle and lower classes frequently went out to work or did work at home in addition to child rearing and housekeeping. Some aided their husbands with a craft or business and frequently carried on alone after being widowed. Single women in urban areas ran their own businesses, and there are numerous examples of single women who managed their own farms.

During this period, the few women whose writings are known to us are largely silent about the roles they were assigned and the images with which they were described. There are, however, a few examples of clear-cut protest against the church's degradation of women and the culture's belief that a woman's main function was procreation. There are also more indirect challenges to the accepted status of medieval women in church and society from the pens and lives of some of Christianity's most revered saints—the female mystics of the thirteenth and fourteenth centuries.

Christine de Pisan

The fifteenth-century Frenchwoman Christine de Pisan was left a widow at the age of twenty-five and was able to earn a living through writing. She produced two popular prose works on women, *The Book of the City of Ladies* and *The Book of Three Virtues*, as well as poetry. Much of her writing was in protest against the violent attacks on women by medieval churchmen and noblemen. Christine de Pisan supplied ample evidence to show that women were modest, gentle, and loving. Her argument is even more credible because she chooses examples of women not only from the distant mythological past but also from recent history. She points out that as a group women do not wage war and do not oppress other people. Adam, furthermore, is just as guilty as Eve in bringing sin into the world; and in the New Testament, women, not men, remain faithful to Jesus during his trial and death. While she does not denigrate the contemplative life, Christine de Pisan urges her readers to take action to improve their lives and the society around them.

Isotta Nogarola

Another woman of the same century, Isotta Nogarola of Verona, Italy, aspired to a life of humanist scholarship. Although she acquired a wide knowledge of classical studies, including Latin, by the time she was eighteen, her efforts were not encouraged. Learned men failed to take her seriously, enemies accused her of sexual promiscuity and incest, and her female friends shunned and ridiculed her. Nogarola was forced to conclude that only the virgin life would give her the freedom and social approval she needed to pursue her studies. From 1441 until her death in 1466 she lived virtually in seclusion on her own property. She studied and wrote on topics related to Christianity and eventually gained praise from prominent men for her saintly and scholarly life. They could approve of an intellectual woman who had taken a vow of chastity, but not one who was marriageable or married.

One of Isotta Nogarola's surviving works, a debate with the Venetian statesman Foscarini, deals with the question of Eve's responsibility for original sin. She points out that Eve only disobeyed Adam, whereas Adam disobeyed God. The heart of her case, however, is that Adam had greater intelligence and thus should have resisted the serpent. While Nogarola wished to protest against the excessive burden of guilt that the church had placed on Eve, she does this by accepting her own culture's definition of the nature of women: Eve cannot be blamed because she is by nature weak and ignorant and no match for the cunning serpent.

The Female Mystics

Medieval women were well represented in the tradition of mysticism that flourished between 1100 and 1450 as part of a wider religious revival. During periods of intense meditation and prayer, or sometimes profound suffering, the mystics believed that they experienced God in a direct and unmediated way. Female mystics often experienced visions, voices, and powerful emotions as they encountered the holy. They also routinely bypassed the male priesthood, receiving the Eucharist directly from Christ and knowledge directly from God. Scholars exploring the reasons why women were so numerous in this tradition have suggested that strict isolation in convents and anchorages gave them exceptional opportunities for meditation. It is also possible that their spiritual practices—repetitive prayer, austere asceticism, contemplation of paintings—stimulated mystical experiences.[28]

The visions and revelations of at least some of these women can be known firsthand because of their writings. Dictated by Hildegard, the twelfth-century abbess of the convent at Bingen, the *Scivias* contains illustrated descriptions and interpretations of her visions. In *Revelations of Divine Love*, Julian of Norwich, a fifteenth-century anchorite, described a series of visions and revelations she received during an illness. A century earlier, Catherine of Siena wrote about similar experiences in *The Dialogue of St. Catherine of Siena*. Gertrude the Great, Mechtild of Hackeborn, and Mechtild of Madgeburg also had reports of their visions and spiritual experiences at the community of Helfta committed to writing. In all cases, these mystics were part of a wider community that gave them books, taught them to write, took down their dictation, and recommended and preserved their works.[29] The nuns of Helfta, Germany, for example, were encouraged to study the Bible and the works of the church fathers by their Dominican spiritual advisors; Julian had access to the library of Augustinian canons near her anchorage.

The content of this mystical writing varies from woman to woman but there are certain common features. There is a free use of bridal imagery to describe the relationship between the Christian and Jesus Christ, which removes the culturally determined boundaries separating men and women. Men must conceive of themselves as the brides of Christ, and in some mystical writing women must assume the identity of the male lover of the Lady Love Christ.[30] There is also considerable emphasis in mystical writing on the physical suffering and humanity of Christ, which some scholars claim offers a more positive image of women. It was from a woman that his flesh came and it was women who were most identified with the physical and material. Physicality thus linked women to Christ and allowed them to claim to be conduits of his grace.[31] Perhaps most significant in mystical writing, especially by women, is that both God and Jesus are described in female and feminine terms. One of the nuns of Helfta frequently refers to God as the mother of humanity to show that God's justice is tempered by love and comfort. Hildegard speaks of God as the bright fiery outermost area of a great cosmic egg.

But Julian of Norwich reconceptualizes God more powerfully and originally than any writer before her. Like Anselm and Bernard of Clairvaux, Julian sees important parallels between Jesus and the physical care an earthly mother gives her child. Jesus has given birth to the believer through his cruel death and pain and he feeds the believer with his body. Julian however engages in a complex exploration of the nature of God, identifying Christ the Mother as the Second Person of the Trinity on an equal footing with God the Father and the Holy Spirit. It is Christ the Mother who tends to us while on earth, watching over spiritual development, chastising us when necessary and enclosing us in the unconditional love of God. "And though, possibly, an earthly mother may suffer her child to perish, our heavenly Mother Jesus can never suffer us who are his children to perish. For he is almighty, all-wisdom and all-love."[32]

The female mystics, apart from bringing a feminine dimension to the images used for God, represented an important avenue for an active ministry in the church beyond traditional roles for women. Frances Beer in fact argues that mysticism was more liberating than convent life as a path to self-fulfill-ment and leadership.[33] The mystics taught and preached, cared for the poor and sick, and campaigned against immorality in the church. Their voices were raised in letters, sermons, counseling sessions, and personal visits. This aspect of their lives has tended to get less attention than their contemplative and mystical experiences. Catherine of Siena, for example, took on a public mission to people in need in Siena and broadened her work in 1374 to embrace the reform and unification of the church. She was a tireless letter writer, advo-cating a crusade and an end to war in Italy. Catherine was most successful in strengthening the resolve of Pope Gregory XI to return to Rome and to the spiritual leadership of the whole church after decades of his residence in France. From her own writings it is possible to argue that Catherine saw her-self as a female apostle, given the mission to carry a message of reconciliation through letter writing, public proclamation, and personal confrontation.[34]

One study by Caroline Bynum on the mystic nuns at Helfta stresses their role of authority among both men and women.[35] Although they held no offi-cial administrative positions, the nuns were sought out as spiritual advisers by lay men and women, clergy, monks, and other women at Helfta. The com-munity believed, for example, that the mystics could provide information on the condition of people who had already died. Perhaps most significantly, the visions of women like Gertrude of Helfta sometimes enabled them to per-form priestly duties like the forgiveness and absolution of sins. In her visions, Gertrude was told by God who had been forgiven and she was commanded to announce this absolution to the people involved. Also in their visions, the nuns were commissioned by God to serve and to teach (often understood as preaching) what had been revealed to them. Those nuns who compiled the visions and life of Mechtild of Hackeborn described her in the following way: "She gave teaching with such abundance that such a one has never been seen in the monastery and we fear, alas, will never be seen again. The sisters gath-ered around her as around a preacher to hear the word of God."[36]

Why did the church—laity and clergy—accept these female mystics as speaking with divine authority? For some, the extreme asceticism of the mystics set them apart as holy especially when, for example, they could survive for long periods without food, were struck with crying fits, or revealed stigmata (bodily marks resembling the wounds of Christ). Also, the experiences of these women were compatible with the role of female prophet, a viable one within the medieval understanding of theology. Women could teach and preach, write and speak if they were specially chosen and filled with the Holy Spirit. Their words were the product of inspiration, a special gift rather than the result of learning. These women stress repeatedly that they were unworthy and unlettered, or, in the words of Hildegard, "a poor little female figure."[37] They wrote only because they had a directive from God who turned their weakness into strength. And so long as their words corroborated the teachings of the church, they could expect the approval of the clergy. Women who claimed to bear messages from God, however, always risked being accused of bearing messages from the Devil—especially if they were not clearly under the control of men.

Margery Kempe

Many of the themes noted above are apparent in the life of Margery Kempe, an Englishwoman born and married into the merchant class of King's Lynn in the fifteenth century. Kempe has left us an account of her answered prayers, visions, and prophetic insights, which she believed to come from God, in *The Book of Margery Kempe*, generally regarded as the earliest autobiography in the English language. Her spiritual experiences persuaded her to alter her lifestyle dramatically. After bearing fourteen children, she persuaded her husband to agree to a celibate marriage, believing that sex was an insuperable obstacle to her spiritual life. She undertook a number of journeys to shrines and holy places, including Santiago de Compostella and the Holy Land.

Kempe's mysticism took a shape different from that of Julian of Norwich or Catherine of Siena or many other women mystics. In the estimate of one historian, her mysticism is for the ordinary woman.[38] There was no heroic asceticism. Deeply influenced by a devotional tradition in England, which was centered on heartfelt love for Mary and Jesus, her visions involve intimate domestic scenes and ordinary conversations with both. Margery also redefines virginity to make it spiritual, something that can be won through grace and holiness. Even married women could thus aspire to this status. Here she draws on the saintly women from the continent of Europe (Birgitta, Dorothy of Mantau) who were married with children. She also shared with some of the continental mystics the flamboyant habit of noisy and prolonged fits of weeping, which, at the Church of the Holy Sepulchre, were so violent that they astonished the people around her.

Medieval Christianity presents us with strong male voices praising the virgin but also condemning women for their association with the flesh and sin. Yet it also has given us, for the first time in Christian history, an array of female voices. Women write and their works endure. We hear direct and indirect protests against their status as they seek both to serve God and to develop their talents. We also have a picture of their conscious and unconscious efforts to circumvent some patriarchal limitations in order to find meaning and dignity in their lives. Within Catholic Christianity, the images of virgin and witch will continue to shape the status of women for centuries. The Protestant Reformation brings a new emphasis on women as obedient wives and devoted mothers, a shift that is explored in the next chapter.

Readings for Chapter 2

2.1 REJECTING PATRIARCHAL MARRIAGE

The text of The Life of Christina of Markyate, *about a celebrated English ascetic, is probably a fourteenth-century abridgment of the story originally written two centuries earlier by an unknown Benedictine monk from St. Albans. Born into a wealthy, noble family of Huntingdon at the end of the eleventh century, Christina vowed to live as a virgin of Christ. Much of her story is an account of her clever and desperate efforts to defy a conspiracy of family members and church authorities to force her to consummate her marriage to Burthred. After spending a year imprisoned in her home, Christina escapes and settles into a hermit life with Roger in his cell at Markyate. She gathers virgin women around her and together they form the nucleus of a female monastery at Markyate, of which Christina becomes prioress. Parts of the text given below describe her parents' unsuccessful use of flattery, force, and church law to intimidate her into submission. She is accused of bringing dishonor upon the family by her obstinacy and disobedience. Christina, however, has a firm sense of where her loyalty rests, and she summons the courage to argue with her superiors accordingly.*

Source: The Life of Christina of Markyate: A Twelfth-Century Recluse. *Edited and translated by C. H. Talbot, 49–63. Oxford: Clarendon Press, 1959.*

See finally how she acted, how she behaved herself at what is called the Gild merchant, which is one of the merchants' greatest and best-known festivals. One day, when a great throng of nobles were gathered together there, Autti and Beatrix held the place of honor, as being the most important amongst them. It was their pleasure that Christina, their eldest and most worthy daughter, should act as cup-bearer to such an honorable gathering. Wherefore they commanded her to get up and lay aside the mantle which she was wearing, so that, with her garments fastened to her sides with bands and her sleeves rolled up her arms, she should courteously offer drinks to the nobility. They hoped that the compliments paid to her by the onlookers and the accumulation of little sips of wine would break her resolution and prepare her body for the deed of corruption. Carrying out their wishes, she prepared a suitable defense against both attacks. Against the favors of human flattery she fixed in her memory the thought of the Mother of God, and for this purpose she was not a little helped by the hall where the gathering took place, for because of its size it had several entrances. One of these before which Christina had frequently to pass looked out on the monastery of the blessed Mother of God. . . . Against the urge to drunkenness, she opposed her burning thirst. What wonder is there that she felt dry, since though she had been pouring out wine all day for others to drink their fill, she had tasted nothing? But in the evening, when it was late and she was fainting with the heat and thirst, she drank a little water and thus satisfied both desires at the same time.

But as her parents had been outwitted in this, they tried something else. And at night they let her husband secretly into her bedroom in order that, if he found the maiden asleep, he might suddenly take her by surprise and overcome her. But even through that providence to which she had commended herself, she was found dressed and awake, and she welcomed the young man as if he had been her brother. And sitting on her bed with him, she strongly encouraged him to live a chaste life, putting forward the saints as examples. She recounted to him in detail the story of St. Cecilia and her husband Valerian, telling him how, at their death they were accounted worthy to receive crowns of unsullied chastity from the hands of an angel. Not only this: but both they and many others after them had followed the path of martyrdom and thus, being crowned twice by the Lord, were honored both in heaven and on earth. "Let us, therefore," she exhorted him, "follow their example, so that we may become their companions in eternal glory. Because if we suffer with them, we shall also reign with them. Do not take it amiss that I have declined your embraces. In order that your friends may not reproach you with being rejected by me, I will go home

with you: and let us live together there for some time, ostensibly as husband and wife, but in reality living chastely in the sight of the Lord. But first let us join hands in a compact that neither meanwhile will touch the other unchastely, neither will look upon the other except with a pure and angelic gaze, making a promise that in three or four years' time we will receive the religious habit and offer ourselves . . . to some monastery which providence shall appoint." When the greater part of the night had passed with talk such as this, the young man eventually left the maiden. When those who had got him into the room heard what had happened, they joined together in calling him a spineless and useless fellow. And with many reproaches they goaded him on again, and thrust him into her bedroom another night, having warned him not to be misled by her deceitful tricks and naive words nor to lose his manliness. Either by force or entreaty he was to gain his end. And if neither of these sufficed, he was to know that they were at hand to help him: all he had to mind was to act the man.

When Christina sensed this, she hastily sprang out of bed and clinging with both hands to a nail which was fixed in the wall, she hung trembling between the wall and the hangings. Burthred meanwhile approached the bed and, not finding what he expected, he immediately gave a sign to those waiting outside the door. They crowded into the room forthwith and with lights in their hands ran from place to place looking for her, the more intent on their quest as they knew she was in the room when he entered it and could not have escaped without their seeing her. What, I ask you, were her feelings at that moment? How she kept trembling as they noisily sought after her. Was she not faint with fear? She saw herself already dragged out in their midst, all surrounding her, looking upon her, threatening her, given up to the sport of her destroyer. At last one of them touched and held her foot as she hung there, but since the curtain in between deadened his sense of touch, he let it go, not knowing what it was. Then the maiden of Christ, taking courage, prayed to God, saying: "Let them be turned backward, that desire my hurt": and straightway they departed in confusion, and from that moment she was safe. . . .

Her father brought her back there [the Augustinian priory of St. Mary's, Huntingdon] another time, and placing her before Fredebert, the reverend prior, and the rest of the canons of the house, addressed them with these doleful words: "I know, my fathers, I know, and I admit to my daughter, that I and her mother have forced her against her will into this marriage and that against her better judgement she has received this sacrament, yet, no matter how she was led into it, if she resists our authority and rejects it, we shall be the laughing-stock of our neighbors, a mockery and derision to those who are round about. Wherefore, I beseech you, plead with her to have pity on us: let her marry in the Lord and take away our reproach. Why must she depart from tradition? Why should she bring this dishonor on her father? Her life of poverty will bring the whole of the nobility into disrepute. Let her do now what we wish and she can have all that we possess." When Autti had said this, Fredebertus asked him to leave the assembly and with his canons about him began to address the maiden with these words: "We are surprised, Theodora, at your obstinacy, or rather we should say, your madness. We know that you have been betrothed according to ecclesiastical custom. We know that the sacrament of marriage, which has been sanctioned by divine law, cannot be dissolved, because what God has joined together, no man should put asunder. For this a man will leave his father and mother and cleave to his wife. And they shall be two in one flesh. And the apostle says: let the husband render unto the wife due benevolence and likewise also the wife unto the husband. The woman has no power over her own body, but the husband: and likewise also the husband has not power over his own body, but the wife. Unto the married I command, yet not I, but the Lord, let not the wife depart from her husband and let not the husband put away his wife. And we know the commandment given to children: obey your parents and show them respect. These two commandments, about obedience to parents and faithfulness in marriage, are great, much commended in the Old and New Testaments. Yet the bond of marriage is so

much more important than the authority of parents that if they commanded
you to break off the marriage you should
not listen to them. Now, however, that
they order you to do something which
we know on divine authority to be more
important than obedience itself, and
you do not listen to them, you are dou-
bly at fault. Nor should you think that
only virgins are saved: for whilst many
virgins perish, many mothers of families
are saved, as we well know. And since
this is so, nothing remains but that you
accept our advice and teaching and submit yourself to the lawful embraces of
the man to whom you have been legally
joined in marriage."

To these exhortations Christina
replied: "I am ignorant of the scriptures
which you have quoted, father prior. But
from their sense I will give my answers
thereto. My father and mother, as you
have heard, bear me witness that against
my will this sacrament, as you call it,
was forced on me. I have never been a
wife and have never thought of becoming one. Know that from my infancy I
have chosen chastity and have vowed to
Christ that I would remain a virgin: this
I did before witnesses, but even if they
were not present God would be witness
to my conscience continuously. This I
showed by my actions as far as I was
allowed. And if my parents have ordered
me to enter into a marriage which I never
wanted and to break the vow to Christ
which they know I made in my childhood, I leave you, who are supposed to
excel other men in the knowledge of the

scriptures, to judge how wicked a thing
this is. If I do all in my power to fulfil
the vow I made to Christ, I shall not be
disobedient to my parents. What I do, I
do on the invitation of Him whose voice,
as you say, is heard in the Gospel: Every
one who leaves house or brothers or sisters or father or mother or wife or children or possessions for My name's sake
shall receive a hundredfold and possess
eternal life. Nor do I think that virgins
only will be saved. But I say as you do,
and it is true, that if many virgins perish, so rather do married women. And
if many mothers of families are saved,
which you likewise say, and it is true,
certainly virgins are saved more easily."

2.2 HUNTING FOR WITCHES

The Malleus Maleficarum *was published in
1486 by the German inquisitors Heinrich Kraemer and Jacob Sprenger. It was only one of several
treatises on witchcraft produced at the height of the
witch hunt, but it had particular significance in
several respects. It was prefaced by a bull from
Pope Innocent VIII ordering the extirpation of
witchcraft, and thus carried great authority. The
Malleus was also important in that it systematized and transmitted the cumulative popular picture of witchcraft, a picture that included grotesque
rituals, sacrilegious orgies, and devil worship. But
perhaps the most novel feature of this treatise was
its vicious attack on women. In the style of scholastic disputation, the authors raise the question of
why more women than men are witches, and then*

answer it by pointing out that women are feebler in mind and body, carnal, prone to jealousy, and quicker to waver in their faith.

Source: Heinrich Kraemer and Jacob Sprenger. *Malleus Maleficarum.* Translated by Montague Summers, 44–47. New York: Dover, 1971.

But because in these times this perfidy is more often found in women than in men, as we learn by actual experience, if anyone is curious as to the reason, we may add to what has already been said the following: that since they are feebler both in mind and body, it is not surprising that they should come more under the spell of witchcraft.

For as regards intellect, or the understanding of spiritual things, they seem to be of a different nature from men; a fact which is vouched for by the logic of the authorities, backed by various examples from the Scriptures. Terence says: Women are intellectually like children. And Lactantius (*Institutiones* 3): No woman understood philosophy except Temeste. And Proverbs 6, as it were describing a woman, says: As a jewel of gold in a swine's snout, so is a fair woman which is without discretion.

But the natural reason is that she is more carnal than a man, as is clear from her many carnal abominations. And it should be noted that there was a defect in the formation of the first woman, since she was formed from a bent rib, that is, a rib of the breast, which is bent as it were in a contrary direction to a man. And since through this defect she is an imperfect animal, she always deceives.

For Cato says: When a woman weeps she weaves snares. And again: When a woman weeps, she labors to deceive a man. And this is shown by Samson's wife, who coaxed him to tell her the riddle he had propounded to the Philistines, and told them the answer, and so deceived him. And it is clear in the case of the first woman that she had little faith; for when the serpent asked why they did not eat of every tree in Paradise, she answered: Of every tree, etc.—Lest perchance we die. Thereby she showed that she doubted, and had little faith in the word of God. And all this is indicated by the etymology of the word; for *Femina* comes from *Fe* and *Minus*, since she is ever weaker to hold and preserve the faith. And this as regards faith is of her very nature; although both by grace and nature faith never failed in the Blessed Virgin, even at the time of Christ's Passion, when it failed in all men.

Therefore a wicked woman is by her nature quicker to waver in her faith, and consequently quicker to abjure the faith, which is the root of witchcraft.

And as to her other mental quality, that is, her natural will; when she hates someone whom she formerly loved, then she seethes with anger and impatience in her whole soul, just as the tides of the sea are always heaving and boiling. Many authorities allude to this cause. Ecclesiasticus 25: There is no wrath above the wrath of a woman. And Seneca (*Tragedies* 8): No might of the flames or of the swollen winds, no deadly weapon, is so much to be feared as the lust and hatred of a woman who has been divorced from the marriage bed.

This is shown too in the woman who falsely accused Joseph, and caused him to be imprisoned because he would not consent to the crime of adultery with her (Genesis 30). And truly the most powerful cause which contributes to the increase of witches is the woeful rivalry between married folk and unmarried women and men. This is so even among holy women, so what must it be among the others? For you see in Genesis 21 how impatient and envious Sarah was of Hagar when she conceived: how jealous Rachel was of Leah because she had no children (Genesis 30): and Hannah, who was barren, of the fruitful Peninnah (I Kings I): and how Miriam (Numbers 12) murmured and spoke ill of Moses, and was therefore stricken with leprosy: and how Martha was jealous of Mary Magdalen, because she was busy and Mary was sitting down (Luke 10). To this point is Ecclesiasticus 37: Neither consult with a woman touching her of whom she is jealous. Meaning that it is useless to consult with her, since there is always jealousy, that is, envy, in a wicked woman. And if women behave thus to each other, how much more will they do so to men.

Valerius Maximus tells how, when Phoroneus, the king of the Greeks, was dying, he said to his brother Leontius that there would have been nothing lacking to him of complete happiness if a wife had always been lacking to him. And when Leontius asked how a wife could stand in the way of happiness, he answered that all married men well knew. And when the philosopher Socrates was asked if one should marry a wife, he answered: If you do not, you are lonely, your family dies out, and a stranger inherits; if you do, you suffer perpetual anxiety, querulous complaints, reproaches concerning the marriage portion, the heavy displeasure of your relations, the garrulousness of a mother-in-law, cuckoldom, and no certain arrival of an heir. This he said as one who knew. For S. Jerome in his *Contra Iouinianum* says: This Socrates had two wives, whom he endured with much patience, but could not be rid of their contumelies and clamorous vitupera-tions. So one day when they were com-plaining against him, he went out of the house to escape their plaguing, and sat down before the house; and the women then threw filthy water over him. But the philosopher was not disturbed by this, saying, "I knew that the rain would come after the thunder."

There is also a story of a man whose wife was drowned in a river, who, when he was searching for the body to take it out of the water, walked up the stream. And when he was asked why, since heavy bodies do not rise but fall, he was search-ing against the current of the river, he answered: "When that woman was alive she always, both in word and deed, went contrary to my commands; therefore I am searching in the contrary direction in case even now she is dead she may preserve her contrary disposition."

And indeed, just as through the first defect in their intelligence they are more prone to abjure the faith; so through their second defect of inordinate affections and passions they search for, brood over, and inflict various vengeances, either by witchcraft, or by some other means. Wherefore it is no wonder that so great a number of witches exist in this sex.

Women also have weak memories; and it is a natural vice in them not to be disciplined, but to follow their own impulses without any sense of what is due; this is her whole study, and all that she keeps in her memory. So Theophrastus says: If you hand over the whole management of the house to her, but reserve some minute detail to your own judgement, she will think that you are displaying a great want of faith in her, and will stir up strife; and unless you quickly take counsel, she will prepare poison for you, and consult seers and soothsayers; and will become a witch. . . .

It is this which is lamented in Ecclesiastes 7, and which the Church even now laments on account of the great multitude of witches. And I have found a woman more bitter than death, who is the hunter's snare, and her heart is a net, and her hands are bands. He that pleaseth God shall escape from her; but he that is a sinner shall be caught by her. More bitter than death, that is, than the devil: Apocalypse 6:8, His name was Death. For though the devil tempted Eve to sin, yet Eve seduced Adam. And as the sin of Eve would not have brought death to our soul and body unless the sin had afterwards passed on to Adam, to which he was tempted by Eve, not by the devil, therefore she is more bitter than death.

More bitter than death, again, because that is natural and destroys only the body, but the sin which arose from woman destroys the soul by depriving it of grace, and delivers the body up to the punishment for sin.

More bitter than death, again, because bodily death is an open and terrible enemy, but woman is a wheedling and secret enemy.

And that she is more perilous than a snare does not speak of the snare of hunters, but of devils. For men are caught not only through their carnal desires, when they see and hear women: for S. Bernard says: Their face is a burning wind, and their voice the hissing of serpents: but they also cast wicked spells on countless men and animals. And when it is said that her heart is a net, it speaks of the inscrutable malice which reigns in their hearts. And her hands are as bands for binding; for when they place their hands on a creature to bewitch it, then with the help of the devil they perform their design.

To conclude. All witchcraft comes from carnal lust, which is in women insatiable. See Proverbs 30: There are three things that are never satisfied, yea, a fourth thing which says not. It is enough; that is, the mouth of the womb. Wherefore for the sake of fulfilling their lusts they consort even with devils. More such reasons could be brought forward, but to the understanding it is sufficiently clear that it is no matter for wonder that there are more women than men found infected with the heresy of witchcraft. And in consequence of this, it is better called the heresy of witches than of wizards, since the name is taken from the more powerful party. And blessed be the Highest Who has so far preserved the male sex from so great a crime: for since He was willing to be born and to suffer for us, therefore He has granted to men this privilege.

2.3 MARGERY KEMPE

The spiritual biography of Margery Kempe is one of the rare vernacular works by women from the fifteenth century. Born in Kings Lynn in 1373, Kempe married a prominent citizen and bore fourteen children before she and her husband agreed to live celibately. This selection from The Book of Margery Kempe *reveals much about her activities, relationships, and spirituality. She makes a number of pilgrimages to local and foreign holy places, in this case Canterbury. Here, as elsewhere, her emotional outbursts and her pointed condemnation of the monks and priests lead the churchmen to accuse her of heresy. She is rescued not by her husband, who has abandoned her, but by two strangers who appear in answer to her prayers. They in turn ask her to pray for them. Following these incidents, Kempe experiences a period of close communion with God.*

Source: Margery Kempe. *The Book of Margery Kempe, Fourteen Hundred & Thirty-Six.* A modern version by W. Butler-Bowden, 20–22. New York: Devin-Adair, 1944.

On a time, as this creature was at Canterbury in the church amongst the monks, she was greatly despised and reproved because she wept so fast, both by the monks and priests, and by secular men, nearly all day both forenoon and afternoon also, so much indeed that her husband went away from her as if he had not known her, and left her alone amongst them, choose how she might. Further comfort had she none of him that day.

So an old monk, who had been Treasurer with the Queen whilst he was in secular clothing, a rich man, and greatly dreaded by many people, took her by the hand, saying unto her:—

"What canst thou say of God?"

"Sir," she said, "I will both speak of Him, and hear of Him," repeating to the monk a story of Scripture.

The monk said:—"I would thou wert enclosed in a house of stone, so that, there, no man should speak with thee."

"Ah! Sir," she said, "ye should maintain God's servants. Ye are the first that hold against them. Our Lord amend you."

Then a young monk said to her:—"Either thou hast the Holy Ghost, or else thou hast the devil within thee, for what thou speakest to us here is Holy Writ, and that hast thou not of thyself."

Then said this creature:—"I pray you, sir, give me leave to tell you a tale."

Then the people said to the monk:—
"Let her say what she will."

Then she said:—"There was once a man who had sinned greatly against God, and when he was shriven, his confessor enjoined him as part of his penance, that he should for one year hire men to chide him and reprove him for his sins, and he should give them silver for their labor. And one day he came amongst many great men, such as are now here, God save you all, and stood among them as I do now amongst you, despising him as ye do me, the man laughing and smiling and having good game at their words. The greatest master of them said to the man:—

'Why laughest thou, wretch? Thou are greatly despised!'

'Ah! Sir, I have great cause to laugh, for I have many days put silver out of my purse and hired men to chide me for remission of my sin, and this day I may keep my silver in my purse. I thank you all.

'Right so I say to you, worshipful sirs. Whilst I was at home in my own country, day by day with great weeping and mourning, I sorrowed because I had no shame, scorn or contempt, as I was worthy. I thank you all, sirs, highly for what, forenoon and afternoon, I have had in good measure this day, blessed be God for it.'"

Then she went out of the monastery, they following and crying upon her—

"Thou shalt be burnt, false Lollard. Here is a cartful of thorns ready for thee, and a tun to burn thee with."

And the creature stood outside the gates of Canterbury, for it was in the evening, many people wondering at her.

Then said the people:—"Take and burn her!"

She stood still, trembling and quaking full sore in her flesh, without earthly comfort, and knew not where her husband had gone.

Then prayed she in her heart to Our Lord in this manner:—

"Here came I, Lord, for Thy love. Blessed Lord, help me and have mercy on me."

And anon, after she had made her prayer in her heart to Our Lord, there came two fair young men, who said to her:—

"Damsel, art thou neither heretic nor Lollard?"

And she said:—"No, sirs, I am neither heretic nor Lollard."

They asked her, where was her inn. She said she knew not what street; nevertheless it would be at a Dewchman's house. Then these two young men brought her home to her hostel, and made her great cheer, asking her to pray for them, and there she found her husband.

And many people in N . . . had said evil of her whilst she was out, and slandered her over many things she was said to have done whilst she was in the country.

Then, after this, she was in great rest of soul a long while, and had high contemplation day by day, and much holy speech and dalliance with Our Lord Jesus Christ, both forenoon and afternoon with many sweet tears of high devotion, so plenteously and continually, that it was a marvel that her eyes endured, or that her heart should last, without being consumed with the ardor of love, which was kindled with the holy dalliance of Our Lord, when He said to her many times:—

"Dear daughter, love thou Me with all thy heart, for I love thee with all My heart and the might of My Godhead, for thou wert a chosen soul without beginning in My sight and a pillar of Holy Church. My merciful eyes are ever upon thee. It would be impossible for thee to suffer the scorn and contempt that thou shalt have, were not My grace supporting thee."

2.4 JESUS AS MOTHER

Julian of Norwich (b. c. 1342) spent much of her life in an anchorage attached to the Church of St. Julian and St. Edward in the Norwich area. She was sought out as a sympathetic, shrewd, and learned spiritual adviser by many, including Margery Kempe. She was probably still living at home in May 1373 when she experienced a series of mystical "showings" or revelations during a serious illness. After giving her the church's last rites, a priest left Julian with a crucifix that he urged her to meditate upon. The result was fifteen revelations in five hours and an additional one the next day. Twenty years later, she committed her experiences and her reflections upon them to writing in The Sixteen Revelations of Divine Love. *As this document illustrates, her visions of the Trinity and the passion of Christ give rise to extensive meditations particularly on the love of God. Here this love is understood in terms of mother-love.*

Source: Julian of Norwich. *Revelations of Divine Love.* Translated with an introduction by M. L. Del Mastro, 191–93. New York: Doubleday, 1977.

But now it is necessary for me to say a little more about this "spreading forth," as I understood it in our Lord's meaning—how we are brought again, by the motherhood of mercy and grace, into our natural place, for which we were created by the motherhood of natural love. This natural love never leaves us.

Our natural mother, our gracious mother, because he willed to become our mother entirely in everything, took the ground for his work most humbly and most mildly in the maiden's womb. That he showed in the first showing, where he brought that meek maiden before the eye of my understanding in the simple stature she had when she conceived. That is to say, our high God, the sovereign wisdom of all, arrayed himself in this low place and made himself entirely ready in our poor flesh in order to do the service and the office of motherhood himself in all things.

A mother's service is nearest, readiest and surest. It is nearest because it is most natural. It is readiest because it is most loving. And it is surest because it is most true. This office no one but him alone might or could ever have performed to the full.

We realize that all our mothers bear us for pain and for dying, and what is that? But our true mother, Jesus—All love—alone bears us for joy and for endless living, blessed may he be! Thus he sustains us within himself in love and hard labor, until the fulness of time. Then he willed to suffer the sharpest thorns and the most grievous pains there ever were or ever will be, and to die at the last.

When he had done this and so borne us to bliss, all this still could not satisfy his marvelous love. That he showed in these noble, surpassing words of love: "If I could suffer more, I would suffer more." He could not die any more, but he would not stop working.

Therefore it was necessary for him to feed us, for the most precious love of motherhood had made him a debtor to us. A mother can give her child her milk to suck, but our precious mother, Jesus, can feed us with himself. He does so most courteously and most tenderly, with the Blessed Sacrament, which is the precious food of true life. With all the sweet sacraments he sustains us most mercifully and graciously. That is what he meant in these blessed words, where he said, "I am that which holy Church preaches and teaches you," that is to say, "All the health and the life of the sacraments, all the virtue and the grace of my word, all the goodness that is ordained for you in holy Church, that I am."

The mother can hold her child tenderly to her breast, but our tender mother, Jesus, can lead us in friendly fashion into his blessed breast by means of his sweet open side and there show

us something of the godhead and the joys of heaven with a spiritual assurance of endless bliss. This he showed in the ninth revelation, giving the same understanding in the sweet word where he said, "See how I loved you!" Look into his blessed side, rejoicing.

This fair, lovely word "mother" is so sweet and so natural in itself that it cannot truly be said of anyone but him, or to anyone but him, who is the true mother of life and of everything.

To motherhood as properties belong natural love, wisdom and knowledge—and this is God. For though it is true that our bodily bringing forth is very little, low and simple compared to our spiritual bringing forth, yet it is he who does the mothering in the creatures by whom it is done.

The natural loving mother, who recognizes and knows the need of her child, takes care of it most tenderly, as the nature and condition of motherhood will do. And continually, as the child grows in age and size, she changes what she does but not her love. When the child has grown older, she allows it to be punished, breaking down vices to enable the child to receive virtues and grace.

This work, with all that is fair and good, our Lord does in those by whom it is done. Thus he is our mother in nature, by the working of grace in the lower part for love of the higher. And he wills that we know it, for he wills to have all our love fastened to him.

In this I saw that all the debts that we owe, by God's command, to fatherhood and motherhood by reason of God's fatherhood and motherhood, are repaid in the true loving of God. This blessed love Christ works in us. And this was showed in everything, especially in the noble, plenteous words, where he says, "I am what you love."

2.5 PERSUADING A POPE

Catherine Benincasa (d. 1380), the daughter of a Sienese dyer, joined the Third Order of St. Dominic when she was sixteen. She was renowned for her saintly life and gifted with the power of persuasion. Both of these qualities are evident in this letter, which is one of a series written to Pope Gregory XI (1370–1378). Gregory XI was residing in Avignon, France, as his predecessors had done since 1305. This "Babylonian Captivity" of the church by the French government had, in the eyes of many, including Catherine, made the Holy See partisan, avaricious, and virtually impotent. Here Catherine urges Gregory to purge the church of its self-serving priests and rulers and to return to Rome despite the turbulence and violence of Italian city-state politics. The Holy See was finally reestablished there in 1377. Gregory's death a year later, however, began another long period of scandal and turmoil in the church.

Source: Catherine of Siena. "To Gregory XI." In *Saint Catherine of Siena as Seen in Her Letters,* translated, edited, and introduced by Vida D. Scudder, 130–33. London: J. M. Dent, 1911.

Most holy and dear and sweet father in Christ sweet Jesus: I your unworthy daughter Catherine, servant and slave of the servants of Jesus Christ, write to you in His precious Blood. With desire have I desired to see in you the fulness of divine grace, in such wise that you may be the means, through divine grace, of pacifying all the universal world. Therefore, I beg you, sweet my father, to use the instrument of your power and virtue, with zeal, and hungry desire for the peace and honor of God and the salvation of souls. And should you say to me, father—"The world is so ravaged! How shall I attain peace?" I tell you, on behalf of Christ crucified, it befits you to achieve three chief things through your power. Do you uproot in the garden of Holy Church the malodorous flowers, full of impurity and avarice, swollen with pride: that is, the bad priests and rulers who poison and rot that garden. Ah me, you our Governor, do you use your power to pluck out those flowers! Throw them away, that they may have no rule! Insist that they study to rule themselves in holy and good life. Plant in this garden fragrant flowers, priests and rulers who are true servants of Jesus Christ, and care for nothing but the honor of God and the salvation of souls, and are fathers of the poor. Alas, what confusion is this, to see those who ought to be a mirror of voluntary poverty, meek as lambs, distributing the possessions of Holy Church to the poor: and they appear in such luxury and state and pomp and worldly vanity, more than if they had turned them to the world a thousand times! Nay, many seculars put them to shame who live a good and holy life. But it seems that Highest and Eternal Goodness is having that done by force which is not done by love; it seems that He is permitting dignities and luxuries to be taken away from His Bride, as if He would show that Holy Church should return to her first condition, poor, humble, and meek as she was in that holy time when men took note of nothing but the honor of God and the salvation of souls, caring for spiritual things and not for temporal. For ever since she has aimed more at temporal than at spiritual, things have gone from bad to worse. See therefore that God, in judgment, has allowed much persecution and tribulation to befall her. But comfort you, father, and fear not for anything that could happen, which God does to make her state perfect once more, in order that lambs may feed in that garden, and not wolves who devour the honor that should belong to God, which they steal and give to themselves. Comfort you in Christ sweet Jesus; for I hope that His aid will be near you, plenitude of divine grace, aid and support divine in the way that I said before. Out of war you will attain greatest peace; out of persecution, greatest unity; not by human power, but by holy virtue, you will discomfit those visible demons, wicked men, and those invisible demons who never sleep around us.

But reflect, sweet father, that you could not do this easily unless you accomplished the other two things which precede the completion of the other: that is, your return to Rome and

uplifting of the standard of the most holy Cross. Let not your holy desire fail on account of any scandal or rebellion of cities which you might see or hear; nay, let the flame of holy desire be more kindled to wish to do swiftly. Do not delay, then, your coming. Do not believe the devil, who perceives his own loss, and so exerts himself to rob you of your possessions in order that you may lose your love and charity and your coming be hindered. I tell you, father in Christ Jesus, come swiftly like a gentle lamb. Respond to the Holy Spirit who calls you. I tell you. Come, come, come, and do not wait for time, since time does not wait for you. Then you will do like the Lamb Slain whose place you hold, who without weapons in His hand slew our foes, coming in gentleness, using only the weapons of the strength of love, aiming only at care of spiritual things, and restoring grace to man who had lost it through sin.

Alas, sweet my father, with this sweet hand I pray you, and tell you to come to discomfit our enemies. On behalf of Christ crucified I tell it you: refuse to believe the counsels of the devil, who would hinder your holy and good resolution. Be manly in my sight, and not timorous. Answer God, who calls you to hold and possess the seat of the glorious Shepherd St. Peter, whose vicar you have been. And raise the standard of the holy Cross; for as we were freed by the Cross—so Paul says—thus raising this standard, which seems to me the refreshment of Christians, we shall

be freed—we from our wars and divisions and many sins, the infidel people
from their infidelity. In this way you
will come and attain the reformation,
giving good priests to Holy Church. Fill
her heart with the ardent love that she
has lost; for she has been so drained of
blood by the iniquitous men who have
devoured her that she is wholly wan.
But comfort you, and come, father, and
no longer make to wait the servants of
God, who afflict themselves in desire.
And I, poor, miserable woman, can
wait no more; living, I seem to die in
my pain, seeing God thus reviled. Do
not, then, hold off from peace because
of the circumstance which has occurred
at Bologna, but come; for I tell you that
the fierce wolves will put their heads in
your bosom like gentle lambs, and will
ask mercy from you, father.

I say no more. I beg you, father, to
hear and hark that which Fra Raimondo
will say to you, and the other sons with
him, who come in the Name of Christ
crucified and of me; for they are true servants of God and sons of Holy Church.
Pardon, father, my ignorance, and may
the love and grief which make me speak
excuse me to your benignity. Give me
your benediction. Remain in the holy
and sweet grace of God. Sweet Jesus,
Jesus Love.

Chapter 3

WOMEN IN AN ERA OF REFORMATION

Luther, Calvin, and the Status of Women

Marriage

The church into which Martin Luther was born and ordained regarded marriage as a sacrament. As such, it was an indissoluble bond that allowed for the procreation and education of children and acted as a remedy for human lust. Celibacy, however, continued to be regarded as the more pleasing lifestyle in the eyes of God.

Luther altered this medieval understanding of marriage and chastity. He removed marriage from its sacramental status yet simultaneously restored it as a relationship that was favored and indeed commanded by God. In the Protestant tradition, marriage rather than the celibate life became the norm or ideal for all Christians. As a result, the Reformation made a significant impact on the status of women in the domestic arena.[1]

Luther, as did numerous other reformers inspired by his writings, used both theological and biblical grounds to defend his ideas on marriage. Luther rejected the church's idea that God laid down some laws that were binding on all Christians as well as "counsels of perfection" that were intended to be kept only by a small elite in the Christian community. As we saw in chapter 2, the church taught for centuries that people who lived according to the more rigorous laws would earn greater rewards in heaven. Virginity and the ascetic life were seen as examples of these counsels of perfection.

In objecting to this concept, Luther made two important points. First, he argued that God did not lay down two sets of laws for humanity but expected the same obedience from everyone. Second, Luther argued that no human being could ever earn grace from God through obedience to laws. God's grace and salvation were bestowed as gifts upon those who trusted in the righteousness of Christ. Doing good works, performing religious ceremonies, and denying oneself physical pleasures had no bearing on a person's salvation.

Both Luther and Calvin, and a host of other reformers, also argued that marriage was preferable to celibacy on biblical grounds. God had commanded Adam and Eve to be fruitful and multiply. Man and woman were made for the purpose of sexual union according to God's design. They should feel joy and not guilt in their natural inclinations (although Calvin did caution against overindulgence). The reformers looked for inspiration particularly in the pastoral epistles, which show marriage as normal and desirable, and also in the stories of the patriarchs of the Old Testament in which God blesses marital union. The reformers did agree that for a very few Christians who were born without sexual desires, the celibate life was appropriate. These Christians had been given exceptional gifts, however, and they ought not denigrate marriage.

The doctrines of the Lutheran and Calvinist Reformation did not lose sight of medieval ideas on the nature of marriage. They described it as a satisfactory means of procreation and as an acceptable way to deal with human lust. In many writings, marriage was recommended as a way to curb the pervasive fornication to which monks, nuns, and priests were said to be driven. In much reformed literature, however, emphasis was given also to marriage as a spiritual relationship between a man and a woman. Marriage was an arrangement of reciprocal trust and caring, and Calvin carefully coupled his emphasis on female subordination with certain mutual obligations outlined by Paul. Marriage also involved a sharing of duties and reflected the highest form of love known to human beings, the love of God. The reformers also described marriage as a union that both the man *and* the woman were to choose freely.

The honor accorded to marriage in both Lutheran and Calvinist circles had an impact upon the status of women. Since sexuality was no longer viewed as evil, the married woman, at least, was not cast in the role of temptress and seducer. She was seen as fulfilling part of God's design and not as working against God to corrupt the minds and bodies of men.

Since the reformers removed marriage from its sacramental status, divorce became a possibility. The medieval church could only allow for the separation of husband and wife, not their divorce, since it was impossible to dissolve the sacramental bonds of marriage. While the reformed churchmen and the Protestant civil authorities were reluctant to approve of divorces, they acknowledged that in some instances (usually adultery and desertion) such a measure was appropriate. Martin Bucer in Strasbourg even went so far as to extend the grounds for divorce from adultery to spiritual incompatibility. In Geneva, John Calvin insisted that women as well as men be permitted to initiate divorce proceedings.

In giving practical shape to their doctrines, the Lutheran and Calvinist reformers entered into marriages themselves and urged other celibate Christians to do the same. Priests serving the newly formed reformed congregations were encouraged to take wives, although clergy couples in some places were met with rudeness and hostility from a population steeped in the tradition of celibacy and from church leaders who saw marriage as a distraction. The marriage of clergymen affected the status of women in two ways. For some women, it meant a legitimization of a relationship in which they were already involved. It was not uncommon for priests to live with women as mistresses for long periods of time, fathering their children and providing a livelihood for them. Such women, however, were without respect in the community and neither they nor their children had any claim on the priest's estate at the time of his death. Marriage gave these women legal status and rights and eventually security and respect.

Married clergy in both Lutheran and Calvinist circles also meant a new sphere of activity and power for some women as "ministers' wives." As we will shortly discover, the Protestant home became an important center for teaching the gospel and passing on the Christian faith. Within this community of families, the minister's home acquired a preeminent status. Although many modern Christians have difficulty associating the role of the minister's wife with liberation, the sixteenth century provides examples of just such a situation. Women who married Lutheran or Calvinist ministers often found themselves presiding over households that were the centers of cultural and intellectual activities. They offered hospitality to theologians, advice to other clergy, and bed and board to young students. Luther's wife, Katherine von Bora, presided over barnyard, fishpond, orchard, a host of servants, children, sick visitors, student boarders, and church leaders and theologians in their huge Augustinian cloister, which had forty rooms on the first floor alone. Katherine Zell, wife of Strasbourg pastor Matthew Zell, summarized at the end of her life some of the work she had carried out: "I honored, cherished and sheltered many great, learned men, with care, work and expense. . . . I listened to their conversation and preaching, I read their books and their letters and they were glad to receive mine."[2] At the same time, however, clergy wives were expected to excel in obedience and charity as role models for the rest of the community.

The Good Woman as Wife and Mother

Reformed Views on Domestic Life. Women, as we have seen, were not denounced as seducers and corrupters in the Lutheran and Calvinist literature, and they were not treated with scorn and derision. Calvin objected to the vulgar expression that women were "a necessary evil" while Luther took a stand against those who "despised the female sex." Yet the reformers, possibly influenced by their humanist studies, retained a somewhat negative assessment of women. Luther in some of his writing indicates that women were created with weaknesses such as deficient reason, and he could be very harsh when discussing women who failed to be ideal wives and mothers. Some Lutheran leaders even claimed that women turned to witchcraft because they could not cope with life. The solution for them was to trust God and submit to their husbands.[3]

The reformers distinguished between the natural order and the eternal/ spiritual order; men and women were equal in the eternal order because each bore the image of God and each could be redeemed. The natural order was hierarchical and had clearly demarcated roles for men and women. Women pleased God by caring for the home, bearing children, and accepting the rule of men in all spheres of life. This message was conveyed to women through sermons, especially at weddings and funerals, and through works of art such as woodcuts.

For Martin Luther, the subordination of women was the result of woman's sin. Before this divine punishment, men and women were equal in their responsibilities and privileges. Calvin, however, interpreted the Genesis stories through the eyes of Paul in some of his commentaries (but not in his important *Institutes of the Christian Religion*). Calvin argued that woman was created in subjection to man since she was made as his "helper" and since she was made *after* him and *for* him. This original subjection was simply aggravated by her sin: before the Fall her subjection was a free and easy one but after the Fall she was assigned a kind of serfdom. The outcome was that women throughout history were not permitted to exercise authority over men but instead had to be obedient to them. This obedience of course precluded teaching in public or assuming positions of government. Luther, too, stressed subordination, saying that a woman had to take her husband's name and follow him to his place of residence to show her obedience. She was permitted to disobey her husband only when his commands caused her to disobey God. The reformers stressed that the husband was not to oppress his wife with cruelty. If this did occur, however, a woman had to be submissive. She could desert her spouse only if her life was in serious danger.

Luther and Calvin both removed the virgin life of the monastery as an option for women, thus eliminating chances for scholarship, leadership, and triumph over the female nature through holiness. The roles of women were restricted to those of motherhood and homemaking. These tasks, however, were elevated to the status of a "vocation" ordained by God. The church had previously restricted its understanding of vocation to believers who entered religious orders or the priesthood. The reformers insisted, in contrast, that the jobs performed by all baptized Christians were vocations. Women were given the tasks of bearing and rearing children, managing households, and caring for their husbands. These were described to Protestant women as "glorious and ennobling works," which were pleasing in the eyes of God and equal in value and dignity to all other human endeavors.

The role women were to fulfill at home was also enhanced by the Lutheran and Calvinist emphasis on the family as the "school of faith." It was at home that children learned the Bible, the catechism, and basic reformed doctrines. Mothers as well as fathers were responsible for imparting the reformed faith. They were to act, in the words of Luther, as "apostles and bishops" to their children. Calvin claimed that both mother and father were to "rule" their

children. He described the mother as setting the pattern for future generations through the instruction and influence of her sons. She was the parent
who had time to hear Bible and catechism lessons and who could most easily
supervise family worship.

The Protestant Reformation also affected the status of women outside
the home. All Christians, it was said, must learn to read the Bible as the
authoritative guide to faith and practice. Luther therefore called upon the
civil authorities in Germany to establish schools for young girls and boys. In
the Reformation city of Geneva, both girls and boys were sent to school to
learn reading, writing, arithmetic, and the catechism. Although some of the
secular writers of the Renaissance had also stressed the intellectual capabilities of women and recommended their education, the Reformation further
advanced the general improvement of education for both women and men.
The reformers, however, had no intention of opening a wider world to women
or making them critical thinkers. The curriculum focused on subjects such as
sewing, nursing, and Bible study, all aiming at the creation of obedient wives
and competent household managers.

Women in the Life of the Church. On the basis of their belief that the Bible
commanded the subordination of women to men, the Lutherans and Calvinists did not allow women to preach, be ordained, or participate in the governing bodies of the churches. Luther's reasons went beyond the Bible. The
preacher needed "a good voice, good eloquence, a good memory, and other
natural gifts."[4] He did concede that in very unusual circumstances, when no
men were available, a woman might preach as a temporary substitute, and
he cites the biblical examples of Sarah and Rebecca to support his position.
Calvin, likewise, claimed that to punish the unfaithfulness of men, the Holy
Spirit has from time to time raised up women to speak as prophets, and
the Holy Spirit could be expected to do so in the future. Both the Lutherans and the Church of England also continued the Catholic practice of
allowing midwives to baptize babies on the verge of death. Calvin, however,
strongly objected to this practice on the basis of his ideas about baptism and
the administration of the sacraments. He cites several church councils and
follows the line of the theologian Tertullian who stated that women could
not baptize or assume any priestly function. Yet both Luther and Calvin
express ideas about the ministry and church organization that could have

been used to support the full participation of women in the new reformed congregations.[5]

Luther, for example, confidently asserted the doctrine of the priesthood of all believers. By this he meant that all Christians had the responsibility of carrying out certain priestly duties. They were obligated to pray to God on behalf of other believers and to speak the gospel to each other. Luther believed that some Christians should be ordained to preach and to administer the sacraments in a public ministry. Yet when it came to the important duties of prayer and proclamation, both the clergy and the laity had equal responsibilities. The laity included both men and women.

In Calvin's commentary on I Corinthians and in the *Institutes*, he provides insights that could have resulted in a new role for women in the churches.[6] Calvin argued that, unlike doctrine, matters of human governance such as church polity and forms of worship could change according to the expectations of a particular culture. The church had to be sensitive to what was regarded as "proper" and "decorous" in certain circumstances. Calvin included the silence of women in church as a matter of human governance. It is not clear whether Calvin believed that the subordination of woman must endure so long as creation endures.[7] Some historians claim that he sees the church as a place at which the kingdom of God breaks in to the natural order, bringing with it male-female equality.[8]

The Virgin Mary

The image of Mary as theological symbol and object of devotion faded from the beliefs and piety of the reformed churches. One reason for this, of course, was the emphasis in Calvin and Luther on marriage rather than on the celibate life. With the decline of the religious orders, the image of Mary as the pure virgin lost much of its original significance as a prototype for the life of chastity. Also, since the Lutherans and Calvinists emphasized the Bible as the sole authority for faith and practice, they could not find enough about Mary in the New Testament to continue the popular cult that had grown up around her over centuries of Christian history. Some practical changes for women resulted: religious processions honoring Mary, in which women were active, were ended and the feast and fast days celebrating her life and the lives of other female saints were stripped from the calendar.

Catholic Women in an Era of Reform

During the sixteenth and early seventeenth centuries, the Catholic Church experienced a period of revival and reform. The changes that occurred were in part a reaction to Luther and the spread of Protestantism and in part the result of reforming impulses already at work within Catholicism. Historians refer to this movement in Catholicism as the Counter-Reformation. Women played a significant role in the internal, ongoing reform of Catholicism.

The Establishment of New Religious Orders

One aspect of the Counter-Reformation was a series of efforts to establish new types of religious orders for Catholic women. Included in these new orders were the Daughters of Charity (founded by Vincent de Paul and Louise de Marillac), the Ursulines (founded by Angela Merici), and the Institute of the Blessed Virgin (the Ladies of Loretto in the United States, founded by Mary Ward). These new orders were conservative in that their founders retained the virgin life as essential to a life dedicated to God and insisted on a pattern of firm obedience to the male spiritual directors associated with the orders. Yet these women also tried to introduce some radical innovations into Catholic sisterhood.

The new orders were established with the goal of serving other people through nursing, education, and care for the poor. This goal had important effects on the organization of the groups. The women who joined were permitted to be out in society. They were required to spend less time reciting prayers and Daily Offices, which normally occupied much time for nuns. The women wore plain, everyday clothing instead of the traditional habit, and if they lived together in a community, their lives were much less structured than was generally true with cloistered convents. The vows they took were not binding for life but were "reversible." One historian has argued that the confessors/spiritual directors with whom many of the women developed close personal relationships as penitents became male voices of authority sanctioning unconventional behavior.[9]

These innovative groups met with considerable opposition. The Catholic Church was fearful that virgin women in the world would be a source of scandal. The Catholic hierarchy was convinced that the Protestant reformers would be quick to use any kind of immorality on the part of the clergy or nuns against the church. The assumption that virgin women were likely to seduce and corrupt celibate men still prevailed. The lengthy council held at Trent reiterated with force the earlier decrees that women living in religious orders should be cloistered in communities, shut off from the world, and strictly disciplined. Additional opposition to the new orders was based largely on financial considerations. It was argued, for example, that without wealthy patrons and land endowments, these groups could not survive financially. Also, since the women did not take solemn vows binding for life, they could take whatever property or money they had brought to the order with them if they left. The church could not count on inheriting the wealth originally placed at its disposal.

Most of the new orders eventually succumbed to the opposition and dropped many of their innovative features. A cloistered lifestyle and solemn, binding vows were reinstituted. The Ursulines, for example, gradually acquired a distinctive costume, formal vows of consecration, and a system of governance under the control of the church hierarchy. They were transformed ultimately into a community of cloistered nuns under Augustinian Rule. Yet the willingness of the church to permit the Ursulines to continue their work as educators of girls and women within the convent is an indication that the need for nurses and educators sometimes compromised the Council of Trent's emphasis on strict order and discipline.[10] The Daughters of Charity did succeed in getting official approval for much of their original plan with some concessions. They were able to proceed with their hospital service by agreeing to go outside their houses in pairs and by agreeing to wear the traditional habit. The innovative features of the other orders were only slowly allowed to reappear in the nineteenth and twentieth centuries. Despite their eventual repression, however, the new orders provided significant role models of women who were involved publicly in the duties of teaching, nursing, and social work. These tasks were important steps taking women beyond the confines of home and cloister.[11]

Women in Defense of Catholicism

Some historians recently have given attention to the question of how Catholic women, particularly those in convents, reacted to the spread of Lutheranism and Calvinism. Some of the female houses were allowed gradually to cease to exist, while other were permitted to continue even in Protestant territories.

Some nuns fled to Catholic states while others accepted Lutheran theology apart from its rejection of monastic life. Jane Dempsey Douglass describes the experiences of one woman, Sister Jeanne de Jussie, who lived in Geneva during the growth and triumph of Calvinism.[12]

Jussie's writings emphasize the point that Catholic women were much more loyal to their faith than Catholic men. She describes how women endured beatings, broken families, and verbal abuse because they would not accept Protestant ideas. She also writes about the support of some high-ranking Catholic women for her convent. These women of status and wealth came to the aid of the sisters when they were harassed by Protestant men and when their convent was ransacked. The account of Jussie confirms stories from many other regions in Europe that describe how many Catholic sisters strongly resisted the closure of their convents and the disbanding of their orders. In Geneva, the women used the biblical text to refute the arguments of the men who made threats outside their door, casting aspersions on the sisters' chastity and claiming that the women were being held by force. Not only did the sisters object to doctrines such as the Protestant understanding of the Eucharist, but they saw the Protestant glorification of marriage, rather than the convent, as a form of constraint on women.

Jussie's account of the behavior of the Calvinist women in Geneva also shows that they too were active in the spread of reformed doctrine and worship. She writes, for example, about the Calvinist women who worked at their spinning and weaving in full public view on Catholic holy days. She also claims that these women were quick to annoy others with their "preaching." The wife of an apothecary "meddled in preaching" and visited the convent to praise marriage, denounce chastity, and irritate the nuns. Jussie adds an interesting note: This woman was regarded by the Calvinist leaders as illumined by God to teach and preach divine truth, an attitude that contrasts sharply with some of their own words on appropriate roles for women.

Protestant Women Active in Reform

Women were not passive recipients of the Reformation; rather, they responded in word and deed as the Reformation spread throughout Europe. So far as historians can tell, women did not serve as ordained clergy in the Lutheran and

Calvinist churches nor did they contribute to the written body of reformed theology. Yet they conducted a whole range of activities, including preaching, that supported and spread the ideals of Luther and Calvin. They wrote and sometimes published letters advocating Protestant principles. They circulated books containing reformed doctrine, and they sometimes sponsored the publication of such material. They visited influential people to win them over to the cause of the Reformation and, on occasion, conducted church services when clergymen were either absent or unwilling. These activities were curtailed as Protestantism triumphed and became more institutionalized.

Katherine Zell

Katherine Zell married a priest with the knowledge that both she and her husband would be subjected to extreme disapproval for abandoning the celibate life. When her husband was denounced by the Bishop of Strasbourg, Zell took up her pen in his defense. In an open letter to the bishop, she attacked the age-old practice of clerical celibacy. She accused the bishop of being concerned only with his own pocket since he could no longer tax the priests who were living with mistresses. Marriage, Zell claimed, would actually save souls since priests with natural sexual desires would not have to commit the sin of fornication. As she bordered on discussing matters of doctrine in her letter, Zell felt that she had to defend her "unwomanly" behavior. She turned to the Bible for support: "You remind me . . . that the Apostle Paul told women to be silent in church. I would remind you of the word of this same apostle that in Christ there is no longer male nor female and of the prophecy of Joel: 'I will pour forth my spirit upon all flesh and your sons and your *daughters* will prophesy.'"[13]

Zell was dedicated to the cause of reform. In addition to her defense of clerical marriage, she wrote a preface to and published a collection of hymns to enhance congregational participation in the new churches. She also devoted herself to caring for the sick and the imprisoned in Strasbourg as well as the multitudes of refugees who flocked to the city to escape religious warfare.

Argula von Grumbach

The Bavarian noblewoman Argula von Grumbach is also representative of the numerous women who furthered the cause of Protestantism. From a family with a tradition of dissent and scholarship, she became a serious student of the Bible and Lutheran doctrine in the early 1520s. In 1523 the University of Ingolstadt tried a student, Arcasius Seehofer, for his Lutheran sympathies and forced him to recant. Von Grumbach took up her pen on his behalf, arguing with university and secular officials in a series of letters that the Bible was on Seehofer's side and she would prove as much in open debate. The letters provoked official wrath but no reply; instead, von Grumbach's husband was dismissed from his administrative post with the intention that he punish and control her. Despite adverse family circumstances and the inaccessibility of pulpit and lecture platform, von Grumbach was determined to be heard. She turned to the new medium of print and became an advocate for religious books in the German language.

Von Grumbach took seriously Luther's doctrine of the priesthood of all believers, which she believed gave her the right to question those in authority and to come to the Bible with fresh eyes.[14] She recognized that the Bible counsels the silence of women, but she argued that in situations of special urgency, God can raise up humble women to challenge the mightiest: "I send you not a woman's rantings but the Word of God. I write as a member of the Church of Christ against which the gates of hell shall not prevail, as they will against the Church of Rome."[15] She saw herself as filling a prophetic role, as did a long line of biblical women in times of crisis. She in fact saw speaking out as a vital part of discipleship, affirmed in Matthew 10 where all believers are commanded to confess Christ.

French Noblewomen

During Calvin's years in Geneva, he corresponded with a number of French noblewomen whose patronage and power were clearly regarded by the reformer as vital to the success of the Reformation in France. These women may have been attracted to a version of Protestantism that encouraged them to transform the world.[16] They offered aid and support in a number of ways. Despite the hostility that they encountered in many places, the women persuaded others to join the Calvinist group and instructed people who were interested in the ideas of the reformers. Calvinist schools were established for teaching young children, as was an academy for the training of clergy modeled on Calvin's school in Geneva. These Frenchwomen sponsored public debates

and seminars to air Protestant and Catholic views, negotiated aid for Hugue-
nots, and secured for reformers access to people with political power. Perhaps
most significant was the protection they offered to Calvinist believers in a
country where the Reformation was never welcomed and often actively persecuted. The women gave refuge and support to young Calvinist women fleeing
from Catholic families and to reform leaders fleeing from Catholic authorities. Calvinist congregations were allowed to flourish on land owned by these
women and protected by their private armed guards.

PROTESTANT WOMEN OUTSIDE THE MAINSTREAM

The Anabaptists

In several territories throughout Switzerland and Germany, Lutheran and
Calvinist churches gained the support of powerful political leaders. As a result
they became "established" or "national" churches just as Roman Catholicism
was in certain states. The civil authorities enforced the doctrine and worship of the reformed churches and supported them in material ways as well.
The churches, for their part, upheld the prevailing social values and political
structures. The membership of the church was virtually identified with the
citizens of a particular state or territory.

In the sixteenth century, a number of groups appeared that accepted many
of the ideas of Luther and Calvin but wanted more radical change in church
and society. They differed on some theological issues and on matters of lifestyle, but many of the groups making up the Anabaptists, as they were called,
did share some common tendencies. Rejecting a close alliance between church
and political establishment, they believed that the church should include in its
membership only those people who could show clear evidence that they had
received God's saving grace in a definitive conversion experience. This was
the prerequisite for baptism. Believers were expected to model their lives and
communities on the New Testament, especially the Sermon on the Mount.
Condemning war and oath-taking, they evolved eventually into groups such
as the Hutterites, Mennonites, and Amish.

The groups were vigorously opposed not only by the Catholic Church but
also by the Lutherans and Calvinists. Their emphasis on direct inspiration by

the Holy Spirit and individual freedom was seen as a threat to the order of society that Christianity traditionally upheld. One concrete way in which this threat was believed to manifest itself was in the public role women assumed (and were sometimes given) in Anabaptist communities. Certainly they appear in some of these traditions in more varied roles than in either Lutheranism or Calvinism, and they were numerically prominent, frequently making up over one-half of a congregation's members. Opponents often used the fact that the groups were composed chiefly of the "weaker sex" as a point of derision.

Most of the written works from this cluster of traditions come from the pens of its male leaders who questioned many things about sixteenth-century culture but described the marriage relationship and female roles in traditional terms of silence and subordination. The German Anabaptist preacher Balthasar Hubmaier turns to the old dichotomy between body and spirit to stress the carnal and hence evil nature of women. The biblical tradition is used to show that woman was created as man's helper and inferior. Obedience to husbands in the home and men in society is the most frequent counsel.

The writers and their female followers, however, sometimes break away from traditional patterns of thought and action. They occasionally stress that a wife had a right to freedom of conscience in religion and a right to worship as she saw fit. Some writers even urged women to separate from their husbands if they hindered faith, and the Hutterites added religious incompatibility to adultery and desertion as grounds for divorce. The godly had to be separated from the ungodly, yet the Anabaptists clearly struggled with this issue. Some groups urged separation only, some advocated divorce but no remarriage, and still others argued that a woman had to be brought under the control of a new husband as quickly as possible.[17]

What was the reality of life for Anabaptist women in homes and faith communities? They were valued members of households and helped to run businesses, but like other women of the artisan class, their roles were domestic and subordinate. The Hutterites provided some education for girls but restricted it to reading and writing along with spinning and sewing. Female roles in the religious life of the Anabaptists were only marginally different from those in other Protestant traditions.

In order to be faithful to the practices of the New Testament church, some groups revived the office of deacon for women who wished to do charitable work. This occurred, for example, in some Mennonite churches in the Netherlands and in North Germany. The office, however, was merged with that of the widow and was restricted to women who were over sixty and whose husbands had died. They were not ordained to this office but in some places were called "church officers."

Most Anabaptist leaders took the prohibitions of Timothy as the final word and claimed that women should not preach or prophesy. Yet they worked within a theological framework that said that the Holy Spirit could communicate with any believer directly, sidestepping the learned and the ordained. Lay preaching, in fact, was a prominent feature of these movements. Furthermore, the revelation of the Holy Spirit could result in the new interpretation of biblical texts. Historian Joyce Irwin has observed that although the leaders may not have approved of women preaching, their theology left the door ajar.[18]

An emphasis on the work of the Holy Spirit coupled with the chaos of persecution did open temporarily some public and authoritative roles to women. There is evidence that a small number preached, taught, and even baptized in the absence of men. Secret meetings held in homes gave women a chance to shape the group's life, and their sufferings and executions along with men gave them an established role as martyrs in Anabaptist tradition. At their trials, women discussed complicated theological doctrines and demonstrated that they had memorized large sections of the Bible. They were honored as role models of how every Christian should fight evil with nonviolence and weakness.[19]

The Seventeenth Century

Both in England and on the continent of Europe, a number of groups appeared that in some sense carried on the belief of the early radicals that the Anglican, Lutheran, and Calvinist reformations had not gone far enough or had lost their initial moral and spiritual rigor. Examples of such groups include the Quakers, German Pietists, and English Puritans (under whose umbrella historians usually place the Baptists, Congregationalists, and Presbyterians). The beliefs of these radical traditions often included direct communication between God and the believer through the Holy Spirit, a distinctive conversion experience, and moral accountability. And while women in a variety of ways in post-Reformation Europe had been assuming increasingly innovative

and independent religious roles, by the 1640s their religious activism, especially in England, was becoming unusually visible and intense.

What forms did this activism take? Opposed as they were to the established churches, many of these groups were forced to meet in secret. Women
repeatedly offered their homes as gathering places and organized group meetings. A lapse in censorship laws in England in 1641 initiated a flood of doctrinal, devotional, and political pamphlets, many of them written, printed, or
published by women. Some ministers such as the Baptist John Smyth gave
women a vote in the selection of pastor, the excommunication of members,
and other affairs of the congregation. Women also engaged in a cluster of
activities involving public speech. Puritan churches required men and women
to give a public account of their conversion experiences for membership.
Both Puritan and Anglican ministers regularly praised women in funeral sermons who offered spiritual advice to families, neighbors, and even the clergy;
clearly these men valued the support of such women at a time of religious
conflict.[20]

Using biblical precedents and the ancient concept that they were merely
instruments in the hands of God, some women also took on the role of
prophet. This meant a variety of things in the seventeenth century: biblical
exposition, personal testimony, warnings to the unsaved, and exhortation of
the faithful. Lady Eleanor Douglas, for example, "predicted the death of the
Duke of Buckingham, a dark fate for Bishop Laud, and even hinted at the
demise of Charles I. Grace Cary . . . had nothing more specific to tell the King
than to urge him to suppress 'all idolatry, superstition and prophanity.'"[21]
And, finally, there were women who preached, although the content of their
sermons and a clear picture of their number are impossible to know. Mrs.
Attaway, for example, preached against infant baptism in Thomas Lamb's
Baptist church in London while in one General Baptist congregation of the
same city, hundreds of people gathered on Tuesday afternoons to hear women
lecture on spiritual matters.

Quaker women were given the widest opportunities for public expression.
Like many of the other sectarian communities, they believed in the direct
experience of the Holy Spirit, called by them the Inner Light of Christ. The
Inner Light was to be found in all people, and salvation came to those who
followed its leading. Rich or poor, learned or unlearned, male or female—
anyone could be called to preach or prophesy. In England such women

preached wherever crowds were to be found, scandalizing society not only by their speech but also by wearing sackcloth and ashes or simple loincloths to call people to repentance. Women's Meetings for the purpose of disciplining and caring for female members and for approving marriages between members also gave women a voice in the affairs of the group. In the next chapter on colonial America, Quaker women are discussed in more detail.

The reactions of the radical groups and those of the established political and religious authorities to this female activism varied. Upper-class women with political as well as religious messages who could command an audience were often seen as threats and therefore persecuted. Lone women from the ranks of the urban working classes were normally treated to little more than derision if they took up preaching or prophesying. Much depended also on how assiduous the local magistrates were in weeding out religious deviance and what kind of male support the women could count on. Even within their own religious communities, they sometimes met with opposition from those who believed that vocal women brought ridicule and hostility down upon all.

Radical Protestant women of the seventeenth century show no evidence that the women's rights was one of their primary goals. Yet even more than the Anabaptist women discussed above, these women discovered possibilities beyond the roles they were assigned traditionally. They developed their speaking and writing skills, they found adventure and intellectual stimulation, and they experienced contentment in responding to what they regarded as a divine mandate.

Women on the continent of Europe participated in radical groups that channeled dissent more into personal piety and withdrawal from the world, and in so doing opened up the possibility of seeing women in new ways. The Moravians, a branch of German Pietism founded by Count von Zinzendorf and his wife Erdmuthe, used the church of the apostles rather than the norms of society as a model for their congregations. They divided themselves into gender-segregated groups for spiritual nurturing and sometimes communal living. These groups were served by a symmetrical, ordained ministry in which women offered pastoral care to other women. This symmetrical ministry seems to be related to Zinzendorf's idea that God's original creation was androgynous. Although evidence that they preached in worship is very scant, Moravian sisters had an important voice in community rituals: they spoke for new female members, delivered eulogies at funerals, and blessed baby girls. Small group discussions and interviews with their leaders on their continuing religious journeys gave all Moravian women a chance to speak. Zinzendorf gradually came to believe that, while women were to be subordinate to men in temporal affairs, female preaching was not unacceptable. He argued that Jesus had restored male-female equality and the Holy Spirit could call women. This trend toward female equality was reversed after Zinzendorf's death in 1760.

By the eighteenth century, many of these radical groups had disappeared, and those that survived imposed silence and subordination on women as they developed institutionally and sought to come to terms with society around them. The silence and subordination of women in home and church were upheld with vigor and the activities of women were curtailed. Female preaching virtually disappeared. Even preaching by Quaker women was not as extensive as it had been in the movement's early years. The English Quakers reveal ambivalence and complexity in their thinking on gender roles, as the discussions on the Women's Meetings show.[22] In one attempt at compromise, women were encouraged to sacrifice making decisions that would affect the community as a whole in order to preserve control of their work with the sick and poor.[23] At the same time, some men discouraged women from doing too much speaking when a number of men were present.[24] Once they gained toleration from the government, the Quakers conformed more to the surrounding culture in an effort to preserve their privileges.

A few radical movements found an atmosphere of religious toleration and opportunities for growth in the American colonies, particularly in Pennsylvania. One such group was the Ephrata Community (originally German Dunkers), which settled in Lancaster, Pennsylvania. Rooted in German Pietism, the community stressed withdrawal from the world, rejection of a state or national church, individual conversion, and a direct knowledge of God through mystical experiences. In some ways, it also anticipated features of American groups in the nineteenth century that encouraged the participation of women. Conrad Biessel, leader of the community, spoke of a divine female principle, Sophia, as well as the male principle, God. At Ephrata, celibate women lived together in one building, sharing the household work with each other but not doing the chores for men. In addition to spinning and quilting, the women developed artistic and musical skills by practicing calligraphy and singing.

LASTING EFFECTS

Did the Reformation of Calvin and Luther enhance or diminish the status of women in the Christian community? The effects of the Reformation are ambiguous. Women were not given opportunities to teach, preach, or govern the reformed congregations, and they lost the monastery as a sphere of female power and autonomy. It is difficult to find evidence that the reformers made conscious efforts to change the social status of women. Yet the theology of the Reformation terminated the second-class status of marriage and the association of women with evil because of their reproductive functions. In some places, it also brought educational opportunities for women, created divorce laws in their favor, and brought reformed Christians at least to the theoretical threshold of full female participation with the doctrine of the priesthood of all believers.

When we look at the actual activities of women during the era of the Reformation, it is possible to detect certain themes that will appear again as we trace the status of women in American religious history. Women frequently found channels for meaningful participation and dignity despite limitations imposed on them, as did Katherine Zell and the French Protestant noblewomen. Women also tended to be given and assume wider roles in groups that flourished outside of or in opposition to the culturally dominant churches and that emphasized the direct action of the Holy Spirit in human lives.

Readings for Chapter 3

3.1 LUTHER ON MARRIAGE

Martin Luther (1483–1546) had already written and preached on marriage several times when he returned to Wittenberg from the Wartburg in March 1522. His more in-depth treatment in "The Estate of Marriage" probably appeared by the end of that year. Although the exact circumstances behind the work are not clear, Luther may have been responding to practical questions about marriage that had arisen during his absence from Wittenberg and that he encountered on a short tour of surrounding towns. In the treatise he discusses legitimate marriages, grounds for divorce, and the character of Christian marriage. Marriage is an estate ordained by and most pleasing to God. The duties and sorrows it might bring—even death in childbirth—are made "sweet and tolerable" because they are God's will. People are created to reproduce and to fill the earth with children who have been taught by both parents to love God. If they do not respond to these natural impulses, they will become sick in soul and body.

Source: Martin Luther. "The Estate of Marriage." Translated by Walter I. Brandt. In *Luther's Works,* volume 45, edited by Walter I. Brandt, 38–46. Philadelphia: Fortress Press, 1962.

The world says of marriage, "Brief is the joy, lasting the bitterness." Let them say what they please; what God wills and creates is bound to be a laughingstock to them. The kind of joy and pleasure they have outside of wedlock they will be most acutely aware of, I suspect, in their consciences. To recognize the estate of marriage is something quite different from merely being married. He who is married but does not recognize the estate of marriage cannot continue in wedlock without bitterness, drudgery, and anguish; he will inevitably complain and blaspheme like the pagans and blind, irrational men. But he who recognizes the estate of marriage will find therein delight, love, and joy without end; as Solomon says, "He who finds a wife finds a good thing," etc. [Prov. 18:22].

Now the ones who recognize the estate of marriage are those who firmly believe that God himself instituted it, brought husband and wife together, and ordained that they should beget children and care for them. For this they have God's word, Genesis 1 [:28], and they can be certain that he does not lie. They can therefore also be certain that the estate of marriage and everything that goes with it in the way of conduct, works, and suffering is pleasing to God. Now tell me, how can the heart have greater good, joy, and delight than in God, when one is certain that his estate, conduct, and work is pleasing to God?

That is what it means to find a wife. Many *have* wives, but *few find* wives.

Why? They are blind; they fail to see that their life and conduct with their wives is the work of God and pleasing in his sight. Could they but find that, then no wife would be so hateful, so ill-tempered, so ill-mannered, so poor, so sick that they would fail to find in her their heart's delight and would always be reproaching God for his work, creation, and will. And because they see that it is the good pleasure of their beloved Lord, they would be able to have peace in grief, joy in the midst of bitterness, happiness in the midst of tribulations, as the martyrs have in suffering.

We err in that we judge the work of God according to our own feelings, and regard not his will but our own desire. This is why we are unable to recognize his works and persist in making evil that which is good, and regarding as bitter that which is pleasant. Nothing is so bad, not even death itself, but what it becomes sweet and tolerable if only I know and am certain that it is pleasing to God. Then there follows immediately that of which Solomon speaks, "He obtains favor from the Lord" [Prov. 18:22].

Now observe that when that clever harlot, our natural reason (which the pagans followed in trying to be most clever), takes a look at married life, she turns up her nose and says, "Alas, must I rock the baby, wash its diapers, make its bed, smell its stench, stay up nights with it, take care of it when it cries, heal its rashes and sores, and on top of that care for my wife, provide for her, labor at my

trade, take care of this and take care of that, do this and do that, endure this and endure that, and whatever else of bitterness and drudgery married life involves? What, should I make such a prisoner of myself? O you poor, wretched fellow, have you taken a wife? Fie, fie upon such wretchedness and bitterness! It is better to remain free and lead a peaceful, carefree life; I will become a priest or a nun and compel my children to do likewise."

What then does Christian faith say to this? It opens its eyes, looks upon all these insignificant, distasteful, and despised duties in the Spirit, and is aware that they are all adorned with divine approval as with the costliest gold and jewels. It says, "O God, because I am certain that thou hast created me as a man and hast from my body begotten this child, I also know for a certainty that it meets with thy perfect pleasure. I confess to thee that I am not worthy to rock the little babe or wash its diapers, or to be entrusted with the care of the child and its mother. How is it that I, without any merit, have come to this distinction of being certain that I am serving thy creature and thy most precious will? O how gladly will I do so, though the duties should be even more insignificant and despised. Neither frost nor heat, neither drudgery nor labor, will distress or dissuade me, for I am certain that it is thus pleasing in thy sight."

A wife too should regard her duties in the same light, as she suckles the child, rocks and bathes it, and cares for it in other ways; and as she busies herself with other duties and renders help and obedience to her husband. These are truly golden and noble works. This is also how to comfort and encourage a woman in the pangs of childbirth, not by repeating St. Margaret legends and other silly old wives' tales but by speaking thus, "Dear Grete, remember that you are a woman, and that this work of God in you is pleasing to him. Trust joyfully in his will, and let him have his way with you. Work with all your might to bring forth the child. Should it mean your death, then depart happily, for you will die in a noble deed and in subservience to God. If you were not a woman you should now wish to be one for the sake of this very work alone, that you might thus gloriously suffer and even die in the performance of God's work and will. For here you have the word of God, who so created you and implanted within you this extremity." Tell me, is not this indeed (as Solomon says [Prov. 18:22]) "to obtain favor from the Lord," even in the midst of such extremity?

Now you tell me, when a father goes ahead and washes diapers or performs some other mean task for his child, and someone ridicules him as an effeminate fool—though that father is acting in the spirit just described and in Christian faith—my dear fellow you tell me, which of the two is most keenly ridiculing the other? God, with all his angels and creatures, is smiling—not because that father is washing diapers, but because he is doing so in Christian faith.

Those who sneer at him and see only the task but not the faith are ridiculing God with all his creatures, as the biggest fool on earth. Indeed, they are only ridiculing themselves; with all their cleverness they are nothing but devil's fools.

St. Cyprian, that great and admirable man and holy martyr, wrote that one should kiss the newborn infant, even before it is baptized, in honor of the hands of God here engaged in a brand new deed. What do you suppose he would have said about a baptized infant? There was a true Christian, who correctly recognized and regarded God's work and creature. Therefore, I say that all nuns and monks who lack faith, and who trust in their own chastity and in their order, are not worthy of rocking a baptized child or preparing its pap, even if it were the child of a harlot. This is because their order and manner of life has no word of God as its warrant. They cannot boast that what they do is pleasing in God's sight, as can the woman in childbirth, even if her child is born out of wedlock. . . .

It is certainly a fact that he who refuses to marry must fall into immorality. How could it be otherwise, since God has created man and woman to produce seed and to multiply? Why should one not forestall immorality by means of marriage? For if special grace does not exempt a person, his nature must and will compel him to produce seed and to multiply. If this does not occur within marriage, how else can it occur except in fornication or secret sins? But, they say, suppose I am neither married nor immoral, and force myself to remain continent? Do you not hear that restraint is impossible without the special grace? For God's word does not admit of restraint; neither does it lie when it says, "Be fruitful and multiply" [Gen. 1:28]. You can neither escape nor restrain yourself from being fruitful and multiplying; it is God's ordinance and takes its course.

Physicians are not amiss when they say: If this natural function is forcibly restrained it necessarily strikes into the flesh and blood and becomes a poison, whence the body becomes unhealthy, enervated, sweaty, and foul-smelling. That which should have issued in fruitfulness and propagation has to be absorbed within the body itself. Unless there is terrific hunger or immense labor or the supreme grace, the body cannot take it; it necessarily becomes unhealthy and sickly. Hence, we see how weak and sickly barren women are. Those who are fruitful, however, are healthier, cleanlier, and happier. And even if they bear themselves weary—or ultimately bear themselves out—that does not hurt. Let them bear themselves out. This is the purpose for which they exist. It is better to have a brief life with good health than a long life in ill health.

But the greatest good in married life, that which makes all suffering and labor worth while, is that God grants offspring and commands that they be brought up to worship and serve him. In all the world this is the noblest and most precious work, because to God there can be nothing dearer than the salvation of souls. Now since we are all duty bound to suffer death, if need be, that we might bring a single soul to God, you can see how rich the estate of marriage is in good works. God has entrusted to its bosom souls begotten of its own body, on whom it can lavish all manner of Christian works. Most certainly father and mother are apostles, bishops, and priests to their children, for it is they who make them acquainted with the gospel. In short, there is no greater or nobler authority on earth than that of parents over their children, for this authority is both spiritual and temporal. Whoever teaches the gospel to another is truly his apostle and bishop. Mitre and staff and great estates indeed produce idols, but teaching the gospel produces apostles and bishops. See therefore how good and great is God's work and ordinance!

3.2 CALVIN ON THE CREATION OF WOMAN

John Calvin's (1509–1564) commentaries on the books of the Old Testament were written after 1555 when his influence over the city of Geneva was at its height. Calvin, a lawyer and scholar, had been prevailed upon to give the Reformation direction in this city-state. His commentary on Genesis is clearly shaped by his understanding of Paul and his desire to affirm the goodness of marriage. Woman in paradise, therefore, was created as a fit companion for man and as one who also bears the divine image. She was, however, in a state of gentle subjection as his helper. After the Fall—for which, according to Calvin, they shared responsibility—she was cast into bondage and punished with a harsher form of subordination.

Source: John Calvin. *Commentaries on the first Book of Moses Called Genesis,* translated by John King. Volume I:128–30, 171–72. Edinburgh: Calvin Translation Society, 1947.

It is not good that the man should be alone. Moses now explains the design of God in creating the woman; namely, that there should be human beings on the earth who might cultivate mutual society between themselves. Yet a doubt may arise whether this design ought to be extended to progeny, for the words simply mean that since it was not expedient for man to be alone, a wife must be created, who might be his helper. I, however, take the meaning to be this, that God begins, indeed, at the first step of human society, yet designs to include others, each in its proper place. The commencement, therefore, involves a general principle, that man was formed to be a social animal. Now, the human race could not exist without the woman; and, therefore, in the conjunction of human beings, that sacred bond is especially conspicuous, by which the husband and the wife are combined in one body, and one soul; as nature itself taught Plato, and others of the sounder class of philosophers, to speak. But although God pronounced, concerning Adam, that it would not be profitable for him to be alone, yet I do not restrict the declaration to his person alone, but rather regard it as a common law of man's vocation, so that every one ought to receive it as said to himself, that solitude is not good, excepting only him whom God exempts as by a special privilege. Many think that celibacy conduces to their advantage, and, therefore, abstain from marriage, lest they should be miserable. Not only have heathen writers defined that to be a happy life which is passed without a wife, but the first book of Jerome, against Jovinian, is stuffed with petulant reproaches, by which he attempts to render hallowed wedlock both hateful and infamous. To these wicked suggestions of Satan let the faithful learn to oppose this declaration of God, by which he ordains the conjugal life for man, not to his destruction, but to his salvation.

I will make him an help. It may be inquired, why this is not said in the plural number. *Let us make,* as before in the creation of man. Some suppose that a distinction between the two sexes is in this manner marked, and that it is thus shown how much the man excels the woman. But I am better satisfied with an interpretation which, though not altogether contrary, is yet different; namely, since in the person of the man the human race had been created, the common dignity of our whole nature was without distinction, honored with one eulogy, when it was said, "Let us make man"; nor was it necessary to be repeated in creating the woman, who was nothing else than an accession to the man. Certainly, it cannot be denied, that the woman also, though in the second degree, was created in the image of God; whence it follows, that what was said in the creation of the man belongs to the female sex. Now, since God assigns the woman as a help to the man, he not only prescribes to wives the rule of their vocation, to instruct them in their duty, but he also pronounces that marriage will really prove to men the best support of life. We may therefore conclude, that the order of nature implies that the woman should be the helper of the man. The vulgar proverb, indeed, is, that she is a necessary evil; but the voice of God is rather to be heard, which declares that woman is given as a companion and an associate to the man, to assist him to live well. I confess, indeed, that in this corrupt state of mankind, the blessing of God, which is here described, is neither perceived nor nourishes; but the cause of the evil must be considered, namely, that the order of nature, which God had appointed, has been inverted by us. For if the integrity of man had remained to this day such as it was from the beginning, that divine institution would be clearly discerned, and the sweetest harmony would reign in marriage; because the husband would look up with reverence to God; the woman in this would be a faithful assistant to him; and both, with one consent, would cultivate a holy, as well as friendly and peaceful intercourse. Now, it has happened by our fault, and by the corruption of nature, that this happiness of

marriage has, in a great measure, perished, or, at least, is mixed and infected with many inconveniences. Hence arise strifes, troubles, sorrows, dissensions, and a boundless sea of evils; and hence it follows, that men are often disturbed by their wives, and suffer through them many discouragements. Still, marriage was not capable of being so far vitiated by the depravity of men, that the blessing which God has once sanctioned by his word should be utterly abolished and extinguished. Therefore, amidst many inconveniences of marriage, which are the fruits of degenerate nature, some residue of divine good remains; as in the fire apparently smothered, some sparks still glitter. On this main point hangs another, that women, being instructed in their duty of helping their husbands, should study to keep this divinely appointed order. It is also the part of men to consider what they owe in return to the other half of their kind, for the obligation of both sexes is mutual, and on this condition is the woman assigned as a help to the man, that he may fill the place of her head and leader. One thing more is to be noted, that, when the woman is here called the help of the man, no allusion is made to that necessity to which we are reduced since the fall of Adam; for the woman was ordained to be the man's helper, even although he had stood in his integrity. But now, since the depravity of appetite also requires a remedy, we have from God a double benefit: but the latter is accidental. . . .

Unto the woman he said. In order that the majesty of the judge may shine the more brightly. God uses no long disputation; whence also we may perceive of what avail are all our tergiversations with him. In bringing the serpent forward, Eve thought she had herself escaped. God, disregarding her cavils, condemns her. Let the sinner, therefore, when he comes to the bar of God, cease to contend, lest he should more severely provoke against himself the anger of him whom he has already too highly offended. We must now consider the kind of punishment imposed upon the woman. When he says, "I will multiply thy pains," he comprises all the trouble women sustain during pregnancy. . . . It is credible that the woman would have brought forth without pain, or at least without such great suffering, if she had stood in her original condition; but her revolt from God subjected her to inconveniences of this kind. The expression, "pains and conception," is to be taken by the figure *hypallage*, for the pains which they endure in consequence of conception. The second punishment which he exacts is *subjection*. For this form of speech, "Thy desire shall be unto thy husband," is of the same force as if he had said that she should not be free and at her own command, but subject to the authority of her husband and dependent upon his will; or as if he had said, "Thou shalt desire nothing but what thy husband wishes." As it is declared afterwards, "Unto thee shall be his desire" (4:7). Thus the woman, who had perversely exceeded

her proper bounds, is forced back to her own position. She had, indeed, previously been subject to her husband, but that was a liberal and gentle subjection; now, however, she is cast into servitude.

3.3 CATHOLIC WOMEN IN GENEVA

Jeanne de Jussie, a nun in the order of St. Claire, provides evidence that women played an active part in both bringing about and opposing the Reformation. Her chronicle of events in Geneva between 1526 and 1535 includes descriptions of many visits made by Protestants to her convent. On one occasion, the elderly abbess, aided by her vicar, firmly resists the efforts of the city officials to compel the nuns to leave their cloister to attend a debate planned to teach Protestant doctrine. Later, a group of city officials and Protestant ministers enter the convent to persuade the sisters to leave while women outside engage the nuns in debate. Especially vocal is the sister of one of the nuns who would later convert to Calvinism. The nuns of St. Claire eventually found the atmosphere in Geneva so hostile that they reestablished their convent at Annecy, France.

Source: Jeanne de Jussie. *The Rise of Calvinism or the Beginning of the Heresy of Geneva, by the Reverend Sister Jeanne de Jussie, Sometime Nun at Sainte Claire de Genève, and after Her Departure Abbess at the Convent of Anyssi,* edited by Ad.-C. Grivel, with an appended notice by Albert Rilliet, and translated by Allan C. Lane, 124–30, 142–45. Geneva: Imprimerie de Jules-Guillame Fick, 1865–1866.

As, then, the stated deadline approached, the Syndics in person ordered the Father

Confessor of the Sisters of Sainte Claire to appear without fail at the Convent of St. Francis for the debate.

Then on the Friday of the Octave of Corpus Christi at five in the afternoon, when the sisters were gathered in the refectory to have their light meal, the Syndics came to the door along with several other great heretics, telling the mother doorkeeper that they were coming to announce to the Ladies that they had to be present at the debate the following Sunday. The mother door-keeper sent this pitiful news to the sisters at once, and asked that the mother abbess and her vicar should come speak to the men and give an answer. They went there together. Those women who remained in the refectory to keep community were soaked in the abundance of the wine of anguish, and sang compline in tears lamentably. The mother abbess and vicar greeted the Syndics humbly, and these men told them that all the nuns were bound by the command of the Messieurs to appear without fail at the debate. The women answered humbly, "Sirs, you have to excuse us, for we cannot obey this order. All our lives we have been obedient to your lordships and to your commands in what was legitimate for us. But this order we must not obey, for we have taken a vow of holy perpetual enclosure, and we wish to observe it."

The Syndics answered, "We have nothing to do with your ceremonies; you must obey the commands of Messieurs. In any case, solid citizens have been called together for this debate in order to become acquainted with and to demonstrate the truth of the Gospel, because we must come to a unity of faith." "How is that?" said the mother abbess and the vicar. "It is not the profession of women to take part in debates, for such things are not prescribed for women. You don't think that they should take part in debate, seeing that it is even forbidden to uneducated men to get at all involved in explaining holy Scripture. A woman has never been called to debate, nor to give testimony, and in this we do not wish to be the first. It would not do you honor to want to force us to be there."

So the Syndics answered them, "All these reasons are useless to us: you will come there with your father confessors, whether you wish to or not." The mother vicar told them, "Sirs, we beg you in the name of God, turn away from the desire to force us to do such a thing and don't prevent us in any way from going to the service of worship. We certainly don't believe that you are the Syndics, given your simple questions. For we believe the Syndics to be so wise and considered that they would not deign to think of wishing to give us any trouble or displeasure. But these are wicked boys who have no other pastime than to molest the servants of God."

The Syndics said to the lady vicar, "Don't try to trifle with us! Open your doors! We will come in, and then you will see who we are and what authority we have. You have in there five or six young ladies who have lived in the city and when they see us they will tell you just who we are, for we are solid citizens, Governors and Councillors of the city." "In good time," said the mother Vicar, "but for right now you can't come in here, nor can you speak to the ones you want, for they are worshipping at compline, and we wish to go there, too, bidding you a good evening."

The Syndics answered the lady vicar: "They are not all of your mind, for there are some of them that you are holding by force in there, by your traditions and bribes, and who would soon turn to the truth of the Gospel, if it were preached to them. And in order that no one should claim ignorance, the Messieurs have ordered this debate in the presence of everyone and wish that all of you should come there together." "Sirs," said the sisters, "save your grace, for we have all come inspired by the grace of the Holy Spirit and not by constraint in order to do penance and to pray for the world, and not for the sake of laziness. We are not at all hypocrites, as you say, but pure virgins."

So one of the Syndics answered, "You have really fallen from truth, for God has not at all commanded so many rules, which human beings have contrived; and in order to deceive the world and under the tide of religion they are servants of the great Devil. You want us to believe that you are chaste, a thing which is not possible by nature: but you are totally corrupt women."

"What," said the mother vicar, "you who call yourselves Evangelists, do you find in the gospel that you ought to speak ill of someone else? The devil can well take away from what is good, but he has no part in us." The Syndic said, "You name the devil and you make yourselves seem so holy." "It is following your example," she said, "for you name him at your pleasure, and I do it as a reproach." The Syndic said, "Madam Vicar, be quiet and let the others speak who are not at all of your opinion." The mother vicar said, "I am willing. My sisters," she said, "tell the Messieurs our intention." And then the three doorkeepers, the bursar and two cooks, the nurse and several of the old mothers who were there to hear the conclusion all cried out together in full voice, "We speak as she does and wish to live and die in our holy vocation." And then the men were all astonished to hear such cries, telling each other, "Listen, Sirs, what a terrible racket these women inside are making, and what an outcry there is." The mother vicar answered, "Sirs, this is nothing. You will hear much more if you take us to your Synagogue, for when we will all be together, we will make such a noise that we will remain unvanquished." "Now," said the Syndics, "you are in high dudgeon, but you will come there." The mother vicar answered, "We will not." "We will take you there ourselves," they said, "and so you will never go back to your own land, for each of us will take one of you to his house, and we will take her every day to the preaching services, for she must change her wicked life and live according to God. We have lived wickedly in the past. I have been," said the Syndic, "a thief, a bandit and a Sybarite, not knowing the truth of the Gospel until now." The mother vicar answered, "All those works are wicked and against the divine commandment. You do well to amend your life, for you have lived badly. But neither my companions nor I, thanks be to the Lord, have ever committed a murder or any such works so as to need to take up a new life, and so we don't wish to change at all, but to continue in the service of God." And she spoke to them so forcefully along with the mother abbess, and the doorkeeper, that they were all amazed. "Lady Vicar," said the Syndic, "you are very arrogant, but if you make us angry, we will make you sorry." "Sirs," she said, "you can do nothing but punish my body, which is what I most desire for the love of my God. For on behalf of the holy faith, neither my company nor I wish at all to be dissemblers; our Lord wants us to confess him before human beings and if I say something which displeases you, I want to accept the punishment for it all by myself. So that you may know better who I am, and that others may not have unhappiness on my account, my name is Sister Pernette of Montleul, or of Chasteau-fort."

When these evil men saw that they were wasting their time, they left, ending the conversation by saying furiously all together, "We enjoin you all a second time, on behalf of the Messieurs, not to fail to be present with your father confessors next Sunday, early, at the convent of St. Francis at the debate we have mentioned, and we do not intend that someone will have to come to get you," and so they left.

When they had gone away, the reverend mother abbess, the vicar, and the doorkeepers went up to the church with the others and then lifted the cloth from the grille to adore the holy Sacrament which was lying on the altar, as is the very praiseworthy custom. Then, lying prostrate on the ground, all together in a loud voice representing themselves as poor sinners and asking God for mercy—it was enough to break a pious heart, seeking from this good Jesus and the blessed Holy Spirit grace to be able to escape these dangers and perils. . . .

The sister of our poor apostate, hoping to make her leave, was there waiting, and in order to make her come and be perverted, had risen from her childbed, for she had given birth only eight days before. Her heretical husband had carried the child in his arms, and had held it in baptism without any other godparent. When that poor woman saw, I say, that her sister was not coming out at all, she proceeded to go up to the grille with some other women of the city, pretending to want to speak to the sisters in all friendship, to find out what had been done to them by these preachers. Then she asked to speak to her sister. The mother abbess, along with several discreet nuns, spoke to them devoutly, and then a false, serpentine tongue, preaching with sweet words, believing she could do more than the above-mentioned preachers, begins to speak of the Gospel, saying "Poor Ladies, you are very obstinate and blind! Don't you know that God has said that his yoke is easy and light, has said 'Come to me all you who labor and are weary and I will unburden you,' and has not said that one should lock oneself up and torture oneself with harsh penances as you are doing[?]" Then she said words about the holy sacrament which I would shrink from writing, as her "holy" words were quite contrary to salvation. The mother abbess, who knew the Holy Scriptures well, replied to her sharply, as did this poor apostate, but still she showed great friendship and intimacy to her sister, who was making the sisters very suspicious. Some of them went to beg the mother vicar to go there and put an end to their discussion. And she went at once to take the mother abbess by the arms, saying, "My Mother, seeing that these good ladies have changed from one law to another, and have chosen a course opposite to salvation, and to ourselves, you ought not to hear them out." And then she said to the mentioned Lady, "If you wish to converse here about our Lord and in honest words, as in the past, we will speak with you willingly, but we don't want to hear anything at all about these innovations in the law, because it is forbidden to us." Then without further ado she shut the door and left them frustrated. So they were very angry, and shouted there for more than half an hour, saying "Ha, false hypocrites, you despise the Word of God, and want to obey your hypocrites, and ministers of the Devil." And then this poor woman began to say, "You see how they treat my poor sister and keep her subject so that the poor young girl didn't dare declare her heart, however willingly she would listen to us."

And since that day they haven't ceased even a single day from sending someone from their sect to trouble and spy on the poor nuns, and often they would say scurrilous and detestable words. But the mother doorkeeper was sober and discreet and would not speak to them for long at all before she closed her little door. If she was forced to respond, she would have the mother abbess come, and the mother vicar and the sisters would start to pray and our Lord would always let them respond to great effect and they left the visitors conquered and confused. The truth is, they would often threaten the mother vicar with criminal imprisonment, and we sometimes feared that they would in fact do it—but some hesitated, saying, "She is too highly born and could be the cause of some high feeling against the city. Moreover the Duke of Savoy supports them, and so they only pray for him. Besides, we would be reproachable to lay hands on a foolish woman."

Several solid citizens used to come to warn us of the threats that they were making to come and take the young sisters in order to marry them, and especially the poor perverted woman, and to warn us that daily her sister begged the Messieurs and the Council to act. Therefore, some Catholic women from the city, and even some of their relatives, would come to weep, exhorting the nuns to be constant and to have good patience and perseverance, for indeed it had been resolved to oust us from the convent and to separate us from each other shortly.

3.4 WOMEN IN DEFENSE OF THE REFORMATION

This reading is from the first of several letters written by Argula von Grumbach. She defends both the Protestant Reformation and Arcacius Seehofer, a student who was forced to retract his Protestant beliefs. Written on September 20, 1523, and addressed to the University of Ingolstadt, the letter is passionate and uncompromising. It was printed in several editions and widely circulated, but officials at the university never responded to her. Her letter boldly asserts that Scripture rather than church teaching is authoritative. When this principle was denied by those in positions of power, God raised up the weak (including women and young students) to confess this truth. Here she proclaims both the importance of Scripture and her right to determine faith and practice accordingly.

Source: *Argula von Grumbach: A Woman's Voice in the Reformation*, edited by Peter Matheson, 86–90. Edinburgh: T. and T. Clark, 1995.

I beseech you for the sake of God, and exhort you by God's judgement and righteousness, to tell me in writing which of the articles written by Martin or Melanchthon you consider heretical. In German not a single one seems heretical to me. And the fact is that a great deal has been published in German, and I've read it all. Spalatin sent me a list of all the titles. I have always wanted to find out the truth. Although of late I have not been reading any, for I have been occupied with the Bible, to which all of [Luther's] work is directed anyway—to bring us to read it. My dear lord and father insisted on me reading it, giving me it when I was ten years old. Unfortunately I did not obey him, being seduced by the afore-named clerics, especially the Observants who said that I would be led astray.

Ah, but what a joy it is when the spirit of God teaches us and gives us understanding, flitting from one text to the next—God be praised—so that I came to see the true, genuine light shining out. I don't intend to bury my talent, if the Lord gives me grace. 'The Gospel', says Christ, Luke 7, 'is preached to the poor, and blessed is the one who is not offended by me. . . .' As Paul says in I Corinthians 9: 'I preach the unvarnished gospel, lest I abuse my power.' 'I speak truly to you of the light that shines again in the world'. Psalm 118: 'As your word is disclosed it shines forth and gives understanding to the lowly.' Psalm 36: 'In you is the well of life, and in your light we will see light.' John 2: God sought no human witness, 'for he knew what was in everyone'. John 16: 'The spirit will explain who I am.' John 14: 'I am the way, the truth and the life. No one comes to the Father except through me.' And in John 9 the Lord says: 'I am come for judgement upon this world. So that those who do not see should see, and those who do see should be made blind. The Pharisees said: "Are we blind, then?" The Lord answers: "If you were blind you would be without sin. But if you say: We understand, then your sin stands".' And John 8: 'Whoever abides in my word is my disciple.' And in the same chapter: 'Whoever is of God, hears the word of God. Therefore if you do not hear it you are not of God. . . .' And John 10: 'My little sheep know my voice, but a stranger's voice they do not know and so they do not follow him'. Matthew 24: 'Heaven and earth will pass away. But my words will not pass away'. And Isaiah 40: 'The word of God stands for ever'.

Now I don't find such promises from human beings, or papal laws or utterances. 2 Corinthians 1: 'The word of God in his promises is a Yes which excludes any No.' 'From this word was made heaven and earth and all that is in it, and without it nothing was made.' John 1. And God was the word by which the dead were quickened, the sinner converted, the blind made to see, the lame made straight, the dumb to speak and so on. . . . That is a treasury of salvation, not a pit for cash, like the Decretals. Through it life is promised to us. Matthew 4 and John 6.

I cry out with the prophet Jeremiah, chapter 22: 'Earth, earth, earth! Hear the word of the Lord.' I beseech and request a reply from you if you consider that I am in error, though I am not aware of it. For Jerome was not ashamed

of writing a great deal to women, to Blesilla, for example, to Paula, Eustochium and so on. Yes, and Christ himself, he who is the only teacher of us all, was not ashamed to preach to Mary Magdalene, and to the young woman at the well.

I do not flinch from appearing before you, from listening to you, from discussing with you. For by the grace of God I, too, can ask questions, hear answers and read in German. There are, of course, German Bibles which Martin has not translated. You yourselves have one which was printed forty one years ago, when Luther's was never even thought of.

If God had not ordained it, I might behave like the others, and write or say that he perverts (Scripture); that it is contrary to God's will. Although I have yet to read anyone who is his equal in translating it into German. May God, who works all this in him, be his reward here in time and in eternity. And even if it came to pass—which God forfend—that Luther were to revoke his views, that would not worry me. I do not build on his, mine, or any person's understanding, but on the true rock, Christ himself, which the builders have rejected. But he has been made the foundation stone, and the head of the corner, as Paul says in 1 Corinthians 3: 'No other base can be laid, than that which is laid, which is Christ'.

God grant that I may speak with you in the presence of our three princes and of the whole community. It is my desire to be instructed by everyone. Philosophy can avail nothing. As Paul says to the Colossians, chapter 2: 'Be careful of philosophy and the lofty speech of those who are wise in the things of the world.' And what does he say in I Corinthians 1: 'God has made human wisdom folly'? In I Corinthians 3: 'All the wisdom of the world is folly to God.'

Jurisprudence cannot harm me; for it avails nothing here; I can detect no divine theology in it. Therefore I have no fears for myself, as long as you wish to instruct me by writing, and not by violence, prison or the stake. Joel 2: 'Turn again; return to the Lord. For he is kind and merciful.' The Lord laments in the words of Jeremiah 2: 'They have forsaken me, the well of living water, and have dug out broken cisterns which cannot hold any water.'

With Paul, I Corinthians 2, I say: 'I am not ashamed of the gospel which is the power of God to salvation to those who believe.' The Lord says, in Matthew 10: 'Should you be called forward do not worry about what you will say. It is not you who speak. In that same hour you will be given what you have to say. And the spirit of your Father will speak through you.'

3.5 MARRIAGE AND ADULTERY AMONG THE HUTTERITES

Peter Rideman (1506–1556) spent his life as a Servant of the Word in the Church of the Broth- *ers, or Hutterites. In 1540, while visiting Hesse to build up the Anabaptist communities there, he was captured and imprisoned. While confined, he wrote his* Account of Our Religion, *which includes sections on marriage and adultery. Rideman contends that three grades of marriage exist, the highest of which is the marriage between God and the spirit. Implied in this discussion is the Anabaptist claim that a person's obligations to Christ take precedence over obligations to a spouse. Nevertheless, Rideman believes that the marriage of one body with another is a useful analogy to the spiritual union. As such, it is spoken of as a covenant or agreement between a woman who pledges obedience and a man who promises compassion. Like other Anabaptists, Rideman also believes that the marriage bond can be broken by adultery, but not just by adultery in a physical sense. One who ignores the moral imperatives of earthly marriage or who forsakes Christ is guilty of the same sin.*

Source: Peter Rideman. "Concerning Marriage" and "Concerning Adultery." In *Account of Our Religion, Doctrine and Faith Given by Peter Rideman of the Brothers Whom Men Call Hutterites*, translated by the Society of Brothers, 97–102. Rifton, N.Y.: Plough, 1970.

Marriage is a union of two, in which one taketh the other to care for and the second submitteth to obey the first, and thus through their agreement two become one, and are no longer two but one. But if this is to be done in a godly way they must come together not through their own action and choice, but in accordance with God's will and order, and therefore neither leave nor forsake the other but suffer both ill and good together all their days.

Marriage is, however, in three grades or steps. First is that of God with the soul or spirit, then that of the spirit with the body, and thirdly that of one body with another, that is, the marriage of man with woman; which is not the first but the last and lowest grade, and is therefore visible, recognizable and to be understood by all. Now because it is visible, recognizable and to be understood it is a picture, an instruction and indication of what is invisible, that is of the middle and highest grades. For as man is head of the woman, so is the spirit the head of the body, and God is the head of the spirit.

Thus, we see marriage instructeth and leadeth men to God, for if one regardeth and observeth it aright it teacheth us to know God and to cleave to him. Where, however, it is not regarded and observed rightly it leadeth men away from God and bringeth them to death. And since they are few who regard it rightly and many who regard it not aright (still less observe it aright) Paul saith, it is good for a man not to touch a woman lest in their ignorance they lapse and destroy themselves. Therefore we want to speak of marriage insofar as is given us from God to speak.

We say, first, that since woman was taken from man, and not man from woman, man hath lordship but woman weakness, humility and submission, therefore she should be under the yoke of man and obedient to him, even as the woman was commanded by God when he said to her, "The man shall be thy lord." Now, since this is so she should heed her husband, inquire of him, ask him and do all things with and naught without his counsel. For where she doeth this not, she forsaketh the place in the order in which she hath been set by God, encroacheth upon the lordship of the man and forsaketh the command of her Creator as well as the submission that she promised her husband in the union of marriage: to honor him as a wife her husband.

The man, on the other hand, as the one in whom something of God's glory is seen, should have compassion on the woman as the weaker instrument, and in love and kindness go before her and care for her, not only in temporal but also and still more in spiritual things; and faithfully share with her all that he hath been given by God. He should go before her in honesty, courage and all the Christian virtues, that in him she may have a mirror of righteousness, and instigation to blessedness and a leader to God. Where, however, the husband doeth this not or is careless and superficial therein, he forsaketh the glory which was given him by God, as well as God's order. . . .

Marriage is a union of two, in which one taketh the other to care for and the second submitteth to obey the first, and thus through the agreement of both the marriage is confirmed. Contrariwise, where this agreement is broken and transgressed, it mattereth not by whom, the marriage is broken. If the husband preserve not his honor as the glory of God and go before his wife and guide her to blessedness, he hath already broken the marriage with his wife, and if he breaketh it thus with his wife, he soon sinneth in the next grade, namely against his spirit, for he alloweth himself not to be ruled by it but by the flesh, and becometh superficial and forsaketh his lordship; if, however, his spirit is overcome and weakened by the flesh, he falleth in the third grade and breaketh his union with the Creator by whom he is led.

Likewise, if the woman forsake obedience to her husband who faithfully goeth before her, she hath broken and transgressed against the marriage with her husband, that is the union made with him. If she thus sinneth against her husband, she, likewise, goeth on to sin as is said above in all three grades; except where her husband through carelessness hath first broken the marriage with her, become superficial and wanted also to draw her after him. In this case she should let the broken marriage go and hold to that which is unbroken, that is obedience to the Spirit and to God, otherwise she falleth into death, together with her husband.

Where, however, the man doeth his part, but his wife acteth not with but without his counsel, she transgresseth her marriage and union in small things as well as in great things, and taketh from her husband his honor and lordship. If the man permit her to do this he sinneth with her as Adam did with Eve, in that he consented to eat of the forbidden fruit, and both fell to death. For they broke marriage with their Creator and transgressed his order.

The Lord Christ saith concerning adultery, "Whosoever looketh on a woman to lust after her hath committed adultery with her already in his heart." Thirdly, there cometh adultery with the work of the flesh, if one or the other of the partners in marriage go to another man or woman. Where this taketh place, where one committeth adultery in this way, the other should put him or her away and have no more in common with him or her before he or she hath shown real fruits of repentance. For where one mixeth with the transgressor before he or she hath repented, one committeth adultery with the other, even though they were husband or wife before. For it is no longer a marriage, because it is broken until through repentance it is healed, therefore this should be punished by separation as much as the other.

Anne Hutchinson (1591–1643)

Chapter 4

WOMEN AND CHRISTIANITY
IN THE AMERICAN COLONIES

Modified Patriarchy

Most of what we know about colonial views on the nature of women and appropriate behavior for them in the church comes from the writings and sermons of Puritan ministers from New England. The Puritans not only wrote and published a great deal of material, but their works were sold and read throughout the colonies. In this way, they played an important role in determining the character of American religious life, especially in its white Protestant expression. The records of individual congregations from the southern and middle colonies as well as New England supplement these more formal sources. The church records give us some idea of whether or not the theories regarding the role of women were carried out in a practical way, and whether or not women found opportunities to act contrary to these ideals.

What we lack is satisfactory knowledge of how women viewed themselves within the context of the Christian community. Some written works of colonial women, either once left uncataloged or regarded as anonymous by many libraries, are being discovered slowly. They are shedding light on how women responded to their situations in both thought and action. What emerges from all of these sources is not the expected picture of colonial churches as uniformly and rigidly patriarchal. Women are certainly treated and viewed as subordinate to men, yet the religious communities of the colonies reveal active women and a surprising appreciation for the feminine.

The Weaker Sex

In the early decades of the colonial settlements (1630s to 1650s) the ancient image of the "bad woman" so prominent in medieval thought and witchcraft lingered on, especially in New England. Because they were considered physically and intellectually impaired, the minds of women were thought to be incapable of handling anything more than basic learning. Poet Anne Bradstreet had to beg a hearing for her work in 1671 from he who "says my hand a needle better fits."[1] Learning for women was not only inappropriate and futile but also dangerous. Governor John Winthrop was convinced that the wife of John Hopkins of Connecticut had lost her sanity "by occasion of her giving herself wholly to reading and writing" and by meddling in things proper to men.[2]

In a society that valued religious and moral integrity above all else, the accusation that women were spiritually and morally weak was even more serious. Women were regarded as easy prey for sexual seduction and as powerful seducers. It was said that they were prone to lying and more susceptible to doctrinal error and heretical opinions. Woman as the "Devil's dunghill" was an image not entirely out of line with some of colonial thought. Although it was disputed by many, the idea that a woman did not even possess a soul was discussed in colonial literature. The traditional images of Eve and Jezebel informed this view of the gullible woman who had direct contact with the powerful forces of darkness.

The appropriate response to such weakness was to keep women under control or in subjection in all areas of life. Throughout England's new colonies, the ideal wife was described as submissive and obedient to her husband. She yielded to his preferences rather than her own and she devoted her life to his service. As minister John Robinson pointed out, in a harmonious marriage one spouse would lead and the other would follow. Both nature and the Bible left no doubt about who would be the follower. Women also were excluded from positions of leadership in public life. Although they fared better legally than their English sisters and did cast the occasional vote in New

England town meetings, colonial women generally could not vote or hold public office.

Subjection was enforced in the churches of the colonies as well. Church membership was open to women in all of the colonial denominations and women were expected to attend worship regularly. The office of minister was closed to them in the Anglican and Puritan traditions, but the Quakers, as we will see, allowed women a remarkable degree of participation as ministers and missionaries. Women generally did not vote in congregational meetings to call a minister or to discipline a member. They were also discouraged from speaking in such meetings. There are records of congregations that even forbade women to sing in the worship service and of churches in which women were seated apart from the men. In Puritan congregations, all candidates for church membership were in theory required to give a public declaration of their conversion. Some ministers, however, insisted that women only speak privately about their conversions for fear that they would violate the New Testament command of silence. Finally, women were thought to be incapable of theological study or discussion and were required to defer to male church members or their husbands in matters of belief.

Exceptions to Silence, Subjection, and the Evil Woman

Yet Puritans were ambivalent about women and this is clear in their pulpit oratory. As one historian observes, they placed restrictions on women while allowing them "to travel a distance in religion."[3] A part of this new approach was the development of a more positive image of women in New England at the end of the seventeenth century. The concept of spiritual and moral equality between men and women began to replace the image of woman as inclined to false beliefs and sin. Despite their hostility toward the Roman Catholic veneration of Mary, some Puritan clergy began to use the mother of Jesus as a positive counterpart to Eve, the seductive temptress. The prominent New England minister Cotton Mather wrote, "As a woman had the Disgrace to go first in that horrid and woeful transgression of our first Parents, . . . so a Woman had the Glory of bringing into the World that Second Adam, who is the Father of all our Happiness."[4] Even Eve was given some positive features: the curses of subordination and painful childbirth that she brought on women had given them added incentives to turn to the consolations of

Christianity in this life. Women therefore gradually came to be regarded as the spiritual and moral equals of men. They shared the same sinful nature, had the same opportunities for salvation, and faced the same obstacles to faith in everyday life. In John Bunyan's popular allegory of the Puritan life, *The Pilgrim's Progress*, Christiana, Christian's wife, makes an identical but less celebrated journey to the celestial city.

The realities of life in colonial society probably played some part in this shift in thinking. Cotton Mather led the way in the transition. He, like his colleagues, had to deal with the fact that his congregation was made up of more women than men. The admission of new female members generally began to exceed that of males in the 1660s, and by the early part of the eighteenth century there were two women for every one man in many congregations. Puritan leaders explained this by the fear women had of death in childbirth or by the extra time they had to pursue matters of faith. Contemporary historians explain this as a possible result of growing role divergence: men could establish their identities in business and politics whereas women could only look to home and church. They also suggest that conversion was more of a challenge to men, who were asked to give up their culturally prescribed role of dominance in order to submit themselves to Christ.[5]

Women throughout the colonies also provided essential services to the growing new settlements. Their economic roles in farm and plantation households put them in positions of practical equality with male family members. Although the subordination commanded in the Genesis story continued to be the spoken ideal, the Gal. 3:28 emphasis on equality was closer to the truth in many colonial homes.

Puritan views on the nature and role of women were also shaped by the theological framework of the Reformation. The reformers' emphasis on the goodness of marriage and their praise for women as devoted wives and mothers tended to mitigate the long-standing belief that the female nature was inclined to evil and more radically separated from the grace of God. These shifts in thinking had tangible results. Puritan leaders gave women they deemed virtuous high visibility in their community and set them up as role models. Funeral sermons and other clerical treatises do not contain specific definitions of feminine virtues as distinct from masculine. Such distinctions emerged later as a formidable influence on women as America moved into the nineteenth century. A century earlier, however, women as "new creatures in

Christ" were encouraged to take up many of the same kinds of pious activities as their male counterparts.

Of particular interest are the outpourings of admiration for women who were not only good household managers but who lived out their faith by reading, writing, and talking to other people about the things of God. Women in the clerical families of Benjamin Colman and Cotton Mather were encouraged to read the Bible as well as other devotional books and works on church history and theology. Colman's daughter, Jane, studied theology systematically. Mather presented all the women who had cared for his wife during her final illness with a book as a token of his gratitude. He taught his daughters shorthand so that they could take notes on sermons, and, as did many other Puritan ministers, he encouraged women to write for the cause of salvation. Sermon notes, private thoughts on Bible passages, and daily diaries often stayed within the privacy of a woman's home. On occasion, however, the written works of women were published by their admiring pastors or quoted in sermons before an entire congregation.

A virtuous woman, like a pious man, was also praised for conversing on religious subjects. Religious conversation sometimes extended beyond immediate family to groups of female neighbors who gathered together to discuss the Christian faith. Mather writes approvingly of one such group of women who met in 1706 to pray and discuss their religious experiences. Benjamin Wadsworth likewise praised Bridget Usher for promoting pious and "savoury" conversation.

Marriage, which featured prominently in Puritan sermons, was also revised in light of more positive images of women. The model of dominant husband and submissive wife received some modification, as did the prominent belief that marriage was nothing more than an approved channel for the satisfaction of male lust and the procreation of children. The Puritans increasingly came to place more emphasis on the elements of love, trust, and mutuality and less on subjection. Spouses were commonly referred to as friends, partners, and companions. The English Puritan John Milton, author of *Paradise Lost*, even argued that when these elements were not present, a true marriage did not exist. Certainly New England began to echo phrases such as "delight in each other's eyes" and "the desire of thine eyes" when they spoke of marriage in the early 1700s. Along with this mutuality in marriage, the Puritans elevated the importance of the household. It became a "little Church," a place of learning vital to the creation of a godly and stable society.[6] No Puritan denied that the husband was head of the household and his wife his subordinate. But the role of women took on special significance, and something approaching equality, in the teaching of children.

The elevation of marriage to a relationship of some spiritual depth had an interesting counterpart in the way the relationship between God and human beings was expressed in Puritan piety, especially after 1690. Marriage was used as a popular analogy for the way in which God and the Christian were joined. Both were loving unions between sovereign and subordinate parties. Marriage brought duties and privileges to a wife just as salvation brought duties and privileges to a believer. The Christian, like the ideal wife, was to avoid anything that would arouse Christ's anger. The Christian was to observe Christ's rules and be loyal and pure in the relationship. In turn, Christ would behave like a loving husband toward his good wife. Women, as passive brides and obedient wives, became role models for all Christians. In this way they acquired a new community status.[7] Ministers encouraged their congregations to learn humility and receptiveness from the women in their midst.

The subordination of women did not rule out their engagement in a whole range of activities. Wenham Church in Massachusetts is an example of a congregation open to the participation of women, and women were prepared to take full advantage of this liberality even in the 1640s. When a married couple left the congregation, the wife was given her own letter of dismission. Many churches required that women give accounts of their conversion experiences to men in private, and men would then read the reports to the congregation. Wenham Church, however, was counted among those who insisted upon a full, public, and articulate profession of faith by all members. The congregational records show that one woman, Joan White, publicly spoke for this privilege and many other issues. She took an active role in governing the church and it appears that her ideas were acted upon. Women are also recorded as liberal benefactors in many colonial congregations; they also provided hospitality to traveling ministers and worked behind the scenes to establish new congregations and get ministers hired and fired.

By the end of the eighteenth century, views on the nature of women and their place in American society and churches shifted again. The Puritan inclination to see male and female as spiritual equals leading similar lives of devotion was altered. It became increasingly common to believe that women were endowed by nature with a whole cluster of characteristics that could be identified as distinctly feminine. These natural attributes defined the "sphere" or area of activity in which women would be happy and competent. Women, for example, were said to be frail, emotional, intuitive, and nurturing. It was also believed that women were naturally more religious and moral than men, something the Puritans would have been quick to refute. Religion and morality along with child rearing therefore were defined as part of the female sphere. While this shift in attitude represents more restrictions and repression in some ways, it also represents a new phase of female influence within the Christian community.

Anne Hutchinson, the "American Jezebel"

The story of Anne Hutchinson and the religious community in Massachusetts Bay reveals some of the themes we have been discussing so far. It involves the deep-seated suspicion that women were easily influenced by false beliefs and that they had tremendous power over other people in spreading those beliefs. It involves the existence of female gatherings in New England for a discussion of the Sunday sermon and for Bible reading. It also involves the radical equality that some women discovered in the Christian gospel and that was hinted at in the agrarian Puritan household.

Hutchinson was born into the family of Francis Marbury, a clergyman highly critical of the Church of England into which he had been ordained. Page Smith has interpreted Hutchinson's later conflict with the New England authorities as the inevitable outcome of a special father-daughter relationship nurtured by the Protestant Reformation.[8] The Reformation placed in the father's hands a responsibility for teaching all members of the household to read and think about the Bible as the source of salvation. Hutchinson acquired these academic skills from her father. She developed them by attending faithfully the church of the English Puritan John Cotton. She took notes on Cotton's sermons and gradually acquired a theological education through her own initiative.

When she was twenty-one, she married William Hutchinson and began an unremarkable period of childbearing and rearing. She also engaged in the practices of nursing and midwifery. Her husband, a merchant of some success, was described by Governor John Winthrop as "a man of very mild temper and weak parts, and wholly guided by his wife."[9] These words probably reflect anger at the fact that he remained loyal to his wife through her eventual excommunication and banishment.

In 1634, the Hutchinson family followed Cotton to Massachusetts Bay, where he became the minister of a church in the expanding settlement of Boston. The house they built was directly across from that of Governor Winthrop. Anne Hutchinson maintained her keen interest in Cotton's theology and began to invite a group of women to her home to read the text on which the Sunday sermon was based and then to review the main points of Cotton's presentation. The meetings proved so popular that a second was added and men began to attend. In keeping with the English Puritan custom of domestic meetings to discuss the Bible and theology, her hospitality was at first praised as behavior appropriate for a pious woman. Soon, however, she was accused of taking on a teaching role and heading a movement that threatened the peace and well-being of the entire Massachusetts Bay Colony.

Hutchinson was viewed in Massachusetts as one of the chief perpetrators of Antinomianism, a theological perspective that meant "without or against the law." She denied that she advocated a total freedom from laws for Christians, but she did interpret John Cotton's sermons in such a way as to disturb deeply the Massachusetts settlement. She claimed that grace was an intensely personal experience between God and the individual. To say that good behavior was a necessary preparation for the coming of grace and an inevitable sign that conversion had indeed taken place was to return to salvation by works. More importantly, she claimed that the Holy Spirit who dwelled in the redeemed person would directly guide that person as to what to believe and how to behave. Thus, there was no need for magistrates or clergymen to preside in an authoritative way over the community. Those in power in Massachusetts believed that the age of direct divine revelation had passed; God continued to speak only through intermediaries such as the Bible and the clergy and magistrates who interpreted it. Their authority would be undermined and anarchy would result if each individual followed what he or she identified as "divine urgings." This was particularly troubling to a colony that faced an influx of immigrants and war with neighboring native Americans.[10] Some of Hutchinson's followers, in fact, were led to refuse military service under the leadership of opposition minister John Wilson.

The ministers and magistrates were troubled by the implications of Hutchinson's teachings. They moved against a number of men whom they believed to be Antinomian sympathizers, banishing or disenfranchising them. Hutchinson, however, provoked a particular outburst of wrath not only because of her doctrinal ideas but because she was a woman. Her accusers were fearful of her power to seduce men with her false doctrines and to spread them among gullible women at her weekly meetings. Also, her theology suggested a new kind of social order for the Christian community that would be free of oppressive restrictions on human behavior. This new order without doubt would have allowed a high degree of freedom and participation to women. Hutchinson was already a concrete example of what might occur if Massachusetts took salvation by grace alone seriously. She was demonstrating the consequences to which the Bay Colony authorities feared Antinomianism would lead.

The clergy responded initially by passing a resolution prohibiting Hutchinson from holding any more meetings in her home. This clerical gathering was followed by two trials, one by the civil magistrates and one by the church. In the trials, the issue of Hutchinson's sex was brought up repeatedly. She was formally accused of disturbing the peace by holding meetings in her home, "a thing not tolerable nor comely in the sight of God nor fitting for your sex."[11] She was chided for acting more like a husband than a wife and for neglecting her family and encouraging other women to do the same.

Hutchinson showed herself to be a formidable debater and able theologian in the course of her civil trial. She used the Bible in her defense, pointing out that the New Testament specifically approved of older women teaching and counseling younger women at home. She also turned to precedents for women preaching in the history of the church, particularly mentioning a woman from the Isle of Ely in England. The meetings that included men, she assured the court, were addressed only by men. Just when it seemed like the case against her was collapsing, however, Hutchinson made the startling claim that God spoke to her directly. To the magistrates, such an admission revealed the depth and gravity of her error.

In the spring of 1638, Hutchinson was both excommunicated from the congregation in Boston and banished from the colony. Already well into another pregnancy, she moved with her family to Rhode Island, where they enjoyed an atmosphere more tolerant of religious diversity. The Massachusetts clergy and magistrates convinced themselves that Hutchinson had repeated the ancient pattern of woman consorting with Satan and then infecting those around her with evil. In the excommunication decree she was "delivered up to Satan" and the news that she had given birth to a badly deformed and dead fetus was seen as the final proof of her spiritual condition. This conclusion was further confirmed when it was learned that Mary Dyer, one of Hutchinson's supporters, had also delivered a premature and dead fetus. Hutchinson had acted as midwife at the birth, which John Winthrop described in salacious, albeit secondhand, detail. Hutchinson's death at the hands of Mohegans (a Native American band) in 1643 was viewed as God's final punishment.

One notable aspect of Hutchinson's life in New England is the large number of women who found meaning in her teachings and who surrounded her with a community of support. Some of her followers were certainly attracted by her skills in folk medicine and midwifery, but it is possible that many were also attracted to her new perspective on the social order.[12] Were these women consciously trying to acquire more rights and a wider role for themselves in Massachusetts society? Were they drawn to Hutchinson unconsciously or intuitively out of deep but unspoken frustrations with their lot in life? These questions are matters of debate and speculation. Hutchinson, however, remains the first well-known woman on the North American continent to raise questions about the appropriate status of women in church and society.

We also must note the fact that Hutchinson was only one of a number of women in New England who tried to participate in the reformulation of Puritan doctrine and who was prosecuted for failing to comply with clerical authority. In many cases, they showed a spirit of independent judgment on the basis of a direct revelation from God. Anne Eaton of New Haven, for example, was excommunicated six years after Hutchinson for refusing to acknowledge the validity of infant baptism. Lady Deborah Moody was forced to flee to Long Island for similar opinions, and Mary Oliver was deported to England for questioning the conversion experience as a requirement for church membership. All of these women remind us that the tradition of English dissent in which the Puritans were rooted was very diverse; no one point of view had yet emerged as authoritative.[13] Hutchinson and others affirmed those dissenters who allowed women to take public and prophetic roles. This perspective, however, did not prevail and any impact that women might have had on the development of Puritan doctrine was finally curtailed by the increasing inclination to try rebellious and activist women as witches in New England.

THE REVIVAL TRADITION

In the early years of the eighteenth century, the Protestant churches in the American colonies and Great Britain experienced a period of apathy. Membership obligations were not taken seriously, sermons were academic presentations on good living, and deeply felt piety was missing from the general understanding of Christian life. This tendency was reversed in a period of general religious awakening in both countries. The conversion or rebirth experience became a hallmark of the Christian life, as did devotion to righteous living. Preaching changed in style and content. It became more emotional and less formal in an effort to awaken congregations to their sinfulness and to encourage them to turn to Jesus for salvation. This particular approach to Christianity is described by historians as evangelicalism.

In the American colonies, the First Great Awakening began with outbreaks of conversions in New England and New Jersey. In the 1740s the awakening spread throughout the colonies as a result of the itinerant preaching of the evangelist George Whitefield. The fervor and emotional enthusiasm generated especially by the itinerant preachers troubled many ministers who feared the disruption of church order. One way to disparage revival preaching was to describe it as a "species of insanity" to which women were particularly susceptible, although in reality men and women were converted in equal numbers. This did not change the fact, however, that women continued to out number men on the membership roles of eighteenth-century churches.

Despite the attraction that a new emphasis on sin and salvation held for men, the awakening was especially significant for women in the colonial churches. In this evangelical style of Christianity, women found additional and wider opportunities for participation in the Christian community, demonstrating that the eighteenth century was just as crucial as the nineteenth in transforming gender roles. The conversion experience itself, for example, became a public ritual in which women were encouraged to join. Anne Dutton and Sarah Osborn, described below, were part of a trend in which women wrote and published inspirational literature with the approval of their ministers. John Wesley, an important evangelical leader in England and the founder of Methodism, appointed women as group or "class" leaders and welcomed their public speaking as it took the forms of prayer, personal testimony, exhortation, and exposition on religious literature. Wesley was profoundly influenced by his mother, Susanna, who conducted Sunday evening prayers for large gatherings in the absence of her clerical husband. Wesley also drew upon his knowledge of Moravian practices. Eventually he gave his approval to Sarah Mallet, Mary Fletcher, and other women who wished to engage in "biblical exegesis and application," or preaching, a natural progression from their other activities. Before the end of the eighteenth century, the Free Will Baptists also permitted women to serve as preachers and evangelists. Among these women was Mary Savage, who began to preach in New Hampshire in 1791. In no evangelical community did women find full equality as public leaders. They most commonly nurtured and participated in revival Christianity by building on accepted roles within the family such as leading devotions, writing, and counseling people concerned about salvation. Wesley's views dominated Methodism while he was alive; however, after his death in 1791, a formal and authoritarian view of the ministry and a desire for cultural acceptance gradually prevailed and preaching and leadership were limited to men. Slowly the Baptists also began to prohibit women from preaching, teaching, and praying aloud as the nineteenth century unfolded.

The character of evangelical Christianity in the eighteenth century provides us with some clues as to why women were acquiring a wider role. For one thing, the evangelicals emphasized the experience of conversion that dramatically transformed both women and men. All people who had experienced grace were compelled by God to tell others about it. Authority to speak or write was rooted in God's "warming of the heart" and not in theological education or church approval. Many of the evangelical leaders were also open to experimentation when it came to matters of church life. If the experiments brought more people to Jesus, then they were acceptable. As an experiment, Wesley permitted lay men to preach and it was not long before lay women were included. He believed that the evangelical awakening signaled extraordinary times in which exceptions to the biblical command of silence could be made. But as evangelicals sought institutional strength and respectability in the American religious marketplace, the free movement of the Holy Spirit was downplayed.

Anne Dutton, Writer

Only fragmentary evidence from a wide variety of sources makes up the knowledge we have of the English evangelical Anne Dutton. She was a prolific and talented writer who nurtured the distant American awakening through her letters, poems, and tracts. Her family evidently had sympathy with the emotional piety of British evangelicalism and they exposed her to ministers of the same persuasion. Benjamin Dutton, her second husband, was a Baptist pastor in the same circles in Huntingdonshire, England. Anne Dutton was greatly impressed by the evangelical call to a devout and holy life, and she strongly desired to do some "service in the cause of Christ."[14] She was discouraged, however, by her disabilities (both real and imagined) as a woman and determined simply to serve her husband as efficiently and cheerfully as possible.

In 1747 Benjamin Dutton lost his life at sea while returning from a trip to the American colonies. Anne Dutton, who had already established herself as a serious religious writer, devoted herself to a lifetime of religious activity. She carried on a massive correspondence with converts to evangelical Christianity "in divers parts" but particularly in America. She corresponded with George Whitefield and their relationship became one of mutual respect and support. Whitefield encouraged her to increase her correspondence as a service to new converts, particularly to those in South Carolina.

Dutton, however, did not confine her writing to correspondence but also published numerous poems and tracts and edited a periodical titled *The Spiritual Magazine*. All of her writing was infused with a sense of wonder at the transformation God had carried out in her own life and a sense of obligation to open this experience to others. She believed that writing was a divine vocation to which she was called and that God dictated her words. She had no difficulties therefore in overcoming the opinion of some that women should not write on religious topics. God had called her to "feed His lambs." She often wrote anonymously, not out of modesty or shame, but to make certain that her work was published.

In addition, Dutton did not hesitate to speak out against those ministers who deviated from her understanding of the gospel, writing even to John Wesley to argue against his doctrine of perfection. Of her growing dissatisfaction with one minister she wrote, "I thought it was my Duty to acquaint him with it; and accordingly did it after having sought the Lord about it."[15] Nor was she afraid to usurp the role of pastor in offering counsel and advice to a host of correspondents regarding their religious obligations. Her experience of God's grace gave her a confidence in her worth and destiny that society could not shake.

Another Englishwoman, Selina Hastings, the Countess of Huntingdon, also had an impact on revivalism in the American colonies. She is usually noted for her generous gifts of money to further the work of Wesley and Whitefield. Yet she pioneered women's work in missions and in social reform organizations. She organized a mission to the Cherokee people of Georgia which she directed from a distance. Her relationship with Wesley and Whitefield was characterized by equality and mutual counsel.

Sarah Osborn, Teacher

Women's groups for Bible study, prayer, and discussion proliferated in New England as a result of the First Great Awakening. Jonathan Edwards, one of the leaders of the awakening, advised young female converts who were seeking direction to join such groups. Shortly after the visit by Whitefield to Newport, Rhode Island, in 1741, a number of women in the First Congregational Church "who were awakened to a concern for their souls" proposed to Sarah Osborn that she form a society with them to meet once a week. The women established a set of rules for each member to sign. They collected money for firewood used during meetings and decided on who were to be admitted as new members. The group flourished throughout Osborn's lifetime, sustaining revivals in Newport in the 1750s and 1760s, engineering the call of evangelical Samuel Hopkins to their church, and giving a substantial donation to an African mission project in 1774. Her experience with the Newport society encouraged Osborn to take an active role in the revivals that swept the area in 1766–67.

We know about Osborn's religious activities in Newport because they have been celebrated in a biography of her by her pastor, Samuel Hopkins. He based his biography on her voluminous diaries and autobiographical account of her spiritual journey. An addition of great value to this material, however, is a collection of Osborn's correspondence with a friend, Rev. Joseph Fish, which has been published by Mary Beth Norton.[16] Fish approved of her women's group but was typical in expressing ministerial anxieties about the new roles lay men and women were assuming. In the letters we do not see a woman of ideal piety as celebrated by her pastor, but rather a woman struggling to defend the work she believed God set for her and to understand the criticism she was receiving from people around her.

Osborn's years as a young woman in Newport were riddled with tragedy. She lost her first husband at sea in 1733 after only a short marriage and the birth of a son. She operated a school to support herself and her child until she married Henry Osborn, a successful businessman. When her husband's business failed and he became disabled a few months after their wedding, Osborn was again forced to turn to teaching to support her new family. Although women frequently adopted this method of earning money, they did not escape criticism for working "out of their sphere" even before their sphere was carefully defined. Osborn's letters testify to this. She was particularly troubled by the charge that she was neglecting her family by teaching. She admitted that "some things Might be done with more Exactness than now," but she had female friends she could call on for help and the income was vital to her family's well-being.[17]

Osborn's role as a teacher and her sense of evangelical urgency led to a remarkable expansion of her activities. Her correspondence reveals that in 1765 a group of free black people were meeting in her home on Tuesday evenings and a group of slaves on Sundays. The sessions involved singing, reading, and "plain familiar conversing" about spiritual matters. Word of her compassion for people spread rapidly in Newport, and white people—children and adults, males and females—began crowding into her home on other evenings during the week. In January 1767, the number had reached an extraordinary 525 people in one week.

Her letter to Fish reveals that he as well as others in the community advised her to give up her activities because she was not qualified to take on a leadership role, was stepping dangerously close to forbidden territory by holding discussions with both men and women, and was threatening the social order by making black people proud and disobedient (presumably because the gospel preached equality). Osborn responded to all of these concerns.

She claimed, first, that she did not seek out a public role for herself but that God had thrust it upon her. The men who met in her home taught themselves; she merely provided the opportunity. She asserted that she had tried to get help from the male leaders in the churches, but they were reluctant to get involved. Also, the people of the community preferred Osborn's counsel to that of men. She also wrote that her message was not intended to instill pride in people but instead to give them the internal resources to be faithful and obedient, and she had noticed a change in behavior in her community. Finally, she made an observation that would be echoed by countless other women who saw themselves as integral parts of the Christian community. She found purpose, refreshment, and strength in her evening meetings that simply could not be supplied by the more feminine activities that Fish had recommended.

Sarah Edwards

Evangelical Christianity claimed that conversion had to be followed by a life totally consecrated to God. Conversion meant that a person's priorities in life had to be reordered, placing God first. For women, this sometimes meant that God's call had to be obeyed, even when it took them beyond what society regarded as proper for a woman. Both Anne Dutton and Sarah Osborn had this experience. Sarah Edwards's rebirth gave her a similar kind of power. She was freed by her allegiance to Christ from always having to seek approval from other people. In 1742, Edwards, the wife of theologian and preacher Jonathan Edwards, had an intense, extraordinary experience of religious emotion that lasted for nine days. She described her feelings as those of peace and exultation, which had physical manifestations in periods of fainting, vigorous conversation, and even rising up and leaping with joy. She claimed that she felt swallowed up in the light and beauty of Christ and that she swam in the rays of Christ's love "like the motes swimming in the beams of the sun."[18]

Edwards came to an important realization as a result of her experience of religious ecstasy. God's estimate of her life became the only judgment that mattered. She was freed from the obligation to meet other people's standards, including those of her neighbors and her husband to be a virtuous wife. Her happiness, she claimed, rested entirely in a source that would not disappoint. She had participated in the beauty and love of God and it had "deepened her self-awareness and offered her a freedom and independence that was new, enjoyable and worthy of celebration."[19]

Black Women and Evangelicalism

The preaching of evangelists such as George Whitefield was also met with enthusiasm by black women, slave and free, in the eighteenth century. White colonists were initially reluctant to seek black conversions since they feared that a Christian servant could not be held in bondage. Legislation denying this, however, soon became common in the colonies. Where Christianity was introduced through efforts such as those of the Church of England's Society for the Propagation of the Gospel, black women were converts. Their conversions to Christianity increased significantly with the First Great Awakening.

Motivated by the transforming power of evangelical Christianity, many black women participated creatively in the life of the Christian community in the late eighteenth and early nineteenth centuries. The number of women, for example, who developed reputations as preachers is astonishing. Marilyn Westerkamp believes that these women had developed a habit of questioning the authority of white men, and they simply transferred this habit to the patriarchal assumptions of black church leaders.[20] They all emphasized the work of God in their hearts and their irresistible calls accompanied by signs and voices and other wondrous works. Leaving families behind, they often preached in dangerous circumstances to black and white congregations.

Other women took more traditional paths in trying to show the fruits of conversion. The slave Phillis Wheatley wrote poems and letters on the strength she found in Christianity and penned an elegy for George Whitefield. Katherine Ferguson organized the first Sabbath school for children in New York City. She was concerned that poor, orphaned children learn to read and write even though she did not have these skills herself. She also sought ways to care for poverty-stricken and lonely unwed mothers. A sense of mission also motivated the women of Richard Allen's African Methodist Episcopal Church to serve as nurses during an epidemic of yellow fever in the city of Philadelphia.

QUAKER WOMEN

In 1646 George Fox had a profound religious experience that he felt compelled to communicate. He preached throughout England, gathering around him a nucleus of followers who would eventually become the Society of Friends, or Quakers, a group that made significant progress toward male-female equality. The new religious movement was attractive to women from its beginning. Elizabeth Hooten became one of the first Quaker converts and one of its earliest preachers. She eventually traveled as a missionary to the West Indies and the American colonies. Margaret Fell opened her home as a meeting place for the Quakers, wrote on behalf of the movement, and served as its financial secretary. It is not difficult to determine the features of Quakerism that may have appealed to women in both Britain and America. Claims about the equal spiritual status of men and women were given concrete form in domestic life and in the public arena, particularly in the institutional structures of the Society. The right of women to preach and prophesy in public was recognized, and Women's Meetings provided the first opportunity for Protestant women to participate in community governance.

Most significant was the Quaker practice of opening the preaching ministry to women as well as men. Quakers eliminated the need for a specially trained interpreter of the Bible by claiming that each believer would be led to the truth by the Inner Light. They also eliminated the sacraments as part of worship and therefore eliminated the need to set someone apart to celebrate them; thus, they did not formally ordain people to the ministry. In the weekly Quaker meeting, silence was observed until a member, male or female, felt led by the Spirit to speak. The Quakers did "acknowledge" certain members, again male or female, as being gifted with preaching and counseling skills, and they charged these individuals with spreading the Quaker message and instructing and overseeing the Quaker communities.

The Quakers were criticized for their openness to the preaching ministry of women, and they adopted several strategies in its defense. They believed that the Inner Light of Christ could lead either men or women to prophesy and preach. They also believed that as a community, the spirit of Christ had brought them to a consensus on the importance of gender equality. But their opponents, they were certain, would not be convinced unless they dealt with the biblical texts used traditionally to support women's silence and subordination. George Fox, and later Margaret Fell in her pamphlet "Women's Speaking Justified, Proved and Allowed of by the Scriptures," made three important points related to the Bible: (1) They believed that men and women were equal in status before the Fall in Genesis and were restored to that equality by the redemptive work of Jesus. The subjection of woman to her husband was not a divine command but a symbol of brokenness. (2) They also claimed that the words in Corinthians prohibiting the speaking of women were addressed to a specific group of people who had not experienced God's grace. (3) Finally, both Fox and Fell pointed to numerous women who spoke and taught on religious matters. Mary, for example, was the first to declare that Jesus had risen, and Mary, the mother of Jesus, declared her faith in the Magnificat. The way in which Fox and Fell approached the biblical material was informed by their belief that the Inner Light was always illuminating the Bible in new ways. Traditional interpretations of certain material could be altered drastically under the guidance of the Spirit. Their conclusions anticipated modern feminist interpretation.

Women preachers played a significant part in the spread of Quakerism from England to New England and throughout the American colonies. They received financial support from local societies as well as certificates stating the soundness of their beliefs and the permission of their husbands, although sometimes the societies overrode family opposition. Male missionaries carried similar statements of release from their wives. Leaving a family in the hands of her husband, Patience Brayton, for example, journeyed from Rhode Island to preach in the middle and southern colonies. Jane Hoskins was recorded as preaching in New England as well as Ireland and Barbados. Sophia Hume, after the death of her husband, became an active itinerant preacher in the southern colonies in the eighteenth century and wrote a number of tracts and sermons for publication. Upon her departure to London to do missionary work, the Charles Town Society of Friends placed this tribute in their minutes: "This Day our Antient [*sic*] and Worthy Friend Sophia Hume sailed from hence. . . . We are sensibly convinced that nothing less could induce her to this Service but the strongest persuasion of her Love and Duty to Mankind, in becoming an Instrument in Publishing the Glad Tidings of the Gospel of Life and Salvation by Jesus Christ."[21]

As is clear from the words on Sophia Hume, the Inner Light was a source of strength and power for many Quaker women. They undertook journeys that called for enormous physical endurance. They also defied established authorities who opposed Quakerism by preaching in forbidden towns and territories. Mary Tompkins and Alice Ambrose were pilloried, whipped, and expelled from Virginia, and Mary Dyer, one of Anne Hutchinson's most

faithful supporters, was hanged in Boston in 1660. Dyer refused to cooperate with attempts to get her to stay away from Boston and to get her execution reprieved. It seems that the profound experience of the Inner Light
enabled some Quaker women to make autonomous decisions about their life's
work even when they were hard pressed with family responsibilities. When
they were not preaching, these women assumed traditional roles of homemaker and mother without questioning them. When God called, however, they answered—despite pregnancy, young children, and the needs of
husbands.

While the Quakers believed that each person should follow the inner guidance of Christ, they also recognized that they had to guard against deviant
doctrine and eccentric behavior. They sought, in short, a delicate balance
between individual freedom and group authority. Early in their history separate meetings for men and women were established as governing bodies. The
Spirit would guide each member who would contribute to the collective decisions eventually reached. Both local and regional, the meetings gave women a
chance to participate in communal governance. The members learned leadership skills by collecting and dispersing aid for women in crisis, disciplining
members, approving marriages, and keeping in touch with Quaker women
far away. In the American colonies, where important women's meetings were
flourishing by 1700, space equal to that occupied by the men was incorporated into Quaker meeting houses.

In addition to preaching and governing, Quaker women were also equal
partners in the household, training and disciplining children, and sharing in
all decisions. New forms of the wedding ceremony replaced the traditional
phrase "love, honor, and obey" with words reflecting mutuality. Men, however, continued to dominate politics and business in Quaker communities,
and attitudes toward women expressed by male leaders were sometimes more
complex than historians once believed.[22] Although men generally respected
the decisions of the women's meetings, the very existence of separate meetings
for women and the wisdom of allowing them to speak in mixed public meetings were debated, especially in England.

Because of the initiative of many women and the attitudes of some men,
colonial American religion does not present us with a monolithic picture
of silence and subordination. A handful of seventeenth-century Puritan
women as well as eighteenth-century evangelicals and Quakers were com-

pelled by the experience of conversion to move beyond prescribed roles and self-understandings. Colonial clergymen also began to replace the image of woman as inherently evil with the idea that men and women are equally inclined to sin and possess equal opportunities for redemption. This change in attitude was extended even further in the nineteenth century as the "cult of true womanhood" evolved.

Readings for Chapter 4

4.1 WIVES AS MODEL CHRISTIANS

Benjamin Colman (1673–1747) was one of Boston's leading colonial ministers and an advocate for change in Puritan worship practices. The pastor of Brattle Street Church from 1699 until his death, Colman was active in civic affairs and was offered the presidency of Harvard University. One of his most important publications was a series of discourses on the parable of the ten virgins in Matthew 25. His overall purpose is to remind his audience that death and judgment can strike at any time, and that they must prepare by accepting God's salvation. The bridegroom in the parable represents Jesus, in Colman's eyes, while the wise virgins are those who profess the Christian faith. In the passage below, he compares the marriage relationship to that between Christ and the believer. All Christians are to use good wives as their role models because such women love and honor their husbands and submit themselves in humble obedience.

Source: Benjamin Colman. *Practical Discourses on the Parable of the Ten Virgins: Being a Serious Call and Admonition to Watchfulness and Diligence in Preparing for Death and Judgment*, 8–10. Boston: Rogers and Fowle, 1747.

That the *Relation* wherein Christ proposes and offers himself unto us, agrees in many respects to the conjugal or marriage Relation. As,

First, It is the *nearest,* most intimate and indissoluble. As Marriage makes Two to become *One,* so he that *is joined to the Lord is one Spirit.* . . . There is a spiritual Union by Faith and Love[.] . . . The Marriage Covenant gives way to this, and binds not when it comes into Competition. We must *forsake* and *hate* every *Relative* for the sake of Christ. Because there is no higher *Allusion* known among Men, whereby to express the Union of Believers to Christ, therefore has the Holy Ghost used *this*[.] 'We are Members of his Body, of his Flesh, and of his Bones.['] The Reference is to those Words of *Transport* wherewith *Adam* receiv'd and welcom'd *Eve;* charm'd at her Sight he said, *This is now Bone of my Bone,* etc. And as the Marriage Covenant binds till Death, so is our Union to Christ for Life, *for ever:* Death do's but perfect it. *This God is our God for ever and ever.*

Secondly, Our Relation to Christ is by a most sacred and awful *Covenant:* as of Marriage we read, *she is thy Companion and the Wife of thy Covenant.* There is a free Contract: the Choice is mutual, and so is the Obligation. It is between *two only,* Christ and the Soul; wherein our Faith is plighted, Fidelity engaged, in exclusion of all others.

Thirdly, The *Duties* of this Covenant are like those which a *Wife* engages in her Marriage: for instance, intire, unfeigned, fervent, and perpetual *Love* to Christ. Hence the Church speaks of him in this Style, *Him whom my Soul loveth.* Again, *Subjection and Obedience* are the willing Offering of Love. *As the Church is subject unto Christ, so let the Wife, etc.* This is in Acknowledgment of the Excellency, Preheminence, Authority of Christ, 'For the Husband is the Head of the Wife, even as Christ is the Head of the Church and the Saviour of the Body.[']

Fidelity, Purity, and *Honour* are express'd and evidenc'd in Obedience. All Sin and Disobedience is resented as a defiling our selves with strange and impure Loves. Honour and Worship is due, *as the Wife shou'd see that she reverence her Husband.* Constancy in Love and Obedience to the Death is the grand Engagement of the Covenant; even *as the Wife is bound by the Law as long as her Husband liveth.* All Sin is Treachery and Disloyalty against the Saviour. We are to be perpetual Captives to his Love: *Be thou faithful to the Death!*

Lastly, The *Privileges* of the Covenant in Christ do agree with those to which a Wife is entitled by Marriage. *As,* there is a special Propriety in Christ and in all his Benefits: *My Beloved is mine and I am his.* A Title to his Love, *I am my Beloved's, and his Desire is towards me.* As it is natural and invincible to love our own Bodies; 'for no Man ever yet hated his own Flesh, but loveth and cherisheth it, even as the Lord the Church.[']

The Fruits of this tender Affection are *Provision, Protection,* and *Conduct* from Christ. Is the Husband to provide for the Wife? 'For if any Man provide not for his own, especially those of his own House, he has denied the Faith,['] etc. So are our Wants supply'd by Christ, who cares for us; 'My God shall supply all your Wants, according to his Riches in Glory by Jesus Christ.['] Is the Husband to *protect* and defend the Wife? So the Lord the Church: God having *put all things under his Feet, and given him to be Head over all things to the Church.* Again, Ought the Husband to counsel and *guide* the Wife, which is the proper Office of the *Head?* So the Church is under the Watch and Influence of the Redeemer, who is the eternal *Wisdom* of God, and *wonderful in Counsel.*

Again, By our Covenant Relation to Christ we partake in his *Honours and Inheritance;* as the Wife shares in the Degree and Possessions of the Husband: *For if the Head be honoured,* so are the Members; the Crown is put on the Head, but it dignifies the whole Body: Now ye are the Body of Christ and Members in particular. We are said to be *Heirs with him;* and he has said. 'The Glory which thou gavest me, I have given them.[']

4.2 ANNE HUTCHINSON

In 1635, the public order of the Massachusetts Bay Colony was threatened by a deep division over whether a sanctified life was evidence of conversion and an indispensable part of the salvation process. Leaders of the faction that pressed for a "Covenant of Grace" unrelated to works included Anne Hutchinson (1591–1643) and her brother-in-law, Rev. John Wheelwright. Despite a petition from influential Bostonians on his behalf, Wheelwright was banished from the colony in November 1637, and Hutchinson was shortly thereafter brought to trial before the general court. She was accused not only of advocating false theological ideas but also of behaving in a manner inappropriate for a woman. Specifically, she was accused of holding and teaching at meetings in her home and of refusing to submit to her "parents," the magistrates. Hutchinson further frustrated the court by replying to their questions with questions of her own, forcing them to justify their positions from the Bible. She responded to them in a tone of clever defiance rather than submission.

Source: "The Examination of Mrs. Anne Hutchinson at the Court at Newtown." In Thomas Hutchinson, *The History of the Colony and Province of Massachusetts-Bay*, edited by Lawrence Shaw Mayo, 366–70. Cambridge: Cambridge University Press, 1936.

Mr. Winthrop governor: Mrs. Hutchinson, you are called here as one of those that have troubled the peace of the commonwealth and the churches here; you are known to be a woman that hath had a great share in the promoting and divulging of those opinions that are causes of this trouble, and to be nearly joined not only in affinity and affection with some of those the court had taken notice of and passed censure upon, but you have spoken divers things as we have been informed very prejudicial to the honour of the churches and ministers thereof, and you have maintained a meeting and an assembly in your house that hath been condemned by the general assembly as a thing not tolerable nor comely in the sight of God nor fitting for your sex, and notwithstanding that was cried down you have continued the same, therefore we have thought good to send for you to understand how things are, that if you be in an erroneous way we may reduce you that so you may become a profitable member here among us, otherwise if you be obstinate in your course that then the court may take such course that you may trouble us no further, therefore I would intreat you to express whether you do not assent and hold in practice to those opinions and factions that have been handled in court already, that is to say, whether you do not justify Mr. Wheelwright's sermon and the petition.

Mrs. Hutchinson: I am called here to answer before you but I hear no things laid to my charge.

Gov.: I have told you some already and more I can tell you.

Mrs. H.: Name one Sir.

Gov.: Have I not named some already?

Mrs. H.: What have I said or done?

Gov.: Why for your doings, this you did harbour and countenance those that are parties in this faction that you have heard of.

Mrs. H.: That's matter of conscience. Sir.

Gov.: Your conscience you must keep or it must be kept for you.

Mrs. H.: Must not I then entertain

the saints because I must keep my conscience[?]

Gov.: Say that one brother should commit felony or treason and come to his brother's house, if he knows him guilty and conceals him he is guilty of the same. It is his conscience to entertain him, but if his conscience comes into act in giving countenance and entertainment to him that hath broken the law he is guilty too. So if you do countenance those that are transgressors of the law you are in the same fact.

Mrs. H.: What law do they transgress?

Gov.: The law of God and of the state.

Mrs. H.: In what particular?

Gov.: Why in this among the rest, whereas the Lord doth say honour thy father and thy mother.

Mrs. H.: Ey Sir in the Lord.

Gov.: This honour you have broke in giving countenance to them.

Mrs. H.: In entertaining those did I entertain them against any act (for there is the thing) or what God hath appointed?

Gov.: You knew that Mr. Wheelwright did preach this sermon and those that countenance him in this do break a law.

Mrs. H.: What law have I broken?

Gov.: Why the fifth commandment.

Mrs. H.: I deny that for he saith in the Lord.

Gov.: You have joined with them in the faction.

Mrs. H.: In what faction have I joined with them?

Gov.: In presenting the petition.

Mrs. H.: Suppose I had set my hand to the petition what then?

Gov.: You saw that case tried before.

Mrs. H.: But I had not my hand to the petition.

Gov.: You have councelled them.

Mrs. H.: Wherein?

Gov.: Why in entertaining them.

Mrs. H.: What breach of law is that Sir?

Gov.: Why dishonouring of parents.

Mrs. H.: But put the case Sir that I do fear the Lord and my parents, may not I entertain them that fear the Lord because my parents will not give me leave?

Gov.: If they be the fathers of the commonwealth, and they of another religion, if you entertain them then you dishonour your parents and are justly punishable.

Mrs. H.: If I entertain them, as they have dishonoured their parents I do.

Gov.: No but you by countenancing them above others put honour upon them.

Mrs. H.: I may put honour upon them as the children of God and as they do honour the Lord.

Gov.: We do not mean to discourse with those of your sex but only this; you do adhere unto them and do endeavor to set forward this faction and so you do dishonour us.

Mrs. H.: I do acknowledge no such thing neither do I think that I ever put any dishonour upon you.

Gov.: Why do you keep such a meeting at your house as you do every week upon a set day?

Mrs. H.: It is lawful for me so to do, as it is all your practices and can you find a warrant for yourself and condemn me for the same thing? The ground of my taking it up was, when I first came to this land because I did not go to such meetings as those were, it was presently reported that I did not allow of such meetings but held them unlawful and therefore in that regard they said I was proud and did despise all ordinances, upon that a friend came unto me and told me of it and I to prevent such aspersions took it up, but it was in practice before I came therefore I was not the first.

Gov.: For this, that you appeal to our practice you need no confutation. If your meeting had answered to the former it had not been offensive, but I will say that there was no meeting of women alone, but your meeting is of another sort for there are sometimes men among you.

Mrs. H.: There was never any man with us.

Gov.: Well, admit there was no man at your meeting and that you was sorry for it, there is no warrant for your doings, and by what warrant do you continue such a course?

Mrs. H.: I conceive there lyes a clear rule in Titus, that the elder women should instruct the younger and then I must have a time wherein I must do it.

Gov.: All this I grant you, I grant you a time for it, but what is this to the purpose that you Mrs. Hutchinson must call a company together from their callings to come to be taught of you?

Mrs. H.: Will it please you to answer me this and to give me a rule for them I will willingly submit to any truth. If any come to my house to be instructed in the ways of God what rule have I to put them away?

Gov.: But suppose that a hundred men come unto you to be instructed will you forbear to instruct them?

Mrs. H.: As far as I conceive I cross a rule in it.

Gov.: Very well and do you not so here?

Mrs. H.: No Sir for my ground is they are men.

Gov.: Men and women all is one for that, but suppose that a man should come and say Mrs. Hutchinson I hear that you are a woman that God hath given his grace unto and you have knowledge in the word of God I pray instruct me a little, ought you not to instruct this man?

Mrs. H.: I think I may—Do you think it not lawful for me to teach women and why do you call me to teach the court?

Gov.: We do not call you to teach the court but to lay open yourself.

Mrs. H.: I desire you that you would then set me down a rule by which I may put them away that come unto me and so have peace in so doing.

Gov.: You must shew your rule to receive them.

Mrs. H.: I have done it.

Gov.: I deny it because I have brought more arguments than you have.

Mrs. H.: I say, to me it is a rule.

Mr. Endicot: You say there are some rules unto you. I think there is a contradiction in your own words. What rule for your practice do you bring, only a custom in Boston[?]

Mrs. H.: No Sir that was no rule to me but if you look upon the rule in Titus it is a rule to me. If you convince me that it is no rule I shall yield.

Gov.: You know that there is no rule that crosses another, but this rule crosses that in the Corinthians. But you must take it in this sense that elder women must instruct the younger about their business and to love their husbands and not to make them to clash.

Mrs. H.: I do not conceive but that it is meant for some publick times.

Gov.: Well, have you no more to say but this?

Mrs. H.: I have said sufficient for my practice.

Gov.: Your course is not to be suffered for, besides that we find such a course as this to be greatly prejudicial to the state, besides the occasion that it is to seduce many honest persons that are called to those meetings and your opinions being known to be different from the word of God may seduce many simple souls that resort unto you, besides that the occasion which hath come of late hath come from none but such as have frequented your meetings, so that now they are flown off from magistrates and ministers and this since they have come to you, and besides that it will not well stand with the commonwealth that families should be neglected for so many neighbours

and dames and so much time spent, we see no rule of God for this, we see not that any should have authority to set up any other exercises besides what authority hath already set up and so what hurt comes of this you will be guilty of and we for suffering you.

Mrs. H.: Sir I do not believe that to be so.

Gov.: Well, we see how it is we must therefore put it away from you or restrain you from maintaining this course.

Mrs. H.: If you have a rule for it from God's word you may.

Gov.: We are your judges, and not you ours and we must compel you to it.

Mrs. H.: If it please you by authority to put it down I will freely let you for I am subject to your authority.

Mr. Bradstreet: I would ask this question of Mrs. Hutchinson, whether you do think this is lawful? for then this will follow that all other women that do not are in a sin.

Mrs. H.: I conceive this is a free will offering.

Bradst.: If it be a free will offering you ought to forbear it because it gives offence.

Mrs. H.: Sir, in regard of myself I could, but for others I do not yet see light but shall further consider of it.

Bradst.: I am not against all women's meetings but do think them to be lawful.

Mr. Dudley, dep. gov.: Here hath been much spoken concerning Mrs. Hutchinson's meetings and among other answers she saith that men come not there, I would ask you this one question then, whether never any man was at your meeting?

Gov.: There are two meetings kept at their house.

Dep. gov.: How; is there two meetings?

Mrs. H.: Ey Sir, I shall not equivocate, there is a meeting of men and women and there is a meeting only for women.

Dep. gov.: Are they both constant?

Mrs. H.: No, but upon occasions they are deferred.

Mr. Endicot: Who teaches in the men's meetings none but men, do not women sometimes?

Mrs. H.: Never as I heard, not one.

Dep. gov.: I would go a little higher with Mrs. Hutchinson. About three years ago we were all in peace. Mrs. Hutchinson from that time she came hath made a disturbance, and some that came over with her in the ship did inform me what she was as soon as she was landed. I being then in place dealt with the pastor and teacher of Boston and desired them to enquire other, and then I was satisfied that she held nothing different from us, but within half a year after, she had vented divers other strange opinions and had made parties in the country, and at length it comes that Mr. Cotton and Mr. Vane were of her judgment, but Mr. Cotton hath cleared himself that he was not of that mind, but now it appears by this woman's meeting that Mrs. Hutchinson hath so forestalled the minds of many by their resort to her meeting that now she

hath a potent party in the country. Now if all these things have endangered us as from that foundation and if she in particular hath disparaged all our ministers in the land that they have preached a covenant of works, and only Mr. Cotton a covenant of grace, why this is not to be suffered, and therefore being driven to the foundation and it being found that Mrs. Hutchinson is she that hath depraved all the ministers and hath been the cause of what is fallen out, why we must take away the foundation and the building will fall.

4.3 THE "UNFEMININE ACTIVITIES" OF SARAH OSBORN

After the death of her first husband and the illness of her second husband, Sarah Osborn (1714–1796) kept her family just above poverty by running a small school in Newport, Rhode Island. In the early 1740s, after a visit from revival preachers George Whitefield and Gilbert Tennent, Osborn was invited to form a society of young women to promote Christian piety, which she led for the rest of her life. In the 1766–1767 revival season, she played an even wider and more controversial role. Her house became a gathering place where large groups—male and female, young and old, slave and free—engaged in devotional exercises almost every evening of the week. In this letter of February 28 and March 7, 1767, to her friend and spiritual adviser Reverend Joseph Fish, Osborn defends her work. She makes it clear that God's work would remain undone if she discontinued her gatherings, because pastor and church remained unmoved. She has no intention of "Moving beyond my Line," however, and is eager to see her slave gatherings as a "school" rather than "meeting." To Fish's suggestion that she use her evenings for the more feminine activities of needlework and meditation, Osborn replies that her social activities were much more refreshing and productive.

Source: "Sarah Osborn to the Reverend Joseph Fish, February 28–March 7, 1767." In Mary Beth Norton, "'My Resting Reaping Times': Sarah Osborn's Defense of Her 'Unfeminine' Activities, 1767." *Signs* 2 (Winter 1976): 522–29.

And now believing Zions cause is as dear as ever to my venerable friend, permit me to set my self as a child in the Presence of her Father to Give you the Most Satisfactory account of my conduct as to religious affairs I am capable. I will begin with the Great one respecting the poor Blacks on Lords day Evenings, which above all the rest Has been Exercising to my Mind. And first Let me assure you Sir it would be the Joy of my Heart to commit it into Superior Hands did any arrise for their Help. My Revd Pastor and Brethren are my wittnesses that I Have earnestly Sought, yea in bitterness of Soul, for their assistance and protection. [I] would Gladly be under inspection of Pastor and church and turn things into a safe channel. O forever blessed be my Gracious God that Has Himself vouchsaft to be my protection Hithertoo by Putting His fear into My Heart and thereby Moving me as far as possible in this surprizing day. To avoid Moving

beyond my Line, while I was anxiously desirous the poor creatures should be favrd with some sutable one to pray with them, I was Greatly distresst; but as I could not obtain [help] I Have Given it up and Thay Have not Had above one [prayer] Made with them I believe Sir Since you was here. I only read to them talk to them and sing a Psalm or Hymn with them, and then at Eight o clock dismiss them all by Name as upon List. They call it School and I Had rather it should be calld almost any thing that is good than Meeting, I reluct so much at being that Head of any thing that bears that Name. Pray my dear Sir dont Look upon it as a rejecting your council; that I Have not yet dismist. It is Such a tender point with me while the poor creatures attend with so Much decency and quietness you Might almost Hear as we say the shaking of a Leaf when there is More than an Hundred under the roof at onece (I mean with the young Mens Society in the chamber) for all there was so Many. Yet was not the Net broken Has sometimes been a refreshing thot. They cling and beg for the Priviledge and no weathers this winter stops them from Enjoying it, nor Have I been once prevented from attending them.

I know of no one in the town now that is against me. My dear Mrs. Cheseborough and Mrs. Grant Have both been to see me and thank'd me for persisting Stedily in the path of duty against their discouragements, ownd they were at first uneasy but now rejoicd and wish'd a blessing. Mr. C is quite silent. Every

Intimate brother and friend intreats and charges me not to dismiss So Long as things rest as they are, telling me it would be the worst days work that Ever I did if I should, as God Him Self Has thus Employd me. If any disturbance or disorder Should arise Either to the breaking of Public or family Peace, that would immediately Make the path of duty Plain for dismissing *at once,* but on the contrary Ministers and Magistrates send their Servants and approve. And other Masters and Misstresses frequently send me presents in token of gratitude. Express their thanks Speaking of the good Effects that thro the blessing of the Lord it Has Had upon their Servants. And my dear sir what shall I do? Did not onisemus, a servant and once a vile one too, supply that want of a phyleman? Were Phylemon Present onicimus would soon give way. . . .

As to friday Evning friends, my dear Sir I by no means Set up for their instructor. They come indeed for Mutual Edification and Sometimes condescend to direct part of conversation to me and so far I bear a part as to answer etc. but no otherway. They consist of the Brethren of our own church or congregation and Members of Societies Either that Meet at the deacons or our young Men, all I think Except My only one according to the flesh viz my own Brothers Son Mr Haggar, who sits under Doct Styles. That these Gatherings at our House Sir I Imagine no way tend to Separations rents or diversions but are rather a Sweet

Sementing bond of union that Holds us together in this critical day. My dear Mr Osborn thro infirmity is unable to Go often to the Deacons on Thurdsdays Evenings and is very fond of this friday Nights visit, and they are Sweet refreshing Evenings my resting reaping times and as God Has Gatherd I dare not Scatter. In any wise I trust My reasons for Encouraging rather than dispersing will prevent your thinking me Obstinate in bad sence. I dont reject council; dont Let My Honrd Father think I do. The exercises of the Evening Consist in singing, reading Gods word anotation and other Good Books, prayer in turn twice; and Seven or Eight of them are the Most Excelent Men in prayer I believe few private christians Exceeds them. O I trust our God is in the Midst of us, does pour out on us a Spirit of prayer and Supplication—Some of our female Society went frequently to the other female Society on friday Evenings, and as a Means Gradualy to draw them off with out Objecting against their going because they are Baptist, I Have invited such Here with concent of the brethren and we were 20 in Number Last Evening—feb 28 1767[.] . . .

Thursday afternoon and Evening after catechising (Except the Last thurdsday in Every Month on which our Society Meets) is reserved for transient visiters business or what Ever providence allots. Satterday afternoon is my dear Miss Susa's particular time to visit me. Satterday Evening is reserv'd to ourselves. Now sir, if my Evenings were not thus improved I could not spend them to so much advantage that I know of any other way, for indeed I am not so capable after the Exercises of the day of working at my Needle; that overpowers me vastly more than the duties I am Engagd in. I could not retire the Evening as I could not Endure cold etc. nor can I Long attain to clost fixt Meditation or any Clearness of thot tho I Labour Ever so much for it; I am at that Season Much more capable of social duties then any other. These seem then to refresh recruit and enliven my Exhausted spirits, and companys Most of them are dismist before Nine o clock [so] that I have some time Left for other duties. My family Has the advantage of all these seasons. Except the wensday Evenings *only* Mr Osborn with draws a Little while before they break up, I mean from the young ones. And if my Evenings were not thus filld up they doubtless would be with trancient visitors, and some chat Less to Edification Especialy in this *critical day* would break in, which is by this Means *shut out*, [so] that at present I do acquiese in my time being thus taken up. Thus Sir I have given you the best account of My time I am capable of, but after all, while others are wondring, I find cause daily to bemoan before God the Misspence of precious time and oft appear to my self a very Loiterer a very snail. I fly with Haste from all my poor narrow Scanty performances and bless God I Have a

perfect rightiousness to Plead and Hope to Escape to Heaven after all by the way of a free Pardon—I would now Humbly beg Leave Just to Speak a word as to Jethros advice, which I own to be very Good, but Here my dear Sir Lies the difference. Moses was Head of the people and So Had it in His power to comply with Jethros advice by appointing Elders etc. to take part with Him, but I am rather as a Servant that Has a Great work assignd Him and However unworthy and unequal he may think Himself, and others may think Him, and However ardently He may wish it was in Superior Hands or that His Master would at Least Help Him, yet if He declines He dares not tell Him, well if you dont do it your self it shall go undone for I will not, but rather trys to do what He can till God in his providence point out a way for it to be better done. And God did uphold Moses til He pointed out that way of relief He could comply with. Dont think me obstinate then Sir if I dont know How to Let Go these shoals of fish (to which My dear Susa compares them) that we Hope God [h]as Gatherd ready to be caught in the Gospel Net when Ever it shall please Him to shew His dear Ministers on which side the ship to Let it down for advanight—the Harvest truely appears to be Plenteous but the Labourers are few. O that the Lord of the Harvest may send forth Labourers into His Harvest and crown their Labours with success—

4.4 QUAKER WOMEN MAY SPEAK

Margaret Fell (1614–1702) played a decisive role in the successful Quaker struggle for survival amid religious and political hostility. In addition to being a prolific writer and correspondent, she tirelessly petitioned the English government for tolerance, funded traveling ministers, and made her home, Swarthmoor Hall, a secure place of refuge and worship. She wrote Womens Speaking Justified *in 1666 during one of her periodic imprisonments for holding unauthorized meetings. The pamphlet is a vindication of female preaching. It makes the point that man and woman were created as equals. Furthermore, the redemptive power of Jesus puts enmity between woman and sin, freeing her to speak with divine authority. This redemptive power was given concrete expression when Jesus commissioned women to spread the message that he had risen from the dead.*

Source: Margaret Fell. *Womens Speaking Justified, Proved and Allowed of by the Scriptures,* 1–3, 6–9. London: Pythia, 1989.

But first let me lay down how God himself hath manifested his Will and Mind concerning Women, and unto Women.

And first, when *God created Man in his own Image; in the Image of God created he them. Male and Female; and God blessed them; and God said unto them, Be fruitful, and multiply: and God said, Behold, I have given you of every Herb, etc.* Gen. I. Here God joins them together in his own Image, and makes no such distinctions and differences as men do; for though they be weak, he is strong; and as he said to the Apos-

tle, *His Grace is sufficient, and his strength is made manifest in weakness,* 2 Cor. 12:9. And such hath the Lord chosen, even the weak things of the world, to confound the things which are mighty; and things which are despised, hath God chosen, to bring to nought things that are, I Cor. I. And god hath put no such difference between the Male and Female as men would make.

It is true. *The Serpent that was more subtle then any other Beast of the Field,* came unto the Woman, with his Temptations, and with a lie; his subtly discerning her to be more inclinable to harken to him, when he said, *If ye eat, your eyes shall be opened;* and the Woman saw that *the Fruit was good to make one wise;* there the temptation got into her, and *she did eat, and gave to her Husband, and he did eat also,* and so they were both tempted into the transgression and disobedience; and therefore God said unto Adam, when that he hid himself when he heard his voice, *Hast thou eaten of the Tree which I commanded thee that thou shouldst not eat?* And Adam said, *The Woman which thou gavest me, she gave me of the Tree, and I did eat.* And the Lord said unto the Woman, *What is this that thou hast done?* and the Woman said, *The Serpent beguiled me, and I did eat.* Here the Woman spoke the truth unto the Lord: see what the Lord saith, verse 15 after he had pronounced Sentence on the Serpent; *I will put enmity between thee and the Woman, and between the Seed and her Seed; it shall bruise his heel,* Genesis 3.

Let this Word of the Lord, which was from the beginning, stop the mouths of all that oppose Womens Speaking in the Power of the Lord; for he hath put enmity between the Woman and the Serpent; and if the Seed of the Woman speak not, the Seed of the Serpent speaks; for God hath put enmity between the two Seeds, and it is manifest, that those that speak against the Woman and her Seeds Speaking, speak out of the enmity of the old Serpents Seed; and God hath fulfilled his Word and his Promise, *When the fullness of time was come, he hath sent forth his Son, made of a Woman, made under the Law, that we might receive the adoption of Sons,* Gal. 4:4, 5. . . .

Thus we see that Jesus owned the Love and Grace that appeared in Women, and did not despise it; and by what is recorded in the Scriptures, he received as much love, kindness, compassion, and tender dealing towards him from Women, as he did from any others, both in his life time, and also after they had exercised their cruelty upon him; for Mary Magdalene, and Mary the Mother of Jesus, beheld where he was laid; And when the Sabbath was past, Mary Magdalene, and Mary the Mother of James and Salom, had *brought sweet spices that they might anoint him: And very early in the morning, the first day of the week, they came unto the Sepulchre at the rising of the Sun; and they said among themselves, Who shall roll us away the stone from the door of the Sepulchre? And when they looked, the stone was rolled away, for it was very great;* Mark 16:1, 2, 3, 4. Luke 24:1, 2. and they went down into the Sepulchre; and as Matthew saith, *The Angel rolled away the stone; and he said unto the Women, fear not, I know whom ye seek, Jesus which was Crucified; he is not here, he is risen.* Mat. 28. Now Luke saith thus, *That there stood two men by them in shining apparel, and as they were perplexed and afraid, the men said unto them, He is not here; remember how he said unto you when he was in Galilee, That the Son of Man must be delivered into the hands of sinful men, and be crucified, and the third day rise again; and they remembered his words, and returned from the Sepulchre, and told all these things to the eleven, and to all the rest.*

It was Mary Magdalene, and Joanna, and Mary the Mother of James, and the other Women that were with them, which told these things to the Apostles, *And their words seemed unto them as idle tales, and they believed them not.* Mark this, ye despisers of the weakness of Woman, and look upon your selves to be so wise; but Christ Jesus doth not so, for he makes use of the weak: for when he met the Women after he was risen, he said unto them, All Hail, and they came and held him by the Feet, and worshipped him; then said Jesus unto them, *Be not afraid; go tell my Brethren that they go into Galilee, and there they shall see me,* Mat. 28:10, Mark 16:9. And John saith, when Mary was weeping at the Sepulchre, that Jesus said unto her, *Woman, why weepest thou? what seekest thou? And when she supposed him to be the Gardener, Jesus saith unto her, Mary; she turned her self, and saith unto him Rabboni, which is to say Master; Jesus saith unto her. Touch me not, for I am not yet ascended to my Father, but go to my Brethren, and say unto them, I ascend unto my Father, and your Father, and to my God, and your God,* John 20:16, 17.

Mark this, you that despise and oppose the Message of the Lord God that he sends by Women; what had become of the Redemption of the whole Body of Man-kind, if they had not believed the Message that the Lord Jesus sent by these Women, of and concerning his Resurrection? And if these Women had not thus, out of their tenderness and bowels of love, who had received Mercy, and Grace, and forgiveness of sins, and Virtue, and Healing from him; which many men also had received the like, if their hearts had not been so united and knit unto him in love, that they could not depart as the men did, but sat watching, and waiting, and weeping about the Sepulchre until the time of his Resurrection, and so were ready to carry his Message, as is manifested; else how should his Disciples have known, who were not there?

Oh! blessed and glorified be the Glorious Lord; for this may all the whole body of man-kind say, through the wisdom of man, that never knew God, is always ready to except against the weak; but the weakness of God is stronger than men, and the foolishness of God is wiser than men.

Chapter 5

WOMEN ORGANIZING
FOR MISSION AND REFORM

THE CULT OF TRUE WOMANHOOD

By the middle of the nineteenth century in America, a cluster of ideas on the nature of women and their appropriate role was firmly planted in the popular mind of many Americans. These ideas make up what historians have called the "cult of true womanhood" or the "cult of domesticity."[1] The word "cult" is used to indicate that this was an almost sacred ideal to which many people were devoted. The ideal American woman was described as submissive, morally pure, and pious. She found power and happiness at home in the role of wife and mother, and judged herself as well as other women according to these qualities.

The cult of true womanhood permeated American culture even in remote corners of the frontier. It spread mainly through the publishing industry, which expanded and flourished between 1820 and 1850. The nature and role of women was a prominent topic in women's magazines such as *Godey's Lady's Book,* in novels, and in religious literature.

Domesticity

Domesticity was an essential feature of the ideal woman. Her sphere was the home, where she reigned as a queen over a kingdom. It was carefully

159

distinguished from the male world of politics and business. In most literature, woman's sphere was described as complementary to man's and different from it, not as inferior. The male sphere was a competitive scene of brutal economic and intellectual struggle. In contrast, woman was to make the home a place of stability and calm, a refuge from the outside world. Her tasks were ones of nurturing and support. She was to comfort and cheer her husband, raise her children, manage the housework, and care for the sick. What little time was left over could be devoted appropriately to home decorating, needlework, flower arranging, letter writing, and the reading of inspiring literature. Women had always done household labor; now, however, the home became a distinct and sacred space, worthy of an investment of time, creativity, and identity.[2]

This separation of spheres had roots in American economic history. For much of the colonial period, women played a major role in the production of food, clothing, and household articles such as soap and candles in the home. These products were often supplemented by custom-made items from local craftsmen who also worked at home. A growth in population, the expansion of transportation, and advances in technology, however, began to change this situation. People with money to invest promoted schemes to produce large quantities of products economically and efficiently by focusing the efforts of a person or group of people on one particular product. Some of this specialized production initially took place in homes, but it gradually moved out of the household and into factories. The rewards for work became wages and profits. Farms also became mechanized and began to specialize in large quantities of certain crops that were exchanged for cash. These changes were accompanied by a growth in areas such as banking and insurance. Business and manufacturing therefore became the sphere away from home that was dominated by men. Although some women became factory and farm workers, many others were left in the home with the economically unproductive tasks of child rearing and housework.

The belief that men and women had different spheres in life was reinforced by ideas on the nature of women that were circulated in popular literature. Men and women were said to be endowed by nature with different character traits. Women were more affectionate and emotional as well as less rational; they were compassionate, sensitive, and capable of enormous self-sacrifice. Women were also prone to physical and mental illness. Perhaps most significantly, many nineteenth-century works radically revised the traditional estimate of women and claimed that women were naturally endowed with an inclination toward moral righteousness and "happily formed for religion."[3]

Virtue and Piety

Nineteenth-century America reversed the traditional view of woman as prone to sin in the image of Eve. Women were seen not as morally and spiritually inferior to men, but as superior. They were idealized as paragons of virtue and piety while men were cast in the role of sensual beasts who constantly assaulted female morality. The traditional Christian fear that the lust of woman was insatiable was reversed by the belief that woman was less carnal and sexual than man.

Because of her moral purity, the true woman was given formidable tasks in safeguarding the social order of the new American republic. Through quiet persuasion and diligent example, she was to tame the wild nature of husband and sons and make them into good citizens. She was to throw a "light of purity" upon the naughty world of men. If a woman's virtue was compromised, the results were portrayed in Victorian literature as calamitous. A woman's moral function was so important to society that she was threatened with death and mental illness if she took liberties with her sexuality.

Closely related to the belief in woman's moral superiority and the separation of male and female spheres was the century's glorification of motherhood. Fathers interacted less and less with children as they worked away from home. Many women were left with the responsibility of raising children, which developed into a semisacred vocation and an important source of power. Puritan women were certainly expected to give their children religious knowledge, but they did so in cooperation with their husbands. The new ideal of Republican Motherhood, on which True Womanhood was built, assigned this task almost exclusively to women and added political knowledge to moral and religious teachings.[4] This may have been society's way of compensating women for their diminished economic role.[5] Certainly the glorification of motherhood was influenced by the educational psychology of the time, which claimed that early influences on a child determined that child's later character, and by the disappearance of a state-supported church to guarantee moral instruction. Victorian culture gave mothers the task of producing sons who would become virtuous and active citizens and daughters who would become Republican Mothers. The nation, and indeed the progress of civilization, could not do without them.

Nineteenth-century America not only viewed women as morally superior to men but also as spiritually superior. Religion therefore became an integral part of the domestic sphere over which women were to reign. They were "peculiarly susceptible" to the Christian message. Ministers suggested that women were by nature meek, imaginative, sensitive, and emotional, all qualities that were increasingly coming to be associated with Christian piety. They added that women more readily responded to Christianity out of gratitude for the way in which this faith had elevated their social status. Women thus came to be viewed as imitators of Christ. Like Christ, they brought redemption to the world through their moral virtue and religious fervor. Like Christ, they endured the sufferings of this life with patience and in silence. Encouraged by advice literature and manuals of home design, women promoted religion at home by directing regular family devotions and purchasing or crafting religious articles such as parlor organs and wax crosses.[6]

The ideas on women and religion in the cult of true womanhood were recognizing in theory what was already true in fact. Religion was increasingly being abandoned by some men seeking political power and economic well-being. Women were left to teach the Bible to their children, oversee family prayers, and enforce church attendance. Women themselves also filled the pews and, as we shall see, supported the charitable, mission, and reform movements that the churches sponsored. It is even possible to interpret the identification of women with religion as a way of dealing with conflicting values.[7] Some men pursued wealth and prestige, often in very non-Christian ways, yet they continued to profess belief in the importance of traditional moral and religious values. They may have quieted their consciences by assigning to women those areas of life that they held dear but treated lightly.

Along with being domestic, religious, and moral, America's ideal woman was submissive. She was passive, weak, dependent, and in a state of perpetual childhood. She was to exercise her influence behind the scenes, always deferring to the authority of her husband in the home. Submission was seen as ordained by God; to flout it was to throw the order of the universe into confusion. In many nineteenth-century novels, the qualities of willfulness and independence belong to the world of white men, while white women, children, and black people are celebrated for their submission and the moral power that comes from this. Very little attention, however, was given to the dilemma this created; if women were morally and spiritually superior, why should they be obedient to men?

Effects of the Cult of True Womanhood

Ideal womanhood was not an option for women who worked in factories or domestic service, nor was it applied to immigrant and African American women; they continued to be cast in the role of seductress. But for those who tried to shape their lives according to it, this ideal had both benefits and drawbacks The cult of domesticity did present a formidable obstacle to political, economic, and occupational advancement for women. It also required them to erase their sexuality in order to acquire spiritual and moral status. And women in the eyes of some Victorian Americans were still ultimately responsible for male sin, for they had failed to protect men from their bestial natures.[8] In the end, they still lacked official, institutional power in church and society. Yet women did gain some important advantages, some of which were particularly relevant to their status in the Christian community.

First, educational opportunities beyond the elementary level began to open up for women to give them training in household management and child rearing. Second, the identification of women and religion led some clergymen to reshape Christian beliefs in ways that would be more pleasing to women.[9] Thus, the doctrine of infant damnation was abandoned. Hymns stressed the themes of Christ's love and God's mercy, and pastor Henry Ward Beecher spoke of the maternal love of God that never wavered. Jesus was increasingly interpreted as one who loved his enemies and who sacrificed himself for others, and the Calvinist doctrine of predestination waned. (Some scholars have argued, in fact, that this emphasis on the role of the human will and human initiative eventually led to the resurgence of a heroic, masculine Christianity.)[10] Third, women appeared in a pastoral and authoritative role in bringing their sometimes recalcitrant sons and husbands to conversion.[11] Finally, women acquired a sense of self-worth and an impetus to action from the constant assertion that they were morally and spiritually superior to men. They were prompted to ask why they should not take a more direct way of influencing and elevating society than marriage and motherhood since they were really only a "little lower than the angels."

ORGANIZING FOR CHARITY AND REFORM

A second period of revival swept the United States during the early decades of the nineteenth century. Preachers such as Charles Finney emphasized that conversion had to result in good works and usefulness; after 1800, this meant participation in the work of the many voluntary groups that were springing up. Clergy and laity alike joined to channel the religious enthusiasm of the revivals into associations designed to create a Christian America.

Women were swept into the revival fervor, outnumbering men as new converts to Christianity. Encouraged by their pastors and the groups already formed by evangelical women in Great Britain, American women rejected the idea of the fashionably idle "lady" and joined a multitude of female voluntary societies after 1800. They were brought and bonded together by their common experience of conversion. For the most part, the societies were for religious, benevolent, or reform purposes, or they involved the care and rearing of children. These concerns were not new in women's lives; what was new in the nineteenth century was the level of organization that eventually developed to channel their efforts. Prior to the Civil War, female societies were auxiliaries of existing male groups or autonomous but regional organizations for women. It was in the decades after the Civil War that powerful national groups run and financed by women emerged. Along with evangelicalism, other factors in American culture compelled women to organize. The cult of true womanhood gave women the right and power to extend morality and religion throughout America, as long as they were deferential to male authority. The roles women filled during the Civil War, while husbands and fathers were away, gave women a sense of their capabilities. Educational opportunities grew to help women be better wives and mothers and as industrialization expanded, a growing number of women had the leisure time to pursue voluntary work.

Maternal Societies and Sunday Schools

The maternal societies, which were concerned with the tasks of motherhood, were local groups, which have left few official records. Involving many women from a range of social classes, they began in New England and spread to New York and Ohio in the early nineteenth century. Women met weekly to pray and share their experiences as mothers. The members of the Maternal Association of Dorchester, Massachusetts, "determined to form ourselves into an association for prayer" in order to ask for guidance in discerning "the proper time and manner of administering reproof, correction and instruction in righteousness."[12] But the groups also provided women with current information on mothering, invited guest speakers, established libraries, and sponsored periodicals that were "readers' digests" of advice literature. These groups were in some measure a response to the glorification of motherhood along with the idea that a child's early character could be molded for vice or virtue. Women who participated and who left records of their experiences clearly believed that they had a duty to teach their children religion and morality and the power to shape the future of the nation.

Motivated by this same desire to build Christian civilization, a group of women organized by Joanna Bethune in 1803 began Sunday schools for poor children. They rebuffed criticism that women should not teach the Bible and interfere with the professional teaching ministry. The program flourished and the Female Sunday School Union of New York was formed in 1816, only to adopt later the status of an auxiliary organization to the men's Sunday School Union. At the local level, the Sunday schools offered to many women work that was useful and demanding along with a much-valued companionship with like-minded women, both teachers and students.

Benevolent Associations

Charity always existed in colonial communities but it was local and spontaneous. In the nineteenth century, a change occurred; the care of the sick and the poor, especially in the cities, became the responsibility of organized women's benevolent groups. Often led by women of wealth and status in the community, these groups accumulated and controlled vast sums of money from legacies, bazaars, and solicited contributions. The benevolent groups cared for orphaned children, indigent young women, and widows. They provided food and clothing and, in some places, shelter. Some groups opened schools that taught reading, writing, arithmetic, needlework, and religion. A Female Humane Association was founded in Baltimore to help poor women and run a charity school, while similar organizations emerged in New York and Philadelphia. These women anticipated modern social work not only in their belief that education was a way out of poverty, but also in their use of "lady visitors" who called on women in the slums to teach them, sometimes with condescension, childcare and housekeeping skills and offer material aid. After the Civil War, the benevolent work of African American women provided a safety net of health care, housing, and food for newly freed slaves. In the vanguard of building an infrastructure for black community life, the Daughters of Zion of Avery Chapel in Memphis, for example, hired a black doctor to provide medical care for the congregation.

Reform Associations

Another type of female society, the reform society, emerged in the 1820s and 1830s. The reform groups directed their attention to the creation of a Christian America by changing a particular social structure or pattern of behavior rather than through individual conversions alone. Many of these groups were touched by the nineteenth-century hope that a perfect society, the kingdom of God on earth, was within reach.

Women took part in a wide variety of reform groups. One of their most significant efforts, however, was their work in moral reform. Inspired by the waves of revivals that swept the northeastern states in the 1830s, women in New York and Boston resolved to close the cities' brothels and convert the prostitutes. When conversions proved difficult, the reformers focused on material aid and employment for the women. Their attack on prostitution was overshadowed, however, by the double sexual standard of society. Society condemned and ostracized the prostitute, but her male customers were excused. In contrast, the reformers believed that male sensuality and manipulation had caused the fall of their sisters in the first place. If guilt was to be assigned, it should fall more upon the men than the women.

The moral reform groups spread from the cities throughout New England and New York. They adopted bold tactics in running their organizations and in accomplishing their goals. Members as well as the societies' male missionaries descended upon brothels to pray with and talk to the prostitutes. They aided parents in seeking runaway daughters and were willing to speak out about what society considered "delicate subjects." One woman masqueraded as a laundress in order to gain admittance to a brothel suspected of hiding a runaway. In its crusade to eliminate the double standard, the movement used its newspaper to urge women to shun men in their communities who were suspected of sexual promiscuity. The identities of men known to visit brothels were published along with the names of suspicious employment agencies. Finally, the movement used women as traveling missionaries to organize auxiliaries and soon adopted a policy of hiring only female employees. Women edited the journal as early as 1836 and also did the bookkeeping. While some of the leaders of moral reform were attracted by radical feminism, most women in the movement embraced True Womanhood, arguing that women were morally superior by nature. In a somewhat contradictory manner, however, these reformers refused to excuse men because they were naturally predatory.[13]

Another social ill targeted by the reformers was the sale and consumption of alcohol. For some, the ultimate goal was simply temperance; for others it was total abstinence. Before the Civil War, male and female efforts in this area used the tactics of moral persuasion and individual conversion to stop drinking. Women found a comfortable place in these efforts in auxiliary societies, given beliefs about their nature and sphere. But they were marginalized by men as tactics became more political, and so they created their own movement and organization after the Civil War.

The Woman's Christian Temperance Union, an enormous, independent organization, was preceded in 1873 and 1874 by the Women's Crusade, a campaign of prayer and exhortation in saloons that called upon the owners to convert. Both the Crusade and the W.C.T.U. were supported by women who believed that their moral duty was to save sons and husbands and Christian civilization. They were guarding home and family, which were threatened by alcohol-induced poverty, sexual indulgence, and violence. In doing so, they adopted the "unwomanly" tactics of confrontation, entered the male sphere of the saloon, and soon became aware of the economic and legal disabilities faced by women married to over-indulgent men.

A direct link between revival-grounded reform and feminism can be found by examining the antislavery societies of the 1830s. The campaign to abolish slavery in part grew out of the revival preaching of Charles Finney and his followers. The male antislavery societies were complemented in the 1830s by the growth of over one hundred female societies. To nineteenth-century America, it was not unexpected that the cause of slaves would commend itself to the sensitive and compassionate nature of women. Some women responded with enthusiasm and, as in other reform movements, they expressed particular outrage at the treatment of black women who were sexually exploited and separated from their families. Unlike some of the other reform groups, however, the antislavery movement raised directly the issue of the status of all women.

By joining in arguments against the defenders of slavery, women were led to reflect upon their own situation in American society. The abolitionists argued that all human beings had a right to life, liberty, and happiness, and some women observed that they were a glaring omission. The abolitionists quoted Gal. 3:28 on behalf of the slaves, and some women began to realize that they, too, were included in the biblical promise of equality. The more some women thought about their own status, the more similarities they could see with that of the black slave. White women and free black women also had little power or liberty and they were treated simply as a means to promote the welfare of men. A cry for freedom for the slave therefore was coupled with a call for the liberty of women.

The practices of certain women in the antislavery movement, however, rather than theories, acted as the strongest catalyst for the emergence of the women's rights movement. Sarah and Angelina Grimké, both eloquent speakers with a firsthand knowledge of the conditions of slavery, began to speak to "promiscuous" audiences made up of men and women. This was highly unusual behavior given that even liberal educational programs did not permit women to attend public speaking classes. Lucretia Mott and Elizabeth Cady Stanton asked to be received and seated with the official male delegates to the World Antislavery Convention in London. And a host of women circulated petitions door-to-door in their neighborhoods on behalf of the slaves. These women all believed that the cause of abolition was important enough to require such unconventional activities. They were denounced by men and women within the antislavery movement and without as "unfeminine" and "immoral." Such activities were believed to be beyond woman's divinely ordained sphere. The speaking activities of the Grimké sisters, for example, were strongly condemned in a widely circulated letter written by a group of Congregational clergymen, while Mott and Stanton were compelled to view the London convention from separate seating in an area screened off from the main floor. Although many radical abolitionist women were deeply influenced by evangelicalism's sense of call and mission, they tended to find spiritual homes in groups such as the Quakers and Unitarians/Universalists. Some even abandoned all forms of institutional religion in favor of the "religion of reform."[14]

As a result of these ideas and activities, a serious, public discussion of what came to be called the "woman question" was launched. At issue was whether or not women actually had a special sphere in life with rights and duties that differed from those of men. Sarah Grimké's *Letters on the Equality of the Sexes* laid out issues at stake: it was both absurd and unbiblical to claim that men and women had different natures and different moral duties. An organized movement for women's rights was also launched in Seneca Falls, New York, in 1848 under the leadership of Mott and Stanton. The women involved in this effort at first directed their attention to a broad range of concerns such as jobs, the legal rights of married women, and educational opportunities. As the century progressed, the focus shifted to the issue of women's suffrage.

THE SOCIAL GOSPEL

Women active in benevolence and reform at the end of the nineteenth century sometimes found themselves drawn into the Social Gospel movement, a movement rooted in the realization that individual conversion and charity were not enough to deal with America's problems. The movement embraced the idea that economic, political, and social structures, as well as individual souls, could be sinful and in need of redemption. The kingdom of God, a major theme of the Social Gospel, meant not only a future hope beyond this world but also life in this world. Men led the efforts by writing theology, hymns, and novels, and forming organizations to support changes such as the minimum wage and the right to strike.

For the most part, the Social Gospel leaders did not support suffrage and women's rights, but they encouraged women to take an active role in church and home. The key to a better society was the family, and it was vital that women, with their natural piety and sensitivity, be enlisted to make the ideal middle-class home a reality. Issues that occupied the Social Gospel leaders were shaped by this ideal, as is evidenced by their concern that husbands be paid enough so that wives would not have to earn a wage. Historians have gone beyond this evaluation and interpreted the Social Gospel as part of a broader attempt that swept all denominations to present a more manly and heroic version of Christianity and a more virile image of the ministry. Their goal was to attract men back to the churches.[15]

Women anticipated and sustained the Social Gospel in important and unacknowledged ways. In the 1880s and 1890s, Methodist minister Anna Howard Shaw, for example, used pulpit and platform to give the kingdom of God a grounding in economic and political reality. Despite the belief that economics and politics were man's sphere, some women in the W.C.T.U. began to work for legislation to reform prisons, improve working conditions, and provide childcare for working mothers. Deaconesses included sociology in their training school curricula and drew up plans for urban reforms. As Susan Lindley observes, however, the men of the Social Gospel movement never quite took women seriously as partners in kingdom-building, seeing them mainly as fundraisers and social workers.[16]

FUNDAMENTALISM

Historians usually see fundamentalism as a movement that was born in the 1880s in opposition to modern science, critical views of the Bible, socio-economic turmoil, and the Social Gospel. There is irony in the fact that current examinations of fundamentalism find an affinity with the Social Gospel: both movements were responses to the role confusion Victorian Protestant men were experiencing as well as attempts to win them back to the churches.[17] The rhetoric of those who became fundamentalist leaders reveals anger toward a feminized church, which was increasingly supportive of suffrage, women's education, and the movement of women into the work-place. Christianity needed to be recast as a virile, muscular religion to save it from the destructiveness of liberalism, which included changes in the status of women.

Fundamentalists embraced particular doctrines and reclaimed traditional Victorian views on men and women as strategies in this effort. Biblical iner-rancy became a way to counter the softening of biblical commands on silence and subordination by making them applicable to all places and times. The fundamentalist scheme of history known as dispensationalism declared even Christian women subordinate until Jesus returned to rule after the tribulation and battle of Armageddon. Fundamentalist leaders reasserted the Victorian ideal of true womanhood with its separate spheres. Motherhood and domestic work and obedience were God-given roles for women. But in one way, fundamentalists revised the Victorian stereotype; men, rather than women, possessed spiritual aptitude and a natural inclination toward faith. Fundamentalists, however, were forced to live with an important paradox: women were sinful and in need of male leadership, yet the movement was dependent on women both as members and workers. They crowded the Bible schools and institutes and went on to serve as missionaries and evangelists. They were welcomed because the harvest was great and the workers were few. They were gradually edged out of public roles in the 1920s and 1950s, but even today, scholars find women to be holding unofficial power in many fundamentalist congregations.[18]

WOMEN IN MISSION

Origins of Women's Missionary Organizations

The Boston Female Society for Missionary Purposes, started in 1800 by Mary Webb and fourteen Baptist and Congregationalist friends, marked the beginning of a network of local women's missionary groups. Their primary activities were prayer and fundraising for the cause of missions. Many of them were "cent societies," which met weekly to collect a penny from each member, while others collected fixed annual dues or depended for resources on the sale of handcrafted items. Also, many were auxiliaries of the established male societies, which received and disbursed the contributions; the women, however, were carefully excluded from participating in the decision making of the main societies and sometimes were not even permitted to speak in their own meetings. Initial interest was in home mission work. Funds were raised to send missionaries to visit Native Americans, establish Sunday schools, distribute tracts and Bibles, and aid young men with seminary education. Gradually the focus of the women shifted to overseas missions, particularly in India and China, and a movement was born that would eventually involve more women than all reform groups combined. The fact that women were meeting together outside of the home, even for missionary purposes, at first attracted some criticism. Ministers who encouraged this activity took great pains to assure the public that these women were not speaking to mixed groups nor were they taking any part in the government of the churches. By the 1820s, consequently, the female missionary society had an accepted place in American church life and men were glad for their support.

Work in the Mission Field

If a woman in the early nineteenth century felt called to devote her life to "spreading the light where there was darkness," her only option was to marry a missionary and go overseas as his wife. Her primary task in this mission was to emulate the Victorian ideal woman by offering her husband a serene, well-run, and comfortable home. In addition, she functioned as a teacher of morality and religion for her children and an example of Christian womanhood for the native population around her. She was expected to learn the language and take part in the work only after her household duties had been completed. The missionary wife was given no official status by the mission boards and societies, and she had no vote in running the everyday affairs of the mission station. The *Encyclopedia of Missions*, published at the end of the nineteenth century, mentions only the three wives of Adoniram Judson and contains scattered references to men who had to return home or do such and such a thing because of the health of their wives. Yet for the women in the American churches, the missionary wives made up an elite group of heroines. Women from all over the country wrote to the wives, prayed for them, and raised funds for their special projects. Admiration for the missionary wives, in fact, may have sustained the interest of women at home in world missions and laid the groundwork for the post–Civil War movement despite the fact that they were excluded from power and participation on the denominational boards.[19]

The male mission boards eventually realized that evangelistic work in many cultures would be successful only when the women in those cultures were reached with the Christian message. Often it was the women who were most strongly devoted to non-Christian religions and often they controlled the rituals conducted within the household. Also, in keeping with popular Western views on women, the mission organizers believed that once women in a given culture had accepted the gospel, they would be powerful influences in reaching their husbands and sons. Yet in many countries, women could only be spoken to or approached by other women. In some, women were even physically separated from men, as in the *zenanas* (the section of the house where women were secluded) of India. Missionary wives could do little to alleviate this problem. They were burdened with the tasks of managing home and family in an often hostile environment. They also had little time to learn a new language. The mission societies and boards had to look elsewhere for a solution, and they found it in the single women who were willing to go to the mission field.

The mission boards reluctantly began to send single women overseas in the 1820s. The American Board of Commissioners for Foreign Missions reported that the former black slave, Betsy Stockton, was sent to Hawaii in 1823, where she ran a school. She was attached there to the family of the Rev. Charles Stewart and returned to America with them two years later. In 1827, Cynthia Farrar was sent by the American Board to India as an "assistant missionary" in order to organize schools. By 1860, the American Board had appointed 138 single women to mission work but only thirty of these went overseas. The rest remained in domestic mission work in the United States, since the board mistakenly believed that home missions offered safer and better working conditions. The appointments, however, were sporadic and made with hesitation. The mission boards generally feared criticism and even they were uncertain as to whether or not women could carry out their tasks without the strong guidance and protection of a husband. There was also tension in the field when single women joined the work. Missionary wives suspected them of being "husband hunters" and the missionaries themselves were reluctant to give the women authority or responsibility.

Women Form Their Own Mission Boards

Women in the female missionary societies had been bombarded with the message that they should give time and money to alleviate the spiritual condition and social degradation of their sisters in more "backward" cultures. Ministers and lay men alike stressed the "elevation of your own sex through the medium of your own sex" to many receptive American women.[20] Women, however, began to realize that missions to women and children were receiving only halfhearted attention from the mission boards. Furthermore, women were not given any representation on these boards so that they could influence policy-making decisions. In the early 1860s, therefore, women began to take the initiative and form their own boards. The first was the interdenominational Women's Union Missionary Society in 1861, followed by a board formed by Congregational women. By 1900, there were over forty such bodies in the United States. Some of the boards were totally independent, with complete control over money and policy. Others were independent but worked in close cooperation with men. Still others were subsidiaries of the original male boards. Throughout the history of the women's boards, some men continued to hamper and oppose the new bodies. They had a deep-rooted fear that the boards represented the movement for women's rights and suffrage in disguise.

The women's boards made women a major force in world mission. Their supporters collected large sums of money for missions, a remarkable accomplishment since women found money for their own organizations over and above the family's normal church contributions. They built and ran complex national organizations and adopted current entrepreneurial practices in money management. They introduced creative methods for educating church members about missions and conducted effective publicity campaigns. Tension was, in fact, created between the boards and local societies. As the boards became more professional, they urged women to move to planned giving rather than depend for funds on events like bazaars and luncheons; they also wanted to eliminate local support for specific missionaries and projects, enabling the boards to incorporate donations into long-term strategic plans.

Perhaps most significantly, the women's boards elevated the status of women in the mission field. They won full "missionary" status for the missionary wives as well as an equal vote in the everyday affairs of the mission. They also made mission work overseas an option for large numbers of single women, a choice for Protestant women similar to that offered by the Catholic religious orders. By the early part of the twentieth century, women represented two-thirds of the church's mission force. These women met the challenge of learning new languages and adjusting to new climates and cultures. They also taught, managed schools and clinics, published literature, orchestrated evangelization campaigns, and engaged in preaching as well. Out of the reach of critics and in places where ordination mattered little, women became involved in activities not open to them in the American churches. Murilla Ingalls, for example, carried on her husband's work in China after his death. While she avoided addressing large mixed audiences and liturgical functions, she trained men in theology, biblical studies, and preaching. The home of Presbyterian Isabella Nassau was referred to as the "theological seminary" of one West African mission. She taught young men theology, church history, and "much else" to prepare them for the ministry.

Missions also provided an opportunity for women with professional medical training to use their skills. The women's boards consciously recruited female doctors to care for the health needs of non-Christian women who, in many places, could only be treated by another woman. Their services often extended beyond treatment to the teaching of medicine as well. In their religious and medical activities women not only acquired new roles but also feelings of worth and self-confidence: "The doctor who treated two hundred patients a day . . . and the itinerant preacher who spoke until midnight and was off in her jinrikisha at dawn, felt herself necessary and important."[21]

Two important questions that interest historians involve the impact of women missionaries on the women they ministered to and the relationship between mission societies and feminism. Women missionaries tended to believe that they were bringing a new way of life rather than institutions or doctrines to another people. Their work often involved material well-being, education, and health care, and it helped in some places to end blatant abuses such as female infanticide and footbinding. Accounts of these efforts, however, often overlooked the role of indigenous reformers and the many occasions on which women missionaries imposed western forms of dress, family life, and music on their converts.[22]

The relationship between mission movements and feminism is complex, ambiguous, and the subject of much disagreement. Opportunities to work in the mission field may have diverted the attention of some women from the cause of women's rights in America by giving them opportunities for freedom and professional growth overseas.[23] Their exposure to the extreme abuses of women in other cultures made their own situation in America look desirable. Certainly very few of the women involved in the missionary movement were sympathetic with radical feminism, although some did support women's suffrage. The whole mission movement also was grounded firmly in the ideology of true womanhood, depending as it did on woman's innate capacity for evangelizing and self-sacrifice.[24] Sometimes, however, the goals of feminism and mission work coincided. Beverly Harrison reminds us that we should not underestimate the influence that the female benevolence and mission groups had in changing the ethos of the churches.[25] Some male leaders, such as Presbyterian Robert E. Speer, changed their minds on the status of women and openly called for equality after working with the women who skillfully coordinated the mission work. The mission boards enabled women to engage in work that was useful and important. They expanded the professional opportunities for women and even prompted some women to seek formal church recognition for the ministerial tasks they were already performing. And, finally, some women who were exposed to other cultures began to become more critical of their own, including the way in which women were treated.

Legacy of the Voluntary Societies

How can we summarize the legacy of women's participation in mission and reform?[26] The support of women was vital to the spread of Christianity in the nineteenth century at home and abroad. Women contributed great sums of money and countless hours to the religious and social welfare of many citizens. Their services in bettering the living conditions of people in urban areas met a need that neither government nor business was prepared to consider. In addition, the female associations encouraged and deepened loyalty to and knowledge of the democratic process of government. The voluntary societies, however, were also channels through which women themselves made some gains. The societies clearly improved the lives of women: they engaged in creative and challenging activities, interacted with other women, and brought themselves benefits such as sober husbands and better schools. But assessing the impact of the societies on the cult of true womanhood and the status of women in America is more complex. Sometimes the societies supported and reinforced true womanhood, but as Wendy Deichmann observes, the organizations sometimes interfered with and even replaced the prevailing beliefs in male versus female spheres and natures.[27]

The voluntary groups, for example, gave women a chance to use their physical and mental resources outside the home. Functioning as a bridge between private and public spheres, they emerged at a time when educational opportunities were restricted and when women were being eased out of the few occupations (such as midwifery) they had followed in colonial society.[28] What is important for us to note is that women were encouraged to join these groups by ministers who preached on the "right" of women to work for others. Most clergymen not only believed that women were suited by nature for charity work, but they also stressed that such groups were simply extensions of a woman's role as mother and guardian of morality and religion. Women were welcomed as helpers in the task of Christianizing America, especially since men's interest in religion was diminishing. Women, however, had to stay as helpers. They were to assist the men, doing their work modestly and in subtle and quiet ways. Most of the women in the voluntary groups accepted these ideas of a "woman's place," yet they decided to take full responsibility for their sphere with a vengeance. As reformer Lydia Maria Child observed, "the clergy had changed the household utensil into a living, energetic being and they had no spell to turn it into a broom again."[29]

The voluntary groups also gave women a chance to take on traditional male roles, which enhanced their own sense of self-confidence and self-worth. They served as group officers, published appeals and advertised their cause to the public, learned to conduct business meetings, drew up strategic plans, gave speeches, and collected and disbursed large sums of money. They exercised power and influence within the group's culture, even shaping policy in the male-dominated organizations.

A sense of solidarity with other women and an awareness of the privileged status of men were also nourished by the societies. Women not only identified with the members of their groups but sought reforms on behalf of other women and against the activities of men. Temperance groups spoke out against the drunk husband who victimized his wife, moral reform groups against the male lecher who victimized the young woman, and benevolent societies against the factory owner who took advantage of his female employees. Some historians have argued that temperance was a way women could express their anger and feelings of victimization against men because it pitted the moral purity of women against male bestiality.[30]

Most women involved in religious, reform, and benevolent societies did not move from these activities into what we today identify as feminism. Most women continued to accept the Victorian ideal of true womanhood and to shape their work outside of the home according to it. Others continued to embrace the ideology of true womanhood but also supported women's right to vote, preach, and have limited contact with the public sphere. They did not reject the Christian tradition, arguing that the Bible, when properly interpreted, supported the leadership of women in some circumstances. Making feminism respectable through their decorous dress and pious behavior, they were able to solicit the support of a number of clergymen who opened their churches to the suffragists and celebrated their cause in sermons.[31] Those women, however, who questioned true womanhood and argued for a wide range of rights, such as divorce and access to the professions, were often denounced by some in the Christian community. Many of these women moved away from the major denominations and into more liberal groups such as the Unitarians and Theosophists, although most of them began with the conviction that the essence of the gospel affirmed female equality and the desire to win the support of the clergy.[32] Some, such as Sarah Grimké, abandoned institutional religion entirely in favor of an "eclectic working religion of reform."[33] While they often discarded their traditional religious beliefs, however, many of them retained a strong certainty that what they were doing was both morally right and in keeping with the will of God.

Readings for Chapter 5

5.1 THE CULT OF TRUE WOMANHOOD

Aptly illustrating the mid-Victorian "cult of true womanhood," these excerpts are from a series of public lectures given to audiences of men and women and first published in 1840 by George Washington Burnap (1802–1850). Burnap was pastor of the First Unitarian Church in Baltimore and a distinguished man of letters who frequently contributed to literary journals and lectured in cities along the East Coast. He makes it plain that the domestic sphere is the domain for which women were "originally intended," but he wants to compensate for this by assuring them that they are really the architects of human society and government. Husbands are only able to make the most of their skills in the workplace if they are comforted and cared for at home. Sons can only take their part on the stage of national life if their characters have been carefully molded by a diligent mother.

Source: George W Burnap. *The Sphere and Duties of Woman.* 5th ed. Baltimore: John Murphy, 1854.

We now see woman in that sphere for which she was originally intended, and which she is so exactly fitted to adorn and bless, as the wife, the mistress of a home, the solace, the aid, and the counsellor of that ONE, for whose sake alone the world is of any consequence to her.

If life be increased in cares, so is it also enriched by new satisfactions. She herself, if she be inspired by just sentiments and true affection, perceives that she has attained her true position. Delivered from that tastelessness, which sooner or later creeps over a single life, every power and faculty is called into energetic exercise, and she feels the current of existence to flow in a richer, deeper stream. . . .

The good wife! How much of this world's happiness and prosperity is contained in the compass of these two short words! Her influence is immense. The power of a wife, for good or for evil, is altogether irresistible. Home must be the seat of happiness, or it must be for ever unknown. A good wife is to a man wisdom, and courage, and strength, and hope, and endurance. A bad one is confusion, weakness, discomfiture, despair. No condition is hopeless when the wife possesses firmness, decision, energy, economy. There is no outward prosperity which can counteract indolence, folly, and extravagance at home. No spirit can long resist bad domestic influences. Man is strong, but his heart is not adamant. He delights in enterprise and action, but to sustain him he needs a tranquil mind, and a whole heart. He expends his whole moral force in the conflicts of the world. His feelings are daily lacerated to the utmost point of endurance by perpetual collision, irritation, and disappointment. To recover his equanimity and composure, home must be to him a place of repose, of peace, of cheerfulness, of comfort; and his soul renews its strength and again goes forth with fresh vigor to encounter the labors and troubles of the world. But if at home he find no rest, and there is met by a bad temper, sullenness, or gloom; or assailed by discontent, complaint, and reproaches, the heart breaks, the spirits are crushed, hope vanishes, and the man sinks into total despair.

Let woman know then, that she ministers at the very fountain of life and happiness. It is her hand that lades out with overflowing cup its soul refreshing waters, or casts in the branch of bitterness which makes them poison and death. Her ardent spirit breathes the breath of life into all enterprise. Her patience and constancy are mainly instrumental in carrying forward to completion the best human designs. Her more delicate moral sensibility is the unseen power which is ever at work to purify and refine society. And the nearest glimpse of heaven that mortals ever get on earth is that domestic circle, which her hands have trained to intelligence, virtue, and love; which her gentle influence pervades, and of which her radiant presence is the centre and the sun. . . .

We come in the next place to speak of woman in the most important and responsible relation which she sustains, as the mother. In this relation Providence fully makes up to her the inferiority of her physical powers, the narrowness of her sphere of action, and the alleged inferiority of her intellectual endowments. In the influence she has in forming the character of the young, and training up each rising generation as it comes forward, and assumes the control of the destinies of the world, she has her full share in that power which sways and governs mankind, which makes nations, families, individuals great, prosperous, virtuous, happy,—or mean, degraded, vicious, and wretched. Woman is mistress of the fortunes of the world, by holding in her plastic hand the minds and hearts of those who are to mould the coming age, at that decisive period when the character is determined and fixed in good, or irrecoverably bent on vice and mischief. She governs the world in the capacity of mother, because in the forming period of life, the cords of love and gentleness are stronger and more prevailing than all the chains which mere force has ever forged. She sways the world, because her influence is on the whole paramount in the primary element of all society, the domestic circle. Men go forth to act their parts on the great stage of life, the most gifted to exert vast influence over its affairs, but it is only to act out the character that has been formed at home. Woman then, whose control over the character is almost absolute, presides at the very fountainhead of power.

5.2 THE CAUSE OF MORAL REFORM

The circular reprinted here was drawn up at the organizational meeting of the New York Female Moral Reform Society on May 12, 1834. The society hoped not only to convert New York's prostitutes to Protestant Christianity but also to launch a women's crusade against sexual license in general and the double standard in particular. The circular reveals much about motives and strategies linked to this second grand goal of sexual purity. The crusade is seen clearly as part of God's work of reform in preparation for the coming millennium. Possibly remembering the criticism heaped upon New York's earlier Magdalen Society for dealing with "obscene" issues, the writers urge women not to shy away from speaking out on delicate subjects of great social consequence. They are, however, challenged to go beyond general disapproval. They are to unmask the libertines in their social circles and shun their company. The circular conveys a sense of anger and determination (licentious men are called "vipers" against which the "sisterhood" should fight) that is echoed in Carroll Smith-Rosenberg's argument that these women, frustrated by male domination, wished to define and limit male sexual behavior.[1]

Source: The Constitution and Circular of the New York Female Moral Reform Society; with the Addresses Delivered at Its Organization, 16–18. New York: J. N. Bolles, 1834.

To the Ladies of the United States of every Religious Denomination.

BELOVED SISTERS:—Suffer a word of exhortation on a subject of vital interest to the entire sisterhood: we refer to the sin of LICENTIOUSNESS.

We need not inform you that this sin prevails to an alarming extent in our land. The fact is obvious to all. A moment's reflection will show you that it has woven itself into all the fibres of society, shaping its opinions, modifying its customs, and in one form or other spreading an atmosphere of corruption and death throughout the entire community. Not that all are impure—far from it; but, unconsciously to ourselves even, we breathe the atmosphere of pollution. Sentiments are afloat, customs are in vogue—the creatures of this sin—which strike at the vitals of all that is lovely in female purity and innocence, and so doing, strike at all that is precious in the most endeared and sacred relations of life. If this be not so, whence, we ask, is that sense of danger, that at times and in certain circumstances, so oppresses the mind of the virtuous female? Whence the fact, that the libertine, known to be such, is welcomed to the society of the chaste? Whence that corrupt public sentiment, that pervades all classes of society—the high and the low, the good and the bad, the pure and the impure—and that storms and rages at the least intimation of exposure, and sends forth, as on the wings of the wind, the cry, "hush," "hush," "indelicate," "indelicate," "you will only corrupt the virtuous";—that in effect, blots out the 7th commandment from the decalogue, and proscribes other portions of the word of

God, as too gross and indecent for this age of refinement, and thus practically puts the ban of silence on the pulpit and the press?—Whence all this; whence, especially, this unwonted unity of sentiment, among persons of every description and character? Strange alliance! And what does it evince but the fearful fact, that while men slept the enemy has sowed tares—that these have sprung up unnoticed, to rank maturity, and have thrown a poisonous atmosphere over the entire field. So we believe; and so believing, we feel that it is time for *us*, in common with others, to take our stand on the side of virtue and God, and do what we can to turn back the tide of pollution that is sweeping over the land, and bearing its victims onward, by thousands, to the chambers of death.

And now, beloved sisters, we ask you to take your stand with us. The evil we know is great, and the public sentiment it has created for itself, and behind which it entrenches itself, is mighty. Nevertheless, we have confidence in the gospel; that it is mighty through God, to the pulling down of strong holds. And we believe that its efficacy will not fail in this case. The evil, great as it is, *can be reached,* and the public sentiment behind which it is entrenched, mighty as it is, CAN BE MET AND CHANGED. Already, if we mistake not, is the change begun. The press is beginning to speak. The pulpit, to a greater extent than ever before, is beginning to break its guilty silence. The ministers of God are ceasing to be any longer "partial in the law." It is a matter of rejoicing, of encouragement, and of unfeigned gratitude to God that it is so.

But this sin, we are persuaded, is one in respect to which it is emphatically true, that a radical reform can never be effected without the co-operation of woman. Here, if we mistake not, her influence may be most powerful and efficacious. She may wield a power that can be wielded by no one else. Ask you how?

The answer is—Ist. Let her do what she can to disseminate light on the subject—by conversation—by the circulation of such papers and tracts as are fitted to be a discerner of the thoughts and intents of the heart, and, at the same time, to show the enormity and guilt, and fatal tendencies and results of this sin—though it be only the sin of the heart.

2d. Let her take the ground, so obviously in accordance with truth, that the libertine is no less guilty than his victim, and as such, shall be at once excluded from her society. This you will perceive by the annexed Constitution, is the ground that your sisters in New-York have taken. We ask you—we entreat you—to take the same. We point you to the whole sex, the entire sisterhood, and we say that demon in human shape, that fixed his lascivious eye upon your sister, and wrought her ruin, is the enemy of your sex. Exclude him then at once from all society with you—in self-defence—in defence of the sex, exclude him. He wants but the opportunity, and he will as soon make you his victim as that err-ing, fallen sister. Some of you, perhaps, are mothers. God has blessed you with a family of lovely children—daughters, pure, innocent, the joy of your heart, the objects of your purest, sweetest, strongest affections. But see, the demon has marked your first born as his vic-tim. His wanton eye is already on her. Mothers, away with him—in defence of your beloved children, away with him, we entreat you, from your families, and from the society of your children. Teach them to shun him as they would a viper. He wants but the opportunity, and he will not hesitate to seize upon his vic-tim, and thereby plunge a dagger to your heart. In self-defence—in defence of your families, and we may add, in defence of the whole community, away with such a one from all society and intercourse with you. This done, and the work of Moral Reform is done, and the virtue and peace of the community secured.

Beloved Sisters, we are persuaded that in this simple way, we may wield an influence on this subject that cannot be resisted. If we will but organize our-selves into associations on this principle, and have the moral courage thus to stand up for injured and outraged innocence, not heeding the reproach that may, for a little season, be heaped upon us, we verily believe, that in God, we shall tri-umph. God seems in a special manner, to have committed this work to our hands; and without arrogance, it is not too much to say, that, if we will, we may,

by this simple process, put such a brand of infamy upon the licentious man—we may gather upon him such a withering frown of virtuous indignation, as to save not only the victim, but the destroyer also, and thus put an effectual check to the tide of pollution that is now sweep-ing us away.

And now, sisters, what say you? Under God, the privilege and the responsibility of this holy and blessed work, is yours. It is for you, in a special manner, to say, what shall be done. Oh! then show, we do intreat you, that you have the virtue, the principle, the moral courage, to breast a corrupt and mighty public sentiment, in defence of virtue and religion.

Note to Reading 5.2

1. Carroll Smith-Rosenberg, "Beauty, the Beast and the Militant Woman: A Case Study in Sex Roles and Social Stress in Jacksonian America," *American Quarterly* 23 (October 1971): 564–65.

5.3 EQUAL RIGHTS AND MORAL DUTIES

In 1837, Sarah Grimké (1792–1873) accom-panied her sister Angelina on a tour of New England on behalf of the antislavery movement. Both women attracted large audiences of men and women wherever they spoke, partly because they were former slaveholders and women who, in public lecturing, were stepping beyond conven-tional boundaries. They were viciously attacked for their unwomanly behavior in a pastoral letter issued by the Congregational Ministerial Associa-tion of Massachusetts. Sarah Grimké responded head-on in a series of letters to Mary Parker, president of the Boston Female Anti-Slavery Society. Eventually published as a single tract, the letters chronicle the condition of women throughout the world, analyze their legal position, and examine the inequities they suffer in education and employment. The letter reproduced here responds specifically to the pastoral letter. Using the New Testament as her basis, Grimké argues that women can be neither excused nor prevented from carrying out their moral responsibilities because of human notions of propriety.

Source: Sarah Grimké. *Letters on the Equality of the Sexes and the Condition of Woman,* edited with an introduction by Elizabeth Ann Bartlett, 37–41. New Haven: Yale University Press, 1988.

Haverhill, 7th Mo. 1837

Dear Friend,

When I last addressed thee, I had not seen the Pastoral Letter of the General Association. It has since fallen into my hands, and I must digress from my intention of exhibiting the condition of women in different parts of the world, in order to make some remarks on this extraordinary document. I am persuaded that when the minds of men and women become emancipated from the thraldom of superstition and "traditions of men," the sentiments contained in the Pastoral Letter will be recurred to with as much astonishment as the opinions of Cotton Mather and other distinguished men of his day, on the subject of witchcraft; nor will it be deemed less wonderful, that a body of divines should gravely assemble and endeavor to prove that woman has no right to "open her mouth for the

dumb," than it now is that judges should have sat on the trials of witches, and solemnly condemned nineteen persons and one dog to death for witchcraft.

But to the letter. It says, "We invite your attention to the dangers which at present seem to threaten the FEMALE CHARACTER with wide-spread and permanent injury." I rejoice that they have called the attention of my sex to this subject, because I believe if woman investigates it, she will soon discover that danger is impending, though from a totally different source from that which the Association apprehends,—danger from those who, having long held the reins *of usurped* authority, are unwilling to permit us to fill that sphere which God created us to move in, and who have entered into league to crush the immortal mind of woman. I rejoice, because I am persuaded that the rights of woman, like the rights of slaves, need only be examined to be understood and asserted, even by some of those, who are now endeavoring to smother the irrepressible desire for mental and spiritual freedom which glows in the breast of many, who hardly dare to speak their sentiments.

"The appropriate duties and influence of women are clearly stated in the New Testament. Those duties are unobtrusive and private, but the sources *of mighty power.* When the mild, *dependent,* softening influence of woman upon the sternness of man's opinions is fully exercised, society feels the effects of it in a thousand ways." No one can desire more earnestly than I do, that woman may move exactly in the sphere which her Creator has assigned her; and I believe her having been displaced from that sphere has introduced confusion into the world. It is, therefore, of vast importance to herself and to all the rational creation, that she should ascertain what are her duties and her privileges as a responsible and immortal being. The New Testament has been referred to, and I am willing to abide by its decisions, but must enter my protest against the false translation of some passages by the men who did that work, and against the perverted interpretation by the men who undertook to write commentaries thereon. (I am inclined to think, when we are admitted to the honor of studying Greek and Hebrew, we shall produce some various readings of the Bible a little different from those we now have.)

The Lord Jesus defines the duties of his followers in his Sermon on the Mount. He lays down grand principles by which they should be governed, without any reference to sex or condition.—"Ye are the light of the world. A city that is set on a hill cannot be hid. Neither do men light a candle and put it under a bushel, but on a candlestick, and it giveth light unto all that are in the house. Let your light so shine before men, that they may see your good works, and glorify your Father which is in Heaven" (Matt. 5:14–16). I follow him through all his precepts, and find him giving the same directions to women as to men, never even referring to the distinction now so strenuously

insisted upon between masculine and feminine virtues: this is one of the antichristian "traditions of men" which are taught instead of the "commandments of God." Men and women were CREATED EQUAL; they are both moral and accountable beings, and whatever is *right* for man to do, is *right* for woman.

But the influence of woman, says the Association, is to be private and unobtrusive; her light is not to shine before man like that other brethren; but she is passively to let the lords of the creation, as they call themselves, put the bushel over it, lest peradventure it might appear that the world has been benefitted by the rays of *her* candle. So that her quenched light, according to their judgment, will be of more use than if it were set on the candlestick. "Her influence is the source of mighty power." This has ever been the flattering language of man since he laid aside the whip as a means to keep woman in subjection. He spares her body; but the war he has waged against her mind, her heart, and her soul, has been no less destructive to her as a moral being. How monstrous, how antichristian, is the doctrine that woman is to be dependent on man! Where, in all the sacred Scriptures, is this taught? Alas! she has too well learned the lesson, which MAN has labored to teach her. She has surrendered her dearest RIGHTS, and been satisfied with the privileges which man has assumed to grant her; she has been amused with the show of power, whilst man has absorbed all the reality into himself. He has adorned the creature whom God gave him as a companion, with baubles and gewgaws, turned her attention to personal attractions, offered incense to her vanity, and made her the instrument of his selfish gratification, a plaything to please his eye and amuse his hours of leisure. "Rule by obedience and by submission sway," or in other words, study to be a hypocrite, pretend to submit, but gain your point, has been the code of household morality which woman has been taught. The poet has sung, in sickly strains, the loveliness of woman's dependence upon man, and now we find it reechoed by those who profess to teach the religion of the Bible. God says, "Cease ye from man whose breath is in his nostrils, for wherein is he to be accounted of?" Man says, depend upon me. God says, "he will teach us of his ways." Man says, believe it not, I am to be your teacher. This doctrine of dependence upon man is utterly at variance with the doctrine of the Bible. In that book I find nothing like the softness of woman, nor the sternness of man: both are equally commanded to bring forth the fruits of the Spirit, love, meekness, gentleness, &c.

But we are told, "the power of woman is in her dependence, flowing from a consciousness of that weakness which God has given her for her protection." If physical weakness is alluded to, I cheerfully concede the superiority; if brute force is what my brethren are claiming, I am willing to let them have all the honor they desire; but if they mean to intimate, that mental or moral weakness

belongs to woman, more than to man, I utterly disclaim the charge. Our powers of mind have been crushed, as far as man could do it, our sense of morality has been impaired by his interpretation of our duties; but no where does God say that he made any distinction between us, as moral and intelligent beings.

"We appreciate," say the Association, "the *unostentatious* prayers and efforts of woman in advancing the cause of religion at home and abroad, in leading religious inquirers TO THE PASTOR for instruction." Several points here demand attention. If public prayers and public efforts are necessarily ostentatious, then "Anna the prophetess, (or preacher,) who departed not from the temple, but served God with fastings and prayers night and day," "and spake of Christ to all them that looked for redemption in Israel," was ostentatious in her efforts. Then, the apostle Paul encourages women to be ostentatious in their efforts to spread the gospel, when he gives them directions how they should appear, when engaged in praying, or preaching in the public assemblies. Then, the whole association of Congregational ministers are ostentatious, in the efforts they are making in preaching and praying to convert souls.

But woman may be permitted to lead religious inquirers to the PASTORS for instruction. Now this is assuming that all pastors are better qualified to give instruction than woman. This I utterly deny. I have suffered too keenly from the teaching of man, to lead any one to him for instruction. The Lord Jesus says,—"Come unto me and learn of me" (Matt. 2:29). He points his followers to no man; and when woman is made the favored instrument of rousing a sinner to his lost and helpless condition, she has no right to substitute any teacher for Christ; all she has to do is, to turn the contrite inquirer to the "Lamb of God which taketh away the sins of the world" (John 1:29). More souls have probably been lost by going down to Egypt for help, and by trusting in man in the early stages of religious experience, than by any other error. Instead of the petition being offered to God,—"Lead me in thy truth, and TEACH me, for thou art the God of my salvation" (Ps. 25:5),—instead of relying on the precious promises—"What man is he that feareth the Lord? him shall HE TEACH in the way that he shall choose" (Ps. 25:12)—"I will instruct thee and TEACH thee in the way which thou shalt go—I will guide thee with mine eye" (Ps. 27:2)—the young convert is directed to go to man, as if he were in the place of God, and his instructions essential to an advancement in the path of righteousness. That woman can have but a poor conception of the privilege of being taught of God, what he alone can teach, who would turn the "religious inquirer aside" from the fountain of living waters, where he might slake his thirst for spiritual instruction, to those broken cisterns which can hold no water, and therefore cannot satisfy the panting spirit. The business of men and women, who are ORDAINED OF GOD to preach the unsearchable riches of

Christ to a lost and perishing world, is to lead souls to Christ, and not to Pastors for instruction.

The General Association say, that "when woman assumes the place and tone of man as a public reformer, our care and protection of her seem unnecessary; we put ourselves in self-defence against her, and her character becomes unnatural." Here again the unscriptural notion is held up, that there is a distinction between the duties of men and women as moral beings; that what is virtue in man, is vice in woman; and women who dare to obey the command of Jehovah, "Cry aloud, spare not, lift up thy voice like a trumpet, and show my people their transgression" (Isa. 58:1), are threatened with having the protection of the brethren withdrawn. If this is all they do, we shall not even know the time when our chastisement is inflicted; our trust is in the Lord Jehovah, and in him is everlasting strength. The motto of woman, when she is engaged in the great work of public reformation should be,—"The Lord is my light and my salvation; whom shall I fear? The Lord is the strength of my life; of whom shall I be afraid?" (Ps. 27:1). She must feel, if she feels rightly, that she is fulfilling one of the important duties laid upon her as an accountable being, and that her character, instead of being "unnatural," is in exact accordance with the will of Him to whom, and to no other, she is responsible for the talents and the gifts confided to her. As to the pretty simile, introduced into the "Pastoral Letter,"

"If the vine whose strength and beauty is to lean upon the trellis work, and half conceal its dusters, thinks to assume the independence and the overshadowing nature of the elm," &c. I shall only remark that it might well suit the poet's fancy, who sings of sparkling eyes and coral lips, and knights in armor clad; but it seems to me utterly inconsistent with the dignity of a Christian body, to endeavor to draw such an anti-scriptural distinction between men and women. Ah! how many of my sex feel in the dominion, thus unrighteously exercised over them, under the gentle appellation of *protection*, that what they have leaned upon has proved a broken reed at best, and oft a spear.

Thine in the bonds of womanhood,
Sarah M. Grimké

5.4 MISSIONARY WOMEN STEP BEYOND THEIR SPHERE

Baptist lay leader Helen Barrett Montgomery (1861–1934) was one of the twentieth century's most active speakers, writers, and organizers on behalf of women's foreign missions. The causes to which she devoted herself and her approach to missions were both determined by her passion to break down the "caste of sex" at home and abroad. Among other achievements, she served as the first female president of the Northern Baptist Convention and translated the New Testament from the Greek to create a popular English study edition. In 1910 she wrote Western Women

in Eastern Lands to mark the fiftieth anniversary of women's boards of missions in America. It celebrates their achievements and points to challenges they will be forced to face. Montgomery reminds readers that women physicians played a shining role in advancing the kingdom of God abroad, although they had to battle prejudice from many sources at home. She also speaks directly to the efforts to merge men's and women's mission boards in several denominations. Montgomery objects to this, citing among other concerns the need for men to always be in charge and the possibility that women and children in foreign lands would be neglected as funds shifted to ministerial training and maintenance.

Source: Helen Barrett Montgomery. *Western Women in Eastern Lands: An Outline Study of Fifty Years of Woman's Work in Foreign Missions,* 117–19, 122–29, 268–72. New York: Macmillan, 1910.

One of the striking developments of the woman's century was the entrance of women into the practice of medicine. Their first step in this direction met with bitter opposition. In 1849 Elizabeth Blackwell was admitted to study medicine in Geneva, after knocking in vain at the doors of twelve medical colleges. This great woman, looking out over the few overcrowded avenues of employment open to women, had resolved to "open a new door, to tread a fresh path." The story of her resolute overcoming of hateful persecution and terrible obstacles, of her conquest for herself of the best medical education, is one of the romances of biography. Those who are inclined to give the clergy a monopoly in conservatism and blind opposition to progress, should read the story of the obstacles put in the way of pioneer women physicians by the medical profession. In 1859 the Philadelphia Medical Society passed a resolution of excommunication against any doctor who lectured or taught in the Women's Medical College, and against every graduate of that institution. Yet, in spite of opposition, within six years after Elizabeth Blackwell graduated at Geneva, the first Women's Hospital in all the world had been founded by Dr. Sims in New York, and the first permanent Woman's College of Medicine had been organized in Philadelphia.

We cannot pursue the story of this chapter in the expanding life of women further than to note its bearing on foreign missions. These lion-hearted pioneers in the field of medicine were blazing a trail whose importance they little dreamed. If the contracted ideas of propriety held by the vast majority of men and women in the civilized world of that time had triumphed, one of the most powerful agencies in the Christian conquest of the world would have been wanting. Whether there were to be women physicians was a question of interest in America: but in Asia it was a question of life and death. The women of half the world were shut out from medical assistance unless they could receive it at the hands of women. So with God and nature leading them, the women pioneers pressed out into the untried path; hundreds of more timid souls followed them, and the protesting old world settled back grumbling to get used to the new situation. . . .

While volumes might be written in regard to the evils, absurdities, and cruelties of the medical systems of the non-Christian world, the full horror of the situation would only be reached when the sufferings of women and children were told. Thousands of women die annually because such help as might be given them cannot be had on account of the restricted conditions of their lives. A physician walking in the streets of a city in India recently heard the screams of a woman coming from a fine native house. He asked a servant to say to the master of the house that a physician was passing by who would gladly be of service. The man returned answer that he would rather his wife should die than be relieved by a male physician. . . .

The need for women physicians to relieve the physical sufferings of their own sex was first perceived and first emphasized by missionaries. Both men and women united in the demand which they began to urge upon the home churches; the men found themselves barred from practising among women by caste and custom; the women, teachers and missionaries, had daily pressing upon them the throngs of women and little children who came to get help from the missionary medicine closet that was a part of the equipment of every station. These women often acquired considerable skill in prescribing for minor ailments, and in caring for wounds and burns; but found themselves helpless before the cases that demanded the services of a fully trained physician. . . .

The first response came from a woman, Sarah J. Hale, of Philadelphia. The editor of *Godey's Lady's Book* was the prophet who saw from afar this marvellous movement in the coming kingdom, to which the men and women of her generation were utterly blinded by prejudice and indifference. In 1851 she organized a Ladies' Medical Missionary Society whose object was "to aid the work of foreign missions by sending out young women qualified as physicians to minister to the wants of women in heathen lands." She wrote editorials in the *Lady's Book*,—the *Ladies' Home Journal* of those days—corresponded with influential people, and held parlor meetings. A few clergymen expressed themselves in sympathy; two young ladies just graduated from the Women's Medical College were ready and anxious to go, but the time had not yet come. The project aroused a storm of opposition and ridicule. At that time the old superstitious division between the "spiritual" and the "secular" was rigidly maintained. It was felt to be a waste of precious time and money to send missionaries to deal with anything but the perishing souls of men. The intimate connection between the soul and the body was not fully appreciated. And the example of the Master in the time he devoted to relieving bodily distress was apparently overlooked. Then there was that awful bogy of a woman going out of her *sphere*, even for the saving of life. So Mrs. Hale, after repeated efforts to storm the fort of public preju-

dice, was forced to postpone the desire of her heart to a better day. For twenty years she waited to see the church begin tardily and timidly the task that should have been begun in 1851.

Nothing further was done for seventeen years; then in India itself a medical missionary, Dr. J. L. Humphrey, began to deliver a course of lectures to a class of young women in the orphanage at Bareilly. The initiative in this case came from an educated Hindu gentleman, Pundit Nund Kishore, who knew the dreadful suffering of women in childbirth under the malpractice of ignorant midwives. He offered to defray half the expenses of training these young women if the government could be induced to help. The governor of the province regarded the matter favorably, but so much opposition came from physicians that the project seemed likely to fall through. Then a noble English official became personally responsible for the amount asked from the government, and the first class of nine women was opened at Naini Tal, May 1, 1869, a day that ought to be celebrated by the women of India. A two years' course of study was given to these women; and then four of them were sent up to stand the government examination. So much hung upon their success! Every one said that the scheme was a wild one; that women had neither the brains nor the judgment to successfully pass tests framed for men. But the four timid Indian women stood bravely before the Board of English Physicians (one of them the Inspector-general of Hospitals), answered correctly the questions, bore themselves so quietly, showed such thorough knowledge, that they won the Board and their coveted certificates at the same time. They were certificated in "Anatomy, Midwifery, Pharmacy, and the management of minor surgical cases, including the more common kinds of fractures and dislocations." The Board testified that these young women "answered questions with quickness and precision" and had a knowledge of medicine and surgery "quite equal to the generality of locally entertained native doctors."

At the time that this "lively experiment" was being made in India, Mrs. Thomas of Bareilly was writing to Mrs. Gracey asking her to interest the Philadelphia Branch of the Woman's Union Missionary Society in sending out a "medical lady." Mrs. Gracey read the letter which described the experiment with the native class at Naini Tal at one of the regular meetings of the Branch. We can well imagine the joy of Mrs. Hale, who was at the time president of the Society, when she heard the plan which she had cherished for nearly twenty years proposed and seemingly about to be realized. Inquiries were made at the Woman's Medical College to see if there was a graduate ready to go to India as a medical missionary. The name of Clara Swain of Castile, New York, was given. A letter was written to her which resulted in her accepting the call, after three months of thought and prayer. Meanwhile the women of the Methodist Church had

organized, and the Union Missionary Society most generously surrendered all claim to Miss Swain (who was herself a Methodist), and relinquished the honor of sending the first woman physician to the women of non-Christian lands. This beautiful deed of generous courtesy on the part of the pioneer Woman's Board has never been forgotten by the Methodist women. Miss Swain sailed with Miss Thoburn, the first missionaries to be sent out by the Methodist women of America. . . .

Would it not be better to have one great organization of the entire church to which both men and women contributed? This is the question that is most agitated to-day. Some of the brethren say: "Let the women collect, they are such splendid collectors. We will spend it far more wisely than they can." Others say, "Let us all work together, have men and women on the Board, men and women in the work."

The first plan will commend itself to few women. The opportunity for self-expression and the development that comes through responsibility are as necessary to women as to men. It is not the united wisdom of the men of the church which would be available for this sacred office of direction, but simply that of some individual secretary or secretaries. The modern educated woman has ideas not only on the way to collect money but on the way to spend it, and the purposes for which it should be spent.

The second plan is very attractive. It looks ideal to have one tremendous organization with men and women working side by side. Perhaps the day will come in the growth of the kingdom when this can be, but let us look at all sides of the argument before hastening out of organizations which have been so blessed of God.

In the first place, are men ready for it? Are they emancipated from the caste of sex so that they can work easily with women, unless they be head and women clearly subordinate? Certain facts seem to indicate that in spite of the rapid strides undoubtedly made in this direction we have still a long stretch of unexplored country to be traversed before the perfect democracy of Jesus is reached. When the Religious Education Association was formed, for example, although for years almost the only really scientific work in the Sunday school had been done by women in the primary department, no woman was asked to speak, and none was among the body of officers and backers of the movement. To have two or three women on a Board who are assigned to unimportant committees would hardly be satisfactory to the women. But in the present state of civilization could we look for much more?

Again, would the plan of consolidation work well for the interests of the work? For years the general Boards tried the lump method in gathering their funds; but all of them are supplementing that method to-day. When people were asked to give to some great, intangible faraway thing labelled Foreign Missions, the sense of responsibility was feeble, and the response feeble. To-day we have the "living link" by which a church agrees to become responsible to send one, the "missionary pastor," by which a church supports not only its home pastor but also its pastor on the field, the "substitute" idea, by which a man keeps his substitute working on the other side of the world while he sleeps. There are "station plans" and "specifics" innumerable. The result is dollars for dimes. The Word had to tabernacle among us that we might touch Him; so do causes. Now if we were to give up that intimate, near appeal made by work for women and homes and little children upon the women of the church, would the cause gain or lose? The experience of denominations which have tried consolidation of causes has not been particularly successful. Take cases where domestic and foreign missions are handled by one organization, and compare the per capita gifts with those where separate appeals on the merits of the case are made. Again, suppose that the same plan were tried in other lines. Would it be a gain to combine the Young Women's Christian Association and the Young Men's Christian Association in one vast organization which should jointly collect? Is it not true that in the startling diversity of human interests we must allow causes to make their appeal, and select their supporters by some inner law of affinity? Neither are they rivals. Each supports and furthers the other. Philanthropies depend on the cultivation of the spirit of philanthropy, and each helps to enrich the soil from which good deeds spring. So long as our national bill for chewing gum exceeds our gifts to foreign missions, and our ostrich feather and candy outputs could float the missionary benevolences like skiffs on a river, we need not fear impoverishing the churches by too much importunity.

Again, is there not a distinctive place for this distinctive work? There is always a danger that in the pressing demands of the wider work the women's interests might be overlooked, unless there were organizations specifically formed to care for them. It is only natural and right that the work of establishing churches, training ministers, educating the future leaders, should absorb the energies of men. The constant pressure for funds is so great, the opportunities for reaching the men of the non-Christian community so striking, that it is little wonder if, in the multiplicity of demands, the work for women and children should not be pressed. Men have seen this need of distinctive women's work clearly and have urged it persistently. One missionary now on the field said recently: "Never give up your separate women's organizations; the work for women is sure to suffer if you do. It needs some one continually pushing on that one point."

Once more, is there not a distinctive contribution that the women's organizations may make? We are not like men, but diverse. There is a feminine viewpoint which, to be sure, is only partial, but it is different. Certain methods are tried out, certain experiments made that would not appeal to men, but do to women. Cannot we cooperate all the better in joint undertakings, for having the separate work which each does better alone? Have women no contribution to add to missionary wisdom?

MRS. JARENA LEE.

Preacher of the A, M, E, Church.

Aged 60 years on the 11th day of the 2nd month 1844.

Phila 1844.

Jarena Lee (1783–unknown)
Caption reads "Mrs Jarena Lee. Preacher of the A,M,E, Church.
Aged 60 years on the 11th day of the 2nd month 1844. Phila 1844."
Photo: Library of Congress. Used by Permission.

Chapter 6

NINETEENTH-CENTURY PREACHERS AND SCHOLARS

Women in the Evangelical Tradition

From 1790 until the middle of the nineteenth century, the United States experienced another wave of revivals, called by historians the Second Great Awakening. These revivals rapidly built up the Methodist and Baptist churches and gave an evangelical character to large segments of American Protestantism. According to many estimates, about two-thirds of the new converts were women under the age of thirty.

Why were women so prominent as revival converts during this period? This is an important question given that some historians believe the dramatic revival techniques were meant to draw men back to the churches.[1] They may have been responding to being constantly bombarded with the message that women are by nature more religious than men and have special religious duties. Women may also have felt less and less in control of their lives as they became economically unproductive and as they could no longer depend on parents to arrange marriages. They turned to God therefore as one who would control their destinies and fortunes. Or, by making a commitment to God, women may have been preparing themselves for marriage, which also required submission and the abandonment of frivolous youth.[2]

We normally associate many evangelical groups today with the subordination and silence of women, and women in the nineteenth century, for the most part, filled similarly traditional roles as wives and mothers as well as Sunday school teachers and members of prayer and mission groups. Historians Lucille Sider Dayton and Donald Dayton make an important point, however, in reminding us that there are significant exceptions to this pattern among American evangelicals in the nineteenth century.[3] In addition to the Unitarians, Quakers, and groups discussed in chapter 7, certain evangelical groups gave a significant public role to women. The ideology of true womanhood provided a rationale for these changes, but more important was the character of evangelicalism itself, discussed in chapter 4.

An Expansion of Roles in the Second Great Awakening

Revival preachers called upon all Christians to spread the gospel in response to their conversions. One of the chief ways of doing this for women, of course, was in the role of mother. Religious literature is filled with stories of women who act as powerful agents of salvation for their sons and daughters. Another private means of promoting the revival of religion was letter writing. As Anne Dutton had done in the eighteenth century, women took up their pens to convert their friends and encourage new Christians.

Women often promoted revivals in other more public ways. They frequently held prayer meetings to petition God for the blessing of conversions. Like reform and benevolent groups, evangelical clergymen encouraged the prayer meetings as long as the women behaved "decorously." Women also counseled female converts who were moved to repentance by the revival preachers. But in keeping with the initial revolutionary and iconoclastic character of the awakening, women also admonished sinners, criticized ministers, and preached by expounding on a passage of Scripture and its relevance to hearers.

The evangelist Charles Finney made a notable contribution to widening the role of women in the promotion of revivals. Finney introduced a variety of new techniques to stimulate conversions in his sweep through the northeastern states. One of these new measures was to allow women to speak and pray before "promiscuous" (i.e., variegated) groups composed of men and women. Women in America had generally observed the ban on speaking in mixed assemblies; Finney and his assistants, however, believed that women should not be prevented from speaking about their faith if they felt deeply moved to do so. Conversion and sanctification led to questioning of traditional ways of living and thinking. Finney's policy aroused hostility among his colleagues but he continued it. Between 1843 and 1847, he served as a professor and then president of Oberlin College, the first college in the United States to admit women (which did so since its founding in 1833). Finney, however, did not fight for the ordination of women to positions of power within church structures, and he continued to believe that women normally belonged in the domestic sphere. He did influence women at Oberlin though, including several leaders of the women's rights movement and Antoinette Brown, the first woman to be ordained to the ministry in the Congregational Church.[4]

Finney and his circle were not the only leaders of evangelical Christianity to endorse public speaking by women. Luther Lee, the founder of the Wesleyan Methodist Church, reflected the thinking of John Wesley in his belief that women had a right to preach the gospel. He preached the sermon at the ordination of Antoinette Brown, pointing to female prophets in the Old Testament and women "ministers" in the New Testament. Lee's church was one of a number of smaller Protestant groups such as the Freewill Baptists, Free Methodists, and African Methodists that had broken away from the larger denominations. Probably hundreds of women from such churches were involved in preaching as itinerant evangelists in the first half of the nineteenth century. These communities were chronically short of ministers, but they also were willing to challenge Protestant social conventions— which they regarded as man-made—such as fancy dress for women and ministerial authority. Despite their competence and willingness to travel long distances, these women regularly had to justify their work, even to male preachers in their own churches. Very few of their sermons survive, but those that do reveal a typical evangelical message: repentance, conversion, and holy living.

By the middle of the century, this openness to women began to disappear. Male preachers proliferated, and some leaders of the smaller denominations feared a link between women preachers and the nascent movement for women's political rights. Men were especially concerned about establishing their respectability in the eyes of the larger Protestant mainstream. They began, for example, to require their preachers to have academic degrees. Revivalism in Finneyite circles became structured and professionalized, losing its spirit-oriented character. And evangelicals worked to set themselves apart from sectarian movements such as the Millerites and Shakers by discouraging female speaking and leadership. Carol Smith-Rosenberg suggests that there was also an economic dimension to this conservatism: frontier and agrarian families embraced revolutionary evangelicalism as they moved to towns and cities and struggled to adjust to urban middle-class life, but once they were comfortably settled, they again restricted women to the domestic sphere.[5]

The Holiness Movement

Women continued to find opportunities for public ministry in the Holiness movement, which emerged within evangelical circles as the nineteenth century progressed. It was at first nurtured within the mainline Protestant churches, particularly the Methodist church, as an attempt to revitalize discipline and commitment; gradually, however, separate Holiness denominations emerged. The Holiness movement claimed that God's grace was available not only for salvation but also was given, in a second dramatic experience, to "sanctify" or "perfect" a Christian's life. Holiness Christians believed that God gave them the power to overcome all intentional sin through the outpouring of the Holy Spirit in their lives, which established a harmonious and unbroken fellowship with Christ. Women took advantage of this emphasis on the spirit to work as preachers and itinerant evangelists, although men were not eager to share leadership roles with them.

Phoebe Palmer was a major force behind the movement. She traveled as an evangelist throughout the United States, Great Britain, and Canada, speaking at over three hundred camp and revival meetings. The Tuesday Meetings, which she led in her home, persuaded many churchmen and women to accept sanctification, as did her books and the *Guide to Holiness* magazine, which she edited. Palmer left her imprint on many parts of Protestant life: she simplified the experience of sanctification by making surrender to God more a matter of will than high emotion; she initiated one of the earliest Protestant efforts to minister to people in the slums of New York; and she helped pave the way for Dwight Moody's revivalism by involving lay people in planning and promotion.[6]

One of Palmer's most significant contributions was her 1859 book *The Promise of the Father*, a theological defense of female preaching. The core idea of the book is that the Holy Spirit calls women to speak and pray in the assembly of God's people. Confident in this belief, she approached the biblical texts. To follow the command to silence in I Corinthians 14 would lead to absurdity, while I Timothy 2 meant only that women could not usurp authority over men. As did many evangelicals after her, she insisted that women were channels or agents of the Holy Spirit and were not exercising their own wills or intellects. Palmer also pointed to examples of women who preached in the New Testament and in early Methodism. Church ordination was not needed to confer authority because tangible signs of status such as rhetorical skill and "palpable virtue" were conferred by the Holy Spirit to mark a chosen woman.[7] She even preferred to speak of women "talking to" or "addressing" the congregation to show her distance from "preaching," which depended on the paraphernalia of academic degrees and special costumes.

When Palmer's preaching was attacked during a tour of England in 1859, Catherine Booth defended her. Booth, like many Methodists, was ambivalent about the innovation of female preaching, but she heard and embraced Palmer's holiness message, coming to believe that Eve's burden was lessened because sin was no longer a permanent state. Booth also published a written defense of female preaching, *Female Ministry*, in which she argued in the following terms: "If she have [sic] the necessary gifts, and feels herself called by the Spirit to preach, there is not a single word in the whole book of God to restrain her, but many, very many, to urge and encourage her. God says she SHALL do so, and Paul prescribed the manner in which she shall do it, and Phoebe, Junia, Philip's four daughters, and many other women, actually did preach and speak in the primitive churches."[8] Along with some reinterpretation of the passages commanding silence, Booth also claims that woman's nature makes her especially fit for preaching. Her primary concern, however, was to establish a positive biblical witness for women.

Women participated widely in the churches, making up a high percentage of Holiness ministers well into the twentieth century; the Church of the Nazarene even guaranteed women the right to preach in its constitution of 1894. The founder of the Pilgrim Holiness Church, Seth Rees, claimed that "no Church that is acquainted with the Holy Ghost will object to the public ministry of women."[9] As these groups became larger and better organized, women's preaching was increasingly discouraged; the call of the Holy Spirit was no longer sufficient authority.

The Pentecostal movement, which grew out of the Holiness groups, continued this view on the preaching of women. Evidence of this is the celebrated ministry of the twentieth-century figure Aimee Semple McPherson, minister of the Foursquare Gospel Church, who created her own distinctive version of Pentecostalism. Despite the vivid, theatrical style of her public appearances, McPherson and the Pentecostal community as a whole embraced conventional ideas about male and female spheres. For example, leadership roles such as elder were restricted to men. As historian Edith Blumhofer describes it, women "enjoyed cultural authority but had no institutional voice."[10]

African American Evangelical Women

Important for understanding the experiences of evangelical women are the autobiographies of nineteenth-century black itinerant preachers and missionaries such as Julia Foote, Zilpha Elaw, and Amanda Berry Smith. These women tended to be active in Methodist and Baptist circles. Taking seriously the command of Jesus that disciples go into the world, they traveled widely and spoke to black and white audiences. But their stories are also about spiritual traveling from "non-being to being" and from ignorance to wisdom about their true place in God's scheme.[11]

Their profound evangelical experiences of conversion and sanctification transformed their lives far beyond the promise of eternal salvation. Conversion gave them proof of their humanity and a way to deal with their anger at racism at a time when Americans debated whether African Americans had souls. Conversion also gave them a sense of being children of God to replace their lost African lineage. After sanctification, these women derived an enormous sense of self-worth from the confidence that they were living in harmony with God's will. Like the mystical experience of some women in earlier centuries, African American preachers believed that they received direction from God through visions, intuitions, and dreams. They were guided in small decisions such as which house or church to visit and in more significant ones involving vocation and marriage. The Spirit thus led them to defy social norms, to put marriage and motherhood second, and to claim the right to preach. Often women were reluctant to answer their calls, fearing for their safety and fearing social disapproval. God, however, filled their lives with affirmations of their calling: they were protected from hostile crowds, provided with clothing and shoes for traveling, and struck with illness when they refused to obey. Since these women inhabited a world in which black men had little or no credible authority, they may have found it easier than their white sisters to claim power for themselves.[12]

Many of these themes are found in the life of Methodist evangelist Amanda Berry Smith, who was born in Maryland in 1837. In the midst of a life of domestic service and an unhappy marriage, Smith's call to ministry developed. She received a direct commission when the words "GO PREACH" appeared in her mind in 1870 when she was attending an African Methodist Episcopal Church in Brooklyn. She became one of the century's best-known evangelists, preaching to thousands of black and white audiences at Holiness camp meetings and churches from New Jersey to Maine. She also preached in England, India, and West Africa. Smith had no interest in ordination, believing she was ordained by God, and her work was never supported by a denomination. Yet her appearance in 1872 at the General Conference of the African Methodist Episcopal Church resulted in an acknowledgment of the success of women preachers and an agreement that preaching licenses be issued to women as "female evangelists." Nancy Hardesty and Adrienne Israel conclude that Smith paved the way for hundreds of black women to establish independent, sanctified storefront churches in the early decades of the twentieth century.[13]

Evangelicals and Women's Rights

How did nineteenth-century evangelicals respond to the question of political and social rights for women? As we might expect, they held a wide range of opinions on these issues, opinions that varied from the very traditional to some version of what Carolyn Haynes has identified as Christian feminism.[14] Some wholeheartedly embraced the silence and subordination of women, allowing them only carefully circumscribed activities in groups to promote the gospel. The more traditional Christian feminists supported women's leadership in reform and mission groups as well as female preaching. They believed that access to public roles in the churches was contingent upon the calling of the Holy Spirit. Tending also to embrace the ideals of true womanhood, they believed that the first priority of women was home and family—and in the domestic sphere, they were to be subject to their husbands. Such women were careful to be decorous in their dress and behavior. The more liberal Christian feminists went beyond the support of women in reform and pulpit to urge that they fight for the right to vote. The perspective of these women was also grounded in the ideals of true womanhood. They argued that women, who were morally superior to men, should have political rights and access to certain professions because of their beneficial effect on society. Radical feminism, with its broad agenda of economic and divorce rights was not, on the whole, supported by evangelical women but rather by women in liberal religious communities, many of them outside of the Protestant mainstream.

But regardless of which perspective on women's rights they embraced, evangelical and holiness women modeled behavior that undermined tradition and set the stage for the attainment of a wider range of rights in the twentieth century. Women such as Smith and Palmer traveled across the globe and organized revival meetings. When men heard Palmer and read her books, they were forced to acknowledge her intelligence. Women who spoke from pulpits "claimed space for themselves" and gave the equality of women concrete expression. Just as important, all of these Christian feminists in some way were forced to confront the biblical text and engage in a process of reinterpretation.[15] They began a process of using scholarship to unlock the text and judge it according to conscience or other parts of Scripture.

THE DEBATE OVER WOMEN PREACHING

The opportunity for preaching that some evangelical groups gave to women raised the issue of the proper role of women in the church for all Protestants. The question became even more insistent as women moved into other professions and expanded their public activities of reform and charity. By the end of the century, most denominations had debated whether or not to sanction activities such as speaking in mixed gatherings, serving on governing bodies, preaching, and being ordained. While these discussions took place among different groups at different times, it is possible to isolate the major arguments on both sides of the issue of preaching.[16]

Those in favor of allowing women to preach made several important points. One was that churches could not prohibit what women felt called by the Holy Spirit to do. The supporters of preaching women regarded this as the most persuasive argument, especially in light of the century's emphasis on the work of the Holy Spirit in the world. The black preacher Jarena Lee was able to overcome rejection because of a "holy energy" that burned in her life like a fire, permitting her to step beyond the lines convention had established. Women who did not obey the directions of the Spirit, out of a fear of men, were said to be troubled in their souls and even subject to "fits and seizures." So far as Quaker women and their societies were concerned, they were simply instruments of God's will when exercising a preaching ministry.

The other two arguments focused on showing the doctrinal correctness and expediency of female preaching.[17] First, women were needed in new roles to extend the work of the church. Immigration, urban expansion, and the growth of science all presented challenges to American Christians. Many people felt that the churches could not afford to overlook the skills and energies of women, especially since they had a proven record as "movers and shakers" in existing efforts to spread the gospel and reform society.

Second, the Bible featured prominently in the defense of preaching women since the opposing side also based its important arguments on Scripture. Many writers used a new way of interpreting the Bible, distinguishing between those texts that were local and temporal and those that were normative and eternal. Thus, the New Testament words commanding women to keep silent were written for a particular time and place and were not meant to apply to all circumstances. Instead, Gal. 3:28 was meant to be the guidepost for all Christians when it came to the status of women. Other writers spent time studying the details of Paul's words, claiming that he only prohibited married women from speaking or that he condemned the babbling and not the praying and preaching of women. They felt that to take Paul literally would be absurd. Still others anticipated modern scholarship by pointing to the active preaching ministries of women such as Deborah, the Samaritan woman, and those who "labored" with Paul. Finally, the events at Pentecost, when the Holy Spirit was poured out upon the sons and daughters of the church who then prophesied, were an important guide for the Holiness groups. To many of these Christians, God was again pouring out the Holy Spirit in America, making the preaching of women appropriate.

The arguments against the preaching of women were based first and foremost on biblical material. New Testament teaching on this issue, it was said, was clear and grounded in reasons that were not affected by the passage of time: Woman was created after man and as his helper, and woman brought sin into the world. One writer claimed that "she made a little speech once and that was the world's undoing: now let her keep silence."[18] Furthermore, since the Holy Spirit dictated the Scriptures, that same Spirit could not be self-contradictory and call upon a woman to preach. Women preachers in the Bible were raised up in very exceptional circumstances.

Christians who objected to this wider role for women also argued on the basis of Victorian ideas of true womanhood. Some claimed, for example, that women already played an important role in the churches in their own "sphere" as mothers and as members of female religious groups. Women could be given willingly an active, speaking role in small prayer meetings and in small sex-segregated social gatherings; these meetings, however, were quite different from large "promiscuous" assemblies.

Finally, a host of social and historical reasons were used to attack those who allowed women to preach. A pregnant woman and nursing mother, for example, could not bear the exhausting duty of preaching. Also, how could a woman combine household duties and the demands on a preacher (and the church certainly did not want to discourage marriage)? Then there was the question of proper education in many denominations. Women simply did not have minds suited to theological studies. They were intuitive rather than logical and reasonable, and their preaching therefore would not win back the men so desperately needed by American congregations.

Ordination to the
Ministry of Word and Sacrament

The question of whether or not churches should ordain women to a ministry was also an issue in the nineteenth century. In most Christian traditions, ordination is understood as the setting apart of certain individuals to hold special authority within the congregation, usually authority to preach, administer the sacraments, and supervise the affairs of the congregation. Unlike itinerant evangelism or preaching, ordination meant a place in the institutional structure of the churches. Preaching was an issue that concerned large numbers of nineteenth-century women while far fewer advocated or sought ordination. Margaret Lamberts Bendroth argues that the rewards of ordination were "more symbolic" than substantive and that women had more real power through the missionary organizations.[19]

What progress had been made toward ordination by 1900? Although they had no sacramental ministry, the Unitarians and Universalists ordained over seventy women by 1890. Some Congregationalist churches also made the decision, on the local level, to ordain women. The first was Antoinette Brown, who, in 1853, was ordained to a charge in East Butler, New York. By 1900, there were forty ordained women in Congregationalist churches. Baptist congregations may in theory have decided to ordain women, but it is not clear whether they did so in practice. In both denominations, a woman only had to convince a local parish to accept her; there were no national boards or bishops. Although the Methodist Episcopal Church rejected the requests in 1880 of Anna Howard Shaw and Anna Oliver, the New York Conference of the Methodist Protestant Church, a small branch of the Methodist family, ordained Shaw a short time later. The action, however, was never approved by the church's General Conference. Another branch of the Methodist family, the Wesleyan Methodists, had agreed to ordain women in the 1860s. Despite the fact that the issue was raised in a number of other denominations, groups such as the Lutherans, Presbyterians, and Episcopalians did not admit women to the ordained ministry until well into the twentieth century. An exception was the Nolen Presbytery of the Cumberland Presbyterian Church in Kentucky, which ordained Louisa Woosley in 1889. But in 1894 the church's General Assembly ordered her name retired from the list of ordained pastors and Woolsey was caught in a lengthy denominational conflict.

Generally, women who hoped to be ordained to the ministry in the nineteenth century faced a lonely struggle, even within sympathetic denominations. A Woman's Ministerial Conference was formed in 1882 to provide a network of support for women but it had little power to enact changes. Some theological schools such as those at Oberlin and Boston University admitted women, but aspiring candidates faced strenuous opposition at local and national levels of church life. Only slowly are historians now getting a sense of the pastoral style of these women. Cynthia Tucker's study of Unitarian/ Universalist women in the Midwest reveals the ways in which they applied the ideology of true womanhood to their parishes. They concentrated on

building a family-like support system in their congregations and tended to
the practical needs of their parishioners, but were at the same time marginalized by the denomination's East Coast leadership.[20]

THE DEACONESS MOVEMENT

In many Protestant denominations, professional church work was initially
open to women through the office of deaconess. Nineteenth-century Christians believed that they were restoring a New Testament office. They interpreted the early office, however, as one of service to the community without
any liturgical functions or formal ordination. It is important therefore to dis-
tinguish between these "deaconesses" and the "female deacons" who would
come to have equal duties with the male deacons in the twentieth century.

The movement in the United States was inspired by the deaconess community in Kaiserswerth, Germany, founded by Theodore Fliedner in 1836.
It first appeared in America in 1849 but was not widespread until after the
Civil War when the Lutheran, Episcopalian, Methodist, and Presbyterian
churches made provisions for the position. Women who volunteered to be
deaconesses were set apart by prayer and special training for work as nurses,
social workers, and missionaries. They were particularly influential as social
workers in immigrant communities in which they ran schools, hospitals, and
settlement houses, helping denominations to develop methods to reach the
alienated poor. Living by rules rather than vows, the deaconesses generally
were expected to remain single and take no salary. Eventually some training
programs emerged that focused on parish service such as Christian education
and administration.

For a variety of reasons, the office of deaconess was never very attractive to
women in the United States.[21] It is possible that many women found enough
channels for activity and leadership in the societies for reform and mission.
Also, anti-Catholic sentiment shed suspicion on groups of women who lived
celibately, dressed in plain, dark uniforms, or who, as the Lutheran deaconesses did, lived in motherhouses under strict regulations. They reminded the
Protestant public of "popish" convents and religious orders. There was also
the fear that the office of deaconess would be seen as a stepping-stone to
ordination for women. Those who supported the deaconesses had to empha-

size that women were not ordained to the office and that they were working within their designated sphere by simply extending their responsibilities as mothers and household managers.

Historians today tend to be conflicted about the significance of the position of deaconess for women. It was in part an attempt to provide an acceptable and safe slot for women who wished to minister in public without opening up true lay and ordination rights in the churches. Yet this was also an opportunity for women to hold a formal church office and engage in professional ministry. It also gave women the possibility of a meaningful life "independent of the family role."[22] Schools such as Lucy Meyer's Chicago Training School provided practical training and some theological education. In the twentieth century however, the spread of professionalization, especially in nursing and Christian education, eventually undermined the office of deaconess.

THE WOMAN'S BIBLE

Most Protestants in the nineteenth century took the Bible seriously and believed that there was one single meaning to biblical texts, a meaning most accurately mediated through their clergymen. When women, therefore, tried to get the vote, access to professions, and a wider role in the churches, they were met with the argument that these activities were not only "unnatural" but they were against the commands of the Bible. But would the same conclusion be reached if women themselves interpreted the Bible, bringing to it different experiences and assumptions and a concern for the dignity and rights of women? By raising this question, women began the process of reading the Bible "in light of the oppressive structures of patriarchal society," a process that has given rise to modern feminist hermeneutics.[23]

In the nineteenth century, women's work in biblical scholarship had both a positive and negative orientation. One position of women was to assert that the Bible supported women's rights by lifting up those portions that empowered women and reinterpreting those passages that were most often cited to oppress women. They used a wide variety of strategies in their re-reading of the biblical text. Women such as Phoebe and Deborah who played prominent roles in the Bible were highlighted. Particular words of texts such as "silence" in I Corinthians 14 were probed to find alternative and more precise meanings. An alternative approach taken by some interpreters was to see the text as applying to a particular congregation to solve particular problems. Or, individual texts were set within the larger context of the whole Bible. They were to be judged according to norms established by the teachings of Jesus or the promises at Pentecost that the Spirit would descend on men and women. What this last interpretive principle recognized, essentially, was that some of the biblical material was tied to a particular culture and some was the eternal word of God.

Other women in the nineteenth century, however, gradually began to suggest that it was futile to base women's rights on an external authority as fraught with controversy as the Bible. Equality was a self-evident truth that did not need biblical sanction. Women who embraced this position were more likely, in fact, to be less hopeful about what the Bible had to offer women. *The Woman's Bible* came to represent this more hesitant and skeptical perspective.

The publication of *The Woman's Bible* was not an attempt to purge the Bible of its masculine-oriented language or of the parts that women found degrading. Rather, it was a series of commentaries or observations prepared by a committee of twenty-five women on those parts of the Bible believed to be of special interest to women. The women—all middle class and white— were from a variety of religious backgrounds, including liberal Protestantism, Christian Science, and Theosophy. Part I of their work, dealing with Genesis through Deuteronomy, was published in 1895, and Part II on the rest of the Bible appeared in 1898. *The Women's Bible* was short and in paperback so that as many women as possible could afford to buy it.

Elizabeth Cady Stanton was the chief architect of the publication and wrote many of the commentaries. Her life reflected the experiences shared by most of the women on the committee. They tended to be well educated, disillusioned with traditional Protestant Christianity, and concerned with acquiring a broad range of rights for women and not simply the vote. Stanton grew up in a Presbyterian family in Johnstown, Pennsylvania. She associated the Christian faith with cold churches and gloomy sermons, but she remained grateful to the family's pastor, who thought enough of her ability to teach her Greek. Stanton, however, was also profoundly affected by the words of a young man who had been helped through seminary by the girls' club to which she belonged. After they had provided for his education and given him a new suit upon his graduation, he preached his first sermon on the text, "But I suffer not a woman to teach . . . but to be in silence" (1 Tim. 2:12).

Stanton's concern for the rights of women was shaped by several influences. Listening to the clients of her father, an attorney and judge, Stanton had become aware of the severe legal disabilities of married women. Her own frustration as a mother and housekeeper moved her to rebel against the doctrine of the woman's sphere. Her experiences in the antislavery campaign also made her keenly aware of the obstacles and prejudices women faced. She devoted her life to the cause of women's rights, advocating a wide spectrum of rights for women in the church, the workplace, and the home. She eventually became convinced that little could be done until women collectively recognized their subjection and rejected it. Yet this could not happen until the spell that the Bible had cast upon them was broken. She therefore set about the task of seeing whether or not the Bible was "usable" in the quest for women's rights; she concluded that the Bible did little to dignify women.

The commentaries written by the women Stanton gathered around her were strongly influenced by the movements and events of their world. They reflected the current belief that the Bible was not an infallible letter from God to the human race but was a human book written in a number of cultural contexts. They did not deny, however, that the Bible contained divine truth.

The writers viewed God as a benevolent creator who had established laws for the smooth operation of the world. These laws demanded justice and equal access to liberty and happiness for all human beings. The universe was so ordered that a balance between the feminine and the masculine had to be acknowledged in everyday life. In God, the women believed, they had an ally for their cause. The Bible had to be brought under the judgment of these divinely ordained laws just like all other human enterprises. In biblical passages where women were treated with justice and humanity, it was possible to speak of such material as the "Word of God." Where women were degraded and made subordinate, the Bible could be given no such status. Because this kind of material, which was pervasive, merely reflected the male domination of the cultures in which it developed, Stanton argued that the Bible as a whole could in no way be called inspired.

With these theological ideas in mind, the women took up the task of preparing commentaries on passages that had been assigned to each of them.

The commentaries do several things. They bring to attention and celebrate women who asserted their rights and dignity. They reinterpret some parts in which the message of female equality has been hidden or overlooked. They also expose those sections that they found to devalue women and they question the divine origins of such passages.

Stanton's committee was eager to uncover the patriarchialism that distorted the equality built into God's created order. In commenting on Num. 20:1-16, for example, the reverend Phoebe Hanaford denounced the fact that a woman could not be responsible for her vow to God. She claimed that this passage portrays women as irresponsible children rather than as mature adults with the freedom intended by God: "It is unjust to a man that he should have the added responsibility of his daughter's or wife's word, and it is cruel to a woman because the irresponsibility is enslaving in its influence. It is contrary to true Gospel teaching, for only in freedom to do right can a soul dwell in that love which is the fulfilling of the law."[24] In the discussion of I Corinthians 11, the commentator informs her readers that God did not command women to cover their heads; rather, the command originated in an ancient Hebrew myth about the sons of God being seduced by the daughters of men. Genesis 2–3 showed the perverse influence of male-dominated culture over the biblical author since the creation of the woman is described in a demeaning way and woman is made the scapegoat for man's sin.

Some biblical material did resonate with the principles of justice and equality. Vashti is applauded by *The Woman's Bible* as a woman who threw off the tyranny of her husband and refused to be treated simply as a sex object. The daughters of Zelophehad, who stood up to Moses and argued for their inheritance, are rescued from oblivion. Deborah and Huldah are designated as role models for nineteenth-century women, and Jesus' treatment of women as fully human and worthy of respect is emphasized. Genesis 1 was also treated as divine truth because it reflected the great divine laws of masculine and feminine equality that were built into God's creation: "If language has any meaning, we have in these texts a plain declaration of the existence of the feminine element in the Godhead, equal in power and glory with the masculine"[25]

The New Testament parable of the wise and foolish virgins (Matt. 25:1-12) was also given a significant new interpretation. Jesus, the women claimed, used the story to encourage the self-reliance of women. The wise virgins in their commentary are compared to women who have cultivated their own skills and talents. The foolish virgins are like those women who totally sacrifice themselves to the success of men while burying their own capacities and powers. The latter group will be unprepared to meet the personal crises of life as well as the demands of modern society.

At the time of its publication, *The Woman's Bible* was greeted with hostility and ridicule. Even the National American Woman Suffrage Association passed a resolution denying any association with it. To tamper with the Scriptures was to invite the anger of evangelical women on whom the group had come to depend for support. Modern scholars fault the publication in part for its anti-Semitic tendencies as ancient Israel is repeatedly condemned for its sexism. Yet Stanton and her committee, while not equipped with the same critical tools, anticipated twentieth-century feminist theology and biblical scholarship by reinterpreting the tradition, recognizing the patriarchal context of the biblical writers, and identifying lost traditions affirming women. They also inspired the 1992 *Women's Bible Commentary*, which broadens the identity of the scholars by including diverse racial, social, and ethnic groups but has the same fundamental objective: women interpreting the Bible for themselves.

As in colonial America, some segments of the evangelical community in the nineteenth century encouraged women to preach and speak in public. For most American Christians, however, the case against female preaching was stated plainly in the Bible and supported by the doctrine of separate spheres and female subordination. Yet was this material to be understood as the revealed Word of God? The editors of *The Woman's Bible* answered "no" and instead claimed that divine revelation affirmed the equality and full humanity of women. The debates over preaching and biblical interpretation occurred mainly among American Protestants from the major denominations. There were other significant developments for the status of women in Christianity in nineteenth century, but for these we must look to the Catholic community and to a variety of sectarian groups.

Readings for Chapter 6

6.1 A DEFENSE OF FEMALE PREACHING

The Wesleyan Methodists combined intense revivalism with radical social reform, believing that obedience to the gospel was not genuine unless linked with abolitionism and temperance. Luther Lee (1800–1889) became a prominent leader and architect of this denomination after careers as a preacher and antislavery agent. His support of temperance led him to become an outspoken supporter of a woman's right to speak publicly on behalf of the movement. It was probably through temperance channels that he met Antoinette Brown and was invited to preach at the service of her ordination in 1853 in the First Congregational Church, East Butler, New York. Lee's sermon hinges on the idea that the church, living in the light of Pentecost, had experienced the fulfillment of Joel's promise that God's spirit would someday lead men and women to prophesy. Lee argues that since the Bible contains a multitude of examples that women in Israel and the early church spoke publicly with God's blessing, the prohibitions in 1 Corinthians 14 and 1 Timothy 2 must be local and specific in their application.

Source: Luther Lee. "Woman's Right to Preach the Gospel." In Five Sermons and a Tract by Luther Lee, *edited with an introduction by Donald W. Dayton, 92–95. Chicago: Holrad, 1975.*

This discourse would be defective, should I not pay some attention to those scriptures which some suppose forbade females to exercise their gifts in public. There are, so far as I know, but two texts, that are, or can be relied upon as proof against the right of females to improve in public. They are as follows:

"Let your women keep silence in the churches: for it is not permitted unto them to speak; but they are commanded to be under obedience, as also saith the law. And if they will learn any thing, let them ask their husbands at home: for it is a shame for woman to speak in the church" (I Cor. 14:34, 35).

"Let the women learn in silence with all subjection. But I suffer not a woman to teach, nor to usurp authority over the man, but to be in silence" (I Tim. 2:11, 12).

These two texts, I believe, are all the proof there is to onset the array of texts and arguments which have been adduced in proof of the right of females to preach the gospel. If I were to say, "I do not know what they mean," they could never disprove the fact that females did prophesy and pray in the church, and if explained at all, they must be so explained as to harmonize with that fact. Let us then examine the matter.

If these texts are to be understood as a general prohibition of the improvement of female gifts in public, it must be entire and absolute, and must cut females off from all vocal part in public worship. It will preclude them from singing and vocal prayer. The expression, "Let your women keep silence in the churches," if it touches the case at all, forbids singing and vocal prayer. Can a woman sing and keep silence at the same time? Can she pray vocally, and keep silence at the same time? Such then is the true issue, and as we must meet the issue before the people, it is important that it be presented to them in its true light. Singing is as much a violation of the command to keep silence as praying or preaching. We must then put locks upon the lips of the sisterhood in time of prayer, and compel them to let their harps hang in silence while we, the lords of creation, chant Zion's songs, and leave the song itself devoid of the softer melodies which flow from woman's soul.

Such a construction of these texts most clearly makes them conflict with other portions of divine truth. Glance for a moment at the weight of evidence on the other side. My text affirms, as a broad foundation on which to stand, "There is neither male nor female; for ye are all one in Christ Jesus." Miriam was a prophetess and led the host of women in Israel forth, and when the men sun[g] of Jehovah's triumph, she responded loudly and gloriously in the face of all Israel. Deborah was a prophetess and was a judge of all Israel. Huldah was a prophetess, and dwelt in the College at Jerusalem, and prophesied in the name of the Lord, to king Josiah. "Thus saith the Lord God of Israel." Anna proph-

esied concerning Christ in the temple to all them that looked for redemption in Jerusalem. The prophet Joel foretold that daughters should prophesy under the New Dispensation; and God did pour out his Spirit on females and they spake with other tongues. Philip "had four daughters which did prophesy," sixty years after the birth of Christ. Paul the author of this supposed law of silence imposed upon females, tells us that Phebe was a deaconess or minister of the Church which was at Cenchrea; and commends several other females in the same chapter, who labored in the Lord. Paul also wrote to the church at Philippi, and told them to "help those women that labored in the gospel." And all antiquity agrees that women were set apart to some church office by the imposition of a bishop's hands.

Now, in the face of all this, are we to understand Paul as issuing a command, covering all countries and all ages, absolutely requiring all women to keep silence in the churches, and not to speak a word within the walls of the sanctuary? Those must believe it who can, but I cannot believe it with the light I now have, and must seek some explanation, which will, in my view, make a better harmony in the word of God.

Every writer should be so construed, if it be possible, as to make him agree with himself, and to do this, Paul must be so understood in these two texts, as to make the sense accord with what he has so plainly taught in other places, that females might and did exercise their gifts in public. Compare with I Corinthians II:5, 6, I3, I4, I5.

"But every woman that prayeth or prophesieth with her head uncovered, dishonoreth her head; for that is even all one as if she were shaven. For if the woman be not covered, let her be covered. Judge in yourselves: is it comely that a woman pray unto God uncovered? Doth not even nature itself teach you, that, if a man have long hair, it is a shame unto him? But if a woman have long hair, it is a glory to her: for her hair is given her for a covering."

Here the apostle most clearly gives directions how women are to pray and prophesy in public, and are we to understand him as first giving directions how females should pray and prophesy, and then in the same letter, absolutely forbid the thing he had given directions how to perform? I cannot believe this, and must seek another exposition. It is clear that women did pray and prophesy in that church, and the apostle told them it must be done with their heads covered, that is wearing the customary veil. This was founded upon the customs of the times, to which it was necessary to conform in order to success, as to appear in public without a veil, in that community, subjected a female to suspicions of a want of virtue. What the apostle calls nature was only the prejudice of education, which has now ceased to exist, or rather never existed among us. The Greek word, *phusis,* here translated *nature,* signifies not only nature, but "constitution, disposition, character, custom,

habit, use." We have no such nature in this country, and as the rule grew out of the then existing customs and prejudices of society, it is no longer binding, and females may appear with or without veils as may suit their taste or convenience. But the point is, that as Paul gives instructions for women to pray and prophesy with their heads covered, he cannot be understood as forbidding them to pray and prophesy under any and all circumstances. But what does the apostle mean when he says it is not permitted for women to speak?

It is certain that he does not speak of female teachers or preachers, as such, for he comprehends the entire membership of the church. The twenty-third verse says, "If therefore the whole church be come together into some place, and all speak with tongues," &c. This proves that the apostle is not treating of teachers as officers, as a distinct class, nor of the eligibility of persons to the office [of] teacher, as distinguished from the membership generally, but of the duties, rights and privileges of the membership in common, as members. If, therefore, the text precludes women from speaking in the church as a general rule, it precludes them, not merely as authorized teachers, but from the right of speaking as common or unofficial members of the church.

In view of the numerous and unanswerable proofs that God did employ females, under the Old and New Covenants, as public instrumentalities of spreading truth, all who hold the doctrine of the absolute equality of males and females, under all circumstances, and in all relations, will as a matter of course, regard these two texts as local and specific in their application, founded upon some peculiarity in the circumstances of the community at that time and in those places, and as having no general bearing on the question. It will be much easier for them to believe that there were circumstances, which were then understood, calling for such a rule, thus specific and local in its bearing, and constituting an exception to the general rule, that women had a right to, and did prophesy; than to believe that the facts that they did teach, scattered, as they are, through a period of more than fifteen centuries, are proved by these two texts to be the exceptions to, and in violation of, a positive law of God, the foundation of which he has laid in nature. The simple admission of such numerous and wide spread exceptions to what is claimed to the law of God, having its foundation in nature, must come but little short of nullification.

6.2 THE ARGUMENT FROM PENTECOST

The Holiness tradition stood apart in its affirmation of women as preachers, and Phoebe Palmer's 1859 book, The Promise of the Father, *was a rich source of argument used to defend this departure from the norm. As historians Donald Dayton and Harold Raser claim, the reader encounters in this book the fountainhead of every contemporary biblical, theological, and historical argument made on behalf of equality in Christian ministry.[1] In this selection, Palmer emphasizes her central argument: Pentecost ushered in the era of the Spirit, and both women and men were called by God to prophesy or preach, as predicted in Joel. The churches could not afford to dismiss female preaching at a time when the Spirit was clearly active and humanity was reaching the last days. In other parts of the book Palmer deals with the problem passages of the New Testament, arguing for their reinterpretation. She also cites examples of female preaching throughout history and concludes with numerous accounts of successful female ministry. She does not argue for women's rights or suffrage, but rather is most concerned that Christians prepare for the coming apocalypse.*

Source: Phoebe Palmer. *The Promise of the Father,* 21 26. 1859. Reprint, New York: Garland, 1985.

Did the tongue of fire descend alike upon God's daughters as upon his sons, and was the effect similar in each?

And did all these waiting disciples, who thus, with one accord, continued in prayer, receive the grace for which they supplicated? It was, as we observe, the gift of the Holy Ghost that had been promised. And was this promise of the Father as truly made to the daughters of the Lord Almighty as to his sons? See Joel 2:28, 29. "And it shall come to pass afterward, that I will pour out my Spirit upon all flesh; and your sons and your daughters shall prophesy, your old men shall dream dreams, your young men shall see visions. And also upon the servants and upon the handmaids in those days will I pour out my Spirit." When the Spirit was poured out in answer to the united prayers of God's sons and daughters, did the tongue of fire descend alike upon the women as upon the men? How emphatic is the answer to this question! "And there appeared unto them cloven tongues, like as of fire, and it sat upon *each of them*." Was the effect similar upon God's daughters as upon his sons? Mark it, O ye who have restrained the workings of this gift of power in the church. "And they were *all* filled with the Holy Ghost, and began to speak as the Spirit gave utterance." Doubtless it was a well nigh impelling power, which was thus poured out upon these sons and daughters of the Lord Almighty, moving their lips to most earnest, persuasive, convincing utterances. Not alone only did Peter proclaim a crucified risen Saviour, but each one, as the Spirit gave utterance, assisted in spreading the good news; and the result of these united ministrations of the Spirit, through human agency, was, that three thousand were, in one day, pricked to the heart. Unquestionably, the whole of this newly-baptized company of one hundred and twenty disciples, male and female, hastened in every direction, under the mighty constrainings of that perfect love that casteth out fear, and great was the company of them that believed.

And now, in the name of the Head of the church, let us ask, Was it designed that these demonstrations of power should cease with the day of Pentecost? If the Spirit of prophecy fell upon God's daughters, alike as upon his sons in that day, and they spake in the midst of that assembled multitude, as the Spirit gave utterance, on what authority do the angels of the churches restrain the use of that gift now? Has the minister of Christ, now reading these lines, never encouraged open female testimony, in the charge which he represents? Let us ask, What account will you render to the Head of the church, for restricting the use of this endowment of power? Who can tell how wonderful the achievements of the cross might have been, if this gift of prophecy, in woman, had continued in use, as in apostolic days? Who can tell but long since the gospel might have been preached to every creature? Evidently this was a *speciality* of the last days, as set forth by the prophecy of Joel. Under the old dispensation, though there was a Miriam, a Deborah, a Huldah, and an Anna, who were prophetesses, the special outpouring of the Spirit upon God's daughters as upon his sons, seems to have been reserved as a characteristic of the last days. This, says Peter, as the wondering multitude beheld these extraordinary endowments of the Spirit, falling alike on all the disciples,—this is that which was spoken by the prophet Joel, "And also upon my servants and upon my handmaidens will I pour out my Spirit."

And this gift of prophecy, bestowed upon all, was continued and recognized in all the early ages of Christianity. The ministry of the Word was not confined to the apostles. No, they had a laity for the times. When, by the cruel persecutions of Saul, all the infant church were driven away from Jerusalem, *except the apostles*, these scattered men and women of the laity "went every where *preaching the word*," that is, proclaiming a crucified, risen Saviour. And the effect was, that the enemies of the cross, by scattering these men and women, who had been saved by its virtues, were made subservient to the yet more extensive proclamation of saving grace.

Impelled by the indwelling power within, these Spirit-baptized men and women, driven by the fury of the enemy in cruel haste from place to place, made all their scatterings the occasion of preaching the gospel every where, and believers were every where multiplied, and *daily* were there added to the church such as should be saved.

Says the Rev. Dr. Taft, "If the nature of society, its good and prosperity, in which women are jointly and equally concerned with men, if, in *many cases*, their fitness and capacity for instructors being admitted to be equal to the other sex, be not reasons sufficient to convince the candid reader of woman's teaching and preaching, because of two texts in Paul's Epistles, (I Cor. 14:34; I Tim. 2:12), let him consult the paraphrase of Locke, where he has proved to a demonstration that the apostle, in these texts, never intended to prohibit women from praying and preaching in the church,

provided they were dressed as became women professing godliness, and were qualified for the sacred office. Nor is it likely that he would, in one part of his Epistle, give directions how a woman, as well as a man, should pray and prophesy in public, and presently after, in the very same Epistle, forbid women, endowed with the gifts of prayer and prophecy, from speaking in the church, when, according to his own explication of prophecy, it is 'speaking unto others for edification, exhortation, and comfort.' Besides, the apostle, in this Epistle to the church at Corinth, says, 'Follow after charity, and desire spiritual gifts, but rather that ye may prophesy.' Again, 'I would that ye all spake with tongues, but rather that ye prophesied.' Here the apostle speaks to the church in general; and the word *all* must comprehend every individual member; and since he had just before given directions about a woman's praying and prophesying, we conclude that his desire extended to women as well as to men. Certainly the word *all* includes both men and women; otherwise the mind of Paul, 'who was made a minister of the Spirit,' would have been more narrow than that of Moses, who was only a minister of the *law*; for when Joshua came and told Moses that Eldad and Medad prophesied in the camp, and desired him to forbid them, Moses said unto him, 'Enviest thou for my sake? Would God that all the Lord's people were prophets, and that he would put his Spirit upon them.' Now, all the Lord's people must certainly comprehend the

Miriams and Deborahs in the camp, as well as the Eldads and Medads."

Dr. Clarke says, (Rom.xvi.12,) "'Salute Tryphena and Tryphosa, who labored in the Lord. Salute the beloved Persis, who labored much in the Lord'—two holy women, who, it seems, were assistants to the apostle in his work, probably by exhorting, visiting the sick, &c. Persis was another woman, who, it seems, excelled the preceding; for of her it is said, she *labored much in the Lord*. We learn from this, that Christian *women*, as well as *men*, labored in the ministry of the word. In those times of simplicity, all persons, whether men or women, who had received the knowledge of the truth, believed it to be their duty to propagate it to the utmost of their power.

"Many have spent much useless labor in endeavoring to prove that these women did not *preach*. That there were some *prophetesses*, as well as *prophets*, in the Christian church, we learn; and that *woman* might pray or prophesy, provided she had her head covered, we know; and that whoever prophesied, spoke unto others to edification, exhortation, and comfort, St. Paul declares, 1 Cor. 14:3. That no preacher can do more, every person must acknowledge; because to edify, exhort, and comfort, are the prime ends of the gospel ministry. If women thus prophesied, then women preached."

Note to Reading 6.2

1. Donald W. Dayton, *Discovering an Evangelical Heritage* (New York: Harper and Row, 1976), 96; and Harold E. Raser, "'Your Daughters Shall Prophesy': Phoebe Palmer's *The Promise of the Father* (1859)—A Manifesto for Equality in Christian Ministry." Address delivered at Nazarene Theological Seminary, March 2003. See www.wynkoopcenter.org/Academic/Essays/Daughters_Prophesy/daughters_prophesy.html.

6.3 AMANDA SMITH'S CALL TO PREACH

Amanda Berry Smith (1837–1915), evangelist and missionary, occupies a position of preeminence among African American female preachers. Embracing the Holiness movement and experiencing entire sanctification, she began her preaching ministry in 1869. Nine years later she left for a decade of missionary work in England, India, and Monrovia. In this selection from her autobiography, she receives a clear call from God to preach in Salem, New Jersey; she receives this call while worshiping in the Fleet Street African Methodist Epicopal (A.M.E.) Church in Brooklyn. She is wearied by the local male A.M.E. preachers who question the validity of her call, discouraged by physical deprivation, and plagued by doubts about her ability to accomplish her task. God, however, provides her with a message and the strength to deliver it. The result is a dramatic two-week revival that restores her confidence.

Source: Amanda Smith. *An Autobiography: The Story of the Lord's Dealings with Mrs. Amanda Smith the Colored Evangelist*, 147–48, 152–59. New York: Oxford University Press, 1988.

We went early, and went into the Sabbath School. At the close of the Sabbath School the children sang a very pretty piece. I do not remember what it was, but the spirit of the Lord touched my heart and I was blessed. My bad feelings had gone for a few moments, and I thought, "I guess the Lord wanted to bless me here." But when we went upstairs I began to feel the same burden and pressure as I had before. And I said, "Oh, Lord, help me, and teach me what this means." And just at that point the Tempter came with this supposition: "Now, if you are wholly sanctified, why is it that you have these dull feelings?"

I began to examine my work, my life, every day, and I could see nothing. Then I said, "Lord, help me to understand what Thou meanest. I want to hear Thee speak."

Brother Gould, then pastor of the Fleet Street Church, took his text. I was sitting with my eyes closed in silent prayer to God, and after he had been preaching about ten minutes, as I opened my eyes, just over his head I seemed to see a beautiful star, and as I looked at it, it seemed to form into the shape of a large white tulip; and I said, "Lord, is that what you want me to see? If so, what else?" And then I leaned back and closed my eyes. Just then I saw a large letter "G," and I said: "Lord, do you want me to read in Genesis, or in Galatians? Lord, what does this mean?" Just then I saw the letter "O." I said, "Why, that means go." And I said "What else?" And a voice distinctly said to me "Go preach." The voice was so audible that it frightened me for a moment, and I said, "Oh, Lord, is that what you wanted me to come here for? Why did you not tell

me when I was at home, or when I was on my knees praying?" But His paths are known in the mighty deep, and His ways are past finding out. On Monday morning, about four o'clock, I think, I was awakened by the presentation of a beautiful, white cross—white as the driven snow—similar to that described in the last chapter. It was as cold as marble. It was laid just on my forehead and on my breast. It seemed very heavy; to press me down. The weight and the coldness of it were what woke me; and as I woke I said: "Lord, I know what that is[.] It is a cross."

I arose and got on my knees, and while I was praying these words came to me: "If any man will come after Me let him deny himself and take up his cross and follow Me." And I said, "Lord, help me and I will. . . ."

I had all the work I could do, and more, at one dollar and twenty-five cents to two dollars a day, until October 1870, when I left my home at God's command, and began my evangelistic work. I did not know then that it meant all that it has been. I thought it was only to go to Salem, as the Lord had showed me. Shortly after this I was off to Salem. Got as far as Philadelphia, where I purposed leaving my little girl with her grandfather, while I went on to Salem. But strange to say, notwithstanding all the light, and clear, definite leading of the Lord, my heart seemed to fail me. I said to myself, "After all, to go on to Salem, a stranger, where I don't know a minister, or anybody. No, I will do some work here in Philadelphia."

So I got some tracts, went away down in the lower part of town, on St. Mary's street, and Sixth, and Lombard, and all in that region. I went into saloons and gave tracts; gave tracts to people on the corners; spoke a word here and there; some laughed and sneered; some took a tract. Then I went to the meetings, and sang and prayed and exhorted. I went about among the sick, and did all I could. And I said, "After all, the Lord may not want me to go to Salem."

After spending a week in Philadelphia I thought I would go home. Friday came, and I thought to myself, "Well, I will go home Saturday." But, Oh! there came such an awful horror and darkness over me. On Friday night, after I had come home from an excellent meeting, I could not sleep, all night. Oh! how I was troubled. I did not know what to do, for I had spent all my money; father did not have much means, and when Mazie and I were at home I generally provided, not only for ourselves, but for all the family; so that my means went almost before I knew it; I had not much, anyhow. But it seemed to me I would die. So I told the Lord if He would spare me till morning, though I had not any money, I would go and see my sister, and if she could lend me a dollar so as to get on to Salem, I would go.

Saturday morning came. I borrowed a dollar, came home, and spent twenty-five cents of it for breakfast; then with what it cost me to ride down to get on the boat, in all about fifteen cents, I had left about sixty cents. My ticket on the boat was fifty cents; I had had some little hymns struck off; we colored people were very fond of ballads for singing.

A little while after I got on the boat, who should come in but Brother Holland, who used to be my pastor eight years before, in Lancaster, Pa. All this had come to pass in the years after I had known him; so that he did not know anything at all about it. He was very glad to see me, and asked me where I was going. I told him the Lord had sent me to Salem. Then I began to tell him my story. How the Lord had led me. How He had called me to His work. Dear old man, he listened to me patiently, and when I had got through he said:

"Well, Sister Smith, you know I don't believe in women preaching. But still, honey, I have got nothing to say about you. You go on. The Lord bless you."

I was dumbfounded; for I thought he was in the greatest sympathy with woman's work, though I had never heard him express himself with regard to it. But I was glad of the latter part of what he said.

It was quite a cool day, and the boat got in about two o'clock in the afternoon. There were no street cars then, as there are now. There was a big omnibus. They didn't let colored people ride inside an omnibus in those days. So I took my carpet bag and had to sit outside on the top of the omnibus.

They didn't let colored people off till all the white people were off, even if they had to go past where they wanted to stop;

so I had to ride round on the omnibus at least three-quarters of an hour before I was taken to where I wanted to go.

The woman's name, where I had been told to go, was Mrs. Curtis. She was a widow, and owned her own house and grounds; she had quite a nice, comfortable little house. But she was a queer genius. Old Father Lewis, who had once been pastor of the A.M.E. Church at Salem, and at this time was pastor of the church at Jersey City Heights, N.J., had recommended me to Sister Curtis, because she was alone and had plenty of room, and he thought it would be so nice for me. It was more than a half mile from the locality in which the colored church was situated, and in which the majority of the colored people lived. But Sister Curtis seemed as though she was frightened at me. I told her who had sent me to her house, and how the Lord had called me to His work, and all my story of the Lord's doing. She listened, but was very nervous. Then she said she didn't know what in the world she would do, for she hadn't anything but some hard bread to give me to eat, and she hadn't any sugar; and I said, "Well, no matter for that. I can eat hard bread, and I can drink tea without sugar, if you can only accommodate me till Monday, at least."

Well, she said she could keep me all night, but she didn't like to leave any one in the house on Monday, because she generally went away to wash; and she generally had the cold pieces given her from the hotel where she went to wash

dishes, and that was all she could give me to eat.

She knew how we colored people are about eating; we do like to eat; so I think she told me that thinking she would frighten me; but I agreed to everything. Then I asked her if she could tell me where Brother Cooper, who was then pastor, lived. She said, "Yes, it is about a mile and a half."

I asked her if she would show me which way to go. She did so, but did not give me anything to eat. I was very hungry, but I did not ask her for anything. So I started off about three o'clock, or a little after, and went to see Brother Cooper.

I was tired, and walked slowly, and it was about half-past four when I got up to the little village above. I inquired my way, and was told that Sister Johnson lived right close by Brother Cooper's, and if I would go to her house she could tell me, for it was just through her yard to Brother Cooper's house. So I went. I knocked at the door. The sister was in; several nice looking little children were playing around, and an elegant pot of cabbage was boiling over the fire. My! how nice it did smell; and I did wish and pray that the Lord would put it into her heart to ask me to have something to eat. I hinted all I knew how, but she did not take the hint. I knew by the sound of it that it was done and ought to come off!

I told her my story; told her about Brother Lewis; she was very glad to hear from him. I asked her if I could stay all night, because I felt so tired that I thought I could not walk back to Sister Curtis'. She said at once she could not possibly have me stay all night. Her mother had been dead about three months, and she had taken down the bedsteads, and she was so overburdened with her grief she had never put them up, and they were all lying on the floor.

I told her no matter for that; I could sleep on the floor just as well. No, she did not have room. She could not possibly do it.

Well, I stayed till it was pretty dark[.] It was after six o'clock. The more I talked the more she gave me to see that she was not going to ask me to have any cabbage, or to stay all night.

So I said to her, "Will you tell me where Brother Cooper, the minister, lives?"

"Oh, yes," she said, "I will send one of the children with you."

When I got to Brother Cooper's I knocked, and Brother Cooper came to the door; he was an awful timid man; so he stood at the door, holding it half open and leaning out a little ways, and asked me who I was. I told him that I was Amanda Smith; that the Lord sent me to Salem. Then I went on, standing at the door, telling him how the Lord had led me, and all about it. His wife, who was a little more thoughtful than he, heard me, and she called out to him, and said, "Cooper, why don't you ask the sister to come in." So then he said, "Come in, Sister."

I was awful glad, so I went in. Sister Cooper was getting supper. The table

was set, and I thought, "Maybe, I will get something to eat now."

So I went on and finished my story, and they seemed to be greatly interested; and when the supper was quite ready, she said, "Will you have some supper, Sister Smith?" I thanked her, and told her I would.

While I was eating my supper who should come in but good Brother Holland, that had been on the boat. He said to Brother and Sister Cooper, "I am glad you have Sister Smith here. You needn't be afraid of her, she is all right; I have known her for years. I have not seen her since I was pastor at Lancaster."

Then they brightened up a little bit, and seemed to be a little more natural. My heart was glad. It was quarterly meeting, and Brother Holland was to preach in the morning and Brother Cooper in the afternoon. So Brother Holland said, as he was Presiding Elder, I might speak at night and tell my story[.]

"All right." I said.

After a little talk, Brother Holland left. Sister Cooper said she would be very glad to have me stay all night, but they had no room. They had not been long there, and had only fitted up one room for their own use. They thought they would make out with that for the winter. So then I was obliged to walk a mile and a half back to Sister Curtis'. I did hate to do it, but the Lord helped me.

So I stayed that night at Sister Curtis', and she gave me a little breakfast on Sunday morning, but it was mighty skimpy! But I found out that a good deal of praying fills you up pretty well when you cannot get anything else! On Sunday morning we went to Love Feast, and had a good time. Prior to this I had been asking the Lord to give me a message to give when I went to Salem. I said, "Lord, I don't want to go to Salem without a message. And now you are sending me to Salem, give me the message. What shall I say?"

Two or three times I had gone before the Lord with this prayer, and His word was, "It shall be made known to you when you come to the place what you shall say." And I said, "All right. Lord." So I didn't trouble Him any more till this Sunday morning. The Lord helped Brother Holland preach. When he got through preaching and the collection was taken. Brother Cooper made the announcement that I was there; he said, "There is a lady here, Mrs. Amanda Smith" (he had never seen me before or heard of me, and he was a rather jovial kind of a man, and in making this announcement he said, in a half sarcastic and half joking way), "Mrs. Smith is from New York; she says the Lord sent her"; with a kind of toss of the head, which indicated that he did not much believe it. Oh, my heart fell down, and I said, "Oh! Lord, help. Give me the message."

The Lord saw that I had as much as I could stand up under, and He said, "Say, 'Have ye received the Holy Ghost since ye believed?'" (Acts 9:2). That was the message; the first message the Lord

gave me. I trembled from head to foot.

A good sister took me home with her to dinner. The people all seemed very kind. I felt quite at home when I got with them. We came back in the afternoon and had a wonderful meeting.

At night after Brother Holland had preached a short sermon, he called me up to exhort. As I sat in the pulpit beside him, he saw I was frightened. He leaned over and said, "Now, my child, you needn't be afraid. Lean on the Lord. He will help you."

And He did help me. There was a large congregation. The gallery was full, and every part of the house was packed. I stood up trembling. The cold chills ran over me. My heart seemed to stand still. Oh, it was a night. But the Lord gave me great liberty in speaking. After I had talked a little while the cold chills stopped, my heart began to beat naturally and all fear was gone, and I seemed to lose sight of everybody and everything but my responsibility to God and my duty to the people. The Holy Ghost fell on the people and we had a wonderful time. Souls were convicted and some converted that night. But the meeting did not go on from that.

Thursday night was the regular prayer meeting night. Brother Cooper said I was there, and would preach Thursday night. He was going to give me a chance to preach, and he wanted all the people to come out.

There was no snow, but Oh! it was cold. The ground was frozen. The moon shone brightly, and the wind blew a perfect gale. One good thing, I did not have to go back to Sister Curtis'. Another good sister asked me to her house to stay. She made me very comfortable, but said I would have to be alone most of the day, as she was going to some of the neighbors to help with the butchering, as they do in the country. I was very glad of that, for it gave me a chance to pray. So I fasted and prayed and read my Bible nearly all day. Oh, I had a good time. And then I thought I would visit a neighbor near by, another friend. So I did; and this was a good old mother in Israel. I told her a little of my experience, and then I told her the message the Lord had given me to speak about, and how it would lead to the subject of sanctification.

"My child," she at once said, "don't you say a word about sanctification here. Honey, if you do, they will persecute you to death. My poor husband used to preach that doctrine, and for years he knew about this blessing. But, Oh! honey, they persecuted him to death. You must not say a word about it."

Well, there I was again! So I went home, and the next day I prayed to God all day. I asked Him to give me some other message. If this message was going to do so much damage, I did not want it. But no, the Lord held me to it. Not a ray of light on anything else but that. I didn't know what to do, but I made up my mind it was all I ever would do, so I would obey God and take the consequences. I thought sure from what the dear old mother told me that the results

would be fatal; I didn't know but I would be driven out. But not so. "Obedience is better than sacrifice, and to hearken than the fat of rams." Thursday was a beautiful, bright day; but Oh! cold, bitterly cold. So I got down and prayed and said, "Lord, Thou hast sent me to Salem, and hast given me the message. Now for an evidence that Thou hast indeed sent me, grant to cause the wind to cease blowing at this fearful rate. Thou knowest Lord, that I want people to hear Thy message that Thou hast given me. They will not mind the cold, but the wind is so terrible. Now cause the wind to cease to blow, and make the people come out."

The wind blew all day; all the afternoon. I started to go across the field, about a half mile from where I was, to talk and pray with a friend. On my way back, about five o'clock, as I was crossing a ditch which ran through the field, bordered on either side by a row of hedge trees, and a little plank across it for a kind of a foot bridge, the wind wrapped me round and took me down into the ditch. I could not hold on, could not control myself. I expected to be thrown up against the trees, and I cried out to Him all alone, "Oh! Lord, Thou that didst command the wind to cease on the Sea of Galilee, cause this wind to cease and let me get home."

Just then there came a great calm, and I got up out of that ditch and ran along to the house. By the time we went to church it was as calm as a summer evening; it was cold, but not a bit windy— a beautiful, moonlight night.

The church was packed and crowded. I began my talk from the chapter given, with great trembling. I had gone on but a little ways when I felt the spirit of the Lord come upon me mightily. Oh! how He helped me. My soul was free. The Lord convicted sinners and backsliders and believers for holiness, and when I asked for persons to come to the altar, it was filled in a little while from the gallery and all parts of the house.

A revival broke out, and spread for twenty miles around. Oh! what a time it was. It went from the colored people to the white people. Sometimes we would go into the church at seven o'clock in the evening. I could not preach. The whole lower floor would be covered with seekers—old men, young men, old women, young women, boys and girls. Oh! glory to God! How He put His seal on this first work to encourage my heart and establish my faith, that He indeed had chosen, and ordained and sent me. I do not know as I have ever seen anything to equal that first work, the first seal that God gave to His work at Salem. Some of the young men that were converted are in the ministry. Some have died in the triumph of faith. Others are on the way. I went on two weeks, day and night. We used to stay in the church till one and two o'clock in the morning. People could not work. Some of the young men would hire a wagon and go out in the country ten miles and bring in a load, get them converted, and then take them back.

6.4 PAUL PROHIBITS THE PREACHING OF WOMEN

Nineteenth-century clergyman Cyrus Cort argues that Paul was an outstanding champion of evangelical freedom, yet he clearly opposed preaching by women in gender-mixed assemblies. Paul makes his position clear in 1 Corinthians 14 and 1 Timothy 2. Contradictory passages cited by Cort's opponents could only be construed to support female preaching by violating the meaning of the texts and the integrity of Paul's powers of reasoning.

Source: Cyrus Cort. "Woman Preaching Viewed in the Light of God's Word and Church History." *The Reformed Quarterly Review* 29 (1882): 124–26.

If Christianity was to mark a new departure from the established customs of the Jewish Church on this subject St. Paul would have been pre-eminently the one to enunciate and emphasize the new departure. But where do we find the great Apostle of the Gentiles ranging himself on this question? Not in favor of the right of women to preach or pray in public religious services. On the other hand his epistles furnish the classic passages on the opposite side.

Nothing could be more explicit and emphatic than the teachings of St. Paul on this subject. "Let your women keep silence in the churches; for it is not permitted unto them to speak.... It is a shame for women to speak in the church." "Let the women learn in silence with all subjection. I suffer not a woman to teach or usurp authority over the man but to be in silence" (see I Cor. 14:34, &c. I Tim. 2:11, &c.). We could not prohibit women from preaching in language more plain and positive than that here employed by the Apostle Paul.

He positively forbids women from preaching or speaking in public promiscuous assemblies of the church. If we believe in the inspiration of St. Paul and that the New Testament must be taken as our infallible guide in matters of Christian faith and practice we must oppose woman preaching as a dangerous innovation. Few have the hardihood to call in question the plain meaning of the passages just quoted as they stand by themselves and in their connexion. But there are some professing Christians who try to break the force of these passages by quoting others, which they suppose relate to the same subject. They violate fundamental rules of scriptural interpretation and throw discredit upon the Apostolic teaching by striving to prove that St. Paul allows in one place what he repeatedly forbids in other places. Distinct and positive passages must always rule the meaning of passages that are vague, indirect and doubtful in their meaning and application.

Thus when Paul tells us in the eleventh chapter of First Corinthians that "every woman that prayeth or prophesieth with her head uncovered dishonoreth her head," we are not to infer as some do that Paul admits the right of woman to pray and prophesy or preach provided she has proper covering for her head. If that were a correct and neces-

sary inference then St. Paul would flatly contradict, in the fourteenth chapter of this epistle, what he taught or permitted in the eleventh, and the whole question would be involved in confusion.

Paul was not so careless or unsound a reasoner as that. His writings, on this point especially, are in all respects logical and consistent. If we read the eleventh chapter carefully we will see that he nowhere teaches or admits that it is right and proper for woman to pray or prophesy in public promiscuous assemblies either with or without a veil or covering to her head. He says that even nature teaches that it is unbecoming for her to pray or prophesy with uncovered head, but he does not say or admit that she has a right to pray or prophesy at all in the church. He is there discussing more particularly the matter of dress and the relation of the sexes and not the matter of preaching itself. It was an utter violation of the rules of modesty and female subordination for a woman to pray or prophesy publicly in that manner. Afterwards in the fourteenth chapter, when he comes to the subject of preaching itself and the conduct of public worship, he emphatically forbids woman to speak in the church at all, and declares in the next verse that "It is a shame for woman to speak in the church."

Calvin compares I Cor. 11:4, with I Cor. 14:34, &c., and significantly remarks *apostolus unum improbando alterum non probat*. In condemning the one thing the Apostle does not approve of the other. In censuring particularly the form and manner of the act he does not thereby necessarily say or admit that the act itself would be right and proper under any circumstances. For instance, a minister might say that it is very unbecoming for a set of men or boys to come stalking along the church aisle engaged in boisterous conversation with their hats on during divine service. By such a remark he would not admit that it would be right and proper for them to engage in such conversation with their hats off. So St. Paul, in condemning women for praying and preaching with uncovered head, does not admit their right to pray or preach at all in promiscuous assemblies.

The passage in the eleventh chapter does not contradict or modify the emphatic and distinct deliverance in the fourteenth chapter.

6.5 WOMEN RE-VISION THE BIBLE

Toward the end of her life, Elizabeth Cady Stanton (1815–1902) came to believe that the Bible was the greatest obstacle to women's rights in America. In response she organized a committee of learned women to write commentaries on those portions of the Bible that deal with women. The result was The Woman's Bible, *published in two parts in 1895 and 1898. The commentaries draw attention to the patriarchal character of much of the material while appropriating some of it for feminism. Both commentaries below are from the*

pen of Stanton. Vashti is presented to the reader as a "grand type of woman" who valued her dignity and modesty above obedience to her husband. The thoughts on Jesus' parable of the wise and foolish virgins reject the traditional tendency to see this as a story about eternal salvation and final judgment in favor of the claim that foolish virgins are women who have failed to develop their own minds and spirits.

Source: *The Woman's Bible,* edited by Elizabeth Cady Stanton, Part 2:84–86, 123–26. Reprint. Edinburgh: Polygon, 1985.

Comments on Esther

The kingdom of Ahasuerus extended from India to Ethiopia, consisting of one hundred and twenty-seven provinces, an overgrown kingdom which in time sunk by its own weight. The king was fond of display and invited subjects from all his provinces to come by turns to behold his magnificent palaces and sumptuous entertainments.

He gave two great feasts in the beginning of his reign, one to the nobles and the princes, and one to the people, which lasted over a hundred days. The king had the feast for the men spread in the court under the trees. Vashti entertained her guests in the great hall of the palace. It was not the custom among the Persians for the sexes to eat promiscuously together, especially when the king and the princes were partaking freely of wine.

This feast ended in heaviness, not as Balshazzar's with a handwriting on the wall, nor like that of Job's children with a wind from the wilderness, but by the folly of the king, with an unhappy falling out between the queen and himself, which ended the feast abruptly and sent the guests away silent and ashamed. He sent seven different messages to Vashti to put on her royal crown, which greatly enhanced her beauty, and come to show his guests the majesty of his queen. But to all the chamberlains alike she said, "Go tell the king I will not come; dignity and modesty alike forbid."

This vanity of a drunken man illustrates the truth of an old proverb, "When the wine is in, the wit is out." Josephus says that all the court heard his command; hence, while he was showing the glory of his court, he also showed that he had a wife who would do as she pleased.

Besides seven chamberlains he had seven learned counsellors whom he consulted on all the affairs of State. The day after the feast, when all were sober once more, they held a cabinet council to discuss a proper punishment for the rebellious queen. Memucan, Secretary of State, advised that she be divorced for her disobedience and ordered "to come no more before the king," for unless she was severely punished, he said, all the women of Medea and of Persia would despise the commands of their husbands.

We have some grand types of women presented for our admiration in the Bible. Deborah for her courage and military prowess; Huldah for her learning, prophetic insight and statesmanship,

seated in the college in Jerusalem, where Josiah the king sent his cabinet ministers to consult her as to the policy of his government; Esther, who ruled as well as reigned, and Vashti, who scorned the Apostle's command, "Wives, obey your husbands." She refused the king's orders to grace with her presence his revelling court. Tennyson pays this tribute to her virtue and dignity:

> "Oh, Vashti! noble Vashti!
> Summoned forth, she kept her state,
> And left the drunken king to brawl
> In Shushan underneath his palms. . . ."

Comments on Matthew

In this chapter we have the duty of self-development impressively and repeatedly urged in the form of parables, addressed alike to man and to woman. The sin of neglecting and of burying one's talents, capacities and powers, and the penalties which such a course involve, are here strikingly portrayed.

This parable is found among the Jewish records substantially the same as in our own Scriptures. Their weddings were generally celebrated at night; yet they usually began at the rising of the evening star; but in this case there was a more than ordinary delay. Adam Clarke in his commentaries explains this parable as referring chiefly to spiritual gifts and the religious life. He makes the Lord of Hosts the bridegroom, the judgment day the wedding feast, the foolish virgins the sinners whose hearts were cold and dead, devoid of all spiritual graces, and unfit to enter the kingdom of heaven. The wise virgins were the saints who were ready for translation, or for the bridal procession. They followed to the wedding feast; and when the chosen had entered *"the door was shut."*

This strikes us as a strained interpretation of a very simple parable, which, considered in connection with the other parables, seems to apply much more closely to this life than to that which is to come, to the intellectual and the moral nature, and to the whole round of human duties. It fairly describes the two classes which help to make up society in general. The one who, like the foolish virgins, have never learned the first important duty of cultivating their own individual powers, using the talents given to them, and keeping their own lamps trimmed and burning. The idea of being a helpmeet to somebody else has been so sedulously drilled into most women that an individual life, aim, purpose and ambition are never taken into consideration. They ofttimes do so much in other directions that they neglect the most vital duties to themselves.

We may find in this simple parable a lesson for the cultivation of courage and of self-reliance. These virgins are summoned to the discharge of an important duty at midnight, alone, in darkness, and in solitude. No chivalrous gentleman is there to run for oil and to trim their lamps. They must depend on themselves, unsupported, and pay the penalty of their own improvidence and unwisdom. Perhaps in that bridal procession might have been seen fathers, brothers, friends, for whose service and amusement the foolish virgins had wasted many precious hours, when they should have been trimming their own lamps and keeping oil in their vessels.

And now, with music, banners, lanterns, torches, guns and rockets fired at intervals, come the bride and the groom, with their attendants and friends numbering thousands, brilliant in jewels, gold and silver, magnificently mounted on richly caparisoned horses—for nothing can be more brilliant than were those nuptial solemnities of Eastern nations. As this spectacle, grand beyond description, sweeps by, imagine the foolish virgins pushed aside, in the shadow of some tall edifice, with dark, empty lamps in their hands, unnoticed and unknown. And while the castle walls resound with music and merriment, and the lights from every window stream out far into the darkness, no kind friends gather round them to sympathize in their humiliation, nor to cheer their loneliness. It matters little that women may be ignorant, dependent, unprepared for trial and for temptation. Alone they must meet the terrible emergencies of life, to be sustained and protected amid danger and death by their own courage, skill and self-reliance, or perish.

Woman's devotion to the comfort, the education, the success of men in general, and to their plans and projects, is in a great measure due to her self-abnegation and self-sacrifice having been so long and so sweetly lauded by poets, philosophers and priests as the acme of human goodness and glory.

Now, to my mind, there is nothing commendable in the action of young women who go about begging funds to educate young men for the ministry, while they and the majority of their sex are too poor to educate themselves, and if able, are still denied admittance into some of the leading institutions of learning throughout our land. It is not commendable for women to get up fairs and donation parties for churches in which the gifted of their sex may neither pray, preach, share in the offices and honors, nor have a voice in the business affairs, creeds and discipline, and from whose altars come forth Biblical interpretations in favor of woman's subjection.

It is not commendable for the women of this Republic to expend much enthusiasm on political parries as now organized, nor in national celebrations, for they have as yet no lot or part in the great experiment of self-government.

In their ignorance, women sacrifice themselves to educate the men of their households, and to make of themselves ladders by which their husbands, brothers and sons climb up into the kingdom of knowledge, while they themselves are shut out from all intellectual companionship, even with those they love best; such are indeed like the foolish virgins. They have not kept their own lamps trimmed and burning; they have no oil in their vessels, no resources in themselves; they bring no light to their households nor to the circle in which they move;

and when the bridegroom cometh, when the philosopher, the scientist, the saint, the scholar, the great and the learned, all come together to celebrate the marriage feast of science and religion, the foolish virgins, though present, are practically shut out; for what know they of the grand themes which inspire each tongue and kindle every thought? Even the brothers and the sons whom they have educated, now rise to heights which they cannot reach, span distances which they cannot comprehend.

The solitude of ignorance, oh, who can measure its misery!

The wise virgins are they who keep their lamps trimmed, who burn oil in their vessels for their own use, who have improved every advantage for their education, secured a healthy, happy, complete development, and entered all the profitable avenues of labor, for self-support, so that when the opportunities and the responsibilities of life come, they may be fitted fully to enjoy the one and ably to discharge the other.

These are the women who to-day are close upon the heels of man in the whole realm of thought, in art, in science, in literature and in government. With telescopic vision they explore the starry firmament, and bring back the history of the planetary world. With chart and compass they pilot ships across the mighty deep, and with skilful fingers send electric messages around the world. In galleries of art, the grandeur of nature and the greatness of humanity are immortalized by them on canvas, and by their inspired touch, dull blocks of marble are transformed into angels of light. In music they speak again the language of Mendelssohn, of Beethoven, of Chopin, of Schumann, and are worthy interpreters of their great souls. The poetry and the novels of the century are theirs; they, too, have touched the key-note of reform in religion, in politics and in social life. They fill the editors' and the professors' chairs, plead at the bar of justice, walk the wards of the hospital, and speak from the pulpit and the platform.

Such is the widespread preparation for the marriage feast of science and religion; such is the type of womanhood which the bridegroom of an enlightened public sentiment welcomes to-day; and such is the triumph of the wise virgins over the folly, the ignorance and the degradation of the past as in grand procession they enter the temple of knowledge, and *the door is no longer shut.*

Mary Baker Eddy (1821–1910)
Photo courtesy of The Mary Baker Eddy Collection. Used by permission.

Chapter 7

AMERICAN WOMEN IN CATHOLICISM AND SECTARIANISM

THE HISTORY OF WOMEN IN AMERICAN CATHOLICISM

Roman Catholics were viewed with suspicion in most of the American colonies in the seventeenth and eighteenth centuries. Opportunities for free worship were restricted, and Catholic believers made up only a very small percentage of the American population. American Catholic and French Catholic support for the American Revolution, plus the new republic's promise of freedom of religion, created a new social climate for the Catholic Church at the beginning of the nineteenth century. The century became one of rapid expansion for the church as it developed a hierarchy of bishops and archbishops, opened schools, and published newspapers. Its membership also grew dramatically as a result of waves of immigrants coming from Europe. At the same time, American Catholicism faced major challenges, including continued hostility from some American Protestants, a need to keep the faith alive on the frontier and in the swelling cities, and a new culture that sometimes clashed with a religion shaped in medieval Europe.

Until recently, the role of women in American Catholic history was largely ignored by historians who surveyed either American religion in general or Catholicism in particular. Attempts to incorporate Catholic women into historical studies were limited often to outstanding women who established religious orders in America. Historians, however, are now exploring the impact women have made on the definition, preservation, and adaptation of Catholicism to the complex environment of nineteenth-century America.[1] What has become apparent is that despite their exclusion from the church's hierarchy, Catholic women, lay and religious, carved out independent and significant avenues for service. Many scholars are now studying Catholic sisters, asking questions about their self-perception, their work, and their relationship to society outside the convent walls.[2] Others consider the efforts of lay women as writers and reformers. Still others are exploring the church's official attitudes toward women and women's issues and are raising the question of whether women really shaped their lives accordingly.[3] It is this disconnect between the rhetoric of the Catholic hierarchy and the reality of the lives of women that forms a major theme in the story of the American Catholic Church.

The Cult of True Womanhood: Ideology and Reality

The cult of true womanhood was reflected as much in Catholic views of women as in those of white American Protestants, and Catholic leaders clung to the ideal long after Protestants relinquished it.[4] This ideal was a familiar and acceptable cluster of ideas for Catholic clergy and lay people, and the church continued to endorse it through much of the twentieth century. Both church tradition and the Bible taught that women were to be submissive and domestic. The figure of the Virgin Mary confirmed these characteristics and reinforced the Victorian ideal of women as morally pure, sexless creatures who bring redemption to the sinful world. But some historians also suggest that Irish immigrants in domestic service to Protestant families passed along the ideal to Irish-American relatives who subsequently moved into the middle class and the priesthood.[5] Catholic women were called upon in novels, sermons, and devotional literature to be submissive wives and mothers who could be "regal" and "heroic" in their own sphere but who would endanger civilization and thwart the purposes of God by seeking jobs or the vote or equality with men. Submission and household tasks were the lot even of Catholic sisters and nuns who were expected in some instances to do laundry for nearby priests. Yet while these ideals certainly infused Catholic teaching and behavior, the reality of women's lives often presented a very different picture. Some women lived by the ideals, some challenged or ignored them, and some used them for their own ends, turning the "true woman" into the "new woman" in the decades after the Civil War.

Catholic ideas on the education of women reflected the popular ideal of true womanhood. Mary, the mother of Jesus, was the role model women were encouraged to imitate. She was wife and mother and had no need for academic training. Consequently, many Catholic leaders claimed that the knowledge that came from newspapers and books was unbecoming to a woman. This argument was modified by a significant number of lay and clerical voices urging that women be given "special education" in order to make them better wives and mothers. A curriculum tailored to woman's role and nature was approved for the institutions of higher education that began to appear. Any advanced schooling given to women was to concentrate on teaching them modesty along with domestic and child rearing skills. The female academies, however, became places that nurtured self-confidence along with literacy and knowledge. It was from them that women launched careers as novelists, for example, using their works to promote Catholicism and true womanhood while simultaneously defying the latter through strong female characters and their own career aspirations.[6]

The Catholic adoption of Victorian true womanhood also provided the framework in which the movement for women's suffrage and employment outside the home was regarded. Many of the clergy believed that suffrage would undermine the family and civilization. The bishop of Colorado, Joseph Machebeouf, dismissed the suffragists as "old maids" who had been disappointed in love. Other Catholic leaders regarded suffrage as an "unspiritual abnormality" that would tear woman from her pedestal and leave her stained and bleeding in the dirty world of politics. The National American Woman Suffrage Association in 1900 could count on the support of only six Catholic clergymen. There is also some evidence that the message of the clergy was taken seriously by lay men and women. Only one officer of the women's suffrage association was Catholic and very few became involved in feminist organizations generally. Studies have been conducted showing that in the Massachusetts referendum on suffrage in 1895, the Catholic sections of the state were overwhelmingly against the right of women to vote.

Yet the Catholic relationship to suffrage was complex. While not deviating from popular Victorian views on the special nature and function of women, a few Catholic leaders defended suffrage. Bishop John Spaulding in 1884, for example, believed that pious and pure women could use their votes to elevate American society. The Catholic women's suffrage groups, which sprang up late in the movement, believed that women could use their political power to protect working women and to ensure a moral society, among other things.

Not only was a voting and educated woman a danger to society, so also was a woman who was employed outside the home. Such an arrangement violated the divine order that dictated that a woman give herself totally to the well-being of her husband and children. Employment also put women in positions in which their virtue could be compromised. Yet many Catholic women, particularly immigrants of the late nineteenth century, were forced to seek employment away from home out of economic necessity. Some Catholic leaders urged therefore that men should be paid higher wages on which a family could exist, thus making it unnecessary for women to work. The social activist John Ryan campaigned for a minimum wage for workers that would stop employers from hiring women as cheap sources of labor. Other Catholics such as Leonora Barry urged women to join the Knights of Labor in order to advocate for working conditions befitting the purity and sensitivity of women. While very few Catholic leaders approved of women working outside of the home, many conceded by the end of the nineteenth century that since some women were forced to earn a living, employers should be encouraged to make every effort to protect true womanhood. Catholic leaders were also willing to concede that social work, nursing, and teaching could be construed as being within the bounds of the female sphere.

Middle-class Catholic women who became involved in voluntary societies used similar reasoning. Although reform efforts were overwhelmingly Protestant in the nineteenth century, Catholic women were active in temperance and the settlement movement, a movement in which volunteers lived and worked in poor urban areas to provide services such as clubs, art programs, and well-baby clinics. The latter interest grew out of the poverty of large numbers of Catholic immigrants. Women initially were not welcome in the National Catholic Total Abstinence Union, but by the last decade of the century they were joining this organization and the Woman's Christian Temperance Union in significant numbers in order to guard the sanctity of the family.

Eve Lingers On

Although Protestants had not entirely forgotten the image of Eve as the archetypal woman who sins and seduces, American Catholics placed more emphasis on woman as temptress. Even during the colonial period, when women performed important rituals in the home to keep Catholicism alive, the clergy worried that women were prone to sin, including intermarriage and dancing. These concerns continued through the nineteenth century. Women might be the guardians of virtue and morality, but they could just as easily be the perpetuators of sin. Following the example of the church fathers, American bishops warned women against immodest dress and the use of cosmetics. An early twentieth-century article in a Catholic encyclopedia reverted to the tradition of earlier centuries in claiming woman's moral and spiritual inferiority. Girls and boys were segregated in Catholic schools to prevent the "corruption" of young men. Catholic colleges were also strictly segregated until financial necessity prompted some men's schools to become coeducational. A book on pastoral care at the end of the nineteenth century warned priests not to fall victim to the snares of "American Eves" who came to confess their sins.

AMERICAN WOMEN IN RELIGIOUS ORDERS

Female members of religious orders first came to the United States in the early seventeenth century as a part of European efforts to colonize and Christianize North America. Their membership grew to over 90,000 by 1920 and in the 1970s an official Catholic directory listed 450 different women's orders in the United States. For much of the nineteenth century, sisters outnumbered priests and monks, and they provided the only presence of the church in the lives of many ordinary people. Historians have only recently started examining their contribution to American Catholicism and society as a whole, as well as exploring the significance of convent life in the nineteenth century.

As early as the 1630s, women who belonged to religious orders in the French territories of Quebec and Montreal worked as missionaries to the Native Americans and became involved in a wide variety of educational and nursing enterprises. Spanish American sisters also made significant contributions to the education of young women in North America. The convents and the virgin life continued to function for these women much as they did in the early centuries of Christian history—as places of economic security, female autonomy, self-expression, and the nurturing of faith. Juana Inés de la Cruz, for example, found an outlet for her intellectual and literary skills in a Mexican convent, where she produced plays, poetry, and theological works. Such women often endured harsh climates, destructive fires, and hostile European and native neighbors in order to establish their vision of the Christian life in the new territories.

The scope of the projects undertaken by Catholic sisters in the nineteenth century demonstrated that they were largely unaffected by the Victorian advice that frail woman should be passive and protected. The sisters throughout America founded and ran a multitude of social services in an era when new frontier settlements and rapidly growing cities had no organized social services. There is evidence that in many ways the women accomplished more than the male hierarchy. The sisters provided homes for unwed mothers and delinquent girls, cared for the aged and mentally ill, and opened daycare centers. Their service as schoolteachers and as nurses, however, became hallmarks of Catholic concern for others as well as vehicles for better relationships between Protestant and Catholic Americans. The Catholic Church, in short, was faced with a variety of challenges in the nineteenth century, and women in religious orders did a great deal to aid the church in successfully meeting them.

Educational Endeavors

One important challenge to the church was the preservation of the Catholic faith among dislocated families on the frontier or in urban ethnic ghettos. Children particularly had to be reached and taught basic Catholic beliefs, a task increasingly being neglected by parents. The women of the Catholic orders responded to this desperate need by making teaching one of their chief occupations in America. By 1900, they ran and staffed most of the nearly four thousand parochial schools in the country as well as over six hundred girls' academies. Along with basic educational skills, the sisters taught religion and Christian living to the children. Many of the schools were established and run by sisters from Europe who possessed knowledge of some of the best educational theory available.

In addition to teaching Catholicism to children, the church also had to gain popular acceptance in a country that was largely Protestant and hostile to Catholicism. Outbreaks of anti-Catholic sentiment occurred throughout the century, fired by the sermons and speeches of Protestant leaders who feared that the Catholic faith was a danger to true religion and democracy. The Catholic sisters and their convents were often targets of this hostility. Because of their distinctive dress, sisters were easy to spot on the street and frequently, like Mother Caroline Friess, pelted with mud and insulted. American Protestants were threatened by the aura of mystery that surrounded the convent, with its European customs and "undemocratic" authoritarian structure. They also were hostile to the sisters' "unnatural" celibate lifestyle. The popular press churned out a flood of literature attacking convent life, claiming that rape and infanticide went on behind locked doors. Alleged "ex-nuns" were paraded around the country with "true confessions" about the convents. In Baltimore and St. Louis, mobs attacked convent property. Friess describes in her writings the special robes in which the sisters slept in case they had to escape from their building in the middle of the night.

The teaching services of the sisters did much to rid the American public of anti-Catholic feelings. Protestant as well as Catholic children attended the schools, especially in frontier areas, and formed bonds of respect and affection with their instructors. Parents admired the advanced teaching methods of some of the sisters as well as their dedication to their work. In addition to their teaching services, the nursing services of the sisters also played a major role in winning Catholic credibility during the century.

Nursing

Women from religious orders performed important nursing services in private homes, hospitals, and almshouses. Their willingness to nurse people with contagious diseases and their perseverance in working through epidemics of cholera and yellow fever gained them the admiration of the public. During the Civil War they represented one-fifth of the nurses on the battlefield and they were active in the Spanish American War as well. They not only offered healing skills to many war casualties but also provided counseling and friendship.

Sister Bridget Pleets, a member of an American Indian sisterhood, contacted the relatives of dying soldiers who had written their names and addresses on her apron. Mary Ewens, who has written extensively on the American nuns, believes that the Civil War marked a real watershed in the history of American attitudes toward Catholics. Through actual contact with the work of these women, a large segment of the population saw the Catholic faith in a more favorable light.

The Catholic sisters not only aided the church by teaching its doctrine and making it more acceptable to Americans, they also gave the church a firmer footing in America by recognizing that lay people who often assisted the sisters could make important contributions and that ecclesiastical structures had to adapt to new cultural conditions. The rules governing the women's communities in Europe (which were brought over to the United States) were developed during the Middle Ages, when women were viewed as childlike, irresponsible, and in need of constant supervision. Sisters were "cloistered" or shut away from the rest of the world. Their schools and churches were in adjacent buildings and visitors could, with special permission, see the sisters only in a parlor where they were separated by a grill. In America, however, the school or church might be some distance from the convent. Furthermore, sisters from houses without endowments had to earn a living, which was not compatible with austere asceticism. Many of the orders therefore sought to have their constitutions changed or replaced in order to respond to new demands, giving rise to conflicts with motherhouses and especially the clergy in direct positions of authority. In these disputes the sisters were often victorious because the bishops needed their services.

As it did from the early centuries of the church, the religious order offered certain benefits to women that they could not get elsewhere. Although they might not be considered "proto-feminists," the Catholic sisters have been described as the most "liberated" women in nineteenth-century America.[7] While the sisters did not have the political influence and wealth that some of their predecessors had in medieval times, they still enjoyed many opportunities to use their talents. They owned property, held executive positions, and were often encouraged to acquire an advanced education. They enjoyed the support of other women and frequently were treated as friends and colleagues by the bishops and priests with whom they worked. They were obedient to the clergy over them but not servile or passive—if their mission was threatened, they resisted male authority. They undertook meaningful and useful work and were urged to cultivate every personal gift "for the Creator's honor and glory." Like other women, the sisters were not admitted to the ordained offices of the church. Like their predecessors in the virgin life, the benefits they acquired were contingent upon their vow to hide their femaleness under thick layers of black cloth. Like the Protestant "true women," the sisters lived with the expectation that they be submissive, domestic, and maternal. They did, however, represent an attractive alternative to marriage and motherhood for American Catholic women, and some historians suggest that women who had this "extraordinary" alternative were less likely to get involved with organized feminism and the movement for women's rights.[8]

WOMEN AND SECTARIAN CHRISTIANITY

Sectarian religious communities appeared in many locations in America throughout the nineteenth century. The words "sect" and "sectarian" are used not to degrade or ridicule these groups but to indicate that they withdrew or broke away from the religious tradition that dominated America during this period—evangelical Protestant Christianity. It is also helpful to know that the word "sect" comes from the Latin word *sequi*, which means "to follow." Many of the sectarian groups were founded and led by dominant, charismatic personalities who wielded power and who were regarded as divinely inspired by God. In several groups, these leaders were women.

There are probably many reasons that sectarian groups flourished in nineteenth-century America. Certainly they were influenced by the atmosphere of revival excitement of the awakenings. They may have been expressions of alienation on the part of people who could not conform, for whatever reasons, to the economic and social demands of American culture. Often the sectarian groups claimed that the American churches had compromised too much with the world and Satan and had forsaken the true faith.

While the sectarian groups were critical of mainstream Protestant Christianity, they often adopted and accentuated the beliefs of the traditional churches. Some groups, for example, emphasized the possibility that the Christian, through the blessings of the Holy Spirit, could live a perfect or "sanctified" life free from all intentional sin. Others stressed the second coming of Jesus and in some instances claimed that this had already taken place. Almost all of the groups accepted the idea that God continued to reveal new spiritual truth to believers, which necessitated a reinterpretation of the Bible.

In their search for religious transformation, the sects challenged many aspects of American life including widely accepted views on the nature and role of women. Although they reveal at best an ambiguous feminism, they raise the possibility of female leadership, economic equality, new patterns of marriage and family life, and alternative ways of thinking about God.[9] Scholars have been interested in looking at the history of women in these groups along with why such communities may have appealed to women. They are getting a clearer picture of gender roles, concluding that, while the sects offered women more avenues of participation and personal fulfillment than the religious mainstream, men still ruled. Modified patriarchy continued despite female founders and female imagery for God.

There were many sectarian groups in nineteenth-century America and it is possible to refer to only a handful in exploring these questions. Six groups in particular are relevant to our discussion of women in the Christian tradition. Two of these are movements in which members lived together in communes, holding all property in common and having highly regulated lifestyles and beliefs. The Shakers, founded by the Englishwoman Ann Lee at the end of the eighteenth century, spread their celibate and simple lifestyle from Maine to Kentucky in the next several decades. The Oneida Community (also sometimes called the Perfectionists) in Oneida, New York, led by John Humphrey Noyes, was influenced by the prevailing belief that Christians could overcome all intentional sin. Noyes believed that Oneida represented God's kingdom on earth, where selfishness, sexual inequality, tiresome labor, and death itself would be overcome.

The Shakers dwindled in numbers and the Oneida Community disbanded, but three other sectarian groups that began around the same time and developed wealthy and powerful national organizations still flourish today. The charismatic leader Ellen Gould White founded the Seventh-Day Adventists on the basis of her belief that Jesus would come again if worship was conducted on the Jewish Sabbath. Mary Baker Eddy, the architect of Christian Science and the author of *Science and Health*, launched a new sectarian group called the Church of Christ, Scientist, that claimed that the material world,

including pain and disease, was illusory. God (and the human reflection of
the divine image) was the only reality, and a person could be trained to live
on that level of reality only. The Mormons (formally called the Church of
Jesus Christ of Latter-day Saints) believed that through revelations to Joseph
Smith, Christ's true church, established in North America after the resurrection, was being restored.

Finally, there were the Spiritualists who flourished in the middle of the
nineteenth century. Their belief was in the reality of life after death and in
the ability of the living to communicate with the dead through professional
mediums. Although many people were (and continue to be) serious believers
in Spiritualism, the movement did not succeed in building a national organization of any real power.

Challenges to the Victorian Ideal

Both the Shakers and the Oneida Community dramatically altered the Victorian picture of the ideal woman as wife, mother, and keeper of the hearth.
The family was seen as a stumbling block to these two groups since it diverted
the attention and efforts of women and men away from the good of the community. Even before the Shakers were organized into communes, they had
solved this potential problem by adopting a life of celibacy. Lee claimed that
she had received a vision from Jesus revealing to her that the original sin of
Adam and Eve was sexual intercourse to satisfy their animal lusts. The perfect or sinless life therefore was a life without sexual desire or sexual relations.
The Shaker community included both men and women, but celibacy was
strictly enforced through indoctrination and careful regulation of day-to-
day activities. Shaker hymns repeated the message that "By a pois'nous fleshy
nature, this dark world has long been led."[10] Men and women ate at different
tables, worked separately, used separate stairs to their living quarters, and sat
on opposite sides of the room for worship.

John Humphrey Noyes had a different solution to the problem of the traditional family. He rejected celibacy and instead proposed a system of "complex marriage" in which every man in the community was married to every
woman and vice versa. Noyes claimed that sexual relations was a gift from
God that would not disappear in the kingdom but rather would be extended
to include all the saints instead of just one husband given to one wife. This,

he believed, was the meaning of the phrase in Mark 12:25: "they neither marry nor are given in marriage." The leaders of the community regulated the frequency of sexual liaisons between men and women, insisting that they did not condone "free love" and also making sure that no permanent attachments developed. Women, however, did have choice in establishing relationships, and Noyes expressed particular concern that they be sexually satisfied by their partners, unusual in a culture devoted to men's needs and desires. To reduce the chances of pregnancy, Noyes taught a method of birth control in which the male partner could, through discipline, eliminate the ejaculation of sperm during sexual intercourse.

The practice of polygamy by the Mormons was just as radical in terms of restructuring marriage and family life. Between 15 and 20 percent of Mormon men had more than one wife until the practice was officially banned by the church in 1890. Although it was defended as a way to create community solidarity, polygamy was often bitterly opposed by Mormon first wives. Some women, however, came to see clear advantages in the arrangement: they were promised high exaltation in the next world and they acquired status in this life by being married to exemplary male leaders. They also enjoyed practical advantages such as the companionship and support of other wives and, if installed in separate households, economic and emotional independence.

In addition to challenging the Victorian ideal of the family, the Shakers and residents of Oneida also challenged to some extent the idea of male and female occupational spheres. The communities were self-sufficient, producing the products and food necessary for daily life. They were similar to the preindustrial households of colonial America. In both instances, women had useful and productive work to fill their days. In the Shaker villages, there was a traditional division of labor to protect celibacy and maintain efficiency: women generally did the indoor work and men did the heavier outdoor tasks. Although men tended to have more varied and interesting jobs, there was no indication that one type of work was superior to the other. There is also some evidence that men in Shaker communes carded wool and picked fruit, duties normally assigned to women. Child rearing also became a shared responsibility. Orphans and the children of new converts among the Shakers were cared for by a group of adults.

At Oneida, where men and women freely intermingled, women farmed alongside men and men learned to sew. Women shared some of the outdoor and industrial work with men, driving the teams of horses and working in the machine shops. The Oneida Community discouraged the formation of bonds between mothers and children and relegated their care to men and women of the community in a special wing of the house. These arrangements, however, did not mean equality for women. Men at Oneida received better work assignments and education; women did almost all of the housework and were taught only through the primary level of schooling. When children were turned over to the community, mothers lost an important area of power and identity. Noyes believed that women were inferior to men and thus should do work that was supportive and secondary. He did consult an inner circle of women on community issues, but he retained absolute authority among his followers and depended on a group of men to carry out his directives.

Thinking and Speaking about God

Some of the sectarian groups not only altered basic ideas in the cult of true womanhood but also challenged traditional theological concepts. Both Noyes and the Christian Scientist Eddy insisted that God had masculine as well as feminine dimensions or elements. Eddy emphasized that this did not mean that God had male and female physical characteristics, but rather that God included both the masculine attributes of Intelligence and Truth and the feminine quality of Love. In fact, to the created world God was more feminine than masculine, being known primarily through works of love. She encouraged her followers to reflect the divine image by showing both masculine and feminine characteristics.

Shakers and Mormons also deviated from the traditional association of the divine with maleness. Power, or Father, and Holy Mother Wisdom were ways of identifying the male and female elements in the Godhead for Shakers, while some Mormon writings suggest the existence of a Heavenly Mother, spouse to God the Father. Again, these theologies did not necessarily promote the equality of women. Holy Mother Wisdom was dominated and led by God the Father, and she displayed all the characteristics of the ideal Victorian mother. The Heavenly Mother was largely absent from Mormon preaching and theology, relegated to the shadows of Mormon thinking and pointed to only when the community wished to glorify motherhood.

New Opportunities for Participation

Many sectarian groups offered women opportunities for participation and recognition that went beyond what was available to them in traditional Protestant churches. Although Eddy used men to fill administrative positions, she sent women throughout the country to communicate her message. Augusta Stetson was responsible for establishing the enormously prestigious First Church of Christ, Scientist, in New York. Eddy also employed women as practitioners of healing within the movement, and the rituals of worship in Christian Science churches were led by a male and female reader from the congregation. In the end, however, Eddy saw her authoritative position as unique; other women were offered small roles within carefully prescribed limits, and women's leadership was not promoted as an organizational principle.[11]

Because they wished to keep men and women as segregated as possible, the Shakers created a system of dual leadership, which appears, on the surface, to provide for male-female equality. The Shaker ministry that presided over the community was made up of two women and two men. An equal number of Elders and Eldresses supervised the spiritual life of the Shaker "families" (thirty to ninety people) while Deacons and Deaconesses attended to the practical details of communal life. The reality was, however, that while men and women had equal spiritual authority, temporal power was unevenly distributed.[12] Women oversaw the household work of the other women, while the male leadership oversaw the entire community, supervised Shaker agriculture, wrote theology, handled property, and made business decisions. Women did not assume financial roles until 1880 when they could become trustees. The Shakers used the teaching of Lee to justify these arrangements: man is to be first and woman second in the government of the kingdom. Lee herself had authority only because Jesus Christ was absent. Apart from the controversial years of Lucy Wright's tenure as leader of the Shaker ministry, subsequent "First Elders" were men for most of the nineteenth century.

The Spiritualists also availed themselves of the services of women as well as men in their quest for contact with the spiritual world. Women outnumbered men as mediums, appearing on lecture platforms at a time when public speaking by women was almost unheard of. More in line with cultural norms, they also presided over séance circles around dining room tables. Spiritualists in fact accepted nineteenth-century ideas on the nature of women but turned them into a rationale for female participation.[13] Men had strong wills and rationality that could impede spirit communication while the feminine traits of emotion, passivity, and weak intellect did the opposite. Even the delicate constitution of women was positive, giving rise to periods of illness in which the psyche was cleansed and prepared for contact with the dead. Men, however, presided at Spiritualist meetings, ran the newspaper, and organized the conventions. It was their own ideas, and not those of the spirits, that were conveyed from the podium.

The situation of Mormon women in the nineteenth century differed markedly from that of their twentieth-century sisters who were told to stay home and produce babies.[14] Apart from playing a vital role in keeping households going under dangerous and desperate frontier conditions, Mormon women had important religious duties. They performed healings and blessings and voted on proposals brought before their congregations. The Relief Society, established by Joseph Smith, was an organization for women parallel to the male priesthood; it became a powerful agent not only for charity but also for female pride, unity, and self-expression. A product of intelligence and talent, women's publications flourished in the late nineteenth and early twentieth centuries. Their rhetoric was often traditional, but journals such as the *Exponent* presented positive images of women active in politics and the workplace.

In keeping with centuries of Christian tradition, the sectarian groups were prepared to see women as inspired channels for truth from God. Both Lee and Eddy offered new interpretations of traditional Christian concepts, which were regarded as authoritative by their followers. By the early nineteenth century, Shaker theologians were identifying Lee as the Second Coming of the Christ-Spirit, who had completed the work of Jesus; and during the 1830s young women got a voice in the community by communicating their visions and messages from Holy Mother Wisdom and the dead. Ellen Gould White's visions, committed to writing with the assistance of her husband, not only shaped the beliefs of the Seventh-Day Adventists but also guided her followers in matters of health care, diet, and dress.

Women and the Appeal of Sectarian Christianity

Women generally have outnumbered men among those Americans who became involved with sectarian groups. In Christian Science, for example, roughly three women for every man joined, and women outnumbered men six to one as practitioners of healing. Studies of some Shaker communities in the nineteenth century show two female members for every male on average, although women more dramatically outnumbered men in the age bracket of twenty to forty-five years old. Why were women attracted to sectarian Christianity? While the reasons are numerous, complex, and difficult to discern, it is possible that some of them may directly involve women's status in church and society.

Evidence taken from the direct testimonies and experiences of women helps to uncover some of their motivations.[15] Women believed that by joining groups such as the Shakers and Adventists their search for eternal salvation would be ended. The revival spirit also created an atmosphere of intense religious feelings and yearnings, which were satisfied for some women only in sectarianism. Also, contact with other women, especially in the communal sects, seemed to provide some women with a much-needed sense of sisterhood. Testimonies from Shaker women, for example, reveal their intense enjoyment of conversation with women in their own communities and visits and letters from sisters in other locations. Finally, for mothers, both married and widowed, life in a religious community offered the assurance that, should death strike, their children would be cared for and the family unit would not be broken up. Widows and single women also found more immediate benefits in the economic security offered by the commune.

By joining the sectarian groups, however, women may also have been rebelling, consciously and unconsciously, against their status in Protestant culture and churches.[16] This motivation is difficult to document because women were probably reluctant to express outright their distaste for childbirth or sexual intercourse or housekeeping or masculine language for God. Yet we must at least consider the possibility that they were drawn to sectarianism because they were attracted to rituals that included women, symbols that appreciated the feminine, and styles of living in which they could break the bonds of woman's traditional sphere. The sects also represented a way to challenge undesirable values in American culture. One historian has suggested that Victorian women, nurtured in the values of self-sacrifice and relationship, were drawn to groups that rejected the harsh individualism of American society.[17]

Christian Science and Spiritualism may have been particularly attractive to women who were unconsciously dissatisfied with their traditional roles. It is possible that a cluster of ailments known as "hysteria" in the nineteenth century provided women with a way to escape the duties of household management and sexual intercourse. Christian Science may have "cured" some women of their illness by offering them alternative roles as practitioners, readers, and missionaries.[18] There is also evidence from the journals of Christian Scientists that women found answers to their theological dilemmas in a God who did not cause evil.[19] And in Christian Science women healed and empowered themselves as they conformed their minds to the Mind of God.

Spiritualism, in a different kind of way, may have enabled women to deal with their discontent.[20] In a state of trance and under the control of the spirit world, women who were mediums sometimes assumed masculine roles that were denied to them in everyday life, such as swearing sailors or brilliant scholars. They could flaunt sexual conventions in the intimacy of the séance and "give voice to the unutterable" without condemnation since they were not responsible for what was happening.[21] Some scholars suggest that Spiritualism was popular with women because it gave them an alternative to the belief, constructed by men, that eternal damnation awaited the unsaved. A family torn asunder for eternity was a bitter prospect for women who made children and husbands the focus of their lives. Spiritualism, teaching universal salvation and progress after death, promised a reunion in Summerland (the spirit world) where Victorian family joys would continue.

The openness of some sectarian groups to female leadership and participation raises the question of their relationship to the secular women's rights movement. Both Christian Scientists and Seventh-Day Adventists had little interest in feminism, instead stressing change through spiritual transformation. Spiritualism occupied the opposite ground, arguing emphatically that the spirits were directing the construction of a new world order and women's rights would be a part of this.

But the story is more complex when we look at the Shaker, Oneida, and Mormon communities. Only late in the nineteenth century did Shaker women gain equality with men, sharing fully in business decisions and writing theology; it was also only then that the community supported suffrage. This was not only because women had come to outnumber men, but also because progressive thinkers, disillusioned with other utopian groups, joined the Shakers in noticeable numbers. The life that evolved at Oneida under the authority of Noyes embodied many of the values and practices advocated by secular feminism. Women wore a version of the "bloomer" costume, for example, and the women's rights movement was regarded with approval by Noyes' newspapers. Ultimately, however, Noyes and his followers believed that only the rule of God could bring a better life for women.

Given their hostility to contemporary feminism, it is surprising that the Mormons emerge as vocal and active supporters of women's rights in the nineteenth century. With and without the explicit blessing of the church hierarchy, Mormon women used their own publications and organizations to celebrate the lives of women in nontraditional roles and to explain the personal as well as economic benefits of paid employment. They also defined a vigorous political role for women, lobbying for suffrage and celebrating the election of women to local and state office. Their subordination was, then, balanced by certain powers and privileges, but this would change drastically in the twentieth century and beyond, when men would take control of the women's organizations and publications. Women would be pressured to remained at home and have many children.

American Catholicism and sectarianism, movements outside the Protestant mainstream, reveal familiar themes in the history of women in the Christian tradition. The cult of true womanhood was preached by the Catholic hierarchy and educational establishment, while the virgin life continued to offer some women a chance for autonomy and influence in church and society. At the same time, groups on the fringe of the dominant evangelical Protestant denominations expanded the boundaries of the woman's sphere in radical ways. As America moved into the twentieth century, however, women within the established denominations began to seek and assume new positions of leadership and ministry.

Readings for Chapter 7

7.1 CATHOLIC SISTERS AS AMERICA'S EDUCATORS

Born into a wealthy Bavarian family, Mother Caroline Friess (1824–1892) joined the School Sisters of Notre Dame when she was sixteen. The order had been established by Mother Teresa Gerhardinger to engage in the work of parochial education. In 1847, in response to a request from the Redemptorist priests in America, Friess traveled to the United States with a small party of sisters to relieve the urgent need of teachers for German Catholic immigrants. Friess was eventually charged with establishing a motherhouse in Milwaukee and overseeing the order's American missions, which included by the time of her death over two hundred schools. Friess had to contend with a variety of prejudices that impeded the work of the sisters. Their teaching methods and pragmatic curriculum, however, won them praise among Catholic and Protestant parents alike. She also had to confront—and summon her courage to change—the church's requirement that all consecrated virgins be cloistered.

Source: [Sister Dympna.] *Mother Caroline and the School Sisters of Notre Dame in North America.* Vol. I, 36–41, 46–49. Saint Louis: Woodward and Tiernan, 1928.

The months of July and August, 1848, were spent by the sisters in the convent in Baltimore in preparation for their work in the schools, especially in the study of English, for which Father Neumann provided teachers. On the nineteenth of August, Sister Caroline began the work assigned her by Mother Teresa, that of opening new schools and superintending those already established. Taking with her Sister Edmund and three candidates, she proceeded to Philadelphia where she opened St. Peter's School, August 21, 1848. The Redemptorist Fathers, at whose invitation they had come, gave them a cordial welcome and promised the kindly interest and aid of their parishioners. On the opening day one hundred seventy girls were enrolled; the boys numbered one hundred sixty-two. The latter were taught by lay teachers until 1853 when Brothers of the Christian Schools were obtained for them. In the beginning the sisters in St. Peter's School endured many hardships; poverty and even hunger were borne unflinchingly for several weeks. Conditions were such that they were not permitted to wear their religious garb for some time. . . .

This agitation extended from 1834 to 1844 through several dioceses in a most frightful manner, and in Philadelphia resulted in a civil war. Through the pulpit and the press, fanatics spread inflammatory reports about the horrors committed in convents, the tortures nuns are subjected to when they would escape, and many other common calumnies. New England provided a fertile soil for the growth of this noxious weed. The mob of Boston attacked the Ursuline Convent of Mt. Benedict August 11, 1834, and destroyed it by fire and pillage, ransacking even the sacred graves of the dead.

In Philadelphia, a band of lawless men identifying themselves as Native Americans brought things to a crisis in May, 1844, and again in July of the same year. Their spirit was the spirit of "Knownothingism," rampant in Philadelphia and directed especially against foreigners and Catholics. Fanatical mobs committed ravages and outrages of all kinds. They attacked Catholic citizens and drove them from their homes, which they pillaged and burned. St. Michael's Church and presbytery adjoining, were destroyed by these firebrands. St. Augustine's Church, rectory, and the newly built convent of the Sisters of Charity of the Blessed Virgin Mary, also fell a prey to the flames. The precious library of the Hermits of St. Augustine was plundered, the books piled up and burned. This loss can never be repaired.

The Augustinian rectory that was burned had at the time been converted by the Reverend Father Hurley, O.S.A., into a hospital for the victims of cholera. Out of three hundred and sixty-seven patients whom he helped to nurse, only forty-eight were Catholics; the others were professing Protestants. On the blackened walls of St. Augustine's Church there remained only the inscription

"The Lord Seeth."

Such were the religious riots in Philadelphia, the smouldering fires of which were ready to flame up anew when Sister Caroline introduced the sisters to the Redemptorist Fathers of St. Peter's Church. The sisters were insulted on the streets, pelted with mud. They lived in unvarying dread of being molested at night, kept valises packed within easy reach, and slept in especially prepared robes, that they might appear respectable, if driven into the street by fire or marauders. During the last week of September, Sister Caroline was obliged to leave the sisters a prey to these anxieties, as her presence was required at the opening of St. Philomena's School in Pittsburgh, where the sisters were to enter the ranks of the fast increasing pioneers of Bishop O'Connor's diocese. . . .

Father Starke, C.Ss.R., and the other Redemptorist Fathers of St. Philomena's Church, welcomed the sisters as cordially as their confreres had done in Philadelphia. Bishop O'Connor blessed the school building, and, at the mass, preached to a large congregation, many of whom were parents and relations of the pupils confided to the care of the new teachers. Fortunately, better conditions prevailed here, and the sisters were spared the hardships and sufferings borne by their companions in the city of Brotherly Love! Sister Caroline divided her time among the six schools now established: St. Mary's in Pennsylvania, St. James', St. Michael's and St. Alphonsus' in Baltimore, St. Peter's in Philadelphia, and St. Philomena's in Pittsburgh.

Happily, the blessing of the God of peace and love rested intimately on the indefatigable labors of the Redemptorist Fathers and the School Sisters of Notre Dame. Sister Caroline returned to Philadelphia before Christmas to find that the sisters, who had at first lived in a private house at some distance from the school, now occupied a part of the church basement as a dwelling. Here they were blessed with at least conventual privacy, and with a sense of protection. Sister Caroline devoted no little attention to the class of first communicants. She instructed them in Christian Doctrine, devotional practices, in the virtues of the Christian home, in habits of neatness and clean living, and so successfully that her name and those of her devoted companions became household words among the parishioners, who gladly testified to the happy change wrought in their children during the first year spent in the sisters' school. . . .

The sisters had been in America nearly three years and had borne many sufferings and privations. They had successfully surmounted all obstacles save one—the restriction imposed by the rule of enclosure, rigidly enforced by Mother Teresa, and on which she had insisted in every letter written to the American sisters. Mother Seraphine and her advisers were in sympathy with Mother Teresa, preferring to forgo the founding of new schools rather than submit to constitutional modifications. Mother Seraphine, and those of the same opinion were actuated by the noblest motives of adhering to the spirit and the letter of the constitutions. Mother Teresa was justified in her stand because the Church required all consecrated virgins to be protected by the rule of enclosure, which permitted communication with the outside world only through grills, and because the Holy See would not sanction the rule of a community lax in observing the cloister regulations.

It will be seen from the following incident that Mother Teresa had been accustomed from earliest childhood to the requirements of cloistered life. When she attended the school of the Sisters of St. Peter Fourier, in Stadtamhof, as a very young child, her father carried her to school every morning, placed her in the convent "turn," and waited till the bell announced that his daughter had been taken safely in by one of the sisters. When he called for her every evening she was returned to him in the same manner.

Sister Caroline and her advisers and fellow teachers, having had more opportunity to try out the letter of the constitutions, had, from experience, obtained broader vision, and thus felt assured that, in this instance, the letter of the law ought to be modified to preserve its spirit. They had learned by experience that the poverty of bishops, priests and people in this country was so great that it was an impossibility to have the school and convent built adjacent to the church. Without this arrangement, the sisters might not accompany their pupils to church, nor assist at mass on week days.

For the privilege of hearing mass on Sundays and of receiving the sacraments in the parish church, dispensation had to be obtained from the religious superiors and from the bishop of the diocese. They knew also that it was impossible to confer with parents or with externs, only through the grate. This would oblige the sisters to leave their pupils unattended in the classrooms while escorting callers to the convent parlor. Sister Caroline had studied the question thoroughly before joining the community, and had been advised by bishops and priests to choose the newly established congregation because its founders had expressly stated that the new constitutions would have to be adapted to the exigencies of the times. She knew of the efforts made by St. Francis de Sales to have the Sisters of the Visitation founded as an active order, and that for five years they worked unhampered among the children of the poor before he was obliged to withdraw and place them within the cloister. St. Peter Fourier met with powerful opposition when he insisted that the Sisters of Notre Dame should teach children who came to them in the morning and returned to their homes in the evening. Like the Carmelites in Baltimore, when for twenty years, 1831–1851, they taught school on Aisquith Street—Archbishop Carroll having obtained a dispensation for them from the Holy See—the sisters who taught these poor children were permitted to speak to them only in the classrooms; they were bound to restrict themselves in instructing them.

In neither case were the teachers permitted to speak to their companions within the cloister concerning pupils or their parents. That conditions such as these militated against the Congregation of the School Sisters in America, was quite apparent. Besides, the sisters were permitted to wear their religious habit only when within the convent walls. The Redemptorists, especially Father Neumann and Father Helmprecht, both of whom were enlightened and practical men, had often urged the sisters to seek a modification of the constitutions. Correspondence had effected nothing, except misunderstanding and misinterpretation of the sisters' motives. Mother Teresa ignored their letters, and for a year communication with the Mother House in Europe ceased.

In this predicament, Mother Seraphine determined to assume the responsibility of taking the initiative, in hope of securing a definite decision. It was decided that Sister Caroline should go to Europe to confer with Mother Teresa and Father Siegert and solicit a favorable settlement of this important question.

It required great heroism on the part of the young sister to undertake a voyage to Europe on such an errand. Not only was she obliged to travel without a companion or a maid, but without credentials of any kind, for Mother Seraphine had failed to write a letter of explanation to Mother Teresa, nor had she announced Sister Caroline's visit. How would she convince the sisters in Europe that she had crossed the ocean in obedience to the command of her lawful superior, and that she had been commissioned to represent the American sisters in a matter of supreme importance?

She sailed from New York, July 31, 1850, on the third anniversary of her arrival in America. She became very ill from the effects of the voyage during which violent storms whipped the sea and threatened to submerge the vessel. Word went round among the passengers that the sister on board was too ill to speak to any one, and because she kept her cabin door locked, no one could go to her assistance. A Catholic bishop was on board and went to inquire as to the truth of the rumor. Sister Caroline, after being assured that he was really a prelate of the Church, admitted him, gratefully received advice about accepting the care of the stewardess, and was much encouraged by his fatherly interest in her. He was the Right Reverend Bernard O'Rielly, D.D., of Hartford, Connecticut, on a visit to Rome. Returning from one of these visits he perished at sea, January, 1856.

Sister Caroline reached the Mother House on the Feast of the Assumption, three years from the day of the sisters' arrival at St. Mary's. Her apprehensions were realized; she was received with mistrust by the sisters, who supposed she had run away from America. Father Siegert was the first to accord her full and honest recognition. Mother Teresa did not relent. She assigned Sister Caroline to rooms in the guests' quarters and forbade communication with any of the sisters. This was a sore trial to a person of Sister Caroline's honest and loyal disposition. Finally, she asked for an interview with Archbishop Reisach who had been her friend and director for many years, and who now became her support and comforter in this painful ordeal. Her uncle, Father Friess, assured her that the cause for which she had been sent to plead tended to the glory of God and the good of souls, and must eventually prevail.

In the archbishop and Father Siegert she had two powerful advocates, who succeeded in convincing Mother Teresa that she must either withdraw her sisters from America or avail herself of the provisions made by Bishop Wittmann and Father Job in the constitutions for such emergencies: "If branch houses be established wherein you have no chapel, nor service of your own, there will be no other alternative than to cross your threshold, in order to attend divine service in your parish church. Love of religious modesty that should everywhere accompany you, will then serve as a substitute for the enclosure." These two holy founders had always insisted that the constitutions of the re-established congregation must be adapted to the changed conditions of the times, if the sisters were to accomplish all that the Church expected in the reclaiming of the masses through the education of children.

The negotiations were eminently successful. Not only was the enclosure for the sisters in America mitigated for all practical purposes, but the decision was made to appoint Sister Caroline to the full charge of the American branch of the congregation, with the title of Vicar to the Superior General.

7.2 CATHOLIC SISTERS AS CIVIL WAR NURSES

In May of 1862, the surgeon in charge of the massive Satterlee Military Hospital in West Philadelphia requested the services of twenty-five Daughters of Charity. He showed a deliberate preference for the sisters over other women involved in benevolent work, perhaps because of their reputed nursing skills, perhaps because of their vow of celibacy. Ninety-one sisters were involved at one time or another at Satterlee until the war ended. Their service is recorded in the journal of Sister Gonzaga, part of which forms the first section of this document, and in the detailed diary entries of a group of unnamed sisters. We learn from the sisters that they earned the respect of physicians, clergy, and patients through their efficient and compassionate nursing. We also learn that they did not hesitate to teach the Catholic faith to the curious and uninformed, sometimes dispelling a lifetime of preconceived ideas.

Source: "Notes on the Satterlee Military Hospital, West Philadelphia, Penna.: From 1862 until Its Close in 1865." *American Catholic Historical Society of Philadelphia. Record* 8 (1897): 403–7, 429–32, 439–40.

In May of 1864, the Jubilee was celebrated at Satterlee Hospital. Our poor sufferers were most happy to have it in their power to obtain this great indulgence. Many received the Sacraments who had not approached them for ten, fifteen, and some for twenty-five years. One had been forty years without going to Confession. He had lived on bad terms with his wife, but he sent for her that they might be reconciled before finishing the Jubilee. The soldiers wore with the greatest confidence the Scapular, Miraculous Medal and Agnus Dei, and many attributed their preservation from injury to one or the other of these. A pale young man came one evening to the door of Sister N——'s room for medicine, and, appearing to suffer as he placed his hand on his breast, Sister asked him if the wound was very painful. He answered no, but he knew it would have been mortal but for a pair of Scapulars his mother had placed on his neck before he left home. The bullet had passed through his uniform coat, battered his watch to pieces and lodged in his Scapular, leaving nothing more serious than a little soreness. He now wished to be instructed in regard to them, so that he might be invested with them by the chaplain before he returned to his regiment. Another—a Protestant—said that a friend of his had put the Scapulars on his neck the morning he left home, telling him that the Blessed Virgin would protect him and bring him safe through all dangers if he said a prayer to her every day. He had done so, and although his comrades had fallen on all sides of him, and a shell tore up the ground quite near his feet, he remained unharmed and even fearless. He said to Sister N———: "I wish to be instructed and baptized." But as he was ordered to his regiment there was no time for it. We distributed a great number of medals and Agnus Deis; even Protestants asked for them before returning to the field, promising to wear them with respect and to say their prayers every day, "because," they said, "the Catholic soldiers who wear them escape so many dangers."

Cases of small-pox had occurred in the Hospital from time to time, but the patients were removed as soon as possible to the Small-pox Hospital, which was several miles from the city. The poor fellows were more distressed on account of their being sent away from the Sisters to be nursed than they were on account of the disease. It was heart-rending when the ambulance came to hear the poor fellows begging to be left, even if they had to be entirely alone, provided the Sisters would be near them to have the Sacraments administered in the hour of danger. We offered our services several times to attend these poor sick, but were told that the Government had sent them away to avoid contagion. At last, however, the Surgeon in Charge obtained permission to keep the small-pox patients in the camp some distance from the Hospital. The tents were made very comfortable, with good large stoves to heat them, and "flys" (double covers) over the tops. The next thing was to have the Sisters in readiness, in case their services were required. Every one

was generous enough to offer herself for the duty, but it was thought more prudent to accept one who had had the disease. As soon as the soldiers learned that a Sister had been assigned to the camp, they said: "Well, if I get the small-pox now, I don't care, because one of our Sisters will take care of me." From November, 1864, until May, 1865, we had upward of ninety cases—of whom nine or ten died. *Two* had the Black Small-pox. They were baptized before they died. We had, I may say, entire charge of the poor sufferers, as the physician who attended them seldom paid them a visit, but allowed us to do anything we thought proper for them. The patients were very little marked, and much benefitted by drinking freely of tea made from Saracenia Purpura, or Pitcher Plant. When the weather permitted, I visited those poor fellows almost every day. Like little children, at these times they expected some little treat of oranges, cakes, jellies, apples and such things, which we always had for them. They often said it was the Sisters who cured them and not the doctors, for they believed they were afraid of the disease. Our small-pox patients appeared to think that the Sisters were not like other human beings, or they would not attend such loathsome contagious diseases, which every one else shunned. One day I was advising an application to a man's face for poison—he would not see one of the doctors, because, he said, the doctor did him no good—and I told him this remedy had cured a Sister who was poisoned. The man looked at me in perfect astonishment. "A Sister!" he exclaimed. I answered "Yes." "Why!" said he, "I didn't know the Sisters ever got anything like that." I told him "To be sure they did. They are liable to take disease as well as any one else." "To be sure *not!*" he said, "For the boys often say they must be different from other people, for they do for us what no other person would do. They are not afraid of fevers, small-pox or anything else." The physicians acknowledged that they would have lost many more patients, had it not been for the Sisters' watchful care and knowledge of medicine. The officers as well as the soldiers showed the greatest respect for the Sisters. The Surgeon in Charge, Dr. I. J. Hayes, often remarked with pleasure that the Sisters had such influence over the soldiers. No matter how rudely they might behave, as soon as the Sister of that ward or any other made her appearance, they became quiet and orderly. They have often refused to go on night-watch or detailed duty for the doctor, but never once when the Sister asked it of them. The Surgeon in Charge gave orders upon our first arrival at the Hospital that any want of obedience or respect should be severely punished, but, happily, there was not a single instance of either. One incident will show the good feeling of all towards the Sisters. One of the patients of Ward ———— had been in town on a pass, and had indulged too freely in liquor, but on his return he

went quietly to bed. Sister—not knowing his condition—took him his medicine, touched the bed-clothes to rouse him, and the poor man, being stupid and sleepy, thought his comrades were teasing him. He gave a blow that sent Sister and the medicine across the room. Some of the convalescents seized him by the collar and would have choked him if Sister had not interfered. He was reported and sent under an escort to the guard-house, where the stocks were being prepared for him. Nothing could be done for his release, as the Surgeon in Charge was absent. As soon as he returned, the Sisters begged that the poor man might return to his ward, and be relieved from all punishment as well as from the guard-house. The Surgeon said, as he could refuse nothing to the Sisters, their request was granted, but in order to make a strong impression on the soldiers, he dispatched an order to each ward, which was read at roll-call, to the effect that this man was released only at the earnest entreaty of the Sister Superior and the Sister of the ward. Otherwise, he would have been severely dealt with. When the poor man came to himself and learned what he had done, he begged a thousand pardons of Sister, and promised never to touch liquor again. On Christmas, Easter, Thanksgiving Day, etc., at our request all the prisoners in the guard-house were liberated. The officers often came to us to solicit favors from Dr. Hayes for them, as they "knew he would not refuse the Sisters anything they asked him."

As to the visitors at the Hospital, in the beginning some of them were very much prejudiced, and one day asked Dr. Hayes why he had the Sisters of Charity to nurse in his Hospital, when there were "ever so many" ladies who would be happy to do that service? He answered, because he considered the Sisters of Charity the only women in the world capable of nursing the sick properly. . . .

Lewis Bruce was baptized on January 25, 1865. His conversion was brought about through reading Catholic books. He said he had been taught to believe everything bad of Catholics. As soon as he learned the truth, his faith was so strong that he had no difficulty in believing anything the Church proposes. Before he knew the catechism, as well as after, he reduced to practice the doctrines of the Church with the docility of a child. He showed the sincerity of his conversion by overcoming a naturally stubborn and ungovernable disposition. Everyone noticed the great change in him previous to making his First Communion on March 19th, not quite one month after his baptism. The hand of God is plainly evident in one circumstance relative to that baptism. On Saturday morning he told Sister that the invalid corps to which he belonged was going away on Monday, and he had not been baptized, nor received sufficient instruction. Sister told him to see Father McGrane and tell him the circum-

stances, which he did. But as Father had not met him before, he hesitated about baptizing him, and told him to return on the following Friday. The poor boy repeated this to Sister, and added that he would have to leave on the next morning. Sister went to the chapel, and kneeling before the Blessed Sacrament, placed the poor boy in the Sacred Heart of Jesus, as an assured place of refuge, earnestly beseeching our Lord not to let the poor boy go away until he had received Baptism. Sister received a speedy answer to her prayer. The company did not leave on Monday, but was delayed for some time. The young man not only was baptized, but made his First Communion, and a little later, his Easter Communion also.

Another patient—of Ward H—was Andrew Hopkins, whose baptism we had the consolation to witness in our chapel. He had been a sufferer for two months. As soon as he was able to go about, he became Sister's "extra diet boy" (that means the one who brings the extra diet from the kitchen and performs other little offices for the Sister. They are generally well disposed and simple, docile natures, and there are many such in every ward). From day to day, Andrew would ask Sister questions regarding our religion, to which he generally received brief answers, as his own and Sister's time was so occupied. He generally concluded with something like this: "I wish I was a Christian; but I think that God must never have intended me to become one, for I have tried it so often. There is so much to be done to be a good one, that I often think I could never go through the half of it. I never was baptized, and was always knocked about up to the time I came into the army." He lost his parents while very young, and had no relatives to take an interest in him. Still, he showed signs of a good disposition, and was attracted to the practice of virtue more than many who have had the advantages of a good education. Sister gave him "The Catholic Christian Instructed," telling him to read it, and he would find therein the way to know how to love and serve God, and become a good Christian. After reading it, he believed its teachings, and immediately applied to Father McGrane for Baptism, telling him that he wished to become a Christian, now that he had found out the way. After having a long conversation with him. Father admired his dispositions very much, and told him to come to him that same evening after Vespers, when he gave him an instruction, and immediately baptized him, fearing that he would soon be sent to his regiment. It was really providential, for the next day he received orders to be ready to leave for his regiment within twenty-four hours. He regretted having to leave without being better instructed, that he might be better able—as he said himself—to instruct others whom he might meet who were as he had been. However, he said, he could not complain. Our Lord had done so much for

him, and with what different feelings he could now enter the battlefield! He felt he was a child of God, and had a right to his place in heaven. He went away cheerfully to perform any duty assigned him, offering all to Our Lord in thanksgiving for these favors. Sister gave him a medal, telling him to wear it always, and to place himself under the protection of our Blessed Mother, who would obtain all blessings for him. She also advised him, if his regiment should stop at any place for a considerable time, to apply to the nearest priest for instruction for his First Communion. He was quite delighted at this prospect, and so left for his regiment. Poor Andrew, in the bustle of hospital life, had been almost forgotten when there arrived a letter from the Rev. Mr. Buder, showing us that we were not forgotten by Andrew, and that he did not neglect to profit by Sister's advice, to be instructed in the religion which he had so happily embraced. The following is the letter:

"Covington, Ky.,
"Jan. 5, 1864.

"Sister N———
"Dear Sister: ———

"By the earnest request of one of your good converts, Andrew J. Hopkins, I send these few lines to express his heartfelt gratitude for your kindness to him during his stay in the Hospital, and especially to thank you a thousand times, with your chaplain, who baptized him, for all the instruction and spiritual assistance you have given him. I find him a very earnest and pious young man. I gave him constant instruction until he was able to make his First Communion, since which he has been a second time admitted to that Divine Favor. He asks me to present his compliments to you and your zealous Pastor, and assure him that he has faithfully kept his promises to him. Indeed, I regard him as one of the most pious and sincere converts I have ever known. Be assured, that his gratitude to you will never fail. Such cases afford you the hundredfold reward here below, for it is a great happiness to have drawn a soul to the service of God, and to have taught it to seek the things which are above, and not those which are of the earth. And certainly we have great confidence in the prayers of such souls to obtain for us the grace necessary for our perseverance in these labors of charity by which we serve the Person of Our Saviour in the persons of his poor earthly children. Present my respectful regards to your good chaplain, and also Andrew's earnest thanks. He is quite troubled by forgetting the Reverend gentleman's name. Will you kindly reply to this letter and let me have his name. Andrew also begs me to inquire for John Hughes, a sick soldier in the same ward with him. He has been in daily expectation of being sent to his regiment in East Tennessee. He has been off once, but had to return for want of officers to direct the men. As he may go at any moment, he requests your

reply may be sent to me. With the highest regards, kind Sister, I am

"Your very humble servant in Christ,
"T. R. Butler, V.G.,
        "Pastor of the Cathedral,
        "Covington, Ky. . . ."

September 27th.—Quite an excitement was created about 2 o'clock, caused by the visit of Generals Sigel and Hammond. The former lost a leg in one of the late battles of Gettysburg, and has been since that time under the care of the Sisters in Washington. He is now able to go about on crutches. Dr. Hayes, with the principal surgeons, accompanied them in making the circuit of the Hospital. The patients, who were all eager to see once more their good old generals, who had stood by them so valiantly in the terrible engagement, came out of the wards as best they could, many of them also on crutches, and crowded in the corridors to cheer and welcome them as they passed along. One poor young lad, who was very sick, who Sister thought would feel the privation of not being able to see them, replied to her words of consolation: "Do not feel sorry on my account. I would any time rather see a Sister than a general, for it was a Sister, who came to see me when I was unable to help myself, in an old barn near Gettysburg, where I was. She dressed my wounds and gave me a drink, and took care of me until I came here." The poor boy is a Protestant, and never saw a Sister before that time.

7.3 COMPLEX MARRIAGE IN THE ONEIDA COMMUNITY

Bible Communism, *a systematic exposition of the religious and social theories of the Oneida Association, was published in 1853 in part to dispel false rumors about the group's sexual practices. The theories presented are acknowledged as those of John Humphrey Noyes (1811–1886) and the association from its beginning. Noyes contended that the kingdom of God had been ushered in when Jerusalem was finally destroyed, but only in its heavenly form. The church, therefore, had continued to sustain traditional institutions. It was time for this to change and for the earthly kingdom to begin to take shape. The old order had to give way to new forms of living, but Noyes pointed out that even at Oneida, this would occur gradually.* Bible Communism *presents an ideal rather than a description of reality. The selection below incorporates a number of propositions from the book's chapter on social theory. They argue that the marriage of one man to one woman will give way in the kingdom to the marriage of a believer to all other believers. Sexual intercourse will have its amative or affectionate side exalted over the propagative as the discharge of semen is prevented. Women will be freed from the dangers and burdens of childbearing and labor will no longer be divided along gender lines.*

Source: Bible Communism: A Compilation from the Annual Reports and Other Publications of the Oneida Association and Its Branches, *26–27, 31–32, 40–42, 45–48, 61–62. Brooklyn, N.Y.: Office of the Circular, 1853.*

PROPOSITION V.— In the kingdom of heaven, the institution of marriage which assigns the exclusive possession of one woman to one man, does not exist. Matt. 22:23–30. "In the resurrection they neither marry nor are given in marriage. . . ."

PROPOSITION VI.— In the kingdom of heaven, the intimate union of life and interests, which in the world is limited to pairs, extends through the whole body of believers; i.e. *complex* marriage takes the place of simple. John 17:21. Christ prayed that *all* believers might be one, *even as* he and the Father are one. His unity with the Father is defined in the words, *"All mine are thine, and all thine are mine."* Ver. 10. This perfect community of interests, then, will be the condition *of all*, when his prayer is answered. The universal unity of the members of Christ, is described in the same terms that are used to describe marriage-unity. Compare 1 Cor. 12:12-27, with Gen. 2:24. See also 1 Cor. 6:15-17, and Eph. 5:30-32. . . .

PROPOSITION IX.— The abolishment of sexual exclusiveness is involved in the love-relation required between all believers by the express injunction of Christ and the apostles, and by the whole tenor of the New Testament. "The new commandment is, that we love one another," and that, not by pairs, as in the world, but *en masse*. We are required to love one another *fervently* (1 Peter 1:22) or, as the original might be rendered, *burningly*. The fashion of the world forbids a man and woman who are otherwise appropriated, to love one another burningly—to flow into each other's hearts. But if they obey Christ they must do this; and whoever would allow them to do this, and yet would forbid them (on any other ground than that of present expediency) to express their unity of hearts by bodily unity, would "strain at a gnat and swallow a camel"; for unity of hearts is as much more important than the bodily expression of it, as a camel is bigger than a gnat. . . .

PROPOSITION X.— The abolishment of worldly restrictions on sexual intercourse, is involved in the anti-legality of the gospel. It is incompatible with the state of perfected freedom towards which Paul's gospel of "grace without law" leads, that man should be allowed and required to *love* in all directions, and yet be forbidden to *express* love in its most natural and beautiful form, except in one direction. In fact, Paul says with direct reference to sexual intercourse— "'All things are *lawful* for me,' but all things are not expedient; 'all things are lawful for me,' but I will not be brought under the power of any" (1 Cor. 6:12); thus placing the restrictions which were necessary in the transition period on the basis, not of law, but of expediency and the demands of spiritual freedom, and leaving it fairly to be inferred that in the final state, when hostile surroundings and powers of bondage cease, all restrictions also will cease. . . .

PROPOSITION XVI.— The restoration of true relations between the sexes, is a matter second in importance only to the reconciliation of man to God. The distinction of male and female is that which makes man the image of God, i.e. the image of the Father and the Son. Gen. 1:27. The relation of male and female was the first social relation. Gen. 2:22. It is therefore the root of all other social relations. The derangement of this relation was the first result of the original breach with God. Gen. 3:7; comp. 2:25. Adam and Eve were, at the beginning, in open, fearless, spiritual fellowship, first with God, and secondly, with each other. Their transgression produced two corresponding alienations, viz., first, an alienation from God, indicated by their fear of meeting him, and their hiding themselves among the trees of the garden; and, secondly, an alienation from each other, indicated by their shame at their nakedness, and their hiding themselves from each other by clothing. These were the two great manifestations of original sin—the only manifestations presented to notice in the inspired record of the apostasy. The first thing then to be done, in an attempt to redeem man and reorganize society, is to bring about reconciliation with God; and the second thing is to bring about a true union of the sexes. In other words, religion is the first subject of interest, and sexual morality the second, in the great enterprise of establishing the kingdom of God on earth. . . .

PROPOSITION XVII.— Dividing the sexual relation into two branches, the amative and propagative, the amative or love-relation is first in importance, as it is in the order of nature. God made woman because "he saw it was *not good for* man to be alone" (Gen. 2:18); i.e. for social, not primarily for propagative purposes. Eve was called Adam's "help-meet." In the whole of the specific account of the creation of woman, she is regarded as his companion, and her maternal office is not brought into view. Gen. 2:18–25. Amativeness was necessarily the first social affection developed in the garden of Eden. The second commandment of the eternal law of love,—"thou shalt love thy neighbor as thyself" —had amativeness for its first channel; for Eve was at first Adam's only neighbor.—Propagation, and the affections connected with it, did not commence their operation during the period of innocence.—After the fall, God said to the woman,—"I will greatly multiply thy sorrow and thy conception"; from which it is to be inferred that in the original state, conception would have been comparatively infrequent. . . .

PROPOSITION XIX.— The propagative part of the sexual relation is in its nature the *expensive* department. 1. While amativeness keeps the capital stock of life circulating between two, propagation introduces a third partner. 2. The propagative act, i.e. the emission of the seed, is a drain on the life of man, and when habitual, produces disease. 3. The infirmities and vital expenses of woman during the long period of pregnancy, waste her constitution. 4. The awful agonies of child-birth heavily tax the life of woman. 5. The cares of the nursing period bear heavily on woman. 6. The cares of both parents, through the period

of the childhood of their offspring, are many and burdensome. 7. The labor of man is greatly increased by the necessity of providing for children. A portion of these expenses would undoubtedly have been curtailed, if human nature had remained in its original integrity, and will be, when it is restored. But it is still self-evident, that the birth of children, viewed either as a vital or a mechanical operation, is in its nature expensive; and the fact that multiplied conception was imposed as a curse, indicates that it was so regarded by the Creator. . . .

PROPOSITION XX.— The amative and propagative functions of the sexual organs are distinct from each other, and may be separated practically. They are confounded in the world, both in the theories of physiologists and in universal practice. The amative function is regarded merely as a bait to the propagative, and is merged in it. The sexual organs are called "organs of reproduction," or "organs of generation," but not organs of love or organs of union. But if amativeness is, as we have seen, the first and noblest of the social affections, and if the propagative part of the sexual relation was originally secondary, and became paramount by the subversion of order in the fall, we are bound to raise the amative office of the sexual organs into a distinct and paramount function. It is held in the world, that the sexual organs have two distinct functions, viz., the urinary and the propagative. We affirm that they have *three*—the urinary, the propagative, and the amative, i.e., they are conductors, first of the urine, secondly of the semen, and thirdly of the social magnetism. And the amative is as distinct from the propagative, as the propagative is from the urinary. In fact, strictly speaking, the organs of propagation are *physiologically* distinct from the organs of union in both sexes. The testicles are the organs of reproduction in the male, and the uterus in the female. These are distinct from the organs of union. The sexual conjunction of male and female, no more necessarily involves the discharge of the semen than of the urine. The discharge of the semen, instead of being the main act of sexual intercourse, properly so called, is really the sequel and termination of it. Sexual intercourse, pure and simple, is the conjunction of the organs of union, and the interchange of magnetic influences, or conversation of spirits, through the medium of that conjunction. The communication from the seminal vessels to the uterus, which constitutes the propagative act, is distinct from, subsequent to, and not necessarily connected with, this intercourse. (On the one hand, the seminal discharge can be voluntarily withheld in sexual connection; and on the other, it can be produced without sexual connection, as it is in masturbation. This latter fact demonstrates that the discharge of the semen and the pleasure connected with it, is not essentially social, since it can be produced in solitude; it is a personal and not a dual affair. This, indeed, is evident from a physiological analysis of it. The pleasure of the act is not produced by contact and interchange of life with the female, but by the action of the seminal fluid on certain internal nerves of the male organ. The appetite and that which satisfies it, are both within the man, and of course the pleasure is personal, and may be obtained without sexual intercourse.) We insist then that the amative function—that which consists in a simple union of persons, making "of twain one flesh," and giving a medium of magnetic and spiritual interchange—is a distinct and independent function, as superior to the reproductive as we have shown amativeness to be to propagation. . . .

PROPOSITION XXIV.— In vital society, labor will become attractive. Loving companionship in labor, and especially the mingling of the sexes, makes labor attractive. The present division of labor between the sexes separates them entirely. The woman keeps house, and the man labors abroad. Men and women are married only after dark and during bedtime. Instead of this, in vital society men and women will mingle in both of their peculiar departments of work. It will be economically as well as spiritually profitable, to marry them indoors and out, by day as well as by night. When the partition between the sexes is taken away, and man ceases to make woman a propagative drudge, when love takes the place of shame, and fashion follows nature in dress and business, men and women will be able to mingle in all their employments, as boys and girls mingle in their sports; and then labor will be attractive. . . .

PROPOSITION XXV.— We can now see our way to victory over death. Reconciliation with God opens the way for the reconciliation of the sexes. Reconciliation of the sexes emancipates woman, and opens the way for vital society. Vital society increases strength, diminishes work, and makes labor attractive, thus removing the antecedents of death. First, we abolish sin; then shame; then the curse on woman of exhausting child-bearing; then the curse on man of exhausting labor; and so we arrive regularly at the tree of life, (as per Gen. 3).

7.4 THE EXPERIENCE OF POLYGAMY

Martha Cragun Cox (1852–1932) left a handwritten autobiography of her experiences as a homesteader, schoolteacher, and wife in a polygamous marriage in Utah. Her parents were farmers from Indiana who converted to the Church of Jesus Christ of Latter-day Saints and settled eventually in southern Utah where Martha spent most of her life. She gives an account of her struggles to become a teacher and with her decision to enter a plural marriage. In these vignettes she describes her decision to become the third wide of Isaiah Cox in 1869, the reaction of friends and family, and the nature of daily life in a polygamous household.

Source: Kenneth W. Godfrey, Audrey M. Godfrey, and Jill Mulvay Derr. *Women's Voices: An Untold History of the Latter-day Saints, 1830–1900*, 278–80, 285–86. Salt Lake City: Deseret, 1982.

I Decide to Try Plural Marriage

My decision to marry into a plural family tried my family all of them, and in giving them trial I was sorely tried. I had studied out the matter—I know the principal [*sic*] of plural marriage to be correct—to be the highest, holiest order of marriage. I knew too, that I might fail to live the holy life required and lose the blessings offered. If I had not learned before to go to the Lord with my burden I surely learned to go to him now. Having decided to enter this order it seemed I had passed the Rubicon. I could not go back, though I fain would have done so rather than incur the hatred of my family. If the Lord would have manifested in answer to my sleepless nights of prayer that the principle of plural marriage was wrong and it was not the will of Heaven that I should enter it, I felt I should be happy. But it only made me miserable beyond endurance when I tried to recede from the decision I had made to enter it. My only relief was in prayer, and prayer only strengthened my resolve to leave father, mother and all for—I scarcely knew what. I was sorry sometimes that I had taken up the question at all, but having assumed it I could not recede, and I found relief only in prayer when the Holy Spirit gave me inspiration and made it plain to me that it was the only source thru which I could attain salvation.

When the final decision was made known to my family that I could not recede from my purpose the storm broke upon my head. It was not a marriage of love, they claimed and in saying so they struck me a blow. For I could not say that I had really loved the man as lovers love, though I loved his wives and the spirit of their home. I could not assure my family that my marriage was gotten up solely on the foundation of love for man. The fact was that I had asked the Lord to lead me in the right way for my best good and the way to fit me for a place in his kingdom. He had told me how to go and I must follow in the pathe he dictated and that was all there was to it. . . .

Tests in Plural Marriage

It had always seemed to me that plural marriage was the leading principle among the L.D.S. and when I came to know how generally my action in going into it was denounced, especially the fact that I had married into poverty, I was saddened as well as surprised. When in my mind I took a survey of our little town I could locate but a very few men, not one in fifty of the whole city who had entered it at all. One who had been my admiring friend said: "It is all very well for those girls who cannot very well get good young men for husbands to take married men, but *she* (me) had no need to lower herself for there were young men she could have gotten." And she and other friends "cold-shouldered" me and made uncomplimentary remarks. The good kind women whom I had chosen to share the burdens of life

with gave me strength and comfort with their sympathy and love, and I retired within the home and like the porcupine rolled myself into a ball when my enemies approached and showed them my quills only. But when thinking it over soberly I would come to the conclusion that the public dealt with me as charitably as I could expect it to do, and I blamed no one not even my own family for their coolness toward me.

I began to realize my own imperfections now, and I am grateful to my Father that I had wisdom from Him to see [and] know them. Adopting the rules and regulations of my husband's family—an order already established—I had to submit to an almost entire reversal of my nature and habits. The greatest foe I had to meet was the hot Irish temper that had always swayed me when occasion aroused it. . . .

Home Regulations

We had our work so systematized and so well ordered that we could with ease do a great deal. One would for a period superintend the cooking and kitchen work with the help of the girls. Another make beds and sweep, another comb and wash all the children. At 7:30 all would be ready to sit down to breakfast. Lizzie was the dressmaker for the house and she was always ready to go to her work at eight or nine o'clock. She was also the best saleswoman of the house. She generally did most of the buying, especially the shoes. She was a good judge of leather. Auntie did darning and repairing. I seldom patched anything. She did it all for me. She never ironed the clothes. I did most of that. When wash day came all hands were employed except the cook. On that day we liked the boiled pudding. Noon saw our family wash on the line.

We usually bought cloth by the bolt and whoever needed most was served first. In fact we had in our home an almost perfect United Order. No one can tell the advantages of that system until he has lived it. We enjoyed many privileges that single wifery never knew. We did not often all go out together. One always stayed at home and took care of the children and the house. In that way we generally came home with a correct idea of what was given in the sermon.

Whenever one was indisposed she was not obliged to tie up her head and keep serving about the house but she could go to her room and be down knowing that her children and all her share of the work would be attended to. No one was obliged to bend over the wash tub when she was delicate in health or condition. All stepped into the breach and helped each other.

We acted as nurses for each other during confinement. We were too poor to hire nurses. One suit or outfit for new babies and confined mothers did for us all, and when one piece wore it was supplied by another. For many years we lived thus working together cooking over the same large stove with the same great ket-

tles, eating at the same long table without a word of unpleasantness or a jar in our feelings portrayed. The children we bore while we lived together in that poor home loved each other more than those that came to us after the raid on polygamists came on and we were obliged to separate and flee in different directions.

To me it is a joy to know that we laid the foundation of a life to come while we lived in that plural marriage that we three who loved each other more than sisters, children of one mother love, will go hand in hand together down through all eternity. That knowledge is worth more to me than gold and more than compensates for all the sorrow I have ever known.

7.5 SHAKER WOMEN IN COMMUNITY

Journalist Charles Nordhoff (1830–1901) provides a valuable account of Shaker life in The Communistic Societies of the United States. *A newspaper assignment led him to visit a number of communal groups to observe among other things their daily routines, industries, systems of government, religious creeds and practices, and history. He weaves into his description of the Shakers some observations on the roles assumed by women. Women were clearly included in the authoritative ministry that was to teach, guide, and direct on matters temporal and spiritual. They were appointed as ministers, elders, and deacons but were also delegated the more traditionally female tasks of mending clothing and cooking.*

Source: Charles Nordhoff. *The Communistic Societies of the United States from Personal Visit and Observation,* 137–41. New York: Schocken, [1875] 1965.

The government or administration of the Shaker societies is partly spiritual and partly temporal. "The visible Head of the Church of Christ on earth is vested in a Ministry, consisting of male and female, not less than three, and generally four in number, two of each sex. The first in the Ministry stands as the leading elder of the society. Those who compose the Ministry are selected from the Church, and appointed by the last preceding head or leading character; and their authority is confirmed and established by the spontaneous union of the whole body. Those of the United Society who are selected and called to the important work of the Ministry, to lead and direct the Church of Christ, must be blameless characters, faithful, honest, and upright, clothed with the spirit of meekness and humility, gifted with wisdom and understanding, and of great experience in the things of God. As faithful ambassadors of Christ, they are invested with wisdom and authority, by the revelation of God, to guide, teach, and direct his Church on earth in its spiritual travel, and to counsel and advise in other matters of importance, whether spiritual or temporal.

"To the Ministry appertains, therefore, the power to appoint ministers, elders, and deacons, and with the elders to assign offices of care and trust to such brethren and sisters as they shall judge to be best qualified for the several offices to which they may be assigned. Such appointments, being communicated to the members of the Church concerned, and having received the mutual approbation of the Church, or the family concerned, are thereby confirmed and established until altered or repealed by the same authority.

"Although the society at New Lebanon is the centre of union to all the other societies, yet the more immediate duties of the Ministry in this place extend only to the two societies of New Lebanon and Watervliet. [Groveland has since been added to this circle.] Other societies are under the direction of a ministry appointed to preside over them; and in most instances two or more societies constitute a bishopric, being united under the superintendence of the same ministry."

Each society has ministers, in the Novitiate family, to instruct and train neophytes, and to go out into the world to preach when it may be desirable. Each family has two elders, male and female, to teach, exhort, and lead the family in spiritual concerns. It has also deacons and deaconesses, who provide for the support and convenience of the family, and regulate the various branches of industry in which the members are employed, and transact business with those without. Under the deacons are "care-takers," who are the foremen and forewomen in the different pursuits.

It will be seen that this is a complete and judicious system of administration.

It has worked well for a long time. A notable feature of the system is that the members do not appoint their rulers, nor are they consulted openly or directly about such appointments. The Ministry are self-perpetuating; and they select and appoint all subordinates, being morally, but it seems not otherwise, responsible to the members.

Finally, "all the members are equally holden, according to their several abilities, to maintain one united interest, and therefore all labor *with their hands;* in some useful occupation, for the mutual comfort and benefit of themselves and each other, and for the general good of the society or family to which they belong. Ministers, elders, and deacons, all without exception, are industriously employed in some *manual* occupation, except in the time taken up in the necessary duties of their respective callings." So carefully is this rule observed that even the supreme heads of the Shaker Church—the four who constitute the Ministry at Mount Lebanon, Daniel Boler, Giles B. Avery, Ann Taylor, and Polly Reed—labor at basket-making in the intervals of their travels and ministrations, and have a separate little "shop" for this purpose near the church. They live in a house built against the church, and eat in a separate room in the family of the first order; and, I believe, generally keep themselves somewhat apart from the people.

The property of each society, no matter of how many families it is composed, is for convenience held in the name of the trustees, who are usually members of the Church family, or first order; but each family or commune keeps its own accounts and transacts its business separately.

The Shaker family rises at half-past four in the summer, and five o'clock in the winter; breakfasts at six or half-past six; dines at twelve; sups at six; and by nine or half-past are all in bed and the lights are out.

They eat in a general hall. The tables have no cloth, or rather are covered with oil-cloth; the men eat at one table, women at another, and children at a third; and the meal is eaten in silence, no conversation being held at table. When all are assembled for a meal they kneel in silence for a moment; and this is repeated on rising from the table, and on rising in the morning and before going to bed.

When they get up in the morning, each person takes two chairs, and, setting them back to back, takes off the bedclothing, piece by piece, and folding each neatly once, lays it across the backs of the chairs, the pillows being first laid on the seats of the chairs. In the men's rooms the slops are also carried out of the house by one of them; and the room is then left to the women, who sweep, make the beds, and put every thing to rights. All this is done before breakfast; and by breakfast time what New-Englanders call "chores" are all finished, and the day's work in the shops or in the fields may begin.

Each brother is assigned to a sister, who takes care of his clothing, mends when it is needed, looks after his washing, tells him when he requires a new garment, reproves him if he is not orderly, and keeps a general sisterly oversight over his habits and temporal needs.

In cooking, and the general labor of the dining-room and kitchen, the sisters take turns; a certain number, sufficient to make the work light, serving a month at a time. The younger sisters do the washing and ironing; and the clothes which are washed on Monday are not ironed till the following week.

Nannie Helen Burroughs (1879–1961)
Photo: © Bettmann/CORBIS. Used by permission.

Chapter 8

THE MOVE TOWARD
FULL PARTICIPATION

Historians of many dimensions of human life often refer to World War I as a watershed. Philosophy, technology, and theology in the 1920s and 1930s were markedly different from their Victorian counterparts. In a sense, the war was also a watershed for women in the Christian community. In the decade that followed, discussion of the "woman question" in the churches reached a new level of intensity, and a sustained movement was begun advocating full participation for women in churches based on the authority of office rather than personal charisma. Although that movement subsequently faltered and faded, it has resulted in the current growing acceptance of women in a full range of ecclesiastical duties and roles.

Events both inside and outside the Christian community gave rise to this burst of interest in the status of women. Women had shown skill and initiative in filling a variety of jobs while men served in the armed forces. Their war relief efforts, particularly in fundraising and nursing, enhanced their status in the public eye. Even before the war, the number of women in medicine, law, and teaching had begun to make small but significant increases. The Nineteenth Amendment, giving women the right to vote, was ratified in August

1920, raising questions about what women would do with their newfound political power. What was important overall for women in churches was what Catherine Wessinger calls the "social expectation" of equality, or the increasing access women had to education, property, and economic resources.[1] Finally, the churches became aware of a new critical approach to the Bible, which had originated in Germany. The new or "higher" criticism emphasized the historical circumstances out of which the New Testament restrictions on women grew and questioned their appropriateness for the twentieth century.

THE EXPANSION OF
DENOMINATIONAL ROLES

The right to play a role as lay women in denominational governance beyond the informal influence of deaconess and missionary was a goal before ordination. This concern emerged at different times in different churches and often initially involved the right to address publicly "mixed" or male audiences, particularly at national gatherings. Often they did so in connection with women's missionary work. Black educator Nannie Helen Burroughs, for example, delivered a powerful speech on "How the Sisters Are Hindered from Helping" to the National Baptist Convention in 1901, voicing the frustration of women who were excluded from the denomination's mission work. Her speech was a catalyst for the formation of the Woman's Convention Auxiliary. The WC supported Burroughs's school for black women that taught both the liberal arts and skills in areas such as domestic science, printmaking and social work. Another example is Katharine Bennett of the Women's Board of Home Missions who, in 1916, became the first woman to deliver a formal report before the General Assembly of the Presbyterian Church in the U.S.A.

Speaking privileges evolved into a claim to the right to vote at all levels of institutional life and election or appointment to lay offices. In the early 1900s, women were included as lay participants in the conferences of the Methodist Episcopal Church. In the 1920s and 1930s, delegate status was opened to women in some Lutheran synods and in the Methodist Episcopal Church South. Helen Barrett Montgomery was elected President of the Northern Baptist Convention in 1921. Even the conference on Faith and

Order in Lausanne, Switzerland, included seven women who gathered with hundreds of men to discuss the crucial theological differences separating Protestant denominations.

Very few women sought ordination in the 1920s although there were small gains in those denominations that did open ordination to women. By 1927, there were one hundred women serving as ordained pastors of Congregational churches and there were slightly more in the Disciples of Christ. The Cumberland Presbyterian Church continued to ordain a handful of women, and the Unitarians and Universalists held to their practices established in the nineteenth century. Two larger denominations—the Methodist Episcopal Church and the Presbyterian Church in the U.S.A.—took significant steps toward full clerical rights for women.

In 1920 the Methodists again granted local preaching licenses to women, and by 1924 opened ordination as elders to women, enabling them to preach, conduct worship, administer the sacraments, and perform marriages. The women elders, however, were to restrict their activities to a local congregation; they could not be admitted to an annual conference, which would have to assure them a position. By 1928, there were sixteen women serving local congregations as ordained elders.

The Presbyterian Church in the U.S.A. in 1922 voted to ordain women as deacons in local churches. They were to exercise the same rights and fulfill the same responsibilities as the male deacons. (Several years earlier, the United Presbyterian Church of North America had taken the same step.) Many members of the Presbyterian Church in the U.S.A., however, believed that women should be granted representation in the church courts and should be admitted to the ordained ministry. A committee was established by the General Assembly to study the status of women, and women themselves organized several efforts to secure ordination rights. A 1929 overture giving women full equality was not approved at the presbytery level, but an overture allowing them to be ordained as elders was passed. Sarah L. Dickson, a religious educator from the Presbytery of Milwaukee, Wisconsin, was the first woman in the denomination to be ordained as an elder.

These changes in ordination policies were accompanied by some changes in the admission policies of theological seminaries. By the late nineteenth and early twentieth centuries, a few schools admitted women to a full theological curriculum. These included Boston University's School of Theology, Oberlin School of Theology, and Union Theological Seminary (New York), which graduated its first woman, Emilie Grace Briggs, in 1897. In 1920, Hartford Seminary admitted women without the explicit declaration that they did not intend to enter the ordained ministry.

SIGNS OF RETRENCHMENT

In the period following World War I, the positions of deaconess and missionary continued to be the only professional options for women in many denominations. There were attempts to make the position of deaconess more attractive to women by upgrading the image and educational requirements for the job. In many instances, however, the position retained the connotation of subservient and second-class "errand girl." In 1920, the Episcopal Church, guided by the Church of England, regarded the deaconess as a member of the clergy and as the recipient of Holy Orders. The decision was reversed, however, in 1930.

Women continued to be active both as the staff and the support network of home and foreign missions. They became a major force in world missions, outnumbering men in the mission field by two to one by 1929. Yet the work of women in the first quarter of the twentieth century was overshadowed by efforts to merge some of the mission boards controlled by women with the denominational boards controlled by men. These efforts, for example, succeeded in the Presbyterian Church in the U.S.A. in 1923 and two years later in the Congregational churches. The women's boards were eliminated at the national level and their budgets were combined with those of the male-dominated associations. At the same time the women's missionary training colleges were closed or absorbed into the theological seminaries, which began to teach practical subjects such as religious education and to supervise student fieldwork. Religious education, a response to the liberal emphasis on spiritual development, became popular as an alternative career opportunity for women.

The main reason voiced for these changes was the efficiency that centralization would bring. The mission historian R. Pierce Beaver suggests that churchmen feared the diversion of funds away from the family's regular contributions to the church. He also suggests that the expense of the mission work directed by the male-dominated boards invited unfavorable comparison with the low cost of the women's boards.[2] Gender rivalry in general and resentment over the perceived feminization of the church likely played a role as well.[3]

Although women generally were not unwilling to cooperate with the mergers, they had important reservations. They objected to the fact that they had not been consulted when the changes were being discussed. They feared that the money they contributed to mission work with women and children would be used for other projects. Perhaps most significant, they sensed that they were losing considerable power in the churches by giving up their executive status and by being relegated to minority committee positions and fundraising enterprises.

In many instances, fears about women were well founded. They did acquire positions on the new national mission boards, and in the Disciples of Christ they even represented 50 percent of the membership. In the Presbyterian Church, however, they became a minority voice with only fifteen of the forty seats on the Board of National and Foreign Missions. In the Presbyterian Church, women also had to struggle immediately with the church's tendency to use presbytery and synod funds given by women for purposes other than missions. The mergers and subsequent protests, however, at least prompted a discussion of the status of women in several denominations. The Presbyterian Church's General Assembly even commissioned a special study of the "unrest" among the church's women. This result was "unintentional and ironic"; women had been up to this point satisfied with a separate but autonomous sphere.[4]

It should be noted that the first decades of the twentieth century brought increased restrictions on the involvement of women in other groups within the Christian tradition. The Quakers, for example, abolished separate women's meetings and incorporated women into the society's general meetings. As part of a general repression of Catholic lay people, the relative freedom enjoyed by many American nuns in the nineteenth century to adapt their lifestyles to the needs of the American environment was curtailed. The new orders dedicated to service were brought under canon law, and previously ignored or tolerated activities were prohibited. Contact with the outside world was carefully limited. The sisters were removed from the care of babies and maternity cases in hospitals and forbidden to teach in coeducational schools. They were especially warned not to form "particular friendships" with men in the church.

The freedom found by women in the Holiness and Pentecostal groups also diminished in the twentieth century. This was partly caused by the influence of fundamentalism, which hardened its restrictions on women by insisting that Paul's command of silence was absolute and immutable and that female subordination was part of God's creative plan. Women were described in harsh terms as the natural allies of Satan and liberalism; their quest for rights was considered part of the chaos of the end times. Holiness and Pentecostal believers also tried to conform more closely to the practices of the mainline denominations and American culture in general. Their desire to be acceptable and to flourish led them to discourage women preachers and to establish theological seminaries for the creation of a professional ministry. And scholars point out that the initial Pentecostal and Holiness enthusiasm for equality was a limited one, based on the need for preachers in the last days and in the extraordinary call of the Holy Spirit. Such trends greatly reduced the number of women ministers in the Holiness and Pentecostal churches; at present, as one historian puts it, these groups hold to the principle of ordination but waver in practice.[5]

The 1930s brought little progress in the struggle to elevate the status of women in the Christian community and in the wider society. This stagnation can be attributed partly to the virtual disappearance of an active feminist movement in the United States.[6] The suffrage movement was successful because of the support of large numbers of women who continued to accept the Victorian ideal of true womanhood. They regarded the ballot box as a way to extend their maternal and moral influence, and once that goal was reached they retreated to the kitchen and the nursery. They had little interest in economic issues or in the acquisition of equality for women in the workplace. Added to this resurgence of the cult of true womanhood were the economic conditions of the 1930s. Few churches were inclined to hire women for any kind of position when so many men were competing for few jobs.

POSTWAR CHANGES

Like World War I, World War II created conditions that gave rise to new discussions and studies of the status of women in the Christian community. Women did many kinds of jobs that had been looked upon previously as male domains because of a shortage of available men. The Christian churches were no exception in this willingness to accept women in unusual roles. In Europe, women with theological training were ordained in certain churches and became pastors in the absence of men. A shortage of men even prompted the Anglican bishop of Hong Kong to ordain Reverend Li Tim-Oi to the priesthood, although her ordination was rejected by the English church hierarchy and she subsequently resigned. Events in the churches of Europe and elsewhere stimulated the American churches again to examine the status of women.

The American denominations were goaded into action by some additional factors. The 1950s saw a period of growth in church membership and building. The need for clergy and trained lay professionals made at least some leaders more open to the inclusion of women, although many of them agreed to ordination only because they believed few women would seek it.[7] Also, the churches were encouraged to consider the status of women by the newly formed World Council of Churches. A study of women in American religious life was conducted in preparation for the first meeting of the council in 1948. The findings from the United States and other countries were later interpreted and published by Kathleen Bliss in a landmark book, *The Service and Status of Women in the Churches*.[8] The book documented the lowly place occupied by women in the churches and their virtual nonexistence in positions of leadership and authority.

Ordained women throughout the 1950s and 1960s continued to be few in number. Some significant changes were occurring, however, in the Protestant world. The African Methodist Episcopal Church voted to ordain women in 1948. In 1956, the Presbyterian Church in the U.S.A. ordained Margaret E. Towner as a minister in keeping with its new policy granting women full ecclesiastical privileges. After its union with this church two years later, the United Presbyterian Church of North America also acknowledged the right of women to be ordained as elders and ministers. Also in 1956, the United Methodist Church (made up of the Methodist Episcopal Church, the Methodist Protestant Church, and the Methodist Episcopal Church South) granted full conference rights to women. Seminaries such as Harvard Divinity School and Episcopal Divinity School also opened their full theological programs to women.

In several denominations women served in newly created lay professional positions. Although these jobs did not include ordination, they gave women an opportunity to do full-time church work in exchange for a salary and a degree of status. These jobs evolved before World War II at a time when congregations were concerned to hire experts or professionals in particular fields such as education, youth work, or music. These positions were open to men and women although the low pay and status made them female preserves. The Presbyterian Church in the U.S.A. formally recognized these ministries in the position of Commissioned Church Worker in 1938 and, later, the Certified Church Educator. The Lutheran Church's position of Certified Lay Professional was a comparable opportunity for service.

In many cases these professional positions offered very little to women who were seeking equality and full participation in the Christian community. The salaries were usually less than half of what ordained men received, and worker benefits were often nonexistent. Women in such posts were frequently the last hired and first fired on a church staff. They had poorly defined relationships with the decision-making bodies of their denominations. They were considered church professionals yet they had no vote in running the institutions they served. And they often found their tasks frustrating. Women frequently became the "errand girls" of the ordained staff, burdened with the mundane and detailed work that others did not want to do.

A New Agenda for Women

The agenda of the Christian community regarding its female members was set in the 1960s by events in American society. The Civil Rights Act of 1964, which prohibited discrimination on the grounds of sex as well as race, followed closely on the heels of a Presidential Commission that found that women were second-class citizens in almost every area of American life. During this same period, books such as Betty Friedan's *The Feminine Mystique* voiced the frustration and rage of women who were tired of being assigned spheres and roles and images in a society that was supposed to offer dignity and opportunity to all.[9] The issue of the status of women in modern American society was brought before the public, and a movement of radical organized feminism was launched.

Many women in the Christian community embarked upon a program of taking stock in order to evaluate their status in the churches. They discovered that although many legal barriers to full participation had been removed, women were still marginal in the professional ministry. They also became aware of the low salaries and low status of women who were lay professionals, as well as the small number of women in leadership positions at all levels of church life. They recognized the painful reality that the nineteenth-century image of woman as homemaker and moral guardian was still very much alive. As Beverly Harrison observes, the belief that the battle for women's rights had been won in church and society by the collapse of formal barriers was an illusion.[10]

Denominational reports and special studies were important vehicles for this self-discovery and new consciousness. An American Baptist report in 1968, for example, revealed only a small percentage of women on the church's national staff. Most of these women occupied low-level posts as administrative assistants. The number of women in upper-level jobs had actually decreased between 1958 and 1968. A year later a special report to the General Assembly of the United Presbyterian Church acknowledged that a "profound bias" against women continued to exist in the Christian community. A similar statistical study in the United Methodist Church documented the inferior status and limited roles of women, showing among other things that fewer than 1 percent of active, ordained Methodist ministers were women.

Another vehicle that acquainted women with the realities of inequality was the vast body of literature that emerged during the early 1970s on sexism in the churches. Some of this material simply described ecclesiastical inequality, making the observation that women were finding more opportunities for participation and dignity outside rather than inside the Christian community. Other publications tried to analyze the causes of sexual inequality in the churches by probing history and the biased ways in which the biblical material had been interpreted. These publications made women aware that they were confronting images and roles that were deeply rooted in the Judeo-Christian tradition.

Women in many denominations also became conscious of their situation through formal and informal discussions with other women. From seminary lounges to church Bible study groups to preplanned gatherings such as the World Council of Churches' conference on sexism in 1974, women began to share both positive and negative experiences of living and working in the

Christian tradition. Like much of the literature on women, the groups were frequently ecumenical. This kind of communal experience provided some women with a chance to talk about their frustrations, learn that they were not alone, and make a start at building relationships with other women. These group gatherings would eventually provide a new setting for theology in the Christian community.

Black women as a group also began to examine their status in the Christian communities. For centuries they operated as the glue that held the black community together, reflecting their African heritage of economic and religious importance. In the face of profound oppression, they cared about preserving and continuing prayer, education, family life, and the programs of the churches. Yet they realized that they had been systematically excluded from positions of authority and leadership. In black Methodism, for example, women were deaconesses and even influential preachers but had no official place in power structures dominated by men. Rosemary Radford Ruether observes that the black church has been "superpatriarchal" because only in the church did the black man find an opportunity for power, which was denied to him in society at large.[11] Black women may have acquiesced in this because they recognized the degradation white society inflicted on men of color.[12] Eventually, however, women also began to resent the fact that their strength was regarded with humiliation by black men and their experiences were ignored by black theologians.

The outcome of these exercises in self-discovery and awareness was the formation of more permanent organizations within ecclesiastical structures to seek justice for women. The American Baptist Convention, for example, formed its Executive Staff Women in 1969 to study the involvement of women in the churches and then followed this up with a Task Force on Women. A United Methodist Women's Caucus was established to promote the rights and participation of women within that denomination, and in 1973 the Presbyterians organized their Council on Women and the Church to identify issues relevant to the status of women in church and society.

Due in part to changes in the status of women in American culture, the advocacy of such church organizations and the entry of growing numbers of women into seminary and the clergy, the last quarter of the twentieth century was a period of change for men and women in the Christian community. A short analysis of women's involvement in several areas of Christian life—theological education, the ministry, theology and ethics, and liturgy—is presented in the next chapter. Significant numbers of women have begun to appear on church governing bodies and in the ordained ministry. For some of them, breaking institutional barriers and settling into the existing church is sufficient. But others have seen themselves as agents of transformation in both radical and moderate forms. They are attempting to construct a different theology and a different style of ministry, arguing that women will only truly experience inclusion when change comes in how the Christian faith is organized and symbolized. Some of this transformation is spontaneous and unconscious, some is carefully planned and executed. Some women, such as feminist interpreters of the Bible, have had a significant impact while the ultimate effect of feminist influence in areas such as worship is less certain.

Readings for Chapter 8

8.1 UNREST AMONG PRESBYTERIAN WOMEN

In an attempt to deal with numerous divisive issues that threatened the unity of the Presbyterian Church in the U.S.A., the church's general assembly appointed a committee to draw up a list of the causes of unrest. Last on the list was the status of women. In the spring of 1926 the assembly responded by appointing Margaret E. Hodge and Katharine Bennett, both prominent leaders in the women's missionary movement, to investigate the matter further. In November 1927 the women presented their report, later described as "thoughtful and disturbing," to the general council of the assembly. The report was based on a careful study of letters, official documents, and personal consultations with churchwomen. The authors concluded that there was a group of women, "not large but intellectually keen," who were dissatisfied with their exclusion from policy-making bodies in general and from the 1923 process that led to the elimination of separate women's mission boards in particular. Making matters worse was the fact that the reorganization made it possible for local ministers and judicatories to divert the money collected by women to projects they had not chosen.

Source: Katharine Bennett and Margaret E. Hodge. *Causes of Unrest among the Women of the Church,* 10–13, 16–19. Philadelphia, 1927.

The new national missionary organizations seized the imagination of Presbyterian women and in the first decade after they were formed their resources and their service grew amazingly. Each decade saw increasing gifts and greatly augmented interest until today women's local missionary organizations in the Presbyterian Church number 6554 and their annual gifts are in the neighborhood of $3,000,000—the sum total of their gifts during half a century having amounted to about $45,000,000. But this has not been the only contribution made. Women have placed much stress on education and knowledge of the task as a basis for giving. As their specific knowledge of need increased, so their zeal to meet that need grew. For years hundreds of thousands of women have been studying the National and Foreign Mission fields in monthly meetings of their societies, through literature especially prepared for them, and of late years through the Mission text-books. Knowledge has begotten interest, interest has begotten love and love has begotten deep, devoted, understanding prayer. The woman's organization in the church has called for a great body of volunteer workers at mission headquarters, in synodical and presbyterial and local societies,—a group avidly loyal both to the mission field and to the organization which had come into being to support the mission fields.

No small impetus to this service was the fact that women of other churches were similarly organized and working along the same lines. The various national denominational women's organizations before consolidation spread, numbered about seventy-five, representing both Home and Foreign Missions, with about 60,000 auxiliary missionary societies in which over 2,000,000 women are enrolled, the gifts of these groups amounting to eight to ten million dollars annually. When the era of reorganization of Boards and Agencies of the churches came, facts which were recognized but which were not seriously disturbing became important. So long as there was a service into which they could put their strength and affection, the women were willing to ignore the disabilities that faced them in general church work, although similar disabilities had been removed in other activities. But when the church, by action taken by the men of the church with but the slightest consultation with the women, and then only as to methods, decided to absorb these agencies which had been built up by the women, the by-product of such decision was to open the whole question of the status of women in the church. Then women faced the fact that their sex constitute about *60 per cent of the membership of the Presbyterian Church,* but that a woman as an individual has no status beyond a congregational meeting in her local church, and that the long developed and carefully erected agencies which she had cherished could be absorbed without a question being seriously asked of her as to her wishes in this matter. The women looked about into business and professional life and saw women rapidly taking their place side by side with men, with full freedom to serve in any position for which they had the qualifications. They saw the church, which affirmed spiritual equality, lagging far behind in the practical expression of it; they saw democracy in civic work, autocracy in church administrations.

It should not surprise anyone that among thinking women there arose a serious question as to whether their place of service could longer be found in the church when a great organization which they had built could be autocratically destroyed by vote of male members of the church without there seeming to arise in the mind of the latter any question as to the justice, wisdom or fairness of their actions.

Unless we speak most frankly of the conditions as they exist in our own denomination we cannot hope to see eye to eye in this matter. The women of our church, notoriously one of the most conservative, have been placed on the Boards of the church, and it is certain that many of the men in the church have felt that this was a real promotion and that the women should be grateful for this recognition. A prominent clergyman of our denomination said to the writer that there had been a real desire "to be generous to the ladies!" But in facing this situation it must be recalled that the women of the Presbyterian Church had carefully and painstakingly built up large and flourishing organizations, that these organizations were taken from them without their consent, and in some cases in opposition to their wishes, by a purely masculine vote, and that when the new Boards were organized the proportion of women upon them was definitely named. Women were not to be placed there on their merits as are men, but plans were so made that however valuable they might be they should never in the voting outnumber the men of the Boards.

A number of denominations have united their general and women's boards of missions; so far as we know each one that has done this has taken action only after the fullest and freest discussion wherein women both spoke and voted and in some cases a fifty-fifty membership of men and women was provided for. In the Presbyterian Church the women, although they constitute the majority of church members, are allocated to a minority which has apparently no relation to ability to render service but is based entirely on sex.

Where in other than church service women have been denied equal opportunity with men, they have organized separately, but the Presbyterian Church, because of its ecclesiastical plan and its rigidity, having refused her equality of opportunity, also has denied to her the right of separate expression. Within the denomination no compensatory achievements are possible to her.

It has been commented that when women are placed on various church bodies men will no longer remain on them. If there be any truth in this statement then it should be recognized and woman be given the opportunity to move forward alone. "Men and women," said Edward S. Martin, "never work together on a great scale on equal terms on the same employment. When the women come in the men go out, or else lose standing and character." If Mr. Martin voices a common male point of view the sooner it is acknowledged the sooner will some problems be cleared.

The experience of many denominations has seemed to indicate that women are ready to work and can work with men, but that men do not work well with women, and very seldom desire to do so. Is not this position a bit illogical, that the men refuse to allow the women to work alone, but are not prepared to work with them? . . .

To many women all over the country who have striven for the accomplishment of their undertakings for the mission field and who have largely considered these gifts as "extras," the "single budget" has brought perplexities, and in some cases "unrest"; they wish to aid the church loyally, they wish to do the thing that will be for the ultimate good, but when as in many cases a session without consultation with those concerned *orders* that all agencies within the church shall come into the new plan of a "single budget" unrest of a serious kind is often stirred.

Methods of apportioning the money under the single budget vary: in some cases the Woman's Missionary Society is promised its full quota irrespective of whether the church's quota is all secured; this is bad; in other cases the Woman's Missionary Society receives an amount which is the per cent of its apportionment to the church's apportionment. One great difficulty has arisen because so often the church is not so keen about raising its full apportionment as is the Society. We can let a few typical cases speak for themselves as to some results that cause "unrest"; these are quotes from letters from active women workers:

Before our Church used the Budget system, our Missionary Society sent in as its apportionment about $770.—Then the budget system was put in, and the Session asked us to desist from soliciting with them at the time of the every member canvass. The Session agreed to give us $500. in four quarterly payments. They gave us $450. the first year, $375. the second year and now they feel that we should be pro-rated.

Shall we take just what we can get and remain under the budget plan, as the Session feels we should? This is the problem. We are trying to find some way out and so we are writing to you for advice in the matter. We want to do our "bit" but we also realize that a church divided in itself cannot stand.

We are ready to grant that there have been and are cases where the gifts of the women through the Woman's Missionary Society are out of proportion to the Church offerings, but there may be two sides even to this. Cases have been known where the women have prosecuted their task with zeal and the church has lagged.

The frequent efforts of pastors, sessions, trustees, Board representatives and others to supplement deficits in funds by the use of the funds raised by the women for the specific work entrusted to them leads to one of the most often repeated expressions: "Why do not the men promote the work and the securing of funds in the church itself, instead of trying to make up deficits out of the women's designated funds[?]"

A recent report from an active Presbyterian center in which a Conference had been held, sent by an intelligent woman, contained the following words: "They (the men) lost no opportunity to promote the single budget—or to covertly knock the Woman's Missionary Society as a parasite sapping the life of the Church benevolence."

Since reorganization, activities of various kinds on the part of the men have called forth similar comments again and again, and "unrest" has increased. Or should this be noted as due to "uncertainty"—the women do not know where they stand. They were instructed to continue as before, but how can they? Every agency of the church has turned jealous eyes toward their activities and in one way or another many strive to destroy their organization, to utilize their funds,—and yet to ignore them. Among all these distracting influences the women, with no power to enforce decisions, are troubled and wonder more and more if their best service cannot be given outside of the church. The ignoring that existed before consolidation was infinitely more simple than the confusion of today.

Are not the women part of the church? They are indeed.

Then should they not be interested in all phases of the church's work? Yes, indeed, and they are to a remarkable degree, as shown by their giving to the Church budget, but they see keen injustice in the constant pressure to place on 25 per cent of the women of the church heavier financial responsibilities, while at the same time there exists a latent antagonism to the very organization that makes these gifts possible.

Are the women unwilling to accept the control prescribed by Presbyterian law?

Yes and *No.* A good many women were most sympathetic to the statements in the petition referred to before; as follows:

1. The women have no part in determining the policy or defining the faith of the Presbyterian Church. This is contrary to the spirit of both justice and democracy.

2. The biological fact of sex excludes women from a seat in the General Assem-

bly and the other courts of the Church. Intelligence and spirituality should be the determining qualities for a seat in these bodies.

And many women who were not, and are not, ready to subscribe to statements they felt to be radical, nevertheless are of the opinion that the autocratic methods in vogue fail to secure real cooperation, and believe that much of the present confusion could have been avoided had men and women thought together on equal terms in the church's planning.

As women have advanced from "Womanly Woman to Intelligent Being," as Mr. Langdon-Davies says, they are having too many opportunities for service to be content to be relegated to the group which prepares suppers, cares for flowers, does deaconess work and deals with details. They are glad to share in the doing of these and other things which come naturally within the scope of their activities, but they desire to share likewise in the opportunities for larger service. One woman, nationally known, called to lead large undertakings outside of the church, and a devoted member of the Presbyterian Church, wrote that "the Presbyterian church does little less than insult the intelligence of its womanhood; that when she was in the Congregational Church in a prayer meeting she felt that she had to be using her mind to see if she could not make a contribution to the meeting, but that in the Presbyterian Church, all that was expected of her was just to sit.

She was never expected to speak in any regular church service, even of the informal prayer meeting type." It is true that this is not today true of all Presbyterian churches, but it does represent much of Presbyterian habit.

What harm has resulted and may result to the church from the autocratic control by one sex?

Men's methods and women's differ, but both types should be valuable and each support the work of the other. Men generalize; women particularize. Such generalizations commonly accepted are not always true as they sound, but if they be true, both forms of service must be valuable. Men "view with alarm." Women "want to do something about it." Each should supplement the other.

But the chief harm is that women's forward looking has been largely stopped in the Presbyterian Church. Their Boards, and the organizations that stood back of those Boards, were always under careful scrutiny by the women of the Church as to aims and methods and the mission field itself received loving but critical interest that it might always measure to the highest standard. At the time of reorganization these women were recognizing the great new life open to the women of the church and were thinking in terms of larger plans, new forms of service and new emphasis that should embrace more of the activities of the church and enlist more women actively in the service of the church.

8.2 INVESTIGATING THE STATUS OF WOMEN IN THE CHURCHES

The modification of traditional gender roles caused by World War II, particularly in Europe, prompted the World Council of Churches to hold a discussion on the "Life and Work of Women in the Church" at its 1948 meeting. Material gathered for the discussion was then used by Kathleen Bliss in the preparation of her 1952 study, The Service and Status of Women in the Churches. *Part of her work was a detailed examination of the role women were currently playing on local and national governing bodies. She points out that while legal barriers to such participation were generally gone, tradition and custom continued to exclude women. She also notes that women usually appeared first on national religious bodies and only more slowly in local positions. In her concluding chapter, "Change and Opportunity," she makes it clear that women who had experienced success in the secular work world were finding the church, which relegated them to institutional kitchens and nurseries, increasingly unattractive.*

Source: Kathleen Bliss. *The Service and Status of Women in the Churches,* 172–75, 184–87, 197–99. London: SCM, 1952.

The great majority of the Churches in the United States are of European origin: a minority of Churches are American in origin and have a separate existence from Europe, and divisions and mergers have made for variations.

In the Baptist and Congregational Churches women may share in the work of governing the Church locally (though this varies between local churches) and denominationally. In the Southern Baptist Convention, a very large and in many respects conservative Church, there seems to be no place for women locally although they sit in the highest assembly of the Church. The larger of the Congregational bodies has a ruling that one third of the members of national boards and of the biennial meetings of the General Council must be women. This Church reports that about one-tenth of its local churches have women deacons. But "for Congregational, Disciple and American Baptist Churches, the question whether deaconesses are equal to deacons can only be answered by a person knowing a given local church. They may meet with the deacons and share in certain of their tasks; again they may not. Rarely, certainly, do deaconesses serve the Lord's Supper as the deacons do" (by serving the Lord's Supper is meant carrying the elements from the minister's hands to the people, who remain in their seats). Two women have held the office of President of the American Baptist Convention. The Congregational Christian General Council elected a woman moderator in 1948. Seven Presbyterian Churches are listed. The largest of these, the Presbyterian U.S.A., admits women both as deacons and as elders, but their functions differ from church to church; in some they are allowed to serve the Lord's Supper and in others they are not. One of the matters of church order in which the Presbyterian churches are divided is the admission of women to the diaconate and eldership. The Presbyterian Church U.S., the second largest body, will not admit women either as deacons or as elders, though women have served on national boards since 1924. Thirty per cent of the Presbyterian U.S.A. churches which replied said that they had women deacons. The proportion of women among the elders is much smaller, and for this reason there are very few women in the General Assembly (of which the Moderator in 1947 was a woman).

In the Reformed Church of America and in the Evangelical and Reformed Church the government of the local church rests in the Consistory, composed of elders and deacons. The Consistory (called in some Evangelical and Reformed Churches the Church Council) takes responsibility, with the minister, for the spiritual work of the church and also looks after the property and the church charitable work. The Reformed Church of America does not allow women to be members of consistories, and although they have the right to vote, tradition still prevents it in many churches. In the Evangelical and Reformed Church there has been a gradual increase in the number of women in the consistories, some congregations have had them for as long as twenty years, but most of the minority of churches which have them at all have done so only recently, and very few women serve on the higher boards of the Church.

The Churches of the Disciples of Christ closely resemble both Congregational and Presbyterian Churches in church order. Women are admitted as elders and deacons, but the report adds, "The eldership is the point at which the strong tradition of sex equality in the Disciple Churches breaks down. Only 1.1 per cent of Disciple Churches reported women elders—a total of five women in three churches out of 277 reporting. This, however, may be in excess of the proportion in the country as a whole. An exceptionally well informed Disciples minister was surprised to hear that there were any. The reason may probably be that the elders administer the Lord's Supper: the minister does not ordinarily do so."

In the Methodist Churches of the United States women have equal rights with men. About three-quarters of the Churches reported that they had both men and women stewards. Stewards correspond somewhat in function to congregational deacons, but are elected after nomination by the minister. The American report voices the complaint of some Methodist women that older women with means are usually chosen, and the younger, trained woman tends to be passed over. A Methodist Status of Women Commission has been working to get women to accept responsibility and Churches to appoint them as stewards. A higher proportion of local congregations appoint women to local boards in the Methodist than in any other Church. Class leaders, who played and still play in Great Britain so large a share in the development of Methodism as a Church, are not mentioned in the American report, though it is added that most Methodist Churches have "a lay leader who takes a special responsibility with the minister for the spiritual welfare of the Church. Women are eligible but apparently only serve in smaller churches. At the Annual Conference level women have been lay leaders in extremely few cases." The Evangelical United Brethren Churches have class leaders and a small number of Churches have women among them.

The position of women in the Protestant Episcopal Church of America differs markedly from their position in the Church of England. They serve on parish vestries if their diocesan convention decides that they may, and dioceses which permit them to serve appear to be in a minority. There are no examples of women serving as churchwardens, although in some dioceses they are allowed to do so. In 1946 the Episcopal General Convention had a woman delegate for the first time, but later two women were elected as lay representatives by their dioceses and by a majority vote the National Convention refused to allow them to be seated.

Lutheranism in America is divided into a number of Churches, some of them regional, others of them national according to the country of Europe from which their original founders came. The governing body of most Lutheran congregations is the Church Council. In most Lutheran Churches women are not allowed to serve on the Church Council (the governing body of the local church), but in the United Lutheran Church, the largest Lutheran group in the United States, they are allowed to serve unless the constitution of the local church forbids it. In Lutheran, as in Churches of the Congregational type, a meeting of all church members is held once a year, or failing that, such a meeting is summoned when a new minister is to be called or some important decision has to be taken. Women are, as church members, eligible to take part in these meetings and on the whole are taking a growing share in them. It is interesting that one of the smaller Churches, the Augustana Synod, has no women participating in church government at the local level, but a fair proportion of women are found on the regional and national boards of the Church.

Most of the Churches which took part in the American survey replied, in answer to a question, that they thought women were playing a larger part in the affairs of the Churches now than they were in 1940. The question was sent to local churches as well as to denominational headquarters. Tradition against their participation is often far stronger than any legal barrier, and many women reported that it is often enough for the minister to invite all men to be present, or for the leading laymen to make it known that they would not welcome the presence of women for women to forgo their legal rights in the interest of peace and harmony. The custom in many churches of appointing officers for life makes changes difficult. One new trend in the manner in which the government of the local church is carried on is making for the easy participation of women in places where they were before excluded. In a number of denominations it is customary for local churches to set up a church council or executive consisting of representatives of the major organizations in the church. In some denominations the function of such a body is advisory, but in others it is a standing committee, responsible for executive decisions in the congregation, and the trustees of the property, empowered to act for the local church, are appointed from this body. Women are to be found with fair frequency among the trustees of local churches of most denominations. The powers of such a council vary from one local church to another. Women's organizations are represented on the councils by women. The American report draws an interesting comparison between the position which women occupy in the Church and in civic life in the United States. "By and large, in church life women's participation in governing bodies is likely to begin with token representation on national boards or committees. Gradually this is extended to local church committees and then to local church boards. In civic life women are most active at the lower rungs of the ladder. . . ."

There are perhaps two main questions which are implicit in the comments made in the reports. The first is the question whether at this moment in the history of a distracted world the Churches are really making the fullest uses of all their resources of personnel in order to fulfill their mission in the world. Are the gifts and willingness of women being used to the best advantage by the Churches? This book is an attempt to answer that question. By showing what women have done in places where they have been given, or have created, opportunity, it may suggest ways in which the service of women could be enlarged, the life of the Church enriched and its message strengthened. There is no other answer than "Look and judge."

Behind this question lies another, far more difficult to define, let alone to answer. It can perhaps be put partially in this way. Are women, married or not, being helped by the Church to understand the problems of the age as they affect women, to play their part in modern life as Christians and as women? But this question cannot be answered unless there is an understanding of what women are, and what their place in society is. What is needed is that there should start within the Churches, among those who care about this matter, a process of thought about women in modern society, an imaginative act of understanding, and entering into, a total experience. For there has been a revolutionary change in the place of women in society. Women not only live a very different life from that of their grandparents, but—and this is even more important—they think differently about themselves. It has been left on the whole to secular thinkers and writers to try to understand this revolution and such books as *Male and Female* by Margaret Mead, who writes as an anthropologist, and *Le deuxième Sexe* by the French existentialist philosopher, Simone de Beauvoir, are eagerly read because they seek to enter into the total experience of women in the modern world and to provide some signposts in a bewildering scene. But Christian writers are silent except for the quantities of practical little books, many of them valuable within their limited range on Christian marriage and Christian home life. Except for Professor Karl Barth's exegesis of the creation story in the third volume of his *Dogmatik*, there is nothing to put beside the books here mentioned.

The reason for this lack of prophetic imaginative writing from the Christian side is at least in part that the Churches are deeply divided in what they think about the place of women in the modern world and in the Church. The woman who accepts the judgment of men on most subjects, who is happy in the small practical tasks to be found in every congregation and seeks protection from the harsh problems of the modern world, will certainly find a niche for herself in the Church and feel that she belongs. And it is quite right that she should do so. Thousands of women the world over expect the Church to be a place where, free for a short period from the continuous demands of families which look to them for everything, they can find rest and refreshment for the soul, friendship and a simple outlet for their desire to help others. One of the reports summarizes the activities of women in many congregations in the following words. "Serving meals at religious gatherings and social functions, raising money by bazaars and fêtes and devices of all kinds; touring as choirs, concert parties, entertainments and competitions; individual church women hold house functions and afternoon parties, musical luncheons, children's concerts, puppet shows, etc. In many Churches women prepare the Sacramental bread and wine for the communion service." To get the picture quite right one must add that this report also describes other activities, such as organizing the Women's World Day of Prayer and work for the United Nations Association. But none the less, it is true that in a great many Churches women work at projects of the kind quoted with immense energy and organizing power but with decreasing conviction, at least among some. "We rather wonder whether the endless cups of tea which women do and are expected to prepare are the only or even the chief contribution which women have to make to the Church." Here speaks another voice, the voice of the woman who is not caught into the busy round of the life of a vigorous congregation with more than half her self. Beyond her is the woman who simply cannot imagine herself ever being able, whatever her goodwill, to throw herself into the kind of social life which is the *sine qua non* of so many successful congregations. "If women take an active part in the life and work of the Church it very often demands so much time that they have no energy left for friendships and family relationships," says one report. There are large numbers of women who are Christians and members of their Churches, but their share in the life of the Church is limited by their feeling that their main work for Christ lies outside the actual walls of the church in society where they work. Often they feel that their situation is not understood in the Church and they do not get from it the spiritual nourishment which they know themselves to need. They also mark the contrast between the workaday world in which, in very many walks of life, it is true, as one report puts it, that "contributions are judged on their merits and not by whether they come from a man or a woman," and the Church where this is often not the case, where "women are seldom stimulated to use their varied gifts" and where "it is doubtful whether the variety of their gifts is recognized." The woman of an independent cast of mind who has earned her own living and perhaps that of dependents and is accustomed to taking her share in decisions without diffidence usually finds it difficult to be at home in the church. . . .

Such an acceptance of the fact that woman is a worker would cause a very big change in the treatment of women in the Churches. The Churches are most successful with married women, especially older married women: they hardly touch that 30 per cent of women who are economically employed, and this 30 per cent contains a high proportion of women in the prime of life and a significant proportion of women who are more than unskilled labor—skilled responsible workers and potential leaders. Basically women are kept out of certain offices in the Church, and operate mainly in groups with other women, because a certain picture of what a woman is prevails in many church circles. Though few would admit as much, many Christians believe that the woman is a secondary being, an agent enabling and completing man: probing will uncover the existence of ancient taboos about women's impurity, still lurking in most unexpected places. Many of the women who have written in the reports quoted in this book feel a sense of despair about the way in which Bible texts are used to justify and support already held opinions about the place of women in the Church. When Churches are in a desperate position for lack of man-power, all sorts of service is gladly accepted from women: when the situation is eased, theological reasons against women doing this kind of work are at once raised. Some women feel quite as strongly the debasement of theology involved in this procedure as true injustice to women! Other reports speak of gifted women who have gained qualifications in divinity, for whom the Church finds no place. Very many

reports refer to the low pay and status accorded to full time women workers in the Church and to the uncertainty which surrounds their position. There is something of a vicious circle in regard to this: many able women do not enter the direct service of the Church because they know that they will find themselves committed to what one report describes as "a collection of good works" or even to all the odd jobs in a congregation, some of them doubtfully valuable, many of them easily performed by those without training. Therefore among those offering to serve in the Church there are, if the truth be told, a fair sprinkling who are not capable of carrying larger responsibility than is at present given to them, and they supply in some Churches an excuse for not enlarging the sphere of service for women.

If there is one thing more than another that these reports show quite clearly it is the uselessness of theoretical argument about what women can, may or ought to do. Such arguments quickly lead into the quagmire of discussing what woman is, as though she were a given and finalized collection of attributes and limitations. As Simone de Beauvoir points out in the book already cited, man is a continuous becoming, constantly exhibiting new and surprising powers of controlling and indeed creating his environment; and the same is true of woman, that she is not a biologically determined creature, so that one can say what she is because one knows what she has been in the past, when she has had to relate herself to particular social conditions and to live within the sphere that man allowed her. She, like man, is a creature with unrealized resources, and she is far behind man in this historical process of showing what she is, because of centuries in which her life was dominated by the necessity of preserving the race. Therefore, says Simone de Beauvoir, she must "display her possibilities," not stand and argue. Karl Barth has said something much the same, that in this question of women in the Church it is for women to "show what they can do."

8.3 RAISING THE CONSCIOUSNESS OF BAPTIST WOMEN

In 1971, The American Baptist Woman, *a magazine for denominational leaders, published an article urging women to take an honest look at their role in church and society. The author, Lois Blankenship, was one of many women in the 1970s who had grown increasingly frustrated with the way in which women were bound to passive, subservient, domestic roles regardless of their interests and abilities. She chides Christian women for their complicity in this cultural stereotyping, reminding them that every person is called to achieve his or her God-given potential. Role models of women who had broken stereotypical patterns were essential. The women of the church could help with this by coming out of the kitchens and becoming deacons, trustees, and ordained ministers.*

Source: Lois Blankenship. "Woman Looks at Herself." *The American Baptist Woman* 15 (January 1971): 2, 14.

On a national television commercial a harassed-looking housewife is shown trying to sort pieces of laundry. She is confused about which pieces to place in the cold water wash and which in hot water. A comforting man's voice comes on and gently rescues her with the one detergent which he assures her is for all laundry. She smiles, relieved, and says, "Oh, thank you, sir! Now I don't have to *think* anymore."

Was that woman you? Have you, unthinkingly, "bought" the ad-men's bait that women are naive and gullible, which philosophy goes out over the air day after day? Do you ever stop to look at yourself and discover who you are and what you think? Do you really know yourself? Have you reflected about what it means to be a unique person— the only one like you in existence? Do you truly comprehend and appreciate the fact that you are created by God in his own image?

Of course, you know that never in all creation has there been another person with fingerprints like yours, no one else with thoughts like yours nor feelings like yours, and no one else can stand where you stand in your unique relationship to God. He created you to respond to him in your own unique way. He created you for your unique mission in his world. He has created, loved, and called you into full-time service for him.

It is a tenet of the Christian faith that every person is called to achieve his God-given potential in service to his Creator. Sadly, however, numerous women have sold out to traditional society's concepts of persons. Instead of magnifying personhood, that is, love and respect for oneself and for every other person as one's peer, with each called to develop his own unique capacities, our culture tends to dehumanize persons.

This is done in myriad and subtle ways, chief of which is to designate life roles by sex rather than ability and interest. Both men and women are caught in this bondage, but more women tend to accept their bondage and try to convince themselves that it is right and normal. Such conditioning starts almost at birth so that by the time they finish college most women accept the limited alternatives offered them and have lost all motivation to choose others.

A recent child's book illustrates the insidious indoctrination which begins at an early age: "Boys are doctors, girls are nurses; boys are pilots, girls are stewardesses; boys invent things, girls use what boys invent; boys are presidents, girls are first ladies."

No wonder women for years have been willing to consider themselves appendages to their husbands, with their lives lived through their husbands, their futures experienced through their children. Those in the work world have seemed content to receive much less pay for their work than that received by men in the same jobs, and to take the less significant jobs, leaving men all the executive, decision-making opportunities. At an early age they completely swallowed the culture's doctrine that to get along

in society a woman must play a passive, subservient role, no matter with what desires, interests, and abilities God may have endowed her. What wife would feel free to speak out as did Nora in Ibsen's *A Doll's House?*

> HELMER: Before all else you are a wife and mother.
>
> NORA: That I no longer believe. I believe that before all else I am a human being, just as much as you are—or at least that I should try to become one.

Why do women permit the "dumb" image of themselves which TV commercials consistently portray, such as the one described in the opening paragraph? Is it that women have been so brainwashed that they actually see themselves as the maimed persons the ad-men describe? Take another example: the suave man's voice to the housewife, "We all know how it feels to cook something new—it's scary. . . . Let us bring you rice dinners."

Even family life is programmed. Marriage is a property relationship, and children are the products we produce. People exist only as consumers, victims of advertisements which create bigger and bigger appetites for things. Since women handle most of the family's money, they become the prey of the system and sell their souls to the promises of the money gods.

Children begin very young to adopt a philosophy about life and sex roles and begin to shape their own self-images.

We are concerned, as Christians, that they develop a healthy, positive sense of their own worth which is necessary if they are to be able to accept God's demands that they strive to achieve their full potential.

It is very important for them to have adults in their experience who are models of such faithfulness. This need includes both men and women, but at this particular period in history it is important for children to break out of the old stereotypes that women are wives, mothers, teachers, nurses, secretaries, and that men are ministers, doctors, lawyers, scientists, politicians.

We need to expose our children to women who are successful in the fields which previously have been thought of as appropriate only for men, and to women who are engaged in important work in the community. We need also to let them know women who, no matter what their occupation, know what is going on in the world, who are able to discuss issues and are not afraid to express their views.

This means some real changes in the church, and already some are coming. In many churches women have declared their unwillingness to continue to provide offerings while the men decide how to spend them. In large numbers women are coming out of the church kitchens to help make the decisions at the tables. Women trustees and deacons are becoming more numerous.

The time is ripe for women to seek ordination and pulpits. If today's children are to overthrow the traditional stereotypes, then women must accept their status of personhood and stand alongside men to shoulder the responsibilities God places on his people.

The noted author, Pearl Buck, states that men have changed in their expectations of women but most women seem to be unaware of contemporary views of men. She thinks that men have a new estimate of what women can be and should be in relationship to themselves as men. "He has discovered that he likes to talk with intelligent women. Never before has the intelligent and educated woman had so much good male companionship as now."

Fortunately, many women are sensitive to God's call to develop themselves and are assuming new roles to meet today's needs, which are quite different than those our mothers and grandmothers faced. The average American woman now lives to age seventy-four and has her last child at about age twenty-six. When she is thirty-two or thirty-three all her children are in school. Before she is forty her youngest child is out of high school and she is left with nearly thirty-five years of life, ten years of it as a widow.

What she does with these years is significantly vital. They tell much about her image of herself, whether she knows herself as a person of worth apart from what she has done for others or they have done for her. She can, as many women are now doing, go back to school and retrain for useful service.

She can enter politics and give much needed support and status in this field which is all-crucial to our world survival. She can call other women together to change the system which puts women down, and she can help everyone she meets to consider himself or herself a creation of God who can stand up and be counted, who can look every other person in the eye as his or her peer.

In the novel *The Chosen*, the boy Reuven is worried about his father's health. The father tells his son, "We live less than the time it takes to blink an eye, if we measure our lives against eternity. I learned a long time ago that a blink of an eye in itself is nothing. But the *eye* that blinks, *that* is something. A span of life is nothing, but the *person* who lives that span is something. He can fill that tiny span with meaning so its quality is immeasurable though its quantity be insignificant."

Look at yourself, American Baptist woman. What good will you be? What truth will you do?

8.4 THE PATRIARCHAL CHURCH

Mary Daly's The Church and the Second Sex *captured the attention of the public with its forthright condemnation of sexist attitudes and practices in the Christian tradition and threatened Daly's job as a professor at Boston College. Inspired by philosopher Rosemary Lauer's writing on the Catholic Church's treatment of women and*

angered by the passive, subservient role of Catholic sisters at the Second Vatican Council, Daly in 1965 accepted a challenge to write a book on women in the church. She clearly exposed antifeminism, arguing that the traditional notion of God as immutable inhibits social change and reinforces the idea that revelation has been given once and for all in the Bible. Like many Catholics in the wake of the Second Vatican Council, she was hopeful that the church would correct past injustices. A few years later, however, Daly was identifying herself as a post-Christian feminist, urging women to reject rather than attempt to reform such a patriarchal institution.

Source: Mary Daly. *The Church and the Second Sex,* with the "Feminist Post-Christian Introduction" and "New Archaic Afterwords," 179–81. Boston: Beacon, [1968, 1975] 1985.

If the change of atmosphere which is so badly needed is really to come about, the best talents and concerted efforts of many persons working in different areas will be required. In this chapter we shall indicate some theological inadequacies which are at the source of Catholic androcentrism. To become aware of the scope and context of the work of ridding theology of its ancient bias is of first importance, not only for theologians but for all who are interested in the women-Church problem.

Once having taken note of the more obvious misogynistic notions which have become embedded in Christian tradition, one begins to see that the roots of these are profound and that they are interrelated. Theology is comparable to an organism: a disease affecting one part quickly spreads to another part. Moreover, it is not enough to cure a symptom. In fact, instant cures of surface manifestations might simply disguise the fact that the disease is still present at a deeper level, ready to manifest itself in other forms.

From one point of view, antifeminism in Christian thought can be looked upon as a symptom. We shall consider it here from this aspect. This is by no means to deny that misogynism can be and is a psychological origin of the very doctrinal disorders which, in turn, serve to perpetuate it. The cause-effect relationship is not one-way. It is more accurate to describe it as a vicious circle. We are now approaching that circle from the point of view of the internal structure of theology itself. That is, we shall examine those inadequacies in the conceptualizations of basic doctrines which sustain and perpetuate androcentric theological teachings.

Ideas about God

In theology, at the root of such distortions as antifeminism is the problem of conceptualizations, images, and attitudes concerning God. Many intelligent people are not aware of the depth and far-reaching consequences of this problem. It appears to such persons that an image of God as "an old man with a beard" who lives "up in heaven" is too childish to be taken seriously by any adult. They feel certain their own belief is on a level far above these notions, and that the same is true of every educated adult. In actuality their confidence in themselves and in others like them is groundless. They fail to realize what a powerful grip such images have upon the imagination even after they have been consciously rejected as primitive and inadequate. Indeed, shades of "the old man with a beard"—his various metaphysical equivalents—continue to appear even in the most learned speculations of theologians. They appear even more obviously and frequently in the watered-down, popularized versions of these speculations, for example, in text books, religion classes, and sermons.

What does the abiding presence of such images have to do with the problem with which this book is concerned? On one level the answer to this question may be glimpsed when one considers that the image in question is, obviously, of a person of the male sex. Of course, no theologian or biblical scholar believes that God literally belongs to the male sex. However, there are bits of evidence that the absurd idea that God is male lingers on in the minds of theologians, preachers and simple believers, on a level which is not entirely explicit or conscious. One has only to think of the predictable and spontaneous reaction of shock and embarrassment if a speaker were to stand before a group and refer to God as "she." Indeed, many would find it unfitting, not quite "normal" to refer to God as "she," and chances are that if forced to choose between "she" and "it" to refer to the divinity, many would prefer the latter pronoun, which, although unsatisfactory, would appear to them less blasphemous than the feminine.

Even the best theological writing can occasionally reflect the confusion over God and sex, even when a conscious effort is being made to avoid confusion. The following passage, from a well-known scholar, is an interesting specimen:

> We have already noticed that in the Mesopotamian myths sex was as primeval as nature itself. The Hebrews could not accept this view, for there was no sex in the God they worshipped. God is, of course, masculine, but not in the sense of sexual distinction, and the Hebrew found it necessary to state expressly, in the form of a story, that sex was introduced into the world by the creative Deity, who is above sex as he is above all the things which he made.[1]

What is fascinating here is that in a passage which patently explains that the God of the Old Testament is above sex, in which the author goes to great pains to make this clear, we find the bland assertion that "God is, of course, masculine." The meaning is, of course, not clear. In fact, this is the sort of nonsense statement which philosophers of the linguistic analysis school delight in dissecting. What can "masculine" mean if predicated of a Being in which there is no sex? Is this a statement about God or is it rather a statement of the author's and/or the Hebrews' opinion of the male

sex? In any case, the subtle conditioning effected by the widespread opinion that God is masculine, whatever that may mean, is unlikely to engender much self-esteem in women, or much esteem for women.

There are other distortions in traditional notions of the divinity which are quite distinct from vague identifications of God with the male sex, although they may very well be connected with these identifications. Many of these distortions have recently come under criticism by some theologians, who attribute them to an exaggerated influence of Greek philosophy upon Christian thought, and who now advocate a "de-hellenization" of Christian doctrine.[2] It is important to be aware of these perverted notions and of their bearing upon the problems with which we are concerned in this book.

Among the misleading and harmful notions about God which the modern "de-hellenizing" theologians have in mind are certain concepts which occur in connection with "divine omnipotence," "divine immutability," and "divine providence." The classical formulations of the doctrine that God is omnipotent bear with them associations and images which modern man tends to find alienating. This is especially the case because these formulations involve the idea that God is immutable. The picture which comes through is of an all-powerful, all-just God who evidently wills or, at least, permits oppressive conditions to exist. Moreover, this God is said to be changeless. In the face of such a God, man is despairing and helpless. He wonders why he should commit himself to attempting to improve his lot or trying to bring about social justice, if such a God exists.

In fact, then, such notions can and do have the effect of paralyzing the human will to change evil conditions and can inspire callousness and insensitivity. This effect upon attitudes is reinforced by certain ideas of divine providence as a fixed plan being copied out in history. With such a frame of reference, there is a temptation to glorify the *status quo*, to assume that the social conditions peculiar to any given time and place are right simply because they exist. Evidently, if one wishes to arouse theological awareness concerning problems of social justice, such as those which concern women, he should take into account the built-in resistance arising from such thought-patterns.

Scholastic theologians can argue that this is a caricature of the traditional doctrines of divine immutability, omnipotence, and providence. They can point out that classical theology has always stressed charity, that it has always insisted upon man's free-will, which is not destroyed by divine omnipotence. They can point to the thousand refinements in scholastic thought which are ignored in such a representation as we have given. The difficulty, is, however, that these efforts to "save" man's freedom have never been particularly convincing, despite their subtle and

elaborate logic. What comes through to modern man is a picture of God and of man's situation which is paralyzing and alienating.

The Static World-view

The central characteristic of the world-view which results is changelessness. The frame of mind which it engenders is hardly open to theological development and social change. It is therefore not sympathetic to the problem that women and other disadvantaged groups face in relation to the Church and to other cultural institutions. Consistent with this static view is a limited conception of biological nature and of the "natural law"—interpreted as God's will. A mentality conditioned by such ideas instinctively opposes radical efforts to control and transcend the limits imposed by biological nature. The typical conservative theologians who have opposed change in the Catholic Church's position on birth control have this frame of reference. And, of course, it is consistent with this line of thinking that the myth of "immutable feminine nature and masculine nature," which is in reality a pattern of images derived in large measure from social conditioning, be set up as normative.

The resistance which the static world-view presents to ideas of social change is fortified by another idea which must be considered inimical to healthy development. This is the idea that divine revelation was given to man in the past, once and for all, and that it was "closed" at the end of the apostolic age. There can easily follow from this the idea that certain statements in the Bible represent descriptions of an unalterable divine plan, and that these statements must be accepted now and forcibly applied even though the social context in which we find ourselves is vastly different from the situation in biblical times. We have seen in a previous chapter how disastrous this attitude has been in relation to the texts of Paul and to the opening chapters of Genesis concerning women.

Contemporary theologians are beginning to take account of the inadequacies of the old notion of revelation as closed. Of course, there has always been some awareness of these inadequacies since, in fact, there has been doctrinal development in every age. Traditional theologians have tried to reconcile this undeniable fact of development with the doctrine that revelation is "closed" by arguing that content which was implicitly contained in revelation becomes, in the course of time, more explicit. Complex theories have been developed elaborating upon this, but these have been less than completely satisfactory. They tend to overemphasize the need for justification of every change in terms of the past. Some contemporary Catholic theologians, notably Gabriel Moran, are beginning to insist that revelation is an event, and that it exists today as a present event.[3] This implies a radical openness to the facts of contemporary experience. We are in need of such a concept of revelation, which will help to create the atmosphere needed for honest re-examination of contemporary issues, such as the Church's attitude concerning women.

Notes to Reading 8.4

1. John L. McKenzie, *The Two-Edged Sword: An Interpretation of the Old Testament* (Milwaukee: Bruce, 1956), 93–94.

2. See Leslie Dewart, *The Future of Belief* (New York: Herder and Herder, 1966).

3. Gabriel Moran, "The God of Revelation," *Commonweal* 85 (10 February 1967): 499–503.

Letty M. Russell

Chapter 9

AGENTS OF TRANSFORMATION

Women in the Ordained Ministry

Some Protestant churches such as independent fundamentalist congregations and two denominations continue to place legal barriers in the way of women who wish to enter the ordained ministry. In 1984, the Southern Baptist convention passed a resolution opposing the ordination of women, although some local congregations have not complied. The Missouri Synod Lutherans have remained firmly opposed to the ordination of women, believing that placing a woman in any authoritative position violates the order God established for creation. Women can vote and hold congregational offices in both denominations. Mark Chaves argues that these churches want to be seen by the rest of the world as opposing liberalism and modernity, and the refusal to ordain women is a symbol for this. Theological and biblical arguments weigh less heavily in policy discussions.[1]

Roman Catholicism

Most recent discussions of the ordination issue, however, have taken place in reference to the policies of the Catholic and Eastern Orthodox churches. These churches include in their membership over one-half of the Christians in the world. The refusal of the church hierarchies to ordain women has been a source of anguish for many women and an occasion to unite in advocating full participation by women in all of the church offices open to men.

Since the 1960s, Catholic women in the United States, with the support of many men, have been pressing actively for ordination to the priesthood. Although the Saint Joan's International Alliance gave Catholic women an opportunity to work for the goals of feminism since the early twentieth century, the rising feminist consciousness of nuns in the 1960s raised the issue of women's rights on a large scale in the church. The powerful Leadership Conference of Women Religious made some startling assertions that led many Catholic women, married and celibate, to examine their status. The women of the Leadership Conference regarded themselves as "loyal dissenters" who looked to Jesus rather than the Bible, the church's hierarchy, or tradition as the authority for faith and practice. They made efforts to acquaint Catholics with the church's long history of female oppression, and they urged that women participate in the decision-making bodies of the institution. They also supported the opening of all of the church's ministries to any person called by God.

In 1974, the work of the Leadership Conference bore fruit in the form of a meeting held to discuss the ordination of women to the priesthood. Scholarly studies favoring ordination were made available through the conference, and a permanent staff was organized to inform interested Catholics and enlist their support.

The documents and spirit of Vatican II (a worldwide council of Catholic leaders that met from 1962 to 1965 to help the church meet the challenges of the modern world) gave some hope to women who sought ordination. The church condemned discrimination among persons on the basis of sex and affirmed the equality of men and women, although women were still urged to seek fulfillment as wives and mothers. In 1976, however, the Vatican made an official statement declaring that women could not be admitted to the priesthood. The statement did not say that women are inferior to men nor did it resort to ancient fears regarding the uncleanliness of women. Rather, the Vatican claimed that since the priest was the "image," "sign," and "representation" of Jesus before the people of God, a man would have to fill this role since Jesus was a male—there had to be a natural resemblance between the two. It also argued that Jesus never appointed a woman as one of his twelve apostles and that the church has never conferred priestly or episcopal ordination on a woman. The declaration was strongly denounced by theologians and women's groups, and there is some evidence that popular support for the ordination of women increased in the United States as a result.

Theologian Paul Jewett has made a careful study of some other arguments opposing the ordination of women that have circulated in the Catholic, Orthodox, and Anglican churches.[2] He outlines three main points made by the opponents of ordination. First, they often claim that a woman before the altar would distract men from the purpose of worship by arousing sexual feelings in an atmosphere already charged with emotion. Second, the point is made that the priestly office is a position of authority and leadership that cannot be granted to women who have been created as inferior to men. Third, they frequently turn to the "maleness" of God, Jesus, and the twelve apostles to stress that women cannot act as God's representatives on earth.

Aside from activities of groups such as the Leadership Conference, the 1976 Vatican Declaration was also provoked by the decision of the Protestant Episcopal Church to ordain women as priests. This pattern of responding to Anglicanism continued when, in 1994, the papal letter *Ordinatio Sacerdotalis* was issued by Pope John Paul II after the Church of England admitted women to the priesthood. Although it fell short of an infallible decree, the letter used the full weight of authority to confirm the 1976 Declaration. The position of the Vatican was to be held definitively and all debate was to end. In the same year, the church issued a revised catechism that made no concessions to gender-inclusive language and rejected the New Revised Standard Version of the Bible, which used inclusive language.

The issue of women's ordination has not disappeared, however, for the Catholic hierarchy. The Women's Ordination Conference, which works for the ordination of women as priests and bishops to a renewed priestly ministry, has countered in its material that there were women priests in the early church and that a priest represents the humanity of Jesus rather than his maleness. Ordination advocates also argue that many women are not comfortable confiding in and confessing to a male priest. But what really keeps the issue alive is the current shortage of priests in the Catholic community.

To deal with this shortage, a growing number of parishes are served by lay men and women who perform all parish duties including worship, apart from the sacraments. Popularly referred to as "pastors," the women involved are known for developing warm personal relationships with congregants and for encouraging a participatory style of ministry. Both women pastors and altar girls, who were given official approval in 1994, have helped to make a growing number of Catholics comfortable with the ordination of women.

Eastern Orthodoxy

The 1976 Consultation on the Role of Orthodox Women in the Church and in Society held in Agapia, Romania, and the 1988 consultation in Rhodes, Greece, brought together women involved in education, social work, theological study, and the monastic life, and male representatives from the various church hierarchies.[3] The recommendations that emerged from both consultations were based on the belief that women have special feminine gifts that they should be encouraged to use in full partnership with men. They should, for example, have full access to theological education and be able to teach theology, counsel, and write educational materials if qualified. The consultations also urged that the office of deacon be revived for women, complete with the ancient Eastern tradition of ordination and recommended that women be admitted to the orders of reader and acolyte. They also urged that nuns be given a voice in decisions affecting their lives. Those meeting in 1988 reached the conclusion that feminist theology and inclusive language be taken seriously, and the persistence of damaging concepts such as female uncleanliness be recognized. While the earlier gathering did not focus on the ordination issue, the 1988 meeting tried to clarify the basis for an all-male priesthood. The participants pointed out that the church has a special priesthood, in addition to that of all believers, which has always excluded women. Neither Jesus nor the apostles ever ordained a woman. Also, as Jesus was the husband and father of the Church, only men who can fulfill these roles can represent him; rather than arguing that there was no "natural resemblance," church leaders claimed that men and women have different "competencies."

Protestant Churches

Ordination conflicts within Protestant denominations after 1970 became more contentious; grassroots agitation including protests and unauthorized ordinations replaced the top-down advocacy of denominational executives.[4] In November 1970, Elizabeth A. Platz became the first woman to enter the ordained ministry of the Lutheran Church in America (L.C.A.). Her ordination was made possible when the denomination revised its constitution during its Minneapolis, Minnesota, assembly in the summer of that year. The constitutional change was due in no small measure to the initiative of Lutheran Church Women who had come to believe that their long-standing support of women as ministers of Christ and as capable leaders compelled them to support the ordination of women. The L.C.A., the largest Lutheran church body in North America, was the first to ordain women. That same year saw the American Lutheran Church, the second largest Lutheran church body, make the historic change to ordain women at its convention. The A.L.C., too, had ordained a woman before the end of 1970.

The Protestant Episcopal Church opened ordination to women only after a very bitter struggle. The church hierarchy first agreed to ordain women as deacons and simultaneously allowed them to become lay delegates to one of the national governing bodies, the House of Deputies. Eventually a national committee was formed to lobby for full ordination rights. A period of upheaval in the church followed the defeat of such a resolution in 1973 because of a questionable voting process. Meanwhile, a number of women were ordained by sympathetic bishops without the sanction of the church hierarchy in 1974. Two years later women were admitted to the priesthood, although dissident bishops were allowed to refuse to ordain or recognize women as priests if they so chose. The next significant denominational decision was in 1995 when the Christian Reformed Church allowed its regional bodies to ordain women.

The number of women studying in mainline seminaries grew rapidly in the last three decades of the twentieth century, although they have not joined the ranks of the clergy to the same extent as men and they lag behind the percentage of women in other professions. Many women wind up in secular work and drop out of the professional ministry altogether. Those who remain have career patterns markedly different from men.

While many women who are ordained have relatively little trouble in finding their first position, they generally continue to discover that their career lines remain flat. They often take positions as assistants, associates, or pastors of small congregations only to find that their second, third, and subsequent jobs are much the same. They also end up clustered in interim positions, specialized ministries such as chaplaincies, and part-time work. The ordained positions of deacon (Episcopal) and Minister of Religious Education (Unitarian-Universalist) were not intended to keep women in special low-level career tracks, but they have had that effect. In addition, women report salary inequities between 10 and 20 percent lower than male colleagues in identical situations.

The large number of women entering seminaries in the 1970s and 1980s led some scholars to speculate on whether the profession was being "feminized" to the detriment of the status and pay of men.[5] It appears now that diminished status and pay began before significant numbers of women entered the profession. In reality it is women who are hurt by feminization since there is much competition for lower-level positions.[6]

Ordained women still face resistance from many groups in organized church life. Some of this resistance, on the surface at least, can be attributed to traditional views regarding the biblical commands that Christian women be silent and exercise no authority over men. Men are also influenced by their views of women in general and their experiences with female family members. And of course women themselves are often outspoken in their opposition to female ministers and are not afraid of being labeled "sexist." They may, for example, resent professional women or they may have completely internalized the message that women do not have the capacity to lead. In the 1980s, sociologist Edward Lehman suggested that concern for the well-being of the church as an organization lies at the root of much resistance to clergywomen and this continues to be the case.[7] Both Baptist lay people and denominational executives interviewed by Lehman said that while they personally supported clergywomen, they had a strong perception that other people in their congregations would object to a woman, thus upsetting the harmony and stability of the organization. It is impossible to know if increased exposure to clergywomen will put these kinds of objections to rest, but congregations who experience having a woman pastor cite the great benefits her presence brought to the congregation.

Some women have questioned the value of ordination into churches and whether this is really a mark of progress for women. Ordination by definition, they claim, creates an intellectual and sacramental elite that is set apart from, and over and above, other baptized Christians. Also, ordination is part of a ministry defined by men; women are welcomed if they embrace the ministry as it currently exists. Edith Blumhofer points out that equal access to ordination deceives women into thinking that they have equal access to power.[8]

New Perspectives on Ministry

Women who are serving churches as ordained ministers and priests have begun to change the weave and texture of ministry in some cases. There were very few preconceived ideas or stereotypes of what a woman minister would be like; thus, women in ministry have had the opportunity to do things differently. It was once believed that one of the most visible changes would be in the area of leadership style. Women, it was thought, would be less inclined to see themselves as authoritarian leaders set apart in status from lay people. Rather, they would see themselves as part of a ministry in which the whole church shares. They would be more inclined to use a partnership paradigm as a model for ministry rather than the hierarchical pyramid model, drawing out and using the resources of all members of the community. Recent studies of church leadership, however, suggest the need for caution when making such claims. Gender may be only one factor among several—including type of position and racial and ethnic background, for example—that determine leadership style. Women who are white and serving as either senior pastors or in part-time ministries do seem to be more collaborative. Also, while men in large congregations tend to perpetuate hierarchical and authoritarian ministry styles, there is a growing tendency among men in other types of positions to move toward more egalitarian relationships.[9]

Women are also contributing to a new understanding of pastoral care in the churches, although scholars claim that this practice of ministry has been the least affected by feminist and womanist (specifically African American feminist) perspectives. Both men and women appear to regard female pastors as more approachable and less judgmental than male pastors. As a result, church members are more willing to become vulnerable by sharing themselves at a deeper level. Feminist and womanist perspectives urge caregivers to be attentive to the community in which a person is situated, taking into account experiences of oppression on the basis of gender and race. They are also urged to be suspicious of certain pastoral "truths" regarded as applicable to all people. Goals such as healing and reconciliation are supplemented by empowerment and resistance, which all give women resources to fight back against injustices they may experience.[10]

The transformation of preaching by women is also important, if less well defined and dramatic than once thought. In the 1980s, the claim that women preach "in a different voice" was repeatedly made, but it was a claim without clear definition and significant supporting evidence. More recent studies suggest that women have brought their own style to the pulpit and also that men have adopted many of these traits. Through seminary and professional contact, men are moving closer to a preaching style that uses those traits traditionally labeled feminine.

What have women brought to preaching? Their use of language appears to be different. They tend to be more careful about avoiding exclusively masculine language for God and the people of God. They also use what has been called "rapport talk" to establish connections and relationships. This contrasts with the use of language by men to show their knowledge and establish their status. Women use first-person pronouns more frequently, and they qualify their statements throughout their sermons while avoiding emphatic, unambiguous declarations as a form of closure. They draw on personal experiences, telling life stories about motherhood or economic oppression that have not been part of homiletic tradition. And they tend to choose issues and biblical texts that have been ignored. Perhaps most significant for long-term change is their inclination to accept the limits of preaching and to elevate the importance of music, action, and prayer in meaningful worship.[11]

The Ministries of Deaconess and Nun

The position of deaconess has been retained in several denominations and has continued to become more professionalized. Women who enter this ministry are required to be fully trained in areas such as social work or nursing. They are also required to take courses in theology and biblical studies. The position, however, has attracted fewer and fewer women as ordination to the priesthood and ministry has become an option. The United Methodist Church has created an Office of Diaconal Ministry for men and women who minister as lay professionals in education or social work or as ministers of music in local congregations.

The years following Vatican II brought a period of turmoil and self-examination to Catholic women in religious orders. Communities began to grow smaller and the median age began to rise. The number of sisters declined from a peak of 185,000 in 1965 to just over 100,000 in 1990. A high percentage of sisters are now over eighty. What is behind these changes? Women who did not wish to become wives and mothers were offered options by secular society. Women who joined the communities in the 1960s and 1970s were often dissatisfied with the quality of community life, and in some convents almost two-thirds of the new members eventually left the order. The traditional tasks or niche of the sisters in the United States—nursing and the education of immigrants—either became unnecessary or were taken over by lay professionals. And both age and ministry commitments have made it difficult for these women to devote time to recruiting new members.

Vatican II itself played an enormous role in transforming the lives of women who remained in religious orders. The church, the council decreed, should be engaged with the modern world and the need for justice and peace. In light of this change, the sisters became conscious of the fact that most of their twentieth-century work was with the non-poor of America. Through Bible study, prayer, and reading about their founders' intentions, they felt led to become involved with health clinics, prison ministries, and literacy projects. The communities then asked whether their traditional ways of living and working facilitated these new missions, which started a process of renewal that is still going on.

One major change has involved the question of authority in the lives of individual nuns and in the shared life of the community. In the past, the superior of the convent was regarded as the mouthpiece for the will of God. She acted as such by enforcing the community's rule. Now, however, nuns continue to speak of obedience to the will of God, but they also listen to their own consciences and the voice of God in prayer and the Bible as well as church authorities. They are expected to make their own decisions about lifestyle and to take responsibility for these decisions. Often this means that even within a single community there will be several ways of dressing and many ways of working, including some outside the convent walls. Also, many communities now have no superiors and instead make decisions as a group on issues such as how money will be spent.

Some of the ancient concepts associated with the virgin life are beginning to disappear or are being reinterpreted. Nuns, for example, are less frequently seen as the brides of Christ and the symbolic ceremonies using the wedding gown and wedding ring are fading away. Many nuns also recognize that they are not living in true poverty and strive instead to simplify their lives as much as possible. Obedience, as we have seen, now involves a large element of personal choice and responsibility. Many nuns continue to live celibate lives but they have tried not to interpret this as an indictment of sexuality. Rather, they see the celibate life as a way to be free for a life of total service to others. The cloistered nature of convent life has been abolished in many situations. Members of the communities now come and go freely and many communities are open to nonmembers.

Although convent life continues to experience uncertainty and instability, some women have responded in creative ways to the new challenges. When interviewed, many of them agree that they prefer the new approaches to community life, even when long-established traditions are disrupted. They report a deepened spirituality and much warmer relationships with other people.[12]

FEMINIST APPROACHES TO THE BIBLE

Biblical interpretation has been an area of significant and lasting transformation in the Christian community. Biblical studies in many theological programs have been reconfigured to take account of the enormous body of scholarship created by feminist scholars. Shaped by both men and women, feminist interpretation involves multiple methods and points of view, but it always begins with an attitude of suspicion. Are male biblical interpreters, for example, accurately representing what a particular text says? Are biblical writers presenting women as stereotypes or overlooking the important roles they played in ancient Israel or the early church? Feminist scholarship takes another look at the Bible. Feminist scholars examine what can be known about the time, place, purpose, and language of texts, but they also assume that every text is influenced by the standpoint or bias of the interpreter. They clearly state that they wish to be in the service of women, promoting their dignity and equality, their value and well-being.

Before the 1970s, biblical scholarship by women involved in the women's rights movement often took a position of loyalism.[13] They claimed that the Bible affirmed women and was not oppressive; the problem rested solely in the way the material had been interpreted or translated. More recent feminist scholarship, however, has acknowledged the bias of translators and interpreters but moved on to identify the text itself as a more serious problem. It represents, in short, "hostile turf" for women with its multiple layers of patriarchy, some obvious and some not as easy to detect.[14] The overall message of the text is that women exist to benefit men who are in authority over them. Women are portrayed as devious and dangerous, alien and unclean. Their voices are silent and their roles are circumscribed.

Feminist biblical scholars disagree over whether this inherent patriarchy completely undermines the authority of the Bible.[15] Adopting a rejectionist position, some argue that even the seemingly affirmative texts have an undercurrent of patriarchy. The revisionist position, however, argues that the biblical text reflects patriarchy but also contains positive images of women and material that can be used in the service of women. In this way, interpreters create a "canon within a canon," although they are faced with the need to find a way to decide which material is authoritative and which can be discarded. Women who wish to focus on the Bible as the authority for faith and practice solve this problem in a number of ways. Some, for example, judge all material according the prophetic call for justice while others look to the reign of God as revealed through Jesus that mends of brokenness of creation.[16] Some women such as Elisabeth Schüssler Fiorenza regard the Bible as an important source for women but judge even the biblical text by the experiences of women, particularly those of women who worship together.[17] They become collectively the "magisterium" or teaching authority.

Some important examples of revisionist feminist interpretation come from recent scholarship on the Old Testament. One area emphasized involves the numerous "texts of terror" in the legal material and historical narratives.[18] Both the story of Jephthah's daughter (Judg, 11:29-40) and that of Lot's daughters (Gen. 19:4-8) illustrate the extent to which the authority of a father could go. In the first case, a daughter is sacrificed by her father; in the other, young women are offered as objects of gang rape.

In the Old Testament, at the time of her marriage, a woman passed from the authority of her father to that of her husband. Women referred to their husbands as *ba'al* or "master," and they in turn were referred to as the property or possession of their husbands. A man could "dispossess," or divorce, his wife but she could not divorce him. Adultery did impose the identical penalty of death on both men and women, yet since only the female offender could become pregnant, she would be caught and punished more often than her male partner. Also, a man could submit his wife to a humiliating and frightening ordeal (Num. 5:14-28) if he merely suspected her of unfaithfulness.

She did not have a similar right. Adultery was viewed as an offense against a husband by a deceitful wife. If a woman's husband engaged in sexual relations with a single woman outside of marriage, there was no penalty.

Serving, however, as a countertradition to those texts of terror for feminist scholars is the Song of Solomon.[19] The book was probably written in the third century B.C.E., although it seems to include material from an earlier date. It is a poetic description of the love between a man and a woman. It may be in the Old Testament because it reminded the people of Israel of the love God had shown to them. Whatever its origins, the Song of Solomon reflects, for some, an understanding of women that challenges the patriarchal view.

Women dominate this series of love poems. The female partner in the love relationship opens the composition in chapter 1 and closes it in chapter 8. The woman has most of the dialogue in the book—eighty-four verses—while her lover speaks in only forty-nine verses. A group of women referred to as the "daughters of Jerusalem" are appealed to for support in several places. The mothers both of the woman and her partner are also important figures in the composition.

Even more significant is the relationship described here between the woman and the man. The relationship is one of mutuality and equality rather than subordination and dependence (2:16). The woman keeps vineyards and looks after flocks (1:6, 8), tasks the man also assumes. At times, her lover approaches her, and at other times she initiates their lovemaking (3:1-4). She describes the beauty of the male just as he describes her beauty. Their relationship is one of tenderness and respect. They celebrate the joys of sexual attraction and love. Perhaps most significantly, the woman is valued in the poem for more than her reproductive abilities. There is no mention of her as a mother, a role so important in Hebrew culture.

Of all the biblical material, the second and third chapters of Genesis have had the most impact on women in the Christian community. Their subordination has been justified by citing woman's creation after man and as his helper, and her responsibility for bringing sin and death into the world. Feminist scholars disagree on whether these chapters can be reclaimed for women. Phyllis Trible argues that God's original creature, 'adam, was an earth creature without sexual differentiation.[20] Sexual differences are introduced only in verse 23 of the second chapter when the original creature becomes male as a counterpart to the newly created female. She also argues that "helper" does not carry with it an indication of status; God, for example, is frequently referred to as the "helper" of Israel. The woman in the story is portrayed as intelligent and reflective. The text never says that she seduces or deceives, and it does not say that the subordination of women is commanded by God. Rather, Gen. 3:16 can be understood as a sad prediction of the way in which equality will be perverted outside the garden.

Other scholars believe that it is not possible to eliminate patriarchy from the story.[21] They agree with Trible that the woman herself has admirable qualities: she listens, she reasons, she carries out a decision. But there is little else to be redeemed. The word *'adam* means "male creature" since it continues to be used in the story even after male and female are created. Woman is clearly made not for her own sake but to meet the needs of the male as defined by God. The need to procreate was particularly important and is emphasized when the man names the woman "mother of all living." The active role God takes in Genesis 3 in articulating the consequences of sin makes it difficult to see these words as predictions rather than divine commands. The whole story, in fact, focuses on the male—his needs, his conversation with God, and his role in naming God's creation.

THEOLOGICAL EDUCATION

Women have also had an impact on the way theological education is conceived, especially in order to take advantage of the mature body of feminist biblical scholarship. Since the middle of the 1970s, women have become the fastest growing constituency of accredited theological schools in the United States. In 1972, women represented only 4.7 percent of the total number of students enrolled in degree programs leading to ordination. By the 1990s, women represented almost 40 percent of this population. In many schools of the mainline denominations, women comprise almost half of the students studying for the Master of Divinity degree.

Historian Nancy Hardesty has outlined several ways in which seminary communities relate to women.[22] These are stages through which institutions pass, although very few schools have even begun to move in the direction of the last phase described below. Stage one occurs when a handful of women enter a school to prepare for full-time work in a church. Male students are friendly and male faculty members are paternal. The second stage is one in which a growing number of women on the campus sense their marginality both in the seminary and in the churches they are preparing to enter. They form a group or "caucus" to discuss their experiences and express their anger with their situations. Often this results in a time of hostility and resistance from male students, faculty members, and administrators.

The third stage is one into which some mainline Protestant and independent seminaries have moved. Women at this stage become a significant part of the student body and they are added to the faculty. Courses on the history of women in the church and feminist theologies are added to the curriculum. Administrators and faculty members make an effort to avoid language that excludes or degrades women. The presence of women makes all students think about sexuality, balancing work and family life, and the value of new models of ministry that blur the traditional lay/clergy lines.[23] Because these kinds of changes are taking place in some institutions, a significant number of women interviewed since the late 1970s describe their educational experiences as affirming and favorable.

A number of women in the Christian community, however, believe that theological education must move into a fourth phase before women can be fully integrated into the Christian community and their experiences taken seriously. They believe that theological education, in both method and content, currently reflects the perspective of white middle-class men; material about women is at best an "add-on" or "ornamental."[24] Instead, theological education must be completely reconfigured. Some propose a model that is "holistic," "integrated," and "collaborative."[25]

Theological education should be "holistic." It should take seriously the fact that knowledge comes not only through the use of the mind but also through senses, feelings, and intuition. It should value poetry, dance, story, and art as much as analytical prose. Seminary education should be "integrated." This means that the distinctions between practical subjects such as religious education and pastoral care and academic subjects such as theology and biblical studies should be eliminated. Theory and practice should be united, not only in the curriculum but also in the teacher. A person cannot adequately convey the meaning of Jeremiah, for example, without some social involvement of his or her own. Integrated also means that feminist and womanist perspectives become part of foundational courses. Finally, these women wish to abolish the educational model in which an authoritative expert pours selected information into submissive pupils. Theological education therefore should be "collaborative" rather than competitive. They wish to discourage members of the seminary community from hoarding knowledge in order to lord it over others. They believe that research should grow out of practical needs and questions, shared freely and communicated in language understood by a wide spectrum of people.

WORSHIP

Language for God and the People of God

The worship and preaching of the Christian community has been visibly affected by the concern of women over language used for God and the people of God. The implementation of inclusive language is mentioned as a major goal by many women in seminary and the ordained ministry, even among those who do not identify themselves as feminists. They point out that language has been very important in perpetuating sexism. Our current language patterns have grown out of and reflect cultures in which men ruled over women and controlled the power in society. By continuing to use this language, the church legitimates and maintains this social arrangement. Sexist attitudes are reinforced as are patterns of behavior that treat women as less than fully human. Women concerned with the language issue believe that until Christians begin to think and speak in terms of equality, this equality will never be truly implemented in society.

Language used for God is a fundamental part of this concern. The patriarchal context in which the biblical material developed is reflected not only in masculine pronouns for God but also in overwhelmingly masculine metaphors, such as king, father, and shepherd. No one of course would say that God is actually male. In the consciousness of people constantly hearing androcentric (male-centered) language, however, the idea takes hold that this language more adequately defines the divine. Communities soon come to believe that since God is fatherlike or husbandlike, fathers and husbands must be godlike. Women are seen as less perfect or godlike. The male becomes the norm, representing humanity as it should be. The female becomes that which is different or the "other."

Many women also believe that the use of androcentric language referring to the people of God perpetuates negative attitudes toward women. They are frustrated by the preponderance of phrases such as "brotherhood of man," "sons of God," and the "God of Abraham, Isaac, and Jacob" in worship. They do not accept the argument that this language is generic or intended to include both men and women because they see that in practice women have been excluded from full participation in the Christian community.

The use of words like "mankind" and masculine pronouns in liturgies and hymns sends a message that women are not important. Upon hearing and repeating language that makes women invisible, the idea that women have nothing to contribute is reinforced. Men continue to be suspicious of women in positions of power and authority. Women are also bombarded with the message that they are nonpersons in the churches. Women may continue to view themselves as less intelligent and less capable than men and may be reluctant to take on leadership tasks. If they do succeed in acquiring a positive self-image, women often feel resentment and alienation in a worship context that ignores them.

What has been the response of men and women in Christian communities to these concerns? A range of positions has emerged. Some ministers and congregations have opted for tradition, viewing language changes as a trivial matter and never seriously considering them. Many traditionalists typically believe that the language of the Bible and liturgy has been divinely revealed and should not be tampered with.

Although it has taken a generation, other churches, at the denominational and congregational levels, have altered language in church documents, liturgies, hymns, sermons, and even the biblical text. They believe that the language of the Christian community should reflect the church's belief in the dignity and equality of women and men. Many avoid phrases such as "brethren" and "men" when in fact the entire community is being described. Also, some suggest that the use of the pronoun "she" to refer to the church is not appropriate since the church by definition sees itself as a servant body in an inferior position to God, a God who is spoken of in masculine terms. National agencies of the Presbyterian Church published an unofficial inclusive language edition of its confession of 1967. The word "men" is replaced by "all people." Between 1989 and 1991, three major denominations—Methodist, Presbyterian, and Southern Baptist—followed this pattern and published new hymnals eliminating exclusive and archaic language. Thus, "Good Christian Men, Rejoice" becomes "Good Christian Friends, Rejoice" and "Rise Up, O Men of God!" is changed to "Rise Up, O Saints of God!"

Churches concerned about exclusive language are more divided on changing language used for God. Some mainline churches opt for moderate change, using gender neutral metaphors such as "rock," "fire," and "Creator." They also attempt to balance carefully masculine and feminine language for God. The use of feminine and masculine similies describing what God is "like" (for example, God is like a woman who cries out in labor) is one solution, coupled with the assertion that in reality God is neither male nor female. Others interested in transformation prefer to claim that God is both male and female and needs to be described using male and female metaphors; thus, God is both Father and Mother and the Lord's Prayer might begin "Our Father, Our Mother."

Also controversial are efforts to alter the biblical text to make it more inclusive. One of the earliest and more radical publications was the National Council of Churches' *Inclusive Language Lectionary,* an effort to eliminate male bias in the three-year cycle of lectionary readings for each Sunday in the Christian year. The committee tried to get Christians to look at the Bible in a fresh light while remaining faithful to the spirit of the original text and the English cadence of the Revised Standard Version. Similar concerns gave rise to changes in the New Revised Standard Version of the Bible, a recent adaptation of the Psalms and New Testament published for worship by Oxford University Press and Today's International Version of the New Testament.

Some of the most straightforward and least controversial changes involve the words "man," "men," and "brethren," which were made inclusive. In many instances the editors were returning to more correct translations of the Greek and Hebrew texts. In John 16:21, for example, the Greek word "man" should really be translated as "human being." More opposition, however, has been generated by changing language about Jesus and God. Those who prefer more radical changes in biblical and worship texts try to de-emphasize the idea that maleness was in any way decisive for, or a precondition of, the incarnation by substituting "Child of God" for "Son of God" and the "Human One" for the "Son of Man." They also try to avoid pronouns for God entirely by repeating the word "God" or using a variation such as "Yahweh."

Transforming Worship

Beginning in the 1970s, disillusionment with worship and liturgy motivated some women to transform this aspect of Christian life. They objected to the absence of women in leadership roles and in Scripture; they also were frustrated by masculine language and by theological formulae (such as the definition of sin as pride) that ignored the experiences of women. A whole spectrum of opinion among women and men has emerged on how worship should be altered. Some urge modest changes such as the presence of women as worship leaders and the use of gender-neutral language. At the other end of the spectrum are those women who have abandoned Christian worship completely, instead turning to rituals inspired by feminist spirituality groups such as the Wiccans, who are neopagans. In the middle of this spectrum are women who have chosen to "defect in place." They remain connected to churches but find it necessary completely to reinvent worship based on the experiences of women. They are not willing simply to be "added" to Christian rituals handed down by a group of elite men.[26]

"Women's ways of worship" have not been intended for all times and all people; rather, they always involve experimentation and always grow out of very specific contexts or life situations. Nevertheless, a few general characteristics have emerged over the past three decades.[27] Women initiate and write liturgy or orders of worship. The leadership rotates from occasion to occasion and there are many participants within each ritual. Worship space and appropriate sacred objects are redefined; homes and the outdoors are used as sacred settings, and chairs are typically arranged in circles or around circular tables. The women who participate use everyday items from home and nature (woven cloth, shells, milk, honey, bread, dates) to symbolize their faith. Existing liturgical forms may be used, but the content is often changed. Rituals are created to match important experiences in women's lives such as a miscarriage or menopause and to celebrate women in the Bible and history. One *mujerista* (Latina feminist) ritual included a sermon but members of the group were invited into a dialogue with the speaker.[28] All rituals attempt in some way to remember specific instances of injustice and oppression in the lives of the participants and their communities, and many draw enthusiastically from other religious traditions such as Native American and Wiccan.

Two interesting examples of transformed worship emerged in the last decades of the twentieth century—the Women-Church movement and the

Re-Imagining Conference held in 1993. Largely supported by Roman Catholic feminists, Women-Church flourished in the 1980s when women were frustrated by their exclusion from the sacramental priesthood. Women began to experiment with different kinds of worship communities at a grassroots level and in the large assemblies of Catholic's women's organizations. They put into practice many of the same worship principles mentioned above.

A similar kind of experimentation took place at the Re-Imagining Conference held in November 1993 as part of the World Council of Churches Ecumenical Decade of Churches in Solidarity with Women. Over two thousand women (many from mainline denominations) and a few men gathered to discuss theology and participate in innovative worship services. The conference was intended to be a safe place to "re-imagine" theological concepts and worship practices. Jesus' atonement, for example, was connected to his life rather than his death, and the image of a Father-God who willfully killed his own child was rejected by one speaker. The conference rituals, however, caused particular controversy. In an effort to explore new language for God, the participants turned to the biblical figure of Sophia. The personification of God's Wisdom, Sophia provided a female name and image to counter the dominance of God the Father. Sophia was repeatedly invoked during the celebrations that included a ritual meal of milk and honey.

While those attending the conference had no intention of worshiping a goddess who replaced the God of the Bible, to outsiders this was exactly what seemed to be happening. Critics were also angered by what they perceived as a parody of the Lord's Supper. Church members threatened to withhold contributions from sponsoring denominations and one executive of the Presbyterian Church lost her position. The conservative press vilified the conference in particularly strong terms, arguing that the women were guilty of heresy. Some historians have interpreted this strong backlash as a resurgence of anger against the ordination of women; women in leadership positions seemed to be initiating real and dramatic change in a "man's" church.[29]

THE NEED FOR FEMINIST THEOLOGIES

Theology grows out of the experiences of a community of people with God. Yet many women have pointed out that Christian theology reflects the experiences of only one-half of the community, since it has been written and interpreted by men. It is expressed in the language and mental categories of men. As a result, it simply is not adequate for the needs and questions of women who are moving toward equality in the Christian community.

As we saw in chapter 6, *The Woman's Bible* represented an 1895 attempt to challenge male-dominated theology. In her interpretation of the parable of the wise and foolish virgins in Matthew 25, for example, the author suggests that the concept of sin must be reinterpreted to respond to the needs of women. It was meaningless to tell women that they should avoid self-interest. Woman's sin was indulging in too much self-sacrifice and not sufficient self-development. Another author suggested that a Heavenly Mother be added to the image of Heavenly Father. Yet *The Woman's Bible* and its attempts at theological reappraisal were rejected as too radical and threatening to the flourishing suffrage movement that depended on the support of church-women. It was not until the early 1970s that another such reappraisal was begun. A 1971 gathering at Alverno College in Milwaukee, Wisconsin, began an extensive process of women doing theology. The Milwaukee conference was followed by numerous others in which women began to redefine or reject the traditional mind-set of Christianity.

The involvement of women in the theological enterprise is still unfolding. Because many of the details have yet to emerge and because the theological activity of women has taken a wide variety of directions, it is possible to make only a few generalizations.

Altering Traditional Theology and Theological Methods

One point that clearly emerges from this work of women is that many have broken with traditional ways of doing theology. Women have stressed that theology should grow out of the immediate experiences of women that are shared in community. Theology is a continuing process of experience and reflection upon experience. Theology must reflect the struggle for liberation as well as the distinctively female experiences of menstruation, pregnancy, and childbirth.

Women who are doing theology may not, in some instances, be trying to create a systematic body of concepts or images with its own inner logic. Some of them object to the use of the phrase "feminist theology" to describe their work. While many women use the traditional form of analytical prose, others find this form of expression inadequate and are inclined to turn instead to stories, art, and poetry as more satisfactory vehicles of expression.

Feminist theologians have agreed that in the past Christian theology has not supported the liberation of women. A whole new framework of concepts, stories, and images must be created. Some of the basic assumptions or the "hidden agenda" of theology must be changed. One such assumption is the dualistic view of reality on which men have long depended. This approach places one dimension of life over against another or alienated from another rather than seeing things as a whole. Thus, God is seen as alienated from the world, male from female, mind from body, church from world, and humanity from nature.

Another problematic assumption is the hierarchical view of reality that traditional Christianity has often adopted. One party is in a powerful position and the other is dependent or subordinate. God is over and above humanity, the priest is over and above lay people, Christianity is over and above other religions, and men are over and above women. In contrast, feminist theologians stress equality, reciprocity, and mutuality.

Specific images, stories, and concepts (such as sin and redemption) within the traditional framework of Christianity subvert the full equality and dignity of women. We have already touched on many of these stories and images in our survey of Christian history. God is seen as Father, the incarnation of God was in the male Jesus, and the story telling of the origin of sin in the world places the blame on women. Mary, the ideal Christian woman, is sexless and submissive. Also, women regard certain common theological concepts as repressive. The idea that Christians must obey the will of God, for example, has often been used to force women to do the bidding of men. The notion of rewards in heaven has led women to accept their situation in this life with meekness. The belief that self-sacrifice is righteous has inhibited women from developing their own talents, and the atonement minimizes the suffering of other people and their contribution to human salvation.

In deciding how to regard traditional Christianity in the process of doing theology, women reach markedly different conclusions. Some women are led to reject the tradition, others to reform it. Some take a revolutionary position by declaring that Christianity in its images, concepts, and stories is hopelessly sexist and only serves the interests of a society or institution that oppresses women. These women believe that a whole new religion must be constructed in which women "name" reality for themselves. Mary Daly is a widely known representative of this position. She believes that new images, concepts, and stories to replace the old will eventually come out of the feminist experience. She has taken some steps herself toward this reconstruction by suggesting that God no longer be thought of as a "noun" (a specific being) but as a "verb," as an active power or force that women feel within themselves. This view also enables her to speak of incarnation not as something that occurred in the first-century man named Jesus but as something that happens in all women.

Rosemary Radford Ruether has taken the position that the traditional biblical canon is so thoroughly sexist that women must move beyond it in order to construct a meaningful theology. She does admit that traces of female power and affirmation can be found in the biblical material. In *Womanguides: Readings toward a Feminist Theology*, however, she finds it imperative to add to these a wide variety of texts from marginal, unorthodox Christian communities that reflect "questionings of male domination in groups where women did enter into critical dialogue." These texts can be the beginning of a "new community, a new theology, a new canon."[30]

Women such as Elisabeth Schüssler Fiorenza and Letty Russell, however, make an attempt to liberate traditional Christianity from its sexism. They believe that through reform and reinterpretation of the tradition the images, concepts, and stories can be humanized and thus claimed by women as well as by men.

Reformist women in theology have made a start at reinterpreting some of the stories, concepts, and images that form the core of the Christian faith. We have already explored briefly the reinterpretation of stories such as the Genesis account of the creation and the Fall. This kind of exercise is an important part of women doing theology. Women have also reinterpreted many of the stories of the life of Jesus. Inspired by the work of liberation theologians, the primary image for Jesus becomes that of Liberator. He is one who challenges the idea that a male religious elite can "lord it over" the poor and women. Also inspired by liberation theology, sin is redefined as applying not only to the lives of individuals but to social structures and institutions that alienate and exploit others.

God is understood in this reinterpretation process not as an elderly father and judge over and above the world who doles out rewards and punishments; rather, the immanence, or indwelling, of God in the universe is stressed. The image of God as Father is exchanged for the image of God as Spirit or as the Ground of our Being, and both the male and female aspects of God's nature are emphasized.

Concepts and images important to the life of the church are also being reinterpreted in light of the experiences of women. *Diakonia,* or service to the church, is no longer defined as passive subservience but as the claiming of power and authority. The laying on of hands, according to Letty Russell, should not be used to create an authoritarian ordained elite but should be used for anyone who has a calling and an ability to perform a particular service.

Finally, because what is valued as good and right in Christianity is closely connected with theological views, the work of some women in theology has influenced their ethical positions. They have been inclined to reject any ethic built on a hierarchical and dualistic view of reality. They oppose behavior that sees other people or the natural world as "things" to be subjugated and the idea that there is one set of rules for private life and one set for public life. They place little value on physical aggression, valor, or competition and instead emphasize the need for compassion and cooperation. They have tended to be concerned with the immediate and concrete results of behavior rather than with abstract ethical principles. And they have indicted the Christian community for its long silence, rooted in the idea that women are subordinate objects, on issues such as rape, wife abuse, and sexual harassment.

Womanist and Mujerista *Theologies*

The presence of a chorus of voices from minority women was the single most important development in feminist theologies in the 1990s. While agreeing that the experiences of women are an important theological resource, Latina and African American women recognized that there was a world of difference between their experiences and those of white middle-class women who had been constructing theology. As one African American churchwoman put it, "There ain't enough to fit me" in the work of white feminist theologians.[31]

African American women used black theology and feminist theology as stepping stones but found the former to be sexist (denying, for example, the call of black women to preach and exploiting the service of black church women) and the latter, racist. Inspired by novelist Alice Walker, theologian Katie Cannon gave the name "womanist" to a new theological enterprise that recognizes sexism as only one way black women experience oppression. Womanist theologians shape their interpretation of Christian concepts, images, and stories according to the pervasive devaluing of African American women, but they are also influenced by the ways in which these women remain strong, take charge of their lives, love their families, and celebrate the food, music, and community around them. Womanist theology, therefore, focuses not only on the theme of liberation but also survival. Hagar in the Old Testament is used as the model for all women who go into the world to make a living for themselves and their children. Believing that white feminist theology focuses too much on women alone, their theology is also shaped by concern for family and community.

Latina theologians and pastoral caregivers also find feminist theology inadequate as an expression of the poverty, ethnic prejudice, and sexism experienced by Latina women. Inspired by the Spanish word for woman (*mujer*) and the womanist community, they have identified their struggle to take these experiences seriously as *mujerista* theology. This theology, rooted in the popular religion of Latina women, is not concerned with elaborate intellectual systems but with the practical goal of justice. The circumstances of women's everyday lives redefine basic theological concepts. Sin becomes self-effacement and resignation in the face of oppression and an unwillingness to define a better future. Suffering is rejected as a good in itself and the "kingdom of God" is transformed into the "kindom of God," a real place in real time where all have equal access to life and joy.[32]

WHAT COMES NEXT?

We have documented remarkable changes—some might say progress—in the status of women in the Christian tradition, but the story is a complex and often ambiguous one. Was the Reformation good or bad for women? The ascetic life? The veneration of Mary, the Mother of Jesus? Life in communities such as the Shakers or Oneida? Such ambiguity makes short concluding remarks about the past difficult and it clouds the future. Rather than drawing conclusions, we can point to certain themes that have emerged in these chapters and use these themes to raise questions that will shape discussions on women and Christianity well into the future. The movement of women toward equality and full participation, for example, has involved both steps forward and steps backward. These goals have been approximated at various times throughout Christian history only to be followed by periods of retrenchment and repression. The openness of the earliest Christian communities, for example, was followed by a return to custom and subordination. The relative freedom of women in the early monasteries was followed by an erosion of power and a move toward complete cloistering. The era of mission leadership, *The Woman's Bible,* and growing professional participation was followed in the early twentieth century by a time of institutional conservatism and a resurgence of the cult of true womanhood. Since the 1960s, women have made great strides toward claiming a place for themselves in the institutional churches and in the community of biblical scholars and theologians. Language for God has changed in some congregations and women's history is being explored with enthusiasm and care. Yet a question we must ask is whether we have entered a new period of retrenchment in the early twenty-first century. The Roman Catholic Church is headed by a new and traditionalist pope, Benedict XVI, and shows no signs of even discussing the ordination women as priests. Protestant women trained for the parish ministry more often than not wind up in noncongregational ministries or in small churches. And the cultural ethos of America, influenced by groups such as Concerned Women for America, appears increasingly to be turning toward the subordination of women in home and church despite their presence in the workplace.

Another theme that runs throughout this history is the kind of power women seek and claim for themselves. Often this power has been the result of personal charisma and the gifts of leadership or visions or other kinds of mystical experiences. Or it has been what scholars call cultural power rooted in the vital contributions made by large numbers of women to the life of a particular community. Women in the twentieth century, however, sought the formal power of office in institutional structures. The question some have begun to pose is whether women really want and need official positions in institutions that are shaped and still, for the most part, run by men along hierarchical lines. If the answer is "yes," can we expect more significant changes to the ways women conduct ministries? So far, dramatic changes have not been apparent. Will they become so as more women serve as clergy for longer periods of time?

Some interesting themes and questions are raised by specific parts of the Christian tradition considered in this survey. Both the Mormons and large segments of American evangelicalism have firmly embraced and advocated an ideology of submission for women in the last decades of the twentieth century, yet in each community there is a far more liberated past—and a community of women scholars who persist in writing about it. Will this past become more widely known? Will it be used eventually to shape more inclusive policies and practices? Roman Catholic women also present us with intriguing possibilities, especially with reference to the ascetic life. This was historically, as we have seen, a location for women to exercise leadership and wield power. Will this life die out in the twenty-first century? Will professional women, disillusioned in the workplace, breathe new life into contemplative orders as they have already done already in a few places? Will the Roman Catholic Church consider temporary vows to attract younger women so urgently needed as sisters? Also stirring Catholic women is the suggestion that they consider the lay pastorate. The questions remains: will this be a satisfactory alternative to the ordained priesthood?

And finally, there is the Bible. In some ways it has been the main character in this story, appearing in every chapter. Men and women have used it to justify female silence and subordination but also to support equality and creative participation in the Christian community. The chasm between biblical literalism and verbal inspiration on the one hand and a willingness to see some texts as cultural artifacts rather than eternal truth on the other hand grows wider. Will some ground for dialogue emerge? Will American believers find a way to take the Bible seriously but not literally? Will excursions into the history of women alert them to alternative voices and alternative ways of discovering truth? I can think of few outcomes that would be more pleasing to the women whose stories are documented in these pages.

Readings for Chapter 9

9.1 ADMISSION OF WOMEN TO THE PRIESTHOOD

The Vatican's "Declaration on the Question of the Admission of Women to the Ministerial Priesthood" was published in January 1977. It was a response more to ferment within the Catholic Church than to the external forces of the women's liberation movement and Protestant ordination policies. The Second Vatican Council defined the church as the people of God and called for lay involvement in all aspects of church life. A flood of books and articles calling for the ordination of women to the priesthood resulted. The declaration, which presents new reasons to justify existing legislation, concludes that the church "does not consider herself authorized to admit women to priestly ordination." As we see in sections one and two, the basis for this is that Jesus did not call a woman to be one of the Twelve, despite his willingness to break with cultural norms on many occasions. We are reminded by some scholars, however, that the declaration contains hints of indecisiveness and ambiguity. We read, for example, that the facts of Jesus' life "do not make the matter immediately obvious."

Source: "Declaration on the Question of the Admission of Women to the Ministerial Priesthood." In *Women Priests: A Catholic Commentary on the Vatican Declaration,* edited by Leonard Swidler and Arlene Swidler, 38–40. New York: Paulist, 1977.

The Church's Constant Tradition

The Catholic Church has never felt that priestly or episcopal ordination can be validly conferred on women. A few heretical sects in the first centuries, especially Gnostic ones, entrusted the exercise of the priestly ministry to women: this innovation was immediately noted and condemned by the Fathers, who considered it as unacceptable in the Church. It is true that in the writings of the Fathers one will find the undeniable influence of prejudices unfavorable to women, but nevertheless, it should be noted that these prejudices had hardly any influence on their pastoral activity, and still less on their spiritual direction. But over and above considerations inspired by the spirit of the times, one finds expressed—especially in the canonical documents of the Antiochian and Egyptian traditions—this essential reason, namely, that by calling only men to the priestly Order and ministry in its true sense, the Church intends to remain faithful to the type of ordained ministry willed by the Lord Jesus Christ and carefully maintained by the Apostles.

The same conviction animates mediaeval theology, even if the Scholastic doctors, in their desire to clarify by reason the data of faith, often present arguments on this point that modern thought would have difficulty in admitting or would even rightly reject. Since that period and up to our own time, it can be said that the question has not been raised again, for the practice has enjoyed peaceful and universal acceptance.

The Church's tradition in the matter has thus been so firm in the course of the centuries that the Magisterium has not felt the need to intervene in order to formulate a principle which was not attacked, or to defend a law which was not challenged. But each time that this tradition had the occasion to manifest itself, it witnessed to the Church's desire to conform to the model left to her by the Lord.

The same tradition has been faithfully safeguarded by the Churches of the East. Their unanimity on this point is all the more remarkable since in many other questions their discipline admits of a great diversity. At the present time these same Churches refuse to associate themselves with requests directed towards securing the accession of women to priestly ordination.

The Attitude of Christ

Jesus did not call any woman to become part of the Twelve. If he acted in this way, it was not in order to conform to the customs of his time, for his attitude towards women was quite different from that of his milieu, and he deliberately and courageously broke with it.

For example, to the great astonishment of his own disciples Jesus converses publicly with the Samaritan woman (cf. John 4:27); he takes no notice of the state of legal impurity of the woman who had suffered from haemorrhages (cf. Matt. 9:20-22); he allows a sinful woman to approach him in the house of Simon the Pharisee (cf. Luke 7:37ff.); and by pardoning the woman taken in adultery, he means to show that one must not be more severe towards the fault of a woman than towards that of man (cf. John 8:11). He does not hesitate to depart from the Mosaic Law in order to affirm the equality of the rights and duties of men and women with regard to the marriage bond (cf. Mark 10:2-11; Matt. 19:3-9).

In his itinerant ministry Jesus was accompanied not only by the Twelve but also by a group of women: "Mary, surnamed the Magdalene, from whom seven demons had gone out, Joanna the wife of Herod's steward Chuza, Susanna, and several others who provided for them out of their own resources" (Luke 8:2-3). Contrary to the Jewish mentality, which did not accord great value to the testimony of women, as Jewish law attests, it was nevertheless women who were the first to have the privilege of seeing the risen Lord, and it was they who were charged by Jesus to take the first paschal message to the Apostles themselves (cf. Matt. 28:7-10; Luke 24:9-10; John 20:11-18), in order to prepare the latter to become the official witnesses to the Resurrection.

It is true that these facts do not make the matter immediately obvious. This is no surprise, for the questions that the Word of God brings before us go beyond the obvious. In order to reach the ultimate meaning of the mission of Jesus and the ultimate meaning of Scripture, a purely historical exegesis of the texts cannot suffice. But it must be recognized that we have here a number of convergent indications that make all the more remarkable the fact that Jesus did not entrust the apostolic charge to women. Even his Mother, who was so closely associated with the mystery of her Son, and whose incomparable role is emphasized by the Gospels of Luke and John, was not invested with the apostolic ministry. This fact was to lead the Fathers to present her as the example of Christ's will in this domain; as Pope Innocent III repeated later, at the beginning of the thirteenth century, "Although the Blessed Virgin Mary surpassed in dignity and in excellence all the Apostles, nevertheless it was not to her but to them that the Lord entrusted the keys of the Kingdom of Heaven."

9.2 INCLUSIVE LANGUAGE FOR WORSHIP

In 1980, the Division of Education and Ministry of the National Council of Churches of Christ appointed a committee of six men and six women to prepare lectionary readings for public worship using inclusive language. Working with Greek and Hebrew texts, other translations, and commentaries, the committee produced three one-year cycles of readings that recast some of the wording of the Revised Standard Version of the Bible. Specifically,

the committee worked to change the male bias in language for God, Jesus, and human beings. In the excerpts here, which come from the second cycle of readings, "Lord" is changed to "Sovereign" to avoid the common understanding of "lord" as a man with power and authority. In two instances names have been added to the text. Women's names are included where the generation of offspring is discussed, and God is described as "Father and Mother," the one who both begat and gave birth to Jesus. As the humanity of Jesus is what is crucial to salvation, Jesus becomes the "Child of God" in the revised text.

Source: *An Inclusive Language Lectionary: Readings for Year B.* Prepared by the Inclusive Language Lectionary Committee appointed by the Division of Education and Ministry, National Council of the Churches of Christ in the U.S.A., 40, 74, 82. Philadelphia: Westminster, 1984.

Ephesians 1:3–6, 15–18

The writer of the letter to the Ephesians begins by praising God's glorious grace in Jesus Christ.

Blessed be God the Father [*and Mother*] of our Sovereign Jesus Christ, who has blessed us in Christ with every spiritual blessing in the heavenly places, even as God chose us in Christ before the foundation of the world, that we should be holy and blameless before God, who destined us in love to be God's children through Jesus Christ, according to the purpose of God's will, to the praise of God's glorious grace freely bestowed on us in the Beloved.

For this reason, because I have heard of your faith in the Sovereign Jesus and your love toward all the saints, I do not cease to give thanks for you, remembering you in my prayers, that the God of our Sovereign Jesus Christ, the Father [*and Mother*] of glory, may give you a spirit of wisdom and of revelation in the knowledge of God, having the eyes of your hearts enlightened, that you may know what is the hope to which you have been called, what are the riches of God's glorious inheritance in the saints.

Psalm 105:1-11

O give thanks to God, call on God's
     name,
     make known God's deeds among the
        peoples!
Sing to God, sing praises to God,
     tell of all God's wonderful works!
Glory in God's holy name;
     let the hearts of those who seek God
        rejoice!
Seek God and God's strength,
     seek God's presence continually!
Remember the wonderful works that
        God has done,
     God's miracles, and the judgments
        God uttered,
O offspring of Abraham [*and Sarah,*]
        God's servants,
     children of Jacob, [*Rachel, and Leah,*]
        God's chosen ones!

This is the Sovereign One our God,
     whose judgments are in all the earth.
God is mindful of the covenant for ever,
     of the word that God commanded, for
        a thousand generations,
the covenant which God made with
        Abraham,
     God's sworn promise to Isaac,
confirmed to Jacob as a statute,
     to Israel as an everlasting covenant,

saying, "To you I will give the land of
     Canaan
     as your portion for an inheritance."

John 3:14-21

Acceptance or rejection of God's love in Jesus Christ brings its own consequence.

And as Moses lifted up the serpent in the wilderness, so must the Human One be lifted up, that whoever believes in the Human One may have eternal life. For God so loved the world that God gave God's only Child, that whoever believes in that Child should not perish but have eternal life. For God sent that Child into the world, not to condemn the world, but that through that Child the world might be saved. Whoever believes in the Child [*of God*] is not condemned; whoever does not believe is condemned already, for not having believed in the name of the only Child of God. And this is the judgment, that the light has come into the world, and people loved the shadows rather than the light, because their deeds were evil. For all who do evil hate the light, and do not come to the light, lest their deeds should be exposed. But all who do what is true come to the light, that it may be clearly seen that their deeds have been wrought in God.

9.3 FEMINIST LITURGY

Liberating Liturgies is a collection of liturgies celebrated by members and friends of the Women's Ordination Conference. Encouraging improvisation and experimentation, the women share their own experiences, tell their own stories, and speak their own prayers in these rituals. This particular commissioning liturgy shows many of the characteristics of feminist liturgy described in Teresa Berger's Women's Ways of Worship, *including forming a circle together, encouraging all to participate, remembering biblical women and women who have made a difference in their lives, using gender-inclusive language, and moving beyond Scripture to multiple authoritative sources.*

Source: Women's Ordination Conference. *Liberating Liturgies*, 44–47. Fairfax, Va.: Women's Ordination Conference, 1989.

INTRODUCTION: This is a liturgy of commission, representing an effort to bring together a spirit of thanksgiving and celebration at a time that has potential to be painful and troublesome for a Catholic woman, with a remembrance and honoring of "unrecognized" apostles whose testimonies were doubted and whose authenticity was questioned. Among these Paul, who needed to defend his equality with the Jerusalem apostles in his own time, figures prominently. As a symbol of the shared leadership and religious authority with which we sent forth our friend, and as a testimony of her witness to the world, we gave her the cup and plate from which we drank and ate during the liturgy.

OPENING PRAYER: (Together) You have turned our mourning to dancing, dear God. There is great cause to rejoice! (One person then prays spontaneously or uses a short reflective passage to set the tone of the liturgy.)

FIRST READING: Galatians 1:11-24

SECOND READING: Luke 24:9-12

THIRD READING: Gospel of Mary, 18-19:

"When Mary had said this, she fell silent, since it was to this point that the Savior had spoken with her. But Andrew answered and said, 'Say what you wish to say about what she has said. I at least do not believe that the Savior said this. For certainly these teachings are strange ideas.' Peter answered and spoke concerning these same things. He questioned them about the Savior: 'Did he really speak privately with a woman and not openly to us? Are we to turn about and all listen to her? Did he prefer her to us?'

Then Mary wept and said to Peter, 'My brother Peter, what do you think? Do you think I thought this up myself in my heart, or that I am lying about the Savior?'

Levi answered and said to Peter, 'Peter, you have always been hot-tempered. Now I see you contending against the woman like the adversaries. But if the Savior made her worthy, who are you indeed to reject her? Surely the Savior knows her very well. That is why he loved her more than us. Rather, let us be ashamed and put on perfection and separate as he commanded us and preach the gospel, not laying down on any other rule or other law beyond what the Savior said' . . . And they began to go forth to proclaim and to preach." (*Excerpt from* The Nag Hammadi Library in English, *edited by James M. Robinson. Copyright © 1978 by E. J. Brill. Reprinted by permission of Harper and Row, Publishers, Inc.*)

COMMUNAL REMEMBRANCE: (The gifts of the woman being celebrated are remembered here. At this time, participants call upon their collective and individual knowledge of the woman to be commissioned, to share reflections on her particular gifts and on her ministerial strength. Symbols for these gifts might include, for example, a cup of oil to symbolize healing, etc.)

For Hagar and Other Women
Who Sit Unwittingly
Beside Living Water
(Genesis 16)
by Kerry Maloney

Shaken out like the pleats of an ancient
    skirt
my womb is the gateway of wanderings.
Fury and scorn, this slavery of sorrows
and no honor gained in a son's
    annunciation—
I am the handmaid of the Lord,
the handmaid of the Lord.

By wellsprings, I have been found.
Still, I am discovered there.
Hearing words of rebuke and
    gladness—
He told me all I have ever done.
Can this be he?

Can this be he?
Who would believe what I have seen?
(Who would really care?)
"The Lord has given heed to my
    affliction."
This child of exalted father will not be
    slain on altars of faith or principle.

But having seen your face, we will live.
and know
God hears.
Ishmael.

BLESSING OF WATER: Creator Spirit, you hovered over the chaotic waters at the beginning of time to bring peace, order and life out of tumult. Through the waters of the flood, parting sea, baptism, and Jesus' wound, you recreated and delivered your people. Be present again as we bless this water, water in which we are nourished before birth, by which we are cleansed and refreshed, with which we spill tears in sorrow and delight. Loving Mother, bring us newness of life and purpose through this water. We praise you for this simple gift which sustains us, and we thank you for your presence in its unending flow.
(The water is poured into a bowl and a cup from a pitcher.)

BLESSING OF THE WOMAN: (Each participant washes her hands in the newly blessed water in the bowl before encircling the woman who is to be commissioned for apostolic service. When the circle is formed, the participants impose their hands—as one—on the woman's head and pray silently for her.)

SHARING OF BREAD AND WATER: We have received the blessing of (N's) friendship and her ministry. We have celebrated God's choice of her to be the bearer of Good News by blessing her. Let us now share this living water from the cup of blessing and this bread among ourselves as friends. This simple meal, bread and water, is transformed from a symbol of austerity and punishment to a sign of celebration and a foretaste of the celestial banquet by our feasting together today on God's goodness in her gift of (N) to us.

ALL: (After the feast.) You have turned our mourning to dancing, dear God. There is great cause to rejoice!

THE COMMISSION: (N), hear these words. "Tend the flock of God that is your charge, not by constraint but willingly, not for shameful gain but eagerly, not as domineering over those in your charge but being an example to the flock." (I Peter 5:2-4)

9.4 FEMINIST VIEWS OF SIN AND SALVATION

In this section of Human Liberation in a Feminist Perspective, *feminist theologian Letty Russell discusses the willingness of contemporary religious seekers to be flexible in their defi-nitions of sin and salvation. Firmly rooted in the biblical concept of* shalom, *liberation theologians, for example, assert that salvation is much more than individual deliverance from sin and death. It is personal and social well-being, the transformation of economic, political, social, and mental structures. Women, Russell points out, are particularly interested in moving beyond the definition of sin as aggression and lust, which has been emphasized by male theologians, to an understanding of sin as underdevelopment or negation of the self. Women, in their quest for liberation, also find it important to define sin as "the refusal to give others room to breathe and live as human beings."*

Source: Letty M. Russell. *Human Liberation in a Feminist Perspective—A Theology*, 109–13. Philadelphia: Westminster, 1974.

One of the interesting things that has happened to the understanding of salvation today is that, in a world of diversity and change, people feel free to use a variety of definitions of salvation. In the search for meaning every religion and ideology is explored for its offer of liberation, wholeness, and blessing.[1] There is a growing awareness of the wholeness of human beings in their body, mind, and spirit and in their social relationship in today's world. For some this has led to a renewed stress on *shalom* as a gift of total wholeness and well-being in community.[2] The search for peace in a war torn world where each new outbreak of fighting brings not only untold suffering but the threat of total destruction has led others to speak of *shalom* as the symbol of peace and harmony for which they long and work. Others see *shalom* as an expression of wholeness and harmony between humanity and the environment which is being destroyed by a technological society.[3]

Nowhere is the stress on salvation as seen in the motifs of *shalom* clearer than among those searching for ways of expressing the good news of God's traditioning action in situations of oppression, hunger, and alienation in our sorry world. Liberation theologies, which seek to reflect on the praxis of God's liberation in the light of particular circumstances of oppression, are returning to the motifs of liberation and blessing as they are found in the biblical tradition. Without denying that salvation includes the message of individual deliverance from sin and death (Rom. 5–7) they, nevertheless, place emphasis on the total goal of salvation (Rom. 8), which is the gift of *shalom* (complete social and physical wholeness and harmony). Gustavo Gutiérrez says:

> Salvation is not something otherworldly, in regard to which the present life is merely a test. Salvation—the communion of . . . [people] with God and the communion of . . . [people] among themselves—is something which embraces all human reality, transforms it, and leads it to its fullness in Christ.[4]

In these emerging liberation theologies the two overlapping motifs of *shalom* appear again as a description of the usable future. The first motif of *liberation* is seen as the gift of God's action in history, as well as the agenda of those who join together in community to transform the world. For Third World and Fourth World people the motif of liberation expresses an important aspect of the *shalom* for which they seek. Speaking about "The Dialectic of Theology and Life," James Cone reminds us that "Jesus is not a doctrine" but an eternal event of liberation who makes freedom possible. From this context of Christ as Liberator emerges a life of interdependence in the lives of black people. He is the Word of truth in their lives.[5] In the area of justice and economic development, those at work to bring about an evolutionary process for transforming economic, social, political, and mental structures point to a connection with salvation in its implication of freedom. Thus in *Liberation, Development, and Salvation*, René Laurentin says that "development presupposes a liberation from systems in which any development is impossible."[6]

Writers such as Rosemary Ruether and Dorothee Sölle emphasize the same theme. Ruether, in her book *Liberation Theology*, speaks of the destructive character of dualisms such as that between the individual and the collective, and the body and the soul, and sets out to analyze various polarities which are barriers to the theology and praxis of liberation. Sölle speaks of the gospel's business as "liberation of all human beings. Its concern rests with the oppressed, the poor, the crying."[7]

The second motif that overlaps with liberation is the meaning and experience of *shalom* as *blessing*. In the writers concerned with liberation theology this is usually interpreted as *humanization:* the setting free of all humanity to have a future and a hope. The blessings of the Patriarchs are now interpreted in modern contexts as the need for full personal and social well-being, as well as the need for the power to participate in shaping the world.

For those who experience *shalom* as new wholeness and liberation as human beings, *sin* is also viewed as a collective reality. The social as well as the individual responsibility for sin is stressed so that *oppression* is itself viewed as a symbol of the social reality of sin. Dorothee Sölle writes:

> Sin to us is eminently political, a social term: the sins of which Jesus reminds me and which he puts before my eyes are the sins of my own people, of my own white race, of my own bourgeois and propertied class.[8]

Going back to the root meaning of one word for salvation (*yeshu'ah*, from a root meaning "to be broad, or spacious"; "to have room"), sin is interpreted as the denial of this room or space in which to live.[9] Just as Isaiah 49:19-20 symbolizes the oppression of Israel as a land "too narrow for your inhabitants" and Psalm 4:1 speaks of salvation as the gift of "room when I was in distress," liberation

theologies point to sin as the refusal to give others room to breathe and live as human beings. According to Gutiérrez:

> Sin is regarded as a social, historical fact, the absence of . . . [humanhood] and love in relationships among . . . [people], the breach of friendship with God and with other . . . [people], and, therefore, an interior, personal fracture. When it is considered in this way, the collective dimensions of sin are rediscovered.[10]

Women are very much interested in the reinterpretation of the meaning of sin in a feminist perspective. In church traditions sin has been interpreted not only individualistically but also as associated with sex and with women. A forthright rejection of such misogyny, including the misinterpretations of the Adam and Eve story which flow from this perspective, can be seen in many feminist writers. For instance, Mary Daly writes:

> In the mentality of the Fathers, woman and sexuality were identified. Their horror of sex was also a horror of woman. There is no evidence that they realized the projected mechanisms involved in this misogynistic attitude. In fact, male guilt feelings over sex and hypersusceptibility to sexual stimulation and suggestion were transferred to "the other," the guilty sex.[11]

Another area of reinterpretation of the traditions concerning sin which interests feminist writers is the male perspective on what constitutes human sin and temptation. Aggression, lust, and hybris may not be at the top of the list for women who have been enculturated to be submissive. Valarie Saiving Goldstein writes:

The temptations of woman *as woman* are not the same as the temptations of man *as man,* and the specifically feminine forms of sin—"feminine" not because they are confined to women or because women are incapable of sinning in other ways but because they are outgrowths of the basic feminine character structure—have a quality which can never be encompassed by such terms as "pride," and "will-to-power." They are better suggested by such items as triviality, distractibility, and diffuseness; lack of an organizing center or focus; dependence on others for one's own self-definition; tolerance at the expense of standards of excellence; . . . in short, under-development or negation of self.[12]

In various liberation theologies sin is viewed not only as the opposite of liberation or the oppression of others but also as the opposite of humanization or the *dehumanization* of others by means of excluding their perspectives from the meaning of human reality and wholeness.

In summary we can say that salvation today, as well as the understanding of sin today, has regained its social and communal emphasis in writings on liberation theology. Not denying individual responsibility and accountability, they still drive us also to see the dimension of responsibility and accountability in terms of the liberation and blessing for all oppressed and defuturized persons. For many people today, liberation is understood as a gift of God at once personal and social which is only ours as it is constantly shared with others.

Notes to Reading 9.4

1. *Salvation Today and Contemporary Experience: A Collection of Texts for Critical Study and Reflection* (Geneva: World Council of Churches, 1972).

2. Gabriel Fackre, *Do and Tell: Engagement Evangelism in the 70s* (Grand Rapids, Mich.: Eerdmans, 1973), 34; Letty M. Russell, "Shalom in Postmodern Society," in *A Colloquy on Christian Education,* ed. John A. Westerhoff III (United Church Press, 1972), 97–105; *Colloquy,* National Shalom Conference Issue 6 (March 1973).

3. Fackre, *Do and Tell,* 86; *Colloquy, A Curriculum for Peace* 5 (July/August 1972).

4. Gustavo Gutiérrez, *A Theology of Liberation,* trans. and ed. Caridad Inda and John Eagleson (Maryknoll, N.Y.: Orbis, 1972), 151; cf. A. Schoors, *I Am God Your Savior* (Leiden: Brill, 1973).

5. James Cone, "The Dialectic of Theology and Life" (inaugural lecture as professor of theology, Union Theological Seminary, New York City, October 11, 1973); and cf. "Black Theology and Reconciliation," *Christianity and Crisis* 32 (January 22, 1973): 303–8.

6. René Laurentin, *Liberation, Development, and Salvation* (Maryknoll, N.Y.: Orbis, 1972), 53.

7. Rosemary Radford Ruether, *Liberation Theology* (New York: Paulist, 1973), 7–9, 16–22; Dor-

othee Sölle, "The Gospel and Liberation," *Commonweal* (December 22, 1972): 270.

8. Sölle, "The Gospel and Liberation," 273–74; cf. Gordon D. Kaufman, "The Imago Dei as Man's Historicity," *The Journal of Religion* 36 (July 1956): 165–67.

9. A. Richardson, "Salvation, Savior," *Interpreter's Dictionary of the Bible,* vol. 4 (Nashville: Abingdon, 1962), 169; J. Verkuyl, *The Message of Liberation in Our Age* (Grand Rapids, Mich.: Eerdmans, 1970), 17–18.

10. Gutiérrez, *Theology of Liberation,* 175; Ruether, *Liberation,* 8.

11. Mary Daly, *The Church and the Second Sex* (New York: Harper & Row, 1968), 46–47; cf. Ruether, *Liberation,* 95–113.

12. Valarie Saiving Goldstein, "The Human Situation: A Feminine View," *The Journal of Religion* 40 (April 1960): 108–9.

9.5 JESUS IN WOMANIST THEOLOGY

Jacquelyn Grant, a professor of systematic theology and ordained pastor in the African Methodist Episcopal Church, is known for her writing on Jesus and Christology in the womanist tradition. In her essay "Womanist Theology," she argues that the experiences of white women as a theological resource fail to take into account the classism and racism as well as sexism experienced by black women. The word "womanist" reminds us that black women have been serious, outspoken, and radical in their interpretation of Christian tradition, particularly the Bible and Jesus. In this reading from her essay she describes a Jesus who has been claimed by black women.

Source: Jacquelyn Grant. "Womanist Theology: Black Women's Experience as a Source for Doing Theology, with Special Reference to Christology." In *Black Theology: A Documentary History,* vol. 2, edited by James H. Cone and Gayraud S. Wilmore, 281–83. Maryknoll, N.Y.: Orbis, 1993.

Jesus in the Womanist Tradition

Having opened the Bible wider than many White people, Black people, in general, and Black women in particular, found a Jesus who they could claim, and whose claim for them was one of affirmation of dignity and self-respect.

In the experience of Black people, Jesus was "all things."[1] Chief among these however was the belief in Jesus as the divine co-sufferer, who empowers them in situations of oppression. For Christian Black women in the past, Jesus was their central frame of reference. They identified with Jesus because they believed that Jesus identified with them. As Jesus was persecuted and made to suffer undeservedly, so were they. His suffering culminated in the crucifixion. Their crucifixion included rapes, and husbands being castrated (literally and metaphorically), babies being sold, and other cruel and often murderous treatments. But Jesus' suffering was not the suffering of a mere human, for Jesus was understood to be God incarnate. As Harold Carter observed of Black prayers in general, there was no difference made between the persons of the trinity, Jesus, God, or the Holy Spirit. All of these proper names for God were used interchangeably in prayer language. Thus, Jesus was the one who speaks the world into creation. He was the power behind the Church.[2] Black women's affirmation of Jesus as God meant that White people were not God. One old slave woman clearly demonstrates this as she prayed:

> Dear Massa Jesus, we all uns beg Ooner [you] come make us a call dis yere day. We is nutting but poor Etiopian women and people ain't tink much 'bout we. We ain't trust any of dem great high people for come to we church, but do' you is de one great Massa, great too much dan Massa Linkum, you ain't shame to care for we African people.[3]

Implicit in the description "nothing but poor black women" and what follows is the awareness of the public devaluation of Black women. But in spite of that Jesus is presented as a confidant who could be trusted while White people could not be trusted. This woman affirmed the contribution of Abraham Lincoln to the emancipation of Blacks, but rejected Mr. Lincoln as her real or ultimate master. Quite a contrast to the master's (slave owner's) perception of his/her-self.

This slave woman did not hesitate to identify her struggle and pain with those of Jesus. In fact, the common struggle made her know that Jesus would respond to her beck and call.

> Come to we, dear Massa Jesus. De sun, he hot too much, de road am dat long and boggy (sandy) and we ain't got no buggy for send and fetch Ooner. But Massa, you 'member how you walked dat hard walk up Calvary and ain't weary but tink about we all dat way. We know you ain't weary for to come to we. We pick out de torns, de prickles, de brier, de backslidin' and de quarrel and de sin out of you path so dey shan't hurt Ooner pierce feet no more.[4]

The reference to "no buggy" to send for Jesus brings to mind the limited material possessions of pre- and post-Civil War Blacks. In her speech, "Ain't I a Woman," Sojourner Truth distinguished between White women's and Black women's experiences by emphasizing that Black women were not helped into carriages as were White women.[5] In the prayer, this woman speaks of that reality wherein most Blacks didn't even have carriages or buggys. For had she owned one, certainly she'd send it to fetch Jesus. Here we see the concern for the comfort and the suffering of Jesus. Jesus suffers when we sin—when we backslide or quarrel. But still Jesus is identified with her plight. Note that Jesus went to the cross with this Black woman on his mind. He was thinking about her and all others like her. So totally dedicated to the poor, the weak, the downtrodden, the outcast that in this Black woman's faith, Jesus would never be too tired to come. As she is truly among the people at the bottom of humanity, she can make things comfortable for Jesus even though she may have nothing to give him—no water, no food—but she can give tears and love. She continues:

> Come to me, dear Massa Jesus. We all uns ain't got no good cool water for give when you thirsty. You know Massa, de drought so long, and the well so low, ain't nutting but mud to drink. But we gwine to take de munion cup and fill it wid de tear of repentance, and love clean out of we heart. Dat all we hab to gib you good Massa.[6]

The material or physical deprivation experienced by this woman did not reduce her desire to give Jesus the best. Being a Black woman in the American society meant essentially being poor, with no buggy, and no good cool water. Life for Black women was indeed bad, hot and at best muddy. Note that there is no hint that their condition results from some divine intervention. Now, whereas I am not prepared to say that this same woman or any others in that church the next day would have been engaged in political praxis by joining such movements as Nat Turner's rebellion or Denmark Vesey's revolt, it is clear that her perspective was such that the social, political and economic orders were believed to be sinful and against the will of the real master, Jesus.

For Black women, the role of Jesus unraveled as they encountered him in their experience as one who empowers the weak. In this vein, Jesus was such a central part of Sojourner Truth's life that all her sermons made him the starting point. When asked by a preacher if the source of her preaching was the Bible, she responded, "No honey, can't preach from de bible—can't read a letter."[7] Then she explained, "When I preaches, I has jest one text to preach from, an' I always preaches from this one. My text is, 'When I found Jesus!'"[8] In this sermon Sojourner Truth recounts the events and struggles of life from the time her parents were brought from Africa and sold "up an' down, an' hither an' yon. . . ."[9] to the time that she met Jesus within the context of her struggles for dignity of Black people and women. Her encounter with Jesus brought such joy that she became overwhelmed with love and praise:

> Praise, praise, praise to the Lord! An I begun to feel such a love in my soul as I never felt before—love to all creatures. An then, all of a sudden, it stopped, an I said, Dar's de white folks that have abused you, an beat you, an abused your people—think o them! But there came another rush of love through my soul, an cried out loud—Lord, I can love even de white folks![10]

This love was not a sentimental, passive love. It was a tough, active love that empowered her to fight more fiercely for the freedom of her people. For the rest of her life she continued speaking at abolition and women's rights gatherings, and condemned the horrors of oppression.

Notes to Reading 9.5

1. Harold A. Carter, *The Prayer Tradition of Black People* (Valley Forge: Judson, 1976), 50. Carter, in referring to traditional Black prayer in general, states that Jesus was revealed as one who "was all one needs!"

2. Ibid.

3. Ibid., 49.

4. Ibid.

5. Sojourner Truth, "Ain't I a Woman?" in *Feminism: The Essential Historical Writings*, ed. Miriam Schneir (New York: Vintage, 1972).

6. Carter, *The Prayer Tradition*, 49.

7. Olive Gilbert, *Sojourner Truth: Narrative and Book of Life* (1850 and 1875; reprint, Chicago: Johnson, 1970), 83.

8. Ibid., 119.

9. Ibid.

10. Ibid.

ACKNOWLEDGMENTS

Chapter 1

Orante figure. Early Christian fresco. Location: Catacomb of the Giordani, Rome, Italy. Photo © Scala/Art Resource, N.Y. Used by permission.

Excerpts from "The Martyrdom of Saints Perpetua and Felicitas," *The Acts of the Christian Martyrs*, introduction, texts, and translations by Herbert Musurillo (Oxford: Clarendon Press, 1972), are reprinted by permission.

Excerpts from "The Pilgrimage of Egeria" in *A Lost Tradition: Women Writers of the Early Church*, by Patricia Wilson-Kastner et al. (Lanham, Md.: University Press of America, 1981) are reprinted by permission of the publisher.

Excerpts from "The Acts of Paul and Thecla," *The Apocryphal New Testament*, Montague Rhodes James, trans. (Oxford: Clarendon Press, 1924), 277–81, are reprinted by permission.

Chapter 2

Excerpts from *The Life of Christina of Markyate: A Twelfth Century Recluse*, edited and translated by C. H. Talbot (Oxford: Clarendon Press, 1959), are reprinted by permission.

Excerpts from *The Book of Margery Kempe* are copyright by Devin-Adair, Publishers, Inc., Old Greenwich, CT 06870. Permission granted to reprint excerpt from *The Book of Margery Kempe, Fourteen Hundred & Thiry Six*, a modern version by W. Butler-Bowden, 1944. All rights reserved.

Chapter 3

Excerpts from "Concerning Marriage" and "Concerning Adultery" in *Confession of Faith: Account of Our Religion, Doctrine and Faith Given by Peter Rideman of the Brothers Whom Men Call Hutterians*, by Peter Rideman (Rifton, N.Y.: Plough Publishing House, 1970), are reprinted by permission.

Excerpts from Peter Matheson, ed. *Argula von Grumbach: A Woman's Voice in the Reformation* (Edinburgh: T. & T. Clark, 1995), are reprinted by permission of The Continuum International Publishing Group.

Chapter 4

Illustration of Anne Hutchinson © Bettmann/CORBIS. Used by permission.

Chapter 6

Photo of Jarena Lee courtesy of the Library of Congress.

Chapter 7

Photo courtesy of The Mary Baker Eddy Collection. Used by permission.

Excerpts from Kenneth W. Godfrey, Audrey M. Godfrey and Jill Mulvay Derr, *Women's Voice: An Un-Folding History of the Latter Day Saints, 1830–1900*, 278–80, 285–86 (Salt Lake City, Utah: Deseret Book Company, 1982), are reprinted by permission.

Chapter 8

Photo of Nannie Helen Burroughs © Bettmann/CORBIS. Used by permission.

Excerpts from *The Service and Status of Women in the Churches* by Kathleen Bliss (London: SCM Press, 1952) are reprinted by permission.

Excerpts from "Woman Looks at Herself" in *The American Baptist Women*, January 1971, are reprinted by permission of American Baptist Women's Ministries.

Excerpts from *The Church and the Second Sex* by Mary Daly (New York: Harper & Row, 1975) are reprinted by permission.

Chapter 9

Photo of Letty Russell © Yale Divinity School and used by permission.

Excerpts from "Declaration on the Question of the Admission of Women to the Ministerial Priesthood" are from *Women Priests: A Catholic Commentary on the Vatican Declaration*, edited by Leonard Swidler and Arlene Swidler. Copyright © 1977 by The Missionary Society of St. Paul the Apostle in the State of New York. Used by permission of Paulist Press.

Excerpts from *An Inclusive Language Lectionary: Readings for Year B*, copyright © 1987 by the Division of Education and Ministry, National Council of the Churches of Christ in the U.S.A., are used by permission. All rights reserved.

Excerpts from *Liberating Liberties* are reprinted with permission of the Women's Ordination Conference, Fairfax, Virginia, 1989.

Excerpts from *Human Liberation in a Feminist Perspective: A Theology* by Letty M. Russell, copyright © 1974 by Letty M. Russell, are reprinted by permission of Westminster/John Knox Press.

Excerpts from Jacquelyn Grant, "Womanist Theology: Black Women's Experience as a Source for Doing Theology, with Special Reference to Christology," in *Journal of the Interdenominational Theological Center* 13 (Spring 1986), are used by permission.

NOTES

INTRODUCTION

1. Eleanor McLaughlin, "The Christian Past: Does It Hold a Future for Women?" in *Womanspirit Rising: A Feminist Reader in Religion*, ed. Carol P. Christ and Judith Plaskow (San Francisco: Harper and Row, 1979), 96.

2. *Women and Religion in Britain and Ireland: An Annotated Bibliography from the Reformation to 1993* (Lanham, Md.: Scarecrow, 1995).

1. WOMEN AND THE EARLY CHURCHES

1. See for example Karen Jo Torjesen, *When Women Were Priests: Women's Leadership in the Early Church and the Scandal of Their Subordination in the Rise of Christianity* (San Francisco: HarperSanFrancisco, 1993).

2. For a discussion of feminist interpretation of the New Testament as well as the activities of women, see for example these works by Elizabeth Schüssler Fiorenza: *Bread Not Stone: The Challenge of Feminist Biblical Interpretation* (Boston: Beacon, 1984), *In Memory of Her* (New York: Crossroad, 1983), and "Women in the New Testament," *New Catholic World* 219 (November/December, 1976): 256–60.

3. Wolfgang Stegemann, "Paul and the Sexual Mentality of His World," *Biblical Theology Bulletin* 23 (Winter 1993): 161–66; Torjesen, *When Women Were Priests*, 135–54.

4. Leonard Swidler, *Biblical Affirmations of Woman* (Philadelphia: Westminster, 1979), 155.

5. Bernadette J. Brooten, "Early Christian Women and Their Cultural Context: Issues of Method in Historical Reconstruction," in *Feminist Perspectives on Biblical Scholarship*, ed. Adela Collins (Chico, Calif.: Scholars Press, 1985), 65–91.

6. Peter Richardson, "From Apostles to Virgins: Romans 16 and the Roles of Women in the Early Church," *Toronto Journal of Theology* 2 (Fall 1986): 254.

7. Constance Parvey, "The Theology and Leadership of Women in the New Testament," in *Religion and Sexism: Images of Woman in the Jewish and Christian Traditions*, ed. Rosemary Radford Ruether (New York: Simon and Schuster, 1974), 138.

8. See for example Rodney Stark, "Reconstructing the Rise of Christianity: The Role of Women," *Sociology of Religion* 56 (Fall 1995): 232.

9. Francine Cardman, "Women, Ministry, and Church Order in Early Christianity," in *Women and Christian Origins*, ed. Ross Shepard Kraemer and Mary Rose D'Angelo (New York: Oxford University Press, 1999), 300–329.

10. Jane Schaberg, "Luke," in *The Women's Bible Commentary*, ed. Carol A. Newsom and Sharon H. Ringe (Louisville: Westminster John Knox, 1998), 376; Rikki Watts, "Women in the Gospels and Acts," *Crux* 35 (June 1999): 28.

11. Jane Schaberg, "How Mary Magdalene Became a Whore," *Bible Review* 8 (October 1992): 52.

12. Schaberg, "Luke," 380.

13. Elizabeth Castelli, "Paul on Women and Gender," in *Women and Christian Origins*, 221–35.

14. Lone Fatum, "Image of God and Glory of Man: Women in the Pauline Congregations," in *Image of God and Gender Models in Judaeo-Christian Tradition*, ed. Kari Elisabeth Børresen (Oslo: Solum Forlag, 1991), 56–86.

15. Castelli, "Paul on Women and Gender," 228.

16. Rosemary Radford Ruether, "The Subordination and Liberation of Women: St. Paul and Sarah Grimké," *Soundings* 51 (1978): 172.

17. Antoinette Clark Wire, "Theological and Biblical Perspective: Liberation for Women Calls for a Liberated World," *Church and Society* 76 (January/February 1986): 10–16.

18. Stegemann, "Paul and the Sexual Mentality of His World," 161–65.

19. Alvin John Schmidt, *Veiled and Silenced: How Culture Shaped Sexist Theology* (Macon, Ga.: Mercer University Press, 1989), 177–79.

20. Torjesen, *When Women Were Priests*, 53–87.

21. For a full study of Junia, see Eldon Epp, *Junia: The First Woman Apostle* (Minneapolis: Fortress Press, 2005).

22. Virginia Burrus, "Blurring the Boundaries: A Response to Howard C. Kee," *Theology Today* 49 (July 1992): 241.

23. See for example Winsome Munro, "Patriarchy and Charismatic Community in 'Paul'," in *Women and Religion: Papers of the Working Group on Women and Religion, 1972–73*, rev. ed., ed. Judith Plaskow and Joan Arnold Romero (Missoula, Mont.: Scholars Press, 1974), 189.

24. Mary T. Malone, *Women and Christianity*, vol. I, *The First Thousand Years* (Maryknoll, N.Y.: Orbis, 2001), 78.

25. Parvey, "The Theology and Leadership of Women in the New Testament," 118–19, 136; Munro, "Patriarchy and Charismatic Community in 'Paul'," 197–98.

26. Quoted in William Phipps, "The Menstrual Taboo in the Judaeo-Christian Tradition," *Journal of Religion and Health* 19 (Winter 1980): 300.

27. G. L. C. Frank, "Menstruation and Motherhood: Christian Attitudes in Late Antiquity," *Studia Historiae Ecclesiasticae* 19 (1993): 185–208.

28. Hamilton Hess, "Changing Forms of Ministry in the Early Church," in *Sexism and Church Law*, ed. James A. Coriden (New York: Paulist Press, 1977), 55.

29. Torjesen, *When Women Were Priests*, 155–72.

30. Richardson, "From Apostles to Virgins," 257–58.

31. Monique Alexandre, "Early Christian Women," in *From Ancient Goddesses to Christian Saints*, vol. I, *History of Women in the West*, ed. Pauline Schmitt Pantel (Cambridge, Mass.: Belknap Press, 1992), 409–44.

32. *Constitutions of the Holy Apostles*, ed. James Donaldson, in *The Ante-Nicene Fathers:Translations of the Writings of the Fathers Down to A.D. 325*, ed. Alexander Roberts and James Donaldson (Buffalo: Christian Literature Publication, 1886), 7:492.

33. Cardman, "Women, Ministry, and Church Order in Early Christianity," 316–17.

34. Karen L. King, "Early Christian Women as Prophetic Leaders," *Harvard Divinity Bulletin* 24 (1995): 7.

35. Edgar Hennecke and Wilhelm Schneemelcher, eds. *New Testament Apocrypha*, vol. I, *Gospels and Related Writings* (Philadelphia: Westminster, 1963), 256–57.

36. Christine Trevett, "Gender, Authority and Church History: A Case Study of Montanism," *Feminist Theology* 17 (January 1998): 23.

37. Ben Witherington, *Women in the Earliest Churches* (Cambridge: Cambridge University Press, 1988), 192.

38. Texts are reproduced in Patricia Wilson-Kastner et al., *A Lost Tradition: Women Writers of the Early Church* (Washington, D.C.: University Press of America, 1981).

39. Ibid., 19–32.

40. Rebecca Lyman, "Perpetua: A Christian Quest for Self," *Journal of Women and Religion* 8 (Winter 1989): 27.

41. Wilson-Kastner et al., *A Lost Tradition*, 22.

42. Malone, *Women and Christianity*, vol. I, *The First Thousand Years*, 105.

43. Wilson-Kastner et al., *A Lost Tradition*, 19–20.

44. Ibid., 107.

45. See for example Stevan L. Davies, *The Revolt of the Widows: The Social World of the Apocryphal Acts* (Carbondale, Ill.: Southern Illinois University Press, 1980); and Dennis R. MacDonald, *The Legend and the Apostle: The Battle for Paul in Story and Canon* (Philadelphia: Westminster, 1983).

2. VIRGIN AND WITCH: WOMEN IN MEDIEVAL CHRISTIANITY

1. Jane Tibbetts Schulenburg, "The Heroics of Virginity: Brides of Christ and Sacrificial Mutilation," in *Women in the Middle Ages and the Renaissance*, ed. Mary B. Rose (Syracuse, N.Y.: Syracuse University Press, 1986), 29–72.

2. Aideen Hartney, "Manly Women and Womanly Men: The *Subintroductae* and John Chrysostom," in *Desire and Denial in Byzantium: Papers from the 31st Spring Symposium of Byzantine Studies*, ed. Liz James (Aldershot, England: Ashgate, 1999), 46.

3. Dyan Elliott, *Spiritual Marriage: Sexual Abstinence in Medieval Wedlock* (Princeton: Princeton University Press, 1993).

4. Jane Simpson, "Women and Asceticism in the Fourth Century," *Journal of Religious History* 15 (June 1988): 38–60.

5. Jo Ann McNamara, "Muffled Voices," in *Medieval Religious Women*, vol. I, ed. John A. Nichols and Lillian Thomas Shank (Kalamazoo, Mich.: Cistercian, 1984), 27.

6. Quoted in Eleanor McLaughlin, "Equality of Souls, Inequality of Sexes," in *Religion and Sexism: Images of Woman in the Jewish and Christian Traditions*, ed. Rosemary Radford Ruether (New York: Simon and Schuster, 1974), 242.

7. Jean Leclercq, "Solitude and Solidarity: Medieval Women Recluses," in *Medieval Religious Women*, vol. 2, ed. John A. Nichols and Lillian Thomas Shank (Kalamazoo, Mich.: Cistercian, 1987), 73.

8. See Eleanor McLaughlin, "Women, Power and the Pursuit of Holiness," in *Women of Spirit: Female Leadership in the Jewish and Christian Traditions*, ed. Rosemary Radford Ruether and Eleanor McLaughlin (New York: Simon and Schuster, 1979), 100–130.

9. Catherine Wybourne, "Leoba: A Study in Humanity and Holiness," in *Medieval Women Monastics: Wisdom's Wellsprings*, ed. Miriam Schmitt and Linda Kulzer (Collegeville, Minn.: Liturgical Press, 1996), 90.

10. Fannie LeMoine, "Jerome's Gift to Women Readers," in *Shifting Frontiers in Late Antiquity*, ed. Ralph W. Mathisen and Hagith S. Sivan (Aldershot, England: Variorum, 1996), 240.

11. Monique Alexandre, "Early Christian Women ," in *From Ancient Goddesses to Christian Saints*, vol. I, *History of Women in the West*, ed. Pauline Schmitt Pantel (Cambridge, Mass.: Belknap Press, 1992), 439.

12. Elizabeth A. Clark, "Early Christian Women: Sources and Interpretation," in *That Gentle Strength: Historical Perspectives on Women and Christianity*, ed. Lynda L. Coon, et al. (Charlottesville, Va.: University Press of Virginia, 1990), 27–29.

13. Caroline Bynum, "Fast, Feast and Flesh: The Religious Significance of Food to Medieval Women," *Representations* 11 (Summer 1985): 1–25.

14. In addition to Bynum, see Gail Corrington, "Anorexia, Asceticism, and Autonomy: Self-Control as Liberation and Transcendence," *Journal of Feminist Studies in Religion* 2 (Fall 1986): 51–61; and Nadia M. Lahutsky, "Food and Feminism and Historical Interpretations: The Case of Medieval Holy Women," in *Setting the Table: Women in Theological Conversation*, ed. Rita Nakashima Brock, et al. (St. Louis: Chalice Press, 1995), 233–48.

15. McLaughlin, "Women, Power and the Pursuit of Holiness," 102.

16. McLaughlin, "Equality of Souls, Inequality of Sexes," 234–35.

17. This cluster of ideas and stories is examined in detail in Marina Warner, *Alone of All Her Sex: The Myth and Cult of the Virgin Mary* (New York: Knopf, 1976); and Rosemary Radford Ruether, *Mary—The Feminine Face of the Church* (Philadelphia: Westminster, 1977).

18. This question is raised, for example, in McLaughlin, "Equality of Souls, Inequality of Sexes," 245–51.

19. Warner, *Alone of All Her Sex*, 284.

20. Sally Cunneen, "Breaking Mary's Silence: A Feminist Reflection on Marian Piety," *Theology Today* 56 (October 1999): 319–35.

21. Elizabeth Johnson, "Mary and the Female Face of God," *Theological Studies* 50 (September 1989): 500–526.

22. For a discussion of the elements contributing to the popular conception of a witch, see Jeffrey Russell, *A History of Witchcraft* (London: Thames and Hudson, 1980), 41–42.

23. See Russell, *A History of Witchcraft*, 113; Rosemary Radford Ruether, "Persecution of Witches: A Case of Sexism and Ageism?" *Christianity and Crisis* 34 (December 23, 1974): 291; Clarke Garrett, "Women and Witches: Patterns of Analysis," *Signs: Journal of Women in Culture and Society* 3 (Winter 1977): 461–63.

24. *Merriam Webster's Collegiate Dictionary*, 11th ed. (Springfield, Mass.: Merriam-Webster, 2004) s.v. "witch."

25. Joseph Klaits, *Servants of Satan: The Age of the Witch Hunts* (Bloomington, Ind.: Indiana University Press, 1985), 85.

26. This thesis is found, for example, in Sigrid Brauner, *Fearless Wives and Frightened Shrews: The Construction of the Witch in Early Modern Germany*, edited by Robert H. Brown (Amherst, Mass.: University of Massachusetts Press, 1995).

27. See Robin Briggs, *Witches and Neighbors: The Social and Cultural Context of European Witchcraft* (New York: Viking, 1996); Alan Charles Kors and Edward Peters, *Witchcraft in Europe, 400–1700: A Documentary History*, rev. ed. (Philadelphia: University of Pennsylvania Press, 2001); and Merry E. Wiesner, *Women and Gender in Early Modern Europe* (Cambridge: Cambridge University Press, 1993).

28. See for example Elizabeth Petroff, *Body and Soul: Essays on Medieval Women and Mysticism* (New York: Oxford University Press, 1994), 3–24.

29. Rosemary Radford Ruether, *Visionary Women: Three Medieval Mystics,* Facets (Minneapolis: Fortress Press, 2002), 1–5.

30. Paul Rorem, "Lover and Mother: Medieval Language for God and the Soul," in *Women, Gender, and Christian Community,* ed. Jane Dempsey Douglass and James F. Kay (Louisville: Westminster John Knox, 1997), 48–49.

31. Henrietta Leyser, *Medieval Women: A Social History of Women in England, 450–1500* (London: Weidenfeld and Nicolson, 1995), 216.

32. Julian of Norwich, *Revelations of Divine Love,* trans. James Walsh (New York: Harper and Row, 1961), 166–67.

33. Frances Beer, *Women and Mystical Experience in the Middle Ages* (Rochester: Boydell Press, 1992), 10.

34. Karen Scott, "St. Catherine of Siena, 'Apostola',", *Church History* 61 (March 1992): 34–46.

35. Caroline Walker Bynum, *Jesus as Mother: Studies in the Spirituality of the High Middle Ages* (Berkeley: University of California Press, 1982).

36. Quoted in Bynum, *Jesus as Mother,* 225.

37. Ruether, *Visionary Women,* 10.

38. Gerda Lerner, *The Creation of Feminist Consciousness: From the Middle Ages to Eighteen-Seventy* (New York: Oxford University Press, 1993), 84.

3. WOMEN IN AN ERA OF REFORMATION

1. For a discussion of this see David Steinmetz, "Theological Reflections on the Reformation and the Status of Women," *Duke Divinity Review* 41 (Fall 1976): 197–207; Miriam U. Chrisman, "Women and the Reformation in Strasbourg, 1490–1530," *Archive for Reformation History* 63 (1972): 143–67; and Jane Dempsey Douglass, "Women and the Continental Reformation," in *Religion and Sexism: Images of Woman in the Jewish and Christian Traditions,* ed. Rosemary Radford Ruether (New York: Simon and Schuster, 1974), 292–302.

2. Quoted in Chrisman, "Women and the Reformation in Strasbourg," 157.

3. Sigrid Brauner, "Martin Luther on Witchcraft: A True Reformer?" in *The Politics of Gender in Early Modern Europe,* ed. Jean R. Brink, et al. (Kirksville, Mo.: Sixteenth Century Journal Publishers, 1989), 29–42.

4. Martin Luther, "The Misuse of the Mass," in *Luther's Works,* vol. 36, *Word and Sacrament II,* ed. Abdel R. Wentz and Helmut T. Lehman, trans. Frederick C. Ahrens (Philadelphia: Fortress Press, 1959), 152.

5. Douglass, "Women and the Continental Reformation," 297.

6. For this interpretation of Calvin, see Willis DeBoer, "Calvin on the Role of Women, " in *Exploring the Heritage of John Calvin* (Grand Rapids, Mich.: Baker, 1976), 236–72; Jane Dempsey Douglass, "Christian Freedom: What Calvin Learned at the School of Women," *Church History* 53 (June 1984): 155–73.

7. John L. Thompson, *"Creata Ad Imaginem Dei, Licet Secundo Gradu*: Women as the Image of God According to John Calvin," in *Calvin's Work in Geneva,* ed. Richard C. Gamble (New York: Garland, 1992): 125–43.

8. Jane Dempsey Douglass, *Women, Freedom, and Calvin* (Philadelphia: Westminster, 1985).

9. Patricia Ranft, "A Key to Counter-Reformation Women's Activism: The Confessor/Spiritual Director," *Journal of Feminist Studies in Religion* 10 (Fall 1994): 7–26.

10. Ibid., 7–8.

11. Ruth P. Liebowitz, "Virgins in the Service of Christ: The Dispute over an Active Apostolate for Women during the Counter-Reformation," in *Women of Spirit: Female Leadership in the Jewish and Christian Traditions,* ed. Rosemary Radford Ruether and Eleanor McLaughlin (New York: Simon and Schuster, 1979), 146–47.

12. Douglass, "Women and the Continental Reformation," 309–14.

13. Quoted in Roland H. Bainton, *Women of the Reformation in Germany and Italy* (Minneapolis: Augsburg, 1971), 55.

14. Peter Matheson, ed., *Argula von Grumbach: A Woman's Voice in the Reformation* (Edinburgh: T. and T. Clark, 1995), 27–39.

15. Quoted in Bainton, *Women of the Reformation in Germany and Italy,* 100.

16. Charmarie J. Blaisdell, "The Matrix of Reform: Women in the Lutheran and Calvinist Movements," in *Triumph over Silence: Women in Protestant History,* ed. Richard L. Greaves (Westport, Conn.: Greenwood, 1985), 33–34.

17. Keith L. Sprunger, "God's Powerful Army of the Weak," in *Triumph over Silence :Women in Protestant History,* ed. Richard L. Greaves (Westport, Conn.: Greenwood), 62–63.

18. Joyce L. Irwin, *Womanhood in Radical Protestantism, 1525–1675* (New York: Edwin Mellen, 1979), 203.

19. Lois Barrett, "The Role and Influence of Anabaptist Women in the Martyr Story," *Brethren Life and Thought* 37 (Spring 1992): 94–95.

20. Debra L. Parish, "The Power of Female Pietism: Women as Spiritual Authorities and Religious Role Models in Seventeenth-Century England," *Journal of Religious History* 17 (June 1992): 41.

21. Dorothy P. Ludlow, "Shaking Patriarchy's Foundations: Sectarian Women in England, 1641–1700," in *Triumph over Silence*, ed. Greaves, 101.

22. Rebecca Larson, *Daughters of Light: Quaker Women Preaching and Prophesying in the Colonies and Abroad, 1700–1775* (New York: Knopf, 1999), 31–32.

23. H. Larry Ingle, " A Quaker Woman on Women's Roles: Mary Penington to Friends, 1678," *Signs: Journal of Women in Culture and Society* 16 (Spring 1991): 593.

24. Larson, *Daughters of Light*, 39.

4. WOMEN AND CHRISTIANITY IN THE AMERICAN COLONIES

1. Anne Bradstreet, "The Tenth Muse Lately Sprung Up in America," in *The Works of Anne Bradstreet in Prose and Verse*, ed. John Harvard Ellis (Gloucester, Mass.: Peter Smith, 1962), 101.

2. James Kendall Hosmer, ed. *Winthrop's Journal: History of New England 1630–1649* (New York: Scribner, 1908) 2:225.

3. Gerald F. Moran, " 'The Hidden Ones': Women and Religion in Puritan New England," in *Triumph over Silence: Women in Protestant History*, ed. Richard L. Greaves (Westport, Conn.: Greenwood, 1985), 145.

4. Cotton Mather, "*Ornaments for the Daughters of Zion, or The Character and Happiness of a Virtuous Woman*, facsimile reproduction with an introduction by Pattie Cowell (Delmar, N.Y.: Scholars' Facsimiles and Reprints, 1978), 1–2.

5. Susan Hill Lindley, *You Have Stept Out of Your Place: A History of Women and Religion in America* (Louisville: Westminster John Knox, 1996), 22–24.

6. Amanda Porterfield, "Women's Attraction to Puritanism," *Church History* 60 (June 1991): 196–209.

7. See Amanda Porterfield, *Feminine Spirituality in America* (Philadelphia: Temple University Press, 1970), 34; Margaret Masson, "The Typology of the Female as a Model for the Regenerate: Puritan Preaching 1690–1730," *Signs: Journal of Women in Culture and Society* 2 (Winter 1976), 310.

8. Page Smith, *Daughters of the Promised Land: Women in American History* (Boston: Little, Brown, 1970), 35.

9. Hosmer, *Winthrop's Journal*, 1:299.

10. Ronald D. Cohen, "Church and State in Seventeenth-Century Massachusetts: Another Look at the Antinomian Controversy," in *Puritan New England: Essays on Religion, Society and Culture*, ed. Francis J. Bremer, et al. (New York: St. Martin's Press, 1977), 174–78.

11. David D. Hall, ed., *The Antinomian Controversy, 1636–1638: A Documentary History* (Middletown, Conn.: Wesleyan University Press, 1968), 312.

12. See Lyle Koehler, "The Case of the American Jezebels: Anne Hutchinson and Female Agitation during the Years of Antinomian Turmoil, 1636–1640," in *Our Sisters: Women in American Life and Thought*, ed. Jean Friedman and William Shade (Boston: Allyn and Bacon, 1976); Carol V. R. George, "Anne Hutchinson and the Revolution Which Never Happened," in *Remember the Ladies: New Perspectives on Women in American History*, ed. Carol V. R. George (Syracuse: Syracuse University Press, 1975).

13. Marilyn J. Westerkamp, " Anne Hutchinson, Sectarian Mysticism, and the Puritan Order," *Church History* 59 (December 1990): 484–85.

14. Quoted in Stephen Stein, "A Note on Anne Dutton, Eighteenth-Century Evangelical, " *Church History* 44 (December 1975): 487.

15. Ibid., 491.

16. Mary Beth Norton, " 'My Resting Reaping Times': Sarah Osborn's Defense of Her 'Unfeminine' Activities, 1767," *Signs: Journal of Women in Culture and Society* 2 (Winter 1976): 519–29.

17. Ibid., 527.

18. Sereno Edwards Dwight, *The Life of President Edwards* (New York: G. and C. and H. Carvill, 1830), 178.

19. Porterfield, *Feminine Spirituality in America*, 47.

20. Marilyn J. Westerkamp, *Women and Religion in Early America, 1600–1850: The Puritan and Evangelical Traditions* (New York: Routledge, 1999), 125–30.

21. Quoted in Julia Spruill, *Women's Life and Work in the Southern Colonies* (Chapel Hill, N.C.: University of North Carolina Press, 1938; repr., New York: Norton, 1972), 253.

22. H. Larry Ingle, "A Quaker Woman on Women's Roles: Mary Penington to Friends, 1678," *Signs: Journal of Women in Culture and Society* 16 (Spring 1991): 587–93.

5. WOMEN ORGANIZING FOR MISSION AND REFORM

1. Barbara Welter, "The Cult of True Womanhood, 1820–1860," in *Dimity Convictions: The American Woman in the Nineteenth Century* (Athens, Ohio: Ohio University Press, 1976), 21–41; see also Janet Forsythe Fishburn, *The Fatherhood of God and the Victorian Family: The Social Gospel in America* (Philadelphia: Fortress Press, 1981).

2. Susan Hill Lindley, *You Have Stept Out of Your Place: A History of Women and Religion in America* (Louisville: Westminster John Knox, 1996), 52–53.

3. As quoted in Marilyn J. Westerkamp, *Women and Religion in Early America, 1600–1850: The Puritan and Evangelical Traditions* (New York: Routledge, 1999), 135.

4. Lindley, *You Have Stept Out of Your Place*, 50–52.

5. See for example Mary P. Ryan, *Womanhood in America from Colonial Times to the Present*, 3rd ed. (New York: Franklin Watts, 1983), 118; Barbara Harris, *Beyond Her Sphere: Women and the Professions in American History* (Westport, Conn.: Greenwood, 1978), 56–57.

6. Colleen McDannell, *The Christian Home in Victorian America, 1840–1900* (Bloomington, Ind.: Indiana University Press, 1986), 150–55.

7. Welter, "The Cult of True Womanhood, 1820–1860," 21.

8. Westerkamp, *Women and Religion in Early America, 1600–1850*, 134.

9. This is discussed in Barbara Welter, "The Feminization of American Religion, 1800–1860," in *Dimity Convictions*, 83–102; and Ann Douglas, *The Feminization of American Culture* (New York: Knopf, 1977).

10. David S. Reynolds, "The Feminization Controversy: Sexual Stereotypes and the Paradoxes of Piety in Nineteenth-Century America," *New England Quarterly* 53 (1980): 96–106.

11. Westerkamp, *Women and Religion in Early America, 1600–1850*, 131–54.

12. Quoted in R. Pierce Beaver, *American Protestant Women in World Mission: History of the First Feminist Movement in North America*, rev. ed. (Grand Rapids, Mich.: Eerdmans, 1980), 46.

13. Lindley, *You Have Stept Out of Your Place*, 96.

14. Blanche Glassman Hersh, "To Make the World Better: Protestant Women in the Abolitionist Movement," in *Triumph over Silence: Women in Protestant History*, ed. Richard L. Greaves (Westport, Conn.: Greenwood, 1985), 198.

15. Lindley, *You Have Stept Out of Your Place*, 135–47.

16. Ibid., 137–38.

17. See Betty A. DeBerg, *Ungodly Women: Gender and the First Wave of American Fundamentalism* (Minneapolis: Fortress Press, 1990); and Margaret Lamberts Bendroth, *Fundamentalism and Gender: 1875 to the Present* (New Haven, Conn.: Yale University Press, 1993).

18. See Brenda E. Brasher, *Godly Women: Fundamentalism and Female Power* (New Brunswick, N.J.: Rutgers University Press, 1998).

19. Beaver, *American Protestant Women in World Mission*, 54.

20. Lucy H. Daggett, *Historical Sketches of Woman's Missionary Societies in America and England* (Boston: Mrs. L. H. Daggett, 1879), 106.

21. Barbara Welter, "She Hath Done What She Could: Protestant Women's Missionary Careers in Nineteenth-Century America," in *Women in American Religion*, ed. Janet Wilson James (Philadelphia: University of Pennsylvania Press, 1980), 125.

22. Lindley, *You Have Stept Out of Your Place*, 70–89.

23. Welter, "She Hath Done What She Could," 123.

24. Lindley, *You Have Stept Out of Your Place*, 70–89; Patricia Ruth Hill, *The World Their Household: The American Woman's Foreign Mission Movement and Cultural Transformation, 1870–1920* (Ann Arbor, Mich.: University of Michigan Press, 1985).

25. Beverly Wildung Harrison, "Sexism and the Contemporary Church: When Evasion Becomes Complicity," in *Sexist Religion and Women in the Church: No More Silence!*, ed. Alice Hageman (New York: Association Press, 1974), 203.

26. Keith Melder, "Ladies Bountiful: Organized Women's Benevolence in Early Nineteenth-Century America," *New York History* 48 (July 1967): 249; Nancy Cott, *The Bonds of Womanhood: Woman's Sphere in New England, 1780–1835* (New Haven, Conn.: Yale University Press, 1977), 138.

27. Wendy J. Deichmann, "Domesticity with a Difference: Woman's Sphere, Women's Leadership, and the Founding of the Baptist Missionary Training School," *American Baptist Quarterly* 9 (September 1990): 141–57.

28. Hill, *The World Their Household*, 24–25.

29. Lydia Maria Child, "Speaking in the Church," *The National Anti-Slavery Standard* 2 (15 July 1841): 22.

30. See for example Barbara Leslie Epstein, *The Politics of Domesticity: Women, Evangelism, and Temperance in Nineteenth-Century America* (Middletown, Conn.: Wesleyan University Press, 1981).

31. Carolyn Haynes, "Women and Protestantism in Nineteenth-Century America," in *Perspectives on American Religion and Culture*, ed. Peter W. Williams (Malden, Mass.: Blackwell, 1999), 300–318; Evelyn A. Kirkley, "'This Work Is God's Cause': Religion in the Southern Woman Suffrage Movement, 1880–1920," *Church History* 59 (December 1990): 507–22.

32. Beverly Wildung Harrison, "Early Feminism and the Clergy: A Case Study in the Dynamics of Secularization," *Review and Expositor* 72 (Winter 1975): 47.

33. Hersh, "To Make the World Better," 198.

6. NINETEENTH-CENTURY PREACHERS AND SCHOLARS

1. Terry D. Bilhartz, "Sex and the Second Great Awakening: The Feminization of American Religion Reconsidered," in *Belief and Behavior: Essays in the New Religious History*, ed. Robert P. Swierenga and Philip R. VanderMeer (New Brunswick, N.J.: Rutgers University Press, 1991), 117–35.

2. Martha Tomhave Blauvelt, "Women and Revivalism," in *Women and Religion in America*, vol. 1, *The Nineteenth Century*, ed. Rosemary Radford Ruether and Rosemary Skinner Keller (San Francisco: Harper and Row, 1981), 3–4; Nancy Cott, "Young Women in the Second Great Awakening in New England," *Feminist Studies* 3 (1975): 18–19.

3. Donald W. Dayton and Lucille Sider Dayton, "Women as Preachers: Evangelical Precedents," *Christianity Today* 19 (23 May 1975): 4.

4. Nancy Hardesty, *Your Daughters Shall Prophesy: Revivalism and Feminism in the Age of Finney* (Brooklyn, N.Y.: Carlson, 1991).

5. Carroll Smith-Rosenberg, "Women and Religious Revivals: Anti-Ritualism, Liminality, and the Emergence of the American Bourgeosie," in *The Evangelical Tradition in America*, ed. Leonard I. Sweet (Macon, Ga.: Mercer University Press, 1984), 199–231.

6. Charles E. White, *The Beauty of Holiness: Phoebe Palmer as Theologian, Revivalist, Feminist, and Humanitarian* (Grand Rapids, Mich.: Zondervan, 1986), 67–75.

7. Marilyn J. Westerkamp, *Women and Religion in Early America, 1600–1850: The Puritan and Evangelical Traditions* (New York: Routledge, 1999), 152.

8. Catherine Booth, *Female Ministry, or, Woman's Right to Preach the Gospel* (London: 1859; reprint, New York: Salvation Army, 1975), 14.

9. Seth C. Rees, *The Ideal Pentecostal Church* (Cincinnati, Ohio: M. W. Knapp, 1897), 41.

10. Edith Blumhofer, "Women in Evangelicalism and Pentecostalism," in *Women and Church: The Challenge of Ecumenical Solidarity in an Age of Alienation*, ed. Melanie A. May (Grand Rapids, Mich.: Eerdmans, 1991), 3–7.

11. *Spiritual Narratives*, introduction by Sue E. Houchins, Schomburg Library of Nineteenth-Century Black Women Writers (New York: Oxford University Press, 1988), xxxi.

12. See William L. Andrews, ed., *Sisters of the Spirit: Three Black Women's Autobiographies of the Nineteenth Century* (Bloomington, Ind.: Indiana University Press, 1986), 1–24; Jean M. Humez, "'My Spirit Eye': Some Functions of Spiritual and Visionary Experience in the Lives of Five Black Women Preachers, 1810–1880," in *Women and the Structure of Society*, ed. Barbara J. Harris and JoAnn K. McNamara (Durham, N.C.: Duke University Press, 1984), 129–43; Judith Weisenfeld, "We Have Been Believers: Patterns of African-American Women's Religiosity," in *This Far By Faith: Readings in African-American Women's Religious Biography*, ed. Judith Weisenfeld and Richard Newman (New York: Routledge, 1996), 1–17.

13. Nancy Hardesty and Adrienne Israel, "Amanda Berry Smith: A 'Downright Outright Christian,'" in *Spirituality and Social Responsibility: Vocational Vision of Women in the United Methodist Tradition*, ed. Rosemary Skinner Keller (Nashville: Abingdon, 1993), 70.

14. Carolyn Haynes, "Women and Protestantism in Nineteenth-Century America," in *Perspectives on American Religion and Culture*, ed. Peter W. Williams (Malden, Mass.: Blackwell, 1999), 300–318.

15. Ibid., 306; Beverly A. Zink-Sawyer, "From Preachers to Suffragists: Enlisting the Pulpit in the Early Movement for Women's Rights," *ATQ (American Transcendental Quarterly)* 14 (2000): 200.

16. These are discussed in detail in Barbara Brown Zikmund, "The Struggle for the Right to Preach," in *Women and Religion in America*, vol. 1, *The Nineteenth Century*, ed. Rosemary Radford Ruether and Rosemary Skinner Keller (San Francisco: Harper and Row, 1981), 193–241.

17. Gary Selby, "'Your Daughters Shall Prophesy': Rhetorical Strategy in the 19th-Century Debate over Women's Right to Preach," *Restoration Quarterly* 34 (1992): 163–65.

18. Stephen Knowlton, "The Silence of Women in the Churches," *Congregational Quarterly* 9 (October 1867): 332.

19. Margaret Lamberts Bendroth, "Millennial Themes and Private Visions: The Problem of 'Woman's Place' in Religious History," *Fides et Historia* 20 (June 1988): 27.

20. Cynthia Grant Tucker, *Prophetic Sisterhood: Liberal Women Ministers of the Frontier, 1880–1930* (Bloomington, Ind.: Indiana University Press, 1994).

21. Virginia Brereton and Christa Klein, "American Women in Ministry: A History of Protestant Beginning Points," in *Women in American Religion*, ed. Janet Wilson James (Philadelphia: University of Pennsylvania Press, 1980), 179–80.

22. Mary A. Dougherty, "The Methodist Deaconess: A Case of Religious Feminism," *Methodist History* 21 (January 1983): 98.

23. Marla J. Selvidge, *Notorious Voices: Feminist Biblical Interpretation, 1550–1920* (New York: Continuum, 1996).

24. *The Woman's Bible*, Part I, Comments on Genesis, Exodus, Leviticus, Numbers and Deuteronomy (New York: European Publishing Company, 1892; reprint, New York: Arno, 1972), 117.

25. Ibid., 14.

7. AMERICAN WOMEN IN CATHOLICISM AND SECTARIANISM

1. Margaret Susan Thompson, "Women and American Catholicism, 1789–1989," in *Perspectives on the American Catholic Church*, ed. Stephen Vicchio and Virginia Geiger (Westminster, Md.: Christian Classics, 1989), 124.

2. Mary Ewens, "Removing the Veil: The Liberated American Nun," in *Women of Spirit: Female Leadership in the Jewish and Christian Traditions*, ed. Rosemary Radford Ruether and Eleanor McLaughlin (New York: Simon and Schuster, 1979), 256–78; Mary Ewens, *The Role of the Nun in Nineteenth-Century America* (New York: Arno, 1978).

3. James J. Kenneally, "Eve, Mary and the Historians: American Catholicism and Women," in *Women in American Religion*, ed. Janet Wilson James (Philadelphia: University of Pennsylvania Press, 1980), 190–206.

4. Susan Hill Lindley, *You Have Stept Out of Your Place: A History of Women and Religion in America* (Louisville: Westminster John Knox, 1996), 198.

5. Colleen McDannell, "Catholic Domesticity, 1860–1960," in *American Catholic Women: A Historical Exploration*, ed. Karen Kennelly (New York: Macmillan, 1989), 54.

6. James J. Kenneally, *The History of American Catholic Women* (New York: Crossroad, 1990), 23–42.

7. Ewens, "Removing the Veil," 256–57; Thompson, "Women and American Catholicism, 1789–1989," 127.

8. Lindley, *You Have Stept Out of Your Place*, 212.

9. Ann D. Braude, "The Perils of Passivity: Women's Leadership in Spiritualism and Christian Science," in *Women's Leadership in Marginal Religions: Explorations Outside the Mainstream*, ed. Catherine Wessinger (Urbana, Ill.: University of Illinois Press, 1993), 55.

10. Quoted in Charles Nordhoff, *The Communistic Societies of the United States: From Personal Visit and Observation: Including Detailed Accounts of the Economists, Zoarites, Shakers, the Amana, Oneida, Bethel, Aurora, Icarian, and Other Existing Societies, Their Religious Creeds, Social Practices, Numbers, Industries and Present Condition* (New York: Harper and Brothers, 1875; repr. New York: Schocken, 1965), 125.

11. Braude, "The Perils of Passivity," 61.

12. Lawrence Foster, *Women, Family, and Utopia: Communal Experiments of the Shakers, the Oneida Community, and the Mormons* (Syracuse, N.Y.: Syracuse University Press, 1991), 17–42; Marjorie Procter-Smith, "'In the Line of the Female': Shakerism and Feminism," in *Women's Leadership in Marginal Religions*, ed. Wessinger, 23–37.

13. Ann D. Braude, "Spirits Defend the Rights of Women: Spiritualism and Changing Sex Roles in Nineteenth-Century America," in *Women, Religion, and Social Change*, ed. Yvonne Haddad and Ellison Findly (Albany, N.Y.: State University of New York, 1985), 422.

14. Lindley, *You Have Stept Out of Your Place*, 262–70.

15. See D'Ann Campbell, "Woman's Life in Utopia: The Shaker Experiment in Sexual Equality Reappraised 1810–1860," *New England Quarterly* 51 (March 1978): 23–38.

16. See Barbara Brown Zikmund, "The Feminist Thrust of Sectarian Christianity," in *Women of Spirit*, ed. Ruether and McLaughlin, 206–24.

17. See for example Foster, *Women, Family, and Utopia*, 91–102.

18. See for example Margery Fox, "Protest in Piety: Christian Science Revisited," *International Journal of Women's Studies* 1 (July/August 1978): 412–13.

19. Jean A. MacDonald, "Mary Baker Eddy and the Nineteenth-Century 'Public' Woman: A Feminist Reappraisal," *Journal of Feminist Studies in Religion* 2 (1986): 89–111.

20. R. Laurence Moore, "Spiritualist Medium: A Study of Female Professionalism in Victorian America," *American Quarterly* 27 (May 1975): 207.

21. Alex Owen, "Women and Nineteenth-Century Spiritualism: Strategies in the Subversion of Femininity," *Disciplines of Faith: Studies in Religion, Politics, and Patriarchy*, ed. Jim Obelkevich (New York: Routledge, 1987), 130–53.

8. The Move toward Full Participation

1. Catherine Wessinger, ed., *Religious Institutions and Women's Leadership: New Roles Inside the Mainstream* (Columbia, S.C.: University of South Carolina Press, 1996), 6–7.

2. R. Pierce Beaver, *American Protestant Women in World Mission: History of the First Feminist Movement in North America*, rev. ed. (Grand Rapids, Mich.: Eerdmans, 1980), 180–82.

3. Susan Hill Lindley, *You Have Stept Out of Your Place: A History of Women and Religion in America* (Louisville: Westminster John Knox, 1996), 299–300.

4. Ibid., 305.

5. Carl J. Schneider and Dorothy Schneider, *In Their Own Right: The History of American Clergywomen* (New York: Crossroad, 1997), 254.

6. See Barbara Harris, *Beyond Her Sphere: Women and the Professions in American History* (Westport, Conn.: Greenwood, 1978), 127–46.

7. Mark Chaves and James C. Cavendish, "Recent Changes in Women's Ordination Conflicts: The Effect of a Social Movement on Intraorganizational Controversy," *Journal for the Scientific Study of Religion* 36 (December 1997): 578.

8. Kathleen Bliss, *The Service and Status of Women in the Churches* (London: SCM, 1952).

9. Betty Friedan, *The Feminine Mystique* (New York: Norton, 1963).

10. Beverly Wildung Harrison, "Sexism and the Contemporary Church: When Evasion Becomes Complicity," in *Sexist Religion and Women in the Church: No More Silence!*, ed. Alice Hageman (New York: Association Press, 1974), 206.

11. Rosemary Radford Ruether, "Crisis in Sex and Race: Black Theology vs. Feminist Theology," *Christianity and Crisis* 34 (15 April 1974): 69.

12. Lindley, *You Have Stept Out of Your Place*, 177–78.

9. Agents of Transformation

1. Mark Chaves, *Ordaining Women: Culture and Conflict in Religious Organizations* (Cambridge, Mass.: Harvard University Press, 1997).

2. Paul Jewett, *The Ordination of Women* (Grand Rapids, Mich.: Eerdmans, 1980).

3. See *Orthodox Women: Their Role and Participation in the Orthodox Church*, Report on the Consultation of Orthodox Women, 11–17 September 1976, Agapia, Romania (Agapia, Romania: WCC, Subunit on Women in Church and Society, 1976).

4. Mark Chaves, and James C. Cavendish, "Recent Changes in Women's Ordination Conflicts: The Effect of a Social Movement on Intraorganizational Controversy," *Journal for the Scientific Study of Religion* 36 (December 1997): 574–84.

5. "Women Clergy—How Their Presence is Changing the Church: A Symposium by Five Women on the Seminary Campus," *Christian Century* 96 (7 February 1979): 125. Letty Russell's section is subtitled "Clerical Ministry as a Female Profession."

6. Paula D. Nesbitt, *Feminization of the Clergy in America: Occupational and Organizational Perspectives* (New York: Oxford University Press, 1997).

7. Edward Lehman, "Organizational Resistance to Women in Ministry," *Sociological Analysis: A Journal in the Sociology of Religion* 42 (Summer 1981): 101–18.

8. Edith Blumhofer, "A Confused Legacy: Reflections of Evangelical Attitudes toward Ministering Women in the Past Century," *Fides et Historia* 22 (Winter–Spring 1990): 60; Carol E. Becker, "Women in Church Leadership—In But Still Out," *Dialog* 35 (Spring 1996): 144–48; Barbara Brown Zikmund, "Ministry of Word and Sacrament: Women and Changing Understandings of Ordination," in *The Presbyterian Predicament: Six Perspectives*, ed. Milton J. Coalter et al., (Louisville: Westminster John Knox, 1990), 134–58.

9. Patricia Mei Yin Chang, "Female Clergy in the Contemporary Protestant Church: A Current Assessment," *Journal for the Scientific Study of Religion* 36 (December 1997): 570; Catherine Wessinger, ed., *Religious Institutions and Women's Leadership: New Roles Inside the Mainstream* (Columbia, S.C.: University of South Carolina Press, 1996), 13–16; Barbara Brown Zikmund et al., "Women, Men and Styles of Clergy Leadership," *Christian Century* 115 (6 May 1998): 478–80, 482–86.

10. See for example Bonnie J. Miller-McLemore, "Feminist Theory in Pastoral Theology," in *Feminist and Womanist Pastoral Theology*, ed. Brita L: Gill-Austern and Bonnie J. Miller-McLemore (Nashville: Abingdon, 1999), 77–94.

11. See for example Edwina Hunter, "Weaving Life's Experiences into Women's Preaching," *Christian Ministry* 18 (September/October 1987): 14–17; Sharon Kyle, "Truly, Madly, Deeply: Women's Experience of Preaching," *Anvil* 14, no. 4 (1997): 254–61; Leonora Tubbs Tisdale, "Women's Ways of Communicating: A New Blessing for Preaching," in *Women, Gender, and Christian Community*, ed. Jane Dempsey Douglass and James F. Kay (Louisville: Westminster John Knox, 1997), 104–16; Barbara Brown Zikmund, "Women as Preachers: Adding New Dimensions to Worship," *Journal of Women and Religion* 3 (Summer 1984): 12–16.

12. Carole G. Rogers, *Poverty, Chastity, and Change: Lives of Contemporary American Nuns* (New York: Twayne, 1996).

13. Gérald Caron, "The Authority of the Bible Challenged by Feminist Hermeneutics," in *Women Also Journeyed with Him: Feminist Perspectives on the Bible*, ed. Jean-Pierre Prévost, trans. Madeleine Beaumont (Collegeville, Minn.: Liturgical, 2000), 157.

14. Carol A. Newsom and Sharon Ringe, eds., *Women's Bible Commentary* (Louisville: Westminster John Knox, 1998), 2–5.

15. Katheryn Pfisterer Darr, *Far More Precious Than Jewels: Perspectives on Biblical Women* (Louisville: Westminster John Knox, 1991), 35–37.

16. Paul Joyce, "Feminist Exegesis of the Old Testament: Some Critical Reflections," in *After Eve*, ed. Janet Martin Soskice (Basingstoke, England: Marshal Pickering, 1990), 4–5.

17. Caron, "The Authority of the Bible," 161.

18. Phyllis Trible, *Texts of Terror: Literary-Feminist Readings of Biblical Narratives* (Philadelphia: Fortress Press, 1984).

19. Phyllis Trible, *God and the Rhetoric of Sexuality* (Philadelphia: Fortress Press, 1978), 144–65.

20. Ibid., 79–82.

21. Beverly J. Stratton, *Out of Eden: Reading, Rhetoric and Ideology in Genesis 2–3* (Sheffield, England: Sheffield Academic Press, 1995), 85–108.

22. Nancy Hardesty, "Women and the Seminaries," in "Women Clergy—How Their Presence is Changing the Church: A Symposium by Five Women on the Seminary Campus," *Christian Century* 96 (7 February 1979): 122.

23. Christa Ressmeyer Klein, "Women's Concerns in Theological Education," *Dialog* 24 (Winter 1985): 25–31.

24. Sharon H. Ringe, "Women and the Viability of Theological Education," *Ministerial Formation* 70 (July 1995): 19–21.

25. This perspective is most fully represented in Cornwall Collective, *Your Daughters Shall Prophesy: Feminist Alternatives in Theological Education* (New York: Pilgrim, 1980).

26. Miriam Therese Winter et al, *Defecting in Place: Women Claiming Responsibility for Their Own Spiritual Lives* (New York: Crossroad, 1995).

27. Mary Collins, "Principles of Feminist Liturgy," in *Women at Worship: Interpretations of North American Diversity*, ed. Marjorie Procter-Smith and Janet R. Walton (Louisville: Westminster John Knox, 1993), 9–26.

28. Ada María Isasi-Díaz, "On the Birthing Stool: Mujerista Liturgy," in *Women at Worship*, ed. Procter-Smith and Walton, 198.

29. Catherine Keller, "Inventing the Goddess: A Study in Ecclesiastical Backlash," *Christian Century* 111 (6 April 1994): 340–42.

30. Rosemary Radford Ruether, *Womanguides: Readings toward a Feminist Theology* (Boston: Beacon, 1985), x–xi.

31. Delores S. Williams, "Womanist Theology," in *Women's Visions: Theological Reflection, Celebration, Action*, ed. Ofelia Ortega (Geneva: WCC, 1995): 113.

32. Sonja Anne Ingwersen, "Mujerista Theology: A Theology for the Twenty-First Century," *Anglican Theological Review* 80 (Fall 1998): 642–44; Ada María Isasi-Díaz, "Mujerista Theology: A Challenge to Traditional Theology," in *Introduction to Christian Theology: Contemporary North American Perspectives*, ed. Roger A. Badham (Louisville: Westminster John Knox, 1998), 237–52.

SUGGESTIONS
FOR FURTHER READING

INTRODUCTION

Bass, Dorothy. *American Women in Church and Society 1607–1920: A Bibliography*. New York: Auburn Theological Seminary, 1973.

Carroll, Bernice, ed. *Liberating Women's History: Theoretical and Critical Essays*. Urbana, Ill.: University of Illinois Press, 1976.

Christ, Carol P. "The New Feminist Theology: A Review of the Literature." *Religious Studies Review* 3 (October 1977): 203–12.

———. "Women's Studies in Religion." *Bulletin of the Council for the Study of Religion* 10 (February 1979): 3–5.

Clark, Elizabeth, and Herbert Richardson. *Women and Religion: A Feminist Sourcebook of Christian Thought*. New York: Harper and Row, 1977.

Conn, Marie A. *Noble Daughters: Unheralded Women in Western Christianity, 13th to 18th Centuries*. Westport, Conn.: Greenwood, 2000.

Coon, Lynda L., Katherine J. Haldane, and Elisabeth W. Sommer, eds. *That Gentle Strength: Historical Perspectives on Women in Christianity*. Charlottesville, Va.: University Press of Virginia, 1990.

Culver, Elsie T. *Women in the World of Religion*. Garden City, N.Y.: Doubleday, 1967.

Driver, Anne Barstow. "Review Essay: Religion." *Signs: Journal of Women in Culture and Society* 2 (Winter 1976): 434–42.

Fox-Genovese, Elizabeth. "Two Steps Forward, One Step Back: New Questions and Old Models in the Religious History of American Women." *Journal of the American Academy of Religion* 53 (1985): 465–71.

Frazer, Ruth F., ed. *Women and Religion: A Bibliography Selected from the ATLA Religion Database*. 3rd rev. ed. Chicago: American Theological Library Association, 1983.

Greaves, Richard L., ed. *Triumph over Silence: Women in Protestant History*. Westport, Conn.: Greenwood, 1985.

James, Edward T., Janet Wilson James, and Paul S. Boyer, eds. *Notable American Women 1607–1950: A Biographical Dictionary*. 3 vols. Cambridge, Mass.: Belknap, 1971.

Kelly-Gadol, Joan. "The Social Relation of the Sexes: Methodological Implications of Women's History." *Signs: Journal of Women in Culture and Society* 1 (Summer 1976): 809–23.

Lerner, Gerda. *The Creation of Feminist Consciousness: From the Middle Ages to Eighteen-Seventy*. New York: Oxford University Press, 1993.

———. *The Majority Finds Its Past: Placing Women in History*. New York: Oxford University Press, 1979.

Lindley, Susan Hill. *You Have Stept Out of Your Place: A History of Women and Religion in America*. Louisville: Westminster John Knox, 1996.

Malone, Mary T. *Women and Christianity*, Vol. I, *The First Thousand Years*. Maryknoll, N.Y.: Orbis, 2001.

Marty, Martin E., ed. *Women and Women's Issues*. Vol. 12, *Modern American Protestantism and Its World*. Munich: K. G. Saur, 1993.

Mead, Judith, comp. *Resource List*. New York: Council on Women and the Church (Presbyterian Church [U.S.A.]), 1983.

Newsom, Carol A. and Sharon Ringe, eds. *Women's Bible Commentary*. Louisville: Westminster John Knox, 1998.

Oden, Amy, ed. *In Her Words: Women's Writings in the History of Christian Thought*. Nashville, Tenn.: Abingdon, 1994.

O'Faolain, Julia, and Laura Martines. *Not in God's Image: Women in History from the Greeks to the Victorians*. New York: Harper and Row, 1973.

Patrick, Anne E., "Women and Religion: A Survey of Significant Literature, 1965–1974." *Theological Studies* 36 (December 1975): 737–65.

Ruether, Rosemary Radford, ed. *Religion and Sexism: Images of Woman in the Jewish and Christian Traditions*. New York: Simon and Schuster, 1974.

Ruether, Rosemary Radford, and Rosemary Skinner Keller., eds. *Women and Religion in America*. 3 vols. San Francisco: Harper and Row, 1981–1986.

Ruether, Rosemary Radford, and Eleanor McLaughlin, eds. *Women of Spirit: Female Leadership in the Jewish and Christian Traditions*. New York: Simon and Schuster, 1979.

Schmidt, Alvin J. *Veiled and Silenced: How Culture Shaped Sexist Theology*. Macon, Ga.: Mercer University Press, 1989.

Schneider, Carl J., and Dorothy Schneider. *In Their Own Right: The History of American Clergywomen*. New York: Crossroad, 1997.

Selvidge, Marla J. *Notorious Voices: Feminist Biblical Interpretation, 1550–1920*. New York: Continuum, 1996.

Sicherman, Barbara, Carol Hurd Green, Ilene Kantrov, and Harriette Walker, eds. *Notable American Women: The Modern Period: A Biographical Dictionary*. Cambridge, Mass.: Belknap, 1980.

Sklar, Kathryn Kish. "The Last Fifteen Years." In *Women in New Worlds: Historical Perspectives on the Wesleyan Tradition*. Vol. I, edited by Hilah F. Thomas and Rosemary Skinner Keller. Nashville, Tenn.: Abingdon, 1981.

Tucker, Ruth A., and Walter Liefeld. *Daughters of the Church: Women and Ministry from New Testament Times to the Present*. Grand Rapids, Mich.: Academie, 1987.

Wessinger, Catherine, ed. *Religious Institutions and Women's Leadership: New Roles Inside the Mainstream*. Columbia, S.C.: University of South Carolina Press, 1996.

———. *Women's Leadership in Marginal Religions: Explorations Outside the Mainstream*. Urbana, Ill.: University of Illinois Press, 1993.

I. WOMEN AND THE EARLY CHURCHES

Alexandre, Monique. "Early Christian Women." In *From Ancient Goddesses to Christian Saints*. Vol. I, *History of Women in the West*, edited by Pauline Schmitt Pantel, 409–44. Cambridge, Mass.: Belknap, 1992.

Arjava, Antti. "Women in the Christian Empire: Ideological Changes and Social Reality." In *Studia Patristica* 24, 6–9. Louvain: Peeters, 1993.

Barton, Stephen C. "Women, Jesus and the Gospels." In *Who Needs Feminism? Male Responses to Sexism in the Church*, edited by Richard Holloway, 32–58. London: S.P.C.K., 1991.

Beck, Rosalie. "The Women of Acts: Foremothers of the Christian Church." In *With Steadfast Purpose: Essays on Acts in Honor of Henry Jackson Flanders*, edited by Naymond H. Keathley, 279–307. Waco, Tex.: Baylor University, 1990.

Bremmer, Jan N. "Pauper or Patroness: The Widow in the Early Christian Church." In *Between Poverty and the Pyre: Moments in the History of Widowhood*, edited by Jan Bremmer and Lourens van den Bosch, 31–57. New York: Routledge, 1995.

Brooten, Bernadette J. "Early Christian Women and Their Cultural Context: Issues of Method in Historical Reconstruction." In *Feminist Perspectives on Biblical Scholarship*, edited by Adela Yarbro Collins, 65–91. Chico, Calif.: Scholars Press, 1985.

Burrus, Virginia. "Blurring the Boundaries: A Response to Howard C. Kee." *Theology Today* 49 (July 1992): 239–42.

Cardman, Francine. "Acts of the Women Martyrs." *Anglican Theological Review* 70 (April 1988): 144–50.

———. "Women, Ministry, and Church Order in Early Christianity." In *Women and Christian Origins*, edited by Ross Shepard Kraemer and Mary Rose D'Angelo, 300–329. New York: Oxford University Press, 1999.

Carnelley, Elizabeth. "Tertullian and Feminism." *Theology* 92 (January 1989): 31–35.

Caron, Ann Marie. "Women Deaconesses: Historical and Contemporary Explorations." In *Where Can We Find Her? Searching for Women's Identity in the New Church,* edited by Marie-Eloise Rosenblatt, 132–51. Mahwah, N.J.: Paulist, 1991.

Castelli, Elizabeth A. "Gender, Theory, and the *Rise of Christianity*: A Response to Rodney Stark." *Journal of Early Christian Studies* 6 (Summer 1998): 227–57.

——————. "Paul on Women and Gender." In *Women and Christian Origins,* edited by Ross Shepard Kraemer and Mary Rose D'Angelo, 221–35. New York: Oxford University Press, 1999.

Church, F. Forrester. "Sex and Salvation in Tertullian." *Harvard Theological Review* 68 (April 1975): 83–101.

Cotter, Wendy. "Women's Authority Roles in Paul's Churches: Countercultural or Conventional?" *Novum Testamentum* 36 (October 1994): 350–72.

Cunningham, Agnes. "Women and Preaching in the Patristic Age." In *Preaching in the Patristic Age: Studies in Honor of Walter J. Burghardt, S.J.,* edited by David Hunter, 53–72. New York: Paulist, 1989.

D'Angelo, Mary Rose. "(Re) Presentations of Women in the Gospels: John and Mark." In *Women and Christian Origins,* edited by Ross Shepard Kraemer and Mary Rose D'Angelo, 129–49. New York: Oxford University Press, 1999.

Davies, Stevan L. *The Revolt of the Widows: The Social World of the Apocryphal Acts.* Carbondale, Ill.: Southern Illinois University Press, 1980.

Dewey, Joanna. "From Storytelling to Written Text: The Loss of Early Christian Women's Voices." *Biblical Theology Bulletin* 26 (Summer 1996): 71–78.

——————. "Teaching the New Testament from a Feminist Perspective." *Theological Education* 26 (Autumn 1989): 86–105.

——————. "Women in the Synoptic Gospels: Seen But Not Heard?" *Biblical Theology Bulletin* 27 (Summer 1997): 53–60.

Dronke, Peter. *Women Writers of the Middle Ages: A Critical Study of Texts from Perpetua to Marguerite Porete.* Cambridge: Cambridge University Press, 1984.

Eisenbaum, Pamela M. "Is Paul the Father of Misogyny and Antisemitism?" *Cross Currents* 50 (2001): 506–24.

Fatum, Lone. "Image of God and Glory of Man: Women in the Pauline Congregations." In *Image of God and Gender Models in Judaeo-Christian Tradition,* edited by Kari Elisabeth Børresen, 56–137. Oslo: Solum Forlag, 1991.

Frank, G. L. C. "Menstruation and Motherhood: Christian Attitudes in Late Antiquity." *Studia Historiae Ecclesiasticae* 19 (1993): 185–208.

Getty-Sullivan, Mary Ann. *Women in the New Testament.* Collegeville, Minn.: Liturgical, 2001.

Gryson, Roger. *The Ministry of Women in the Early Church.* Collegeville, Minn.: Liturgical, 1976.

Gundry-Volf, Judith M. "Paul on Women and Gender: A Comparison with Early Jewish Views." In *Road From Damascus: The Impact of Paul's Conversion on His Life, Thought and Ministry,* edited by Richard N. Longenecker, 184–212. Grand Rapids, Mich.: Eerdmans, 1997.

Haskins, Susan. *Mary Magdalen: Myth and Metaphor.* New York: Harcourt, Brace, 1994.

Heine, Susanne. *Women and Early Christianity: A Reappraisal.* Translated by John Bowden. Minneapolis: Augsburg, 1987.

Hess, Hamilton. "Changing Forms of Ministry in the Early Church." In *Sexism and Church Law,* edited by James A. Coriden, 43–57. New York: Paulist, 1977.

Hinson, E. Glenn. "Women Among the Martyrs." *Studia Patristica* 25, 423–28. Louvain: Peeters, 1993.

Houts, Margo G. "The Visual Evidence of Women in Early Christian Leadership." *Perspectives* 14 (March 1999): 14–18.

Hughes, Frank Witt. "Feminism and Early Christian History." *Anglican Theological Review* 69 (July 1987): 287–99.

Irvin, Dorothy. "The Ministry of Women in the Early Church: The Archaeological Evidence." *Duke Divinity Review* 45 (1980): 76–86.

Jackson, Glenna S. "The Complete Gospel: Jesus and Women via the Jesus Seminar." *Hervormde Teologiese Studies* 56 (November 2000): 1043–56.

Jansen, Katherine Ludwig. "Maria Magdalena: Apostolorum Apostola." In *Women Preachers and Prophets through Two Millennia of Christianity,* edited by Beverly Mayne Kienzle and Pamela J. Walker, 57–96. Berkeley: University of California Press, 1998.

Jensen, Anne. *God's Self-Confident Daughters: Early Christianity and the Liberation of Women.* Translated by O. C. Dean. Louisville: Westminster John Knox, 1996.

Kee, Howard Clark. "The Changing Role of Women in the Early Christian World." *Theology Today* 49 (July 1992): 225–38.

Kinder, Donald. "Clement of Alexandria: Conflicting Views on Women." *Second Century: A Journal of Early Christian Studies* 7 (Winter 1989–1990): 213–20.

King, Karen L. "Early Christian Women as Prophetic Leaders." *Harvard Divinity Bulletin* 24 (1995): 7.

Klawiter, Frederick C. "The Role of Martyrdom and Persecution in Developing the Priestly Authority of Women in Early Christianity: A Case Study of Montanism." *Church History* 49 (September 1980): 251–61.

Koukoura, Dimitra A. "Women in the Early Christian Church." In *Orthodox Women Speak: Discerning the "Signs of the Times,"* edited by Kyriaki Karidoyanes FitzGerald, 69–74. Geneva: WCC, 1999.

Kraemer, Ross Shepard. *Her Share of the Blessings: Women's Religions among Pagans, Jews, and Christians in the Greco-Roman World.* New York: Oxford University Press, 1992.

Laporte, Jean. *The Role of Women in Early Christianity.* Studies in Women and Religion 7. New York: Edwin Mellen, 1982.

LeMoine, Fannie J. "Apocalyptic Experience and the Conversion of Women in Early Christianity." In *Fearful Hope: Approaching the New Millennium,* edited by Christopher Kleinhenz and Fannie J. LeMoine, 201–6. Madison: University of Wisconsin Press, 1999.

Levine, Amy-Jill. "Second Temple Judaism, Jesus and Women: Yeast of Eden." *Biblical Interpretation* 2 (March 1994): 8–33.

Lieu, Judith. "The 'Attraction of Women' in/to Early Judaism and Christianity: Gender and the Politics of Conversion." *Journal for the Study of the New Testament* 72 (December 1998): 5–22.

Luter, Boyd. "Partnership in the Gospel: The Role of Women in the Church at Philippi." *Journal of the Evangelical Theological Society* 39 (September 1996): 411–20.

———. "Women Disciples and the Great Commission." *Trinity Journal,* no. 2 (Fall 1992): 171–85.

Lyman, Rebecca. "Perpetua: A Christian Quest for Self." *Journal of Women and Religion* 8 (Winter 1989): 26–33.

Maahs, Kenneth H. "Male and Female in Pauline Perspective: A Study in Ambivalence." *Dialogue and Alliance* 2 (Fall 1988): 17–34.

MacDonald, Dennis R. *The Legend and the Apostle: The Battle for Paul in Story and Canon.* Philadelphia: Westminster, 1983.

MacDonald, Margaret Y. "Reading Real Women Through the Undisputed Letters of Paul." In *Women and Christian Origins,* edited by Ross Shepard Kraemer and Mary Rose D'Angelo, 199–220. New York: Oxford University Press, 1999.

McKechnie, Paul. "'Women's Religion' and Second-Century Christianity." *Journal of Ecclesiastical History* 47 (July 1996): 409–31.

Maisch, Ingrid. *Mary Magdalene: The Image of a Woman through the Centuries.* Translated by Linda M. Maloney. Collegeville, Minn.: Liturgical, 1998.

The Martyrdom of Perpetua. Introduction by Sara Maitland. Evesham, England: Arthur James, 1996.

Matter, E. Ann. "Christ, God and Woman in the Thought of St. Augustine." In *Augustine and His Critics: Essays in Honour of Gerald Bonner,* edited by Robert Dodaro and George Lawless, 164–75. London: Routledge, 2000.

Methuen, Charlotte. "The 'Virgin Widow': A Problematic Social Role for the Early Church?" *Harvard Theological Review* 90 (July 1997): 285–98.

———. "Widows, Bishops and the Struggle for Authority in the *Didascalia Apostolorum.*" *Journal of Ecclesiastical History* 46 (April 1995): 197–213.

Munro, Winsome. "Patriarchy and Charismatic Community in 'Paul.'" In *Women and Religion: Papers of the Working Group on Women and Religion, 1972–73,* rev. ed., edited by Judith Plaskow and Joan Arnold Romero, 189–98. Missoula, Mont.: Scholars Press, 1974.

Osiek, Carolyn. "The Women at the Tomb: What Are They Doing There?" *Hervormde Teologiese Studies* 53 (March–June 1997): 103–18.

———. "Women in House Churches." In *Common Life in the Early Church: Essays Honoring Graydon F. Snyder,* edited by Julian V. Hills, 300–315. Harrisburg, Pa.: Trinity Press International, 1998.

Pagels, Elaine. *The Gnostic Gospels.* New York: Random House, 1979.

Parvey, Constance. "The Theology and Leadership of Women in the New Testament." In *Religion and Sexism: Images of Women in the Jewish and Christian Traditions,* edited by Rosemary Radford Ruether, 117–49. New York: Simon and Schuster, 1974.

Patterson, Lloyd. "Women in the Early Church: A Problem of Perspective." In *Toward a New Theology of Ordination: Essays on the Ordination of Women,* edited by Marianne H. Micks, 23–41. Somerville, Mass.: Greeno, Hadden, 1976.

Phipps, William. *Influential Theologians on Wo/Man.* Washington, D.C.: University Press of America, 1980.

———. "The Menstrual Taboo in the Judaeo-Christian Tradition." *Journal of Religion and Health* 19 (Winter 1980): 298–303.

Richardson, Peter. "From Apostles to Virgins: Romans 16 and the Roles of Women in the Early Church." *Toronto Journal of Theology* 2 (Fall 1986): 232–61.

Rogers, Katherin A. "Equal Before God: Augustine on the Nature and Role of Women." In *Nova Doctrina Vetusque: Essays on Early Christianity in Honor of Fredric W. Schlatter, S.J.*, edited by Douglas Kries and Catherine Brown Tkacz, 169–85. New York: Peter Lang, 1999.

Rossi, Mary Ann. "The Passion of Perpetua: Everywoman of Late Antiquity." In *Pagan and Christian Anxiety: A Response to E. R. Dodds*, edited by R. Smith and J. Lounibos, 53–86. Lanham, Md.: University Press of America, 1984.

———. "Priesthood, Precedent and Prejudice: On Recovering the Women Priests of Early Christianity." *Journal of Feminist Studies in Religion* 7 (Spring 1991): 73–94.

Ruether, Rosemary Radford. "Misogynism and Virginal Feminism in the Fathers of the Church." In *Religion and Sexism: Images of Woman in the Jewish and Christian Traditions*, edited by Rosemary Radford Ruether, 150–83. New York: Simon and Schuster, 1974.

———. "The Subordination and Liberation of Women: St. Paul and Sarah Grimké." *Soundings* 51 (1978): 172.

Schaberg, Jane. "How Mary Magdalene Became a Whore." *Bible Review* 8 (October 1992): 30–37, 51–52.

Scholer, David. "'And I Was a Man': The Power and Problem of Perpetua." *Daughters of Sarah* 15 (September/October 1989): 10–14.

Scholer, David, ed. *Women in Early Christianity*. New York: Garland, 1993.

Schottroff, Luise. *Lydia's Impatient Sisters: A Feminist Social History of Early Christianity*. Translated by Barbara and Martin Rumscheidt. Louisville: Westminster John Knox, 1995.

Schulz, Ray R. "A Case for 'President' Phoebe in Romans 16:2." *Lutheran Theological Journal* 24 (December 1990): 124–27.

Schüssler Fiorenza, Elisabeth. *Bread Not Stone: The Challenge of Feminist Biblical Interpretation*. Boston: Beacon, 1984.

———. *In Memory of Her: A Feminist Theological Reconstruction of Christian Origins*. 10th anniversary edition. New York: Crossroad, 1994.

———. "Women in the New Testament." *New Catholic World* 219 (November/December 1976): 256–60.

———. "Word, Spirit and Power: Women in Early Christian Communities." In *Women of Spirit: Female Leadership in the Jewish and Christian Traditions*, edited by Rosemary Radford Ruether and Eleanor McLaughlin, 30–70. New York: Simon and Schuster, 1979.

Scroggs, Robin. "Women and Men in the Early Church." In *We Belong Together: Churches in Solidarity with Women*, edited by Sarah Cunningham, 43–55. New York: Friendship, 1992.

Shaw, Brent. "Women and the Early Church." *History Today* 44 (February 1994): 21–28.

Stark, Rodney. "Reconstructing the Rise of Christianity: The Role of Women." *Sociology of Religion* 56 (Fall 1995): 229–44.

Stegemann, Wolfgang. "Paul and the Sexual Mentality of His World." *Biblical Theology Bulletin* 23 (Winter 1993): 161–66.

Spong, John Shelby. "Misogyny: A Pattern as Ancient as Life" and "Women: Less Than Free in Christ's Church." In *Into the Whirlwind: The Future of the Church*, 73–103. New York: Seabury, 1983.

Sullivan, Lisa M. "'I Responded, I Will Not . . .': Christianity as Catalyst for Resistance in the Passio Perpetuae and Felicitatis." *Semeia* 79 (1997): 63–74.

Swidler, Leonard. *Biblical Affirmations of Woman*. Philadelphia: Westminster, 1979.

———. "Greco-Roman Feminism and the Reception of the Gospel." In *Traditio-Krisis-Renovatio aus theologischer Sicht*, edited by Bernd Jaspert and Rudolf Mohr, 41–55. Marburg: N. G. Elwert, 1976.

Tavard, George. *Women in the Christian Tradition*. Notre Dame, Ind.: University of Notre Dame Press, 1973.

Thorley, John. "Junia, a Woman Apostle." *Novum Testamentum* 38 (January 1996): 18–29.

Thurston, Bonnie Bowman. *The Widows: A Women's Ministry in the Early Church*. Philadelphia: Fortress Press, 1989.

———. *Women in the New Testament: Questions and Commentary*. New York: Crossroad, 1998.

Torjesen, Karen Jo. "The Early Christian Orans: An Artistic Representation of Women's Liturgical Prayer and Prophecy." In *Women Preachers and Prophets through Two Millennia of Christianity*, edited by Beverly Mayne Kienzle and Pamela J. Walker, 42–56. Berkeley: University of California Press, 1998.

———. "Reconstruction of Women's Early Christian History." In *Searching the Scriptures*, vol. 1, edited by Elisabeth Schüssler Fiorenza, 290–307. New York: Crossroad, 1993–94.

———. *When Women Were Priests: Women's Leadership in the Early Church and the Scandal of Their Subordination in the Rise of Christianity*. San Francisco: HarperSanFrancisco, 1993.

Trevett, Christine. "Gender, Authority and Church History: A Case Study of Montanism." *Feminist Theology* 17 (January 1998): 9–24.

Vogt, Kari. "'Becoming Male': A Gnostic and Early Christian Metaphor." In *Image of God and Gender Models in Judaeo-Christian Tradition*, edited by Kari Elisabeth Børresen, 172–87. Oslo: Solum Forlag, 1991.

Watts, Rikki E. "Women in the Gospels and Acts." *Crux* 35 (June 1999): 22–33.

Whelan, Caroline F. "Amica Pauli: The Role of Phoebe in the Early Church." *Journal for the Study of the New Testament* 49 (March 1993): 67–85.

Wilson-Kastner, Patricia et al. *A Lost Tradition: Women Writers of the Early Church.* Washington, D.C.: University Press of America, 1981.

Wire, Antoinette Clark. *The Corinthian Women Prophets: A Reconstruction through Paul's Rhetoric.* Minneapolis: Fortress Press, 1990.

———. "Theological and Biblical Perspective: Liberation for Women Calls for a Liberated World." *Church and Society* 76 (January/February 1986): 7–17.

Witherington, Ben. *Women and the Genesis of Christianity*, edited by Ann Witherington. Cambridge: Cambridge University Press, 1990.

———. *Women in the Earliest Churches.* Cambridge: Cambridge University Press, 1988.

———. *Women in the Ministry of Jesus.* Cambridge: Cambridge University Press, 1984.

2. VIRGIN AND WITCH: WOMEN IN MEDIEVAL CHRISTIANITY

Atkinson, Clarissa. *Mystic and Pilgrim: The Book and the World of Margery Kempe.* Ithaca, N.Y.: Cornell University Press, 1983.

Barry, Jonathan et al. *Witchcraft in Early Modern Europe: Studies in Culture and Belief.* Cambridge: Cambridge University Press, 1996.

Barstow, Anne Llewellyn. *Witchcraze: A New History of the European Witch Hunts.* San Francisco: Pandora, 1994.

Beer, Frances. *Women and Mystical Experience in the Middle Ages.* Rochester: Boydell Press, 1992.

Bhattacharji, Santha. "Independence of Thought in Julian of Norwich." In *Women in Monasticism*, edited by Jean Leclercq et al., 79–92. Petersham, Mass.: St. Bede's, 1989.

Bradford, Clare. "Julian of Norwich and Margery Kempe." *Theology Today* 35 (July 1978): 153–58.

Bradley, Ritamary. "Julian of Norwich: Writer and Mystic." In *An Introduction to the Medieval Mystics of Europe*, edited by Paul E. Szarmach, 195–216. Albany, N.Y.: State University of New York Press, 1984.

Brauner, Sigrid. *Fearless Wives and Frightened Shrews: The Construction of the Witch in Early Modern Germany*, edited by Robert H. Brown. Amherst, Mass.: University of Massachusetts Press, 1995.

Brennan, Margaret. "Enclosure: Institutionalising the Invisibility of Women in Ecclesiastical Communities." In *Women: Invisible in Theology and Church*, edited by Mary Collins and Elisabeth Schüssler Fiorenza, 38–48. Edinburgh, Scotland: T. and T. Clark, 1985.

Briggs, Robin. *Witches and Neighbors: The Social and Cultural Context of European Witchcraft.* New York: Viking, 1996.

Brown, Raymond E. et al., eds. *Mary in the New Testament: A Collaborative Essay by Protestant and Roman Catholic Scholars.* Philadelphia: Fortress Press; New York: Paulist, 1978.

Bynum, Caroline. "Fast, Feast, and Flesh: The Religious Significance of Food to Medieval Women." *Representations* 11 (Summer 1985): 1–25.

———. *Jesus as Mother: Studies in the Spirituality of the High Middle Ages.* Berkeley: University of California Press, 1982.

Cameron, Averil. "Desert Mothers: Women Ascetics in Early Christian Egypt." In *Women as Teachers and Disciples in Traditional and New Religions*, edited by Elizabeth Puttick and Peter B. Clarke, 11–24. Lewiston, N.Y.: Edwin Mellen, 1993.

Castelli, Elizabeth. "Virginity and Its Meaning for Women's Sexuality in Early Christianity." *Journal of Feminist Studies in Religion* 2 (Spring 1986): 61–88.

Clark, Elizabeth. "Ascetic Renunciation and Feminine Advancement: A Paradox of Late Ancient Christianity." *Anglican Theological Review* 63 (July 1981): 240–57.

———. "Early Christian Women: Sources and Interpretation." In *That Gentle Strength: Historical Perspectives on Women and Christianity*, edited by Lynda L. Coon et al., 19–35. Charlottesville, Va.: University Press of Virginia, 1990.

———. "John Chrysostom and the Subintroductae." *Church History* 46 (June 1977): 171–85.

———. "Theory and Practice in Late Ancient Asceticism: Jerome, Chrysostom, and Augustine." *Journal of Feminist Studies in Religion* 5 (Fall 1989): 25–46.

Clark, Gillian. "Women and Asceticism in Late Antiquity: The Refusal of Status and Gender." In *Asceticism*, edited by Vincent L. Wimbush and Richard Valantasis, 33–48. New York: Oxford University Press, 1995.

Cloke, Gillian. "Mater or Martyr: Christianity and the Alienation of Women within the Family in the Later Roman Empire." *Theology and Sexuality* 5 (September 1996): 37–57.

———. *This Female Man of God: Women and Spiritual Power in the Patristic Age, A.D. 350–450.* London: Routledge, 1995.

Corrington, Gail. "Anorexia, Asceticism, and Autonomy: Self-Control as Liberation and Transcendence." *Journal of Feminist Studies in Religion* 2 (Fall 1986): 51–61.

Crisp, Beth R. "Seeking the Feminine: An Exploration of the Spiritual Writings of Hildegard of Bingen and Julian of Norwich." *Pacifica* 10 (October 1997): 310–18.

Cummings, Charles. "The Motherhood of God According to Julian of Norwich." In *Medieval Religious Women*, vol. 2. Edited by John A. Nichols and Lillian Thomas Shank, 305–14. Kalamazoo, Mich.: Cistercian, 1987.

Cunneen, Sally. "Breaking Mary's Silence: A Feminist Reflection on Marian Piety." *Theology Today* 56 (October 1999): 319–35.

Derksen, Loes D. "St. Thomas Aquinas: The Theology of Woman." In *Dialogues on Women: Images of Women in the History of Philosophy*, 43–62. Amsterdam: VU University Press, 1996.

Elliott, Dyan. *Spiritual Marriage: Sexual Abstinence in Medieval Wedlock.* Princeton: Princeton University Press, 1993.

Elm, Susanna. *Virgins of God: The Making of Asceticism in Late Antiquity.* Oxford: Oxford University Press, 1994.

Feldman, Laurie A. "St. Catherine of Siena: An Exploration of the Feminine and the Mystic." *Anima* 4 (Spring 1978): 57–63.

Finnegan, Mary Jeremy. *The Women of Helfta: Scholars and Mystics.* Athens, Ga.: University of Georgia Press, 1991.

Fries, Maureen. "Margery Kempe." In *An Introduction to the Medieval Mystics of Europe*, edited by Paul E. Szarmach, 217–35. Albany, N.Y.: State University of New York Press, 1984.

Galloway, Penelope. "Discreet and Devout Maidens: Women's Involvement in Beguine Communities in Northern France, 1200–1500." In *Medieval Women in Their Communities*, edited by Diane Watt, 92–115. Toronto: University of Toronto Press, 1997.

Garrett, Clarke. "Women and Witches: Patterns of Analysis." *Signs: Journal of Women in Culture and Society* 3 (Winter 1977): 461–70.

Gaventa, Beverly Roberts. "'All Generations Will Call Me Blessed': Mary in Biblical and Ecumenical Perspective." *Princeton Seminary Bulletin* 18 (1997): 251–61.

Gies, Frances, and Joseph Gies. *Women in the Middle Ages.* New York: Crowell, 1978.

Goodman, Anthony. *Margery Kempe and Her World.* Harlow, England: Longman, 2002.

Gould, Graham. "Women in the Writings of the Fathers: Language, Belief and Reality." In *Women in the Church: Papers Read at the 1989 Summer Meeting and the 1990 Winter Meeting of the Ecclesiastical History Society*, edited by W. J. Sheils and Diana Wood, 1–13. Oxford: Basil Blackwell, 1990.

Hartney, Aideen. "Manly Women and Womanly Men: The *Subintroductae* and John Chrysostom." In *Desire and Denial in Byzantium: Papers from the 31st Spring Symposium of Byzantine Studies*, edited by Liz James, 41–48. Aldershot, England: Ashgate, 1999.

Henneau, Marie-Elisabeth, and Jocelyn Wogan-Browne. "Introduction: Liège, the Medieval 'Woman Question' and the Question of Medieval Women." In *New Trends in Feminine Spirituality: The Holy Women of Liège and Their Impact*, edited by Juliette Dor et al., 1–32. Turnhout, Belgium: Brepols, 1999.

Hickey, Anne Ewing. *Women of the Roman Aristocracy as Christian Monastics.* Ann Arbor, Mich.: UMI Research Press, 1987.

Institoris, Henricus, and James Sprenger. *Malleus Maleficarum.* Trans. Montague Summers. New York: Bloom, 1970.

Jantzen, Grace M. "Cry Out and Write: Mysticism and the Struggle for Authority." In *Women, the Book, and the Godly: Selected Proceedings of the St. Hilda's Conference, 1993*, edited by Lesley Smith and Jane H. M. Taylor, 67–76. Rochester: Brewer, 1995.

Johnson, Elizabeth. "Mary and the Female Face of God." *Theological Studies* 50 (September 1989): 500–526.

King, Margaret L. "Isotta Nogarola." In *Italian Women Writers: A Bio-bibliographical Sourcebook*, edited by Rinaldina Russell, 313–21. Westport, Conn.: Greenwood, 1994.

———. "The Religious Retreat of Isotta Nogarola (1418–1466): Sexism and Its Consequences in the Fifteenth Century." *Signs: Journal of Women in Culture and Society* 3 (Summer 1978): 807–22.

Klaits, Joseph. *Servants of Satan: The Age of the Witch Hunts.* Bloomington, Ind.: Indiana University Press, 1985.

Kors, Alan Charles and Edward Peters. *Witchcraft in Europe, 400–1700: A Documentary History.* Rev. ed. Philadelphia: University of Pennsylvania Press, 2001.

Kraemer, Ross S. "The Conversion of Women to Ascetic Forms of Christianity." In *Sisters and Workers in the Middle Ages*, edited by Judith M. Bennett et al., 198–207. Chicago: University of Chicago Press, 1989.

Lagorio, Valerie. "The Continental Women Mystics of the Middle Ages: An Assessment." In *Spirituality of Western Christendom*, vol. 2. Edited by E. Rozanne Elder, 71–90. Kalamazoo, Mich.: Cistercian, 1984.

Lahutsky, Nadia. "Food and Feminism and Historical Interpretations: The Case of Medieval Holy Women." In *Setting the Table: Women in Theological Conversation*, edited by Rita Nakashima Brock et al., 233–48. St. Louis: Chalice, 1995.

Leclercq, Jean. "Monasticism and the Promotion of Women." In *Women in Monasticism*, edited by Jean Leclercq et al., 3–15. Petersham, Mass.: St. Bede's, 1989.

———. "Solitude and Solidarity: Medieval Women Recluses." In *Medieval Religious Women*, vol. 2. Edited by John A. Nichols and Lillian Thomas Shank, 67–83. Kalamazoo, Mich.: Cistercian, 1987.

LeMoine, Fannie. "Jerome's Gift to Women Readers." In *Shifting Frontiers in Late Antiquity*, edited by Ralph W. Mathisen and Hagith S. Sivan, 230–41. Aldershot, England: Variorum, 1996.

Leyser, Henrietta. *Medieval Women: A Social History of Women in England, 450–1500.* London: Weidenfeld and Nicolson, 1995.

The Life of Christina of Markyate. Trans. Monica Furlong. Berkhamsted, England: Arthur James, 1997.

Loades, Ann L. "Feminist Theology: A View of Mary." In *Mary Is for Everyone: Papers on Mary and Ecumenism*, edited by William McLoughlin and Jill Pinnock, 32–40. Leominster, England: Gracewing, 1997.

Lucas, Angela M. *Women in the Middle Ages: Religion, Marriage and Letters.* New York; St. Martin's Press, 1983.

McEntire, Sandra J. "The Journey into Selfhood: Margery Kempe and Feminine Spirituality." In *Margery Kempe: A Book of Essays*, edited by Sandra J. McEntire, 51–69. New York: Garland, 1992.

McLaughlin, Eleanor. "Equality of Souls, Inequality of Sexes: Woman in Medieval Theology." In *Religion and Sexism: Images of Woman in the Jewish and Christian Traditions*, edited by Rosemary Radford Ruether, 213–66. New York: Simon and Schuster, 1974.

———. "Women, Power and the Pursuit of Holiness in Medieval Christianity." In *Women of Spirit: Female Leadership in the Jewish and Christian Traditions*, edited by Rosemary Radford Ruether and Eleanor McLaughlin, 100–130. New York: Simon and Schuster, 1979.

McNamara, Jo Ann. "Muffled Voices: The Lives of Consecrated Women in the Fourth Century." In *Medieval Religious Women*, vol. 1. Edited by John A. Nichols and Lillian Thomas Shank, 11–29. Kalamazoo, Mich.: Cistercian, 1984.

———. *A New Song: Celibate Women in the First Three Christian Centuries.* New York: Haworth, 1983.

McNamer, Sarah. "The Exploratory Image: God as Mother in Julian of Norwich's Revelations of Divine Love." *Mystics Quarterly* 15 (March 1989): 21–28.

Miller, Patrick D. ed. "[Mary]." *Theology Today* 56 (October 1999): 293–78.

Morris, Joan. *The Lady Was a Bishop: The History of Women with Clerical Ordination and the Jurisdiction of Bishops.* New York: Macmillan, 1973.

Moss, Patricia. "Unravelling the Threads: The Origins of Women's Asceticism in the Earliest Christian Communities." *Pacifica* 10 (June 1997): 137–55.

Muessig, Carolyn. "Prophecy and Song: Teaching and Preaching by Medieval Women." In *Women Preachers and Prophets through Two Millennia of Christianity*, edited by Beverly Kienzle and Pamela Walker, 146–58. Berkeley: University of California Press, 1998.

Noffke, Suzanne. *Catherine of Siena: Vision through a Distant Eye.* Collegeville, Minn.: Liturgical, 1996.

Norris, Janice Racine. "Nuns and Other Religious: Women and Christianity in the Middle Ages." In *Women in Medieval Western European Culture*, edited by Linda E. Mitchell, 277–94. New York: Garland, 1999.

Pelikan, Jaroslav. *Mary through the Centuries: Her Place in the History of Culture.* New Haven, Conn.: Yale University Press, 1996.

Petroff, Elizabeth. *Body and Soul: Essays on Medieval Women and Mysticism.* New York: Oxford University Press, 1994.

Power, Eileen. *Medieval Women.* Cambridge: Cambridge University Press, 1975.

Provost, William. "Margery Kempe and Her Calling." In *Margery Kempe: A Book of Essays*, edited by Sandra J. McEntire, 3–16. New York: Garland, 1992.

Quaife, G. R. *Godly Zeal and Furious Rage: The Witch in Early Modern Europe.* New York: St. Martin's, 1987.

Rorem, Paul. "Lover and Mother: Medieval Language for God and the Soul." In *Women, Gender, and Christian Community*, edited by Jane Dempsey Douglass and James F. Kay, 46–54. Louisville: Westminster John Knox, 1997.

Rosof, Patricia. "The Anchoress in the Twelfth and Thirteenth Centuries." In *Medieval Religious Women*, vol. 2. Edited by John A. Nichols and Lillian Thomas Shank, 123–144. Kalamazoo, Mich.: Cistercian, 1987.

Ross, Ellen M. "Spiritual Experience and Women's Autobiography: The Rhetoric of Selfhood in the Book of Margery Kempe." *Journal of the American Academy of Religion* 59 (Fall 1991): 527–46.

Ruether, Rosemary Radford. "Asceticism and Feminism: Strange Bedmates?" In *Sex and God: Some Varieties of Women's Religious Experience*, edited by Linda Hurcombe, 229–50. New York: Routledge, 1987.

————. *Mary—The Feminine Face of the Church.* Philadelphia: Westminster, 1977.

————. "Mary in U.S. Catholic Culture." *National Catholic Reporter* (10 February 1995): 15–17.

————. "The Persecution of Witches: A Case of Sexism and Ageism?" *Christianity and Crisis* 34 (23 December 1974): 291–95.

————. *Visionary Women: Three Medieval Mystics.* Facets. Minneapolis: Fortress Press, 2002.

————. *Women and Redemption: A Theological History.* Minneapolis: Fortress Press, 1998.

Russell, Jeffrey. *History of Witchcraft.* London: Thames and Hudson, 1980.

Scaraffia, Lucetta, and Gabriella Zarri. *Women and Faith: Catholic Religious Life in Italy from Late Antiquity to the Present.* Cambridge, Mass.: Harvard University Press, 1999.

Schulenburg, Jane Tibbetts. *Forgetful of Their Sex: Female Sanctity and Society, ca. 500–1100.* Chicago: University of Chicago Press, 1998.

————. "The Heroics of Virginity: Brides of Christ and Sacrificial Mutilation." In *Women in the Middle Ages and the Renaissance*, edited by Mary B. Rose, 29–72. Syracuse: Syracuse University Press, 1986.

Scott, Karen. "Catherine of Siena and Lay Sanctity in Fourteenth-Century Italy." In *Lay Sanctity, Medieval and Modern: A Search for Models*, edited by Ann W. Astell, 77–90, 211–213. Notre Dame, Ind.: University of Notre Dame, 2000.

————. "St. Catherine of Siena, 'Apostola.'" *Church History* 61 (March 1992): 34–46.

————. "Urban Spaces, Women's Networks, and the Lay Apostolate in the Siena of Catherine Benincasa." In *Creative Women in Medieval and Early Modern Italy*, edited by John Coakley and E. Ann Matter, 105–19. Philadelphia: University of Pennsylvania Press, 1994.

Simpson, Jane. "Women and Asceticism in the Fourth Century." *Journal of Religious History* 15 (June 1988): 38–60.

Stuard, Susan M., ed. *Women in Medieval Society.* Philadelphia: University of Pennsylvania Press, 1976.

Szarmach, Paul, ed. *An Introduction to the Medieval Mystics of Europe.* Albany: State University of New York Press, 1984.

Troup, Cynthia. "Writing About Women and Mysticism." *Pacifica* 8 (June 1995): 201–12.

Vivian, Miriam Raub. "Escaping Women: Paradox and Achievement in Late Roman Asceticism." In *The Formulation of Christianity by Conflict through the Ages*, edited by Katharine Free, 101–25. Lewiston, N.Y.: Edwin Mellen, 1995.

Warner, Marina. *Alone of All Her Sex: The Myth and Cult of the Virgin Mary.* New York: Knopf, 1976.

Wemple, Suzanne F. "Contemplative Life: The Search for Feminine Autonomy in the Frankish Kingdom." *Anima* 6 (Spring 1980): 131–36.

Wiesner, Merry E. *Women and Gender in Early Modern Europe.* Cambridge: Cambridge University Press, 1993.

Willard, Charity Cannon. *Christine de Pizan: Her Life and Works.* New York: Persea, 1990.

Williams, Marty, and Anne Echols. *Between Pit and Pedestal: Women and the Middle Ages.* Princeton: Markus Wiener, 1994.

Wybourne, Catherine. "Leoba: A Study in Humanity and Holiness." In *Medieval Women Monastics: Wisdom's Wellsprings*, edited by Miriam Schmitt and Linda Kulzer, 81–96. Collegeville, Minn.: Liturgical, 1996.

Yoshioka, Barbara. "Whoring After Strange Gods: A Narrative of Women and Witches." *Radical Religion* 1 (Summer/Fall 1974): 6–11.

Zimdars-Swartz, Sandra. *Encountering Mary: From LaSalette to Medjugorje.* Princeton: Princeton University Press, 1991.

3. WOMEN IN AN ERA OF REFORMATION

Bainton, Roland H. *Women of the Reformation, from Spain to Scandinavia.* Minneapolis: Augsburg, 1977.

————. *Women of the Reformation in France and England.* Minneapolis: Augsburg, 1973.

————. *Women of the Reformation in Germany and Italy.* Minneapolis: Augsburg, 1971.

Baldwin, Claude Marie. "John Calvin and the Ethics of Gender Relations." *Calvin Theological Journal* 26 (April 1991): 133–43.

————. "Marriage in Calvin's Sermons." In *Calvin's Work in Geneva*, edited by Richard C. Gamble, 107–16. New York: Garland, 1992.

Barrett, Lois. "The Role and Influence of Anabaptist Women in the Martyr Story." *Brethren Life and Thought* 37 (Spring 1992): 87–96.

————. "Women's History/Women's Theology: Theological and Methodological Issues in the Writing of the History of Anabaptist-Mennonite Women." *Conrad Grebel Review* 10 (Winter 1992): 1–16.

Barstow, Anne Llewellyn. "An Ambiguous Legacy: Anglican Clergy Wives After the Reformation." In *Women in New Worlds: Historical Perspectives on the Wesleyan Tradition*, edited by Hilah F. Thomas and Rosemary Skinner Keller, 97–111. Nashville: Abingdon, 1982.

Blaisdell, Charmarie J. "Angela Merici and the Ursulines." In *Religious Orders of the Catholic Reformation: In Honor of John C. Olin*, edited by Richard L. DeMolen, 99–136. New York: Fordham University Press, 1994.

———. "Calvin's Letters to Women: The Courting of Ladies in High Places." In *Calvin's Work in Geneva*, edited by Richard C. Gamble, 167–84. New York: Garland, 1992.

———. "The Matrix of Reform: Women in the Lutheran and Calvinist Movements." In *Triumph over Silence: Women in Protestant History*, edited by Richard L. Greaves, 13–44. Westport, Conn.: Greenwood, 1985.

Bratt, John. "Role and Status of Women in the Writings of John Calvin." In *Renaissance, Reformation, Resurgence*, edited by Peter DeKlerk, 1–17. Grand Rapids, Mich.: Calvin Theological Seminary, 1976.

Brauner, Sigrid. "Martin Luther on Witchcraft: A True Reformer?" In *The Politics of Gender in Early Modern Europe*, edited by Jean R. Brink et al., 29–42. Kirksville, Mo.: Sixteenth Century Journal Publishers, 1989.

Chrisman, Miriam U. "Women and the Reformation in Strasbourg, 1490–1530." *Archive for Reformation History* 63 (1972): 143–67.

Coudert, Allison P. "The Myth of the Improved Status of Protestant Women: The Case of the Witchcraze." In *The Politics of Gender in Early Modern Europe*, edited by Jean R. Brink et al., 61–90. Kirksville, Mo.: Sixteenth Century Journal Publishers, 1989.

Cunningham, Lawrence S. "Mary in Catholic Doctrine and Practice." *Theology Today* 56 (October 1999): 307–18.

DeBoer, Willis. "Calvin on the Role of Women." In *Exploring the Heritage of John Calvin*, edited by David Holwerda, 236–72. Grand Rapids, Mich.: Baker, 1976.

Douglass, Jane Dempsey. "Christian Freedom: What Calvin Learned at the School of Women." *Church History* 53 (June 1984): 155–73.

———. "Hearing a Different Message: Reforming Women Interpret the Bible." In *Women, Gender and Christian Community*, edited by Jane Dempsey Douglass and James F. Kay, 55–65. Louisville: Westminster John Knox, 1997.

———. "The Image of God in Women as Seen by Luther and Calvin." In *The Image of God: Gender Models in Judaeo-Christian Tradition*, edited by Kari Elisabeth Børresen, 236–66. Minneapolis: Fortress Press, 1995.

———. "Women and the Continental Reformation." In *Religion and Sexism: Images of Woman in the Jewish and Christian Traditions*, edited by Rosemary Radford Ruether, 292–318. New York: Simon and Schuster, 1974.

———. "Women and the Reformation." In *The Many Sides of History: Readings in the Western Heritage*, vol. I. Edited by Steven Ozment and Frank M. Turner, 318–35. New York: Macmillan, 1987.

———. *Women, Freedom, and Calvin*. Philadelphia: Westminster, 1985.

Greaves, Richard L. "The Role of Women in Early English Nonconformity." *Church History* 52 (September 1983): 299–311.

Harrison, Wes. "The Role of Women in Anabaptist Thought and Practice: The Hutterite Experience of the Sixteenth and Seventeenth Centuries." *Sixteenth Century Journal* 23 (1992): 49–69.

Haude, Sigrun. "Anabaptist Women: Radical Women?" In *Infinite Boundaries: Order, Disorder, and Reorder in Early Modern German Culture*," edited by Max Reinhart, 313–28. Kirksville, Mo.: Sixteenth Century Journal Publishers, 1998.

Irwin, Joyce L. *Womanhood in Radical Protestantism 1525–1675*. Vol. I, *Studies in Women and Religion*. New York: Edwin Mellen, 1979.

Joldersma, Hermina. "Argula von Grumbach." In *German Writers of the Renaissance and Reformation, 1280–1580*, edited by James Hardin and Max Reinhardt, 89–96. Detroit: Gale Research, 1997.

Jordon, Sherry. "Women as Proclaimers and Interpreters of the Word." *Currents in Theology and Mission* 24 (February 1997): 33–43.

Karant-Nunn, Susan C. "Reformation Society, Women and the Family." In *The Reformation World*, edited by Andrew Pettegree, 433–60. New York: Routledge, 2002.

Liebowitz, Ruth P. "Virgins in the Service of Christ: The Dispute over an Active Apostolate for Women During the Counter-Reformation." In *Women of Spirit: Female Leadership in the Jewish and Christian Traditions*, edited by Rosemary Radford Ruether and Eleanor McLaughlin, 131–52. New York: Simon and Schuster, 1979.

Ludlow, Dorothy P. "Shaking Patriarchy's Foundations: Sectarian Women in England, 1641–1700." In *Triumph over Silence: Women in Protestant History*, edited by Richard L. Greaves, 93–123. Westport, Conn.: Greenwood, 1985.

Marr, M. Lucille. "Anabaptist Women of the North: Peers in the Faith, Subordinates in Marriage." *Mennonite Quarterly Review* 61 (October 1987): 347–62.

Marshall, Sherrin, ed. *Women in Reformation and Counter-Reformation Europe: Public and Private Worlds*. Bloomington, Ind.: Indiana University Press, 1989.

Matheson, Peter, ed. *Argula von Grumbach: A Woman's Voice in the Reformation.* Edinburgh: T. and T. Clark, 1995.

———. "Breaking the Silence: Women, Censorship, and the Reformation." *Sixteenth Century Journal* 27 (1996): 97–109.

———. "A Reformation for Women? Sin, Grace and Gender in the Writings of Argula von Grumbach." *Scottish Journal of Theology* 49 (1996): 39–55.

Norberg, Kathryn. "The Counter-Reformation and Women Religious and Lay." In *Catholicism in Early Modern History: A Guide to Research*, edited by John W. O'Malley, 133–146. St. Louis: Center for Reformation Research, 1988.

Packull, Werner O. "'We Are Born to Work Like the Birds to Fly:' The Anabaptist-Hutterite Ideal Woman." *Mennonite Quarterly Review* 73 (January 1999): 75–86.

Parish, Debra L. "The Power of Female Pietism: Women as Spiritual Authorities and Religious Role Models in Seventeenth-Century England." *Journal of Religious History* 17 (June 1992): 33–46.

Ranft, Patricia. "A Key to Counter-Reformation Women's Activism: The Confessor-Spiritual Director." *Journal of Feminist Studies in Religion* 10 (Fall 1994): 7–26.

Roelker, Nancy. "The Appeal of Calvinism to French Noblewomen in the Sixteenth Century." *Journal of Interdisciplinary History* 2 (Spring 1972): 391–418.

———. "The Role of Noblewomen in the French Reformation." *Archive for Reformation History* 63 (1972): 168–95.

Scharffenorth, Gerta. *Becoming Friends in Christ: The Relationship Between Man and Woman in Luther.* LWF Studies: Reports and Texts from the Department of Studies. Geneva: Lutheran World Federation, 1983.

Snyder, C. Arnold, and Linda A. Huebert Hecht, eds. *Profiles of Anabaptist Women: Sixteenth-Century Reforming Pioneers.* Waterloo, Ontario: Wilfrid Laurier University Press, 1996.

Sprunger, Keith L. "God's Powerful Army of the Weak: Anabaptist Women of the Radical Reformation." In *Triumph over Silence: Women in Protestant History*, edited by Richard L. Greaves, 45–74. Westport, Conn.: Greenwood, 1985.

Steinmetz, David C. "Theological Reflections on the Reformation and the Status of Women." *Duke Divinity Review* 41 (Fall 1976): 197–207.

Thomas, Keith. "Women and the Civil War Sects." In *Crisis in Europe, 1560–1660*, edited by Trevor Aston, 317–40. New York: Basic, 1965.

Thompson, John L. "*Creata Ad Imaginem Dei, Licet Secundo Gradu*: Women as the Image of God According to John Calvin." In *Calvin's Work in Geneva*, edited by Richard C. Gamble, 137–55. New York: Garland, 1992.

Van der Walt, Barend Johannes. "Women and Marriage. In the Middle Ages, in Calvin, and in Our Own Time." In *John Calvin's Institutes: His Opus Magnum*, 184–236. Potchefstroom, South Africa: Potchefstroom University for Christian Higher Education, 1986.

Vogt, Peter. "A Voice for Themselves: Women as Participants in Congregational Discourse in the Eighteenth-Century Moravian Movement." In *Women Preachers and Prophets through Two Millennia of Christianity*, edited by Beverly Mayne Kienzle and Pamela J Walker, 227–47. Berkeley: University of California Press, 1998.

White, Robert. "Women and the Teaching Office According to Calvin." *Scottish Journal of Theology* 47, no. 4 (1994): 489–509.

Wiesner, Merry E. "The Early Modern Period: Religion, the Family, and Women's Public Roles." In *Religion, Feminism, and the Family*, edited by Anne Carr and Mary Stewart van Leeuwen, 149–65. Louisville: Westminster John Knox, 1996.

———. "Luther and Women: The Death of Two Marys." In *Disciplines of Faith: Studies in Religion, Politics, and Patriarchy*, edited by Jim Obelkevich et al., 295–308. New York: Routledge, 1987.

———. *Women and Gender in Early Modern Europe.* New York: Cambridge University Press, 1993.

———. "Women's Response to the Reformation." In *The German People and the Reformation*, edited by R. Po-Chia Hsia, 148–71. Ithaca: Cornell University Press, 1988.

Wilson, Katharina, ed. *Women Writers of the Renaissance and Reformation.* Athens, Ga.: University of Georgia Press, 1987.

Wright, David. "Women Before and After the Fall: A Comparison of Luther's and Calvin's Interpretation of Genesis 1–3." *Churchman* 98, no. 2 (1984): 126–35.

Zophy, Jonathan W. "We Must Have the Dear Ladies: Martin Luther and Women." In *Pietas et Societas: New Trends in Reformation Social History*, edited by Kyle C. Sessions and Phillip N. Bebb, 141–50. Kirksville, Mo.: Sixteenth Century Journal Publishers, 1985.

4. WOMEN AND CHRISTIANITY IN THE AMERICAN COLONIES

Bacon, Margaret Hope. *Mothers of Feminism: The Story of Quaker Women in America.* 2nd ed. Philadelphia: Friends General Conference, 1995.

Bendroth, Margaret Lamberts. "Feminism, Anne Hutchinson and the Antinomian Controversy, 1634–1638." *Trinity Journal* 2 (1981): 40–48.

Benson, Mary Sumner. *Women in Eighteenth-Century America: A Study of Opinion and Social Usage.* New York: Columbia University Press, 1935. Reprint. New York: A.M.S. Press, 1976.

Calvo, Janis. "Quaker Women Ministers in Nineteenth-Century America." *Quaker History* 63 (Autumn 1974): 75–93.

Chilcote, Paul Wesley. *John Wesley and the Women Preachers of Early Methodism.* Metuchen, N.J.: Scarecrow, 1991.

Cohen, Ronald D. "Church and State in Seventeenth-Century Massachusetts: Another Look at the Antinomian Controversy." In *Puritan New England: Essays on Religion, Society and Culture,* edited by Francis J. Bremer et al., 174–86. New York: St. Martin's Press, 1977.

Cooper, James F. "Anne Hutchinson and the 'Lay Rebellion' against the Clergy." *New England Quarterly* 61 (September 1988): 381–97.

Cowring, Cedric. "Sex and Preaching in the Great Awakening." *American Quarterly* 20 (Fall 1968): 624–44.

Crabtree, Davida Foy. "Controversy in Context: Anne Marbury Hutchinson Against the Massachusetts Bay Colony." *Andover Newton Quarterly* 11 (September 1970): 27–34.

Dunn, Mary Maples. "Latest Light on Women of Light." In *Witnesses for Change: Quaker Women over Three Centuries,* edited by Elisabeth Potts Brown and Susan Mosher Stuard, 71–85. New Brunswick, N.J.: Rutgers University Press, 1989.

Feige, Diana and Franz Feige. "Love, Marriage, and Family in Puritan Society." *Dialogue and Alliance* 9 (Spring–Summer 1995): 96–114.

George, Carol V. R. "Anne Hutchinson and the Revolution Which Never Happened." In *Remember the Ladies: New Perspectives on Women in American History,* edited by Carol V. R. George, 13–37. Syracuse: Syracuse University Press, 1975.

Hall, David D. ed. *The Antinomian Controversy, 1636–1638: A Documentary History.* Middletown, Conn.: Wesleyan University Press, 1968.

Hambrick-Stowe, Charles E. "The Spiritual Pilgrimage of Sarah Osborn (1714–1796)." *Church History* 61 (December 1992): 408–21.

Holliday, Carl. *Women's Life in Colonial Days.* Boston: Cornhill, 1922. Reprint. Detroit, Mich.: Gale Research Co., 1970.

Huber, Elaine C. "'A Woman Must Not Speak': Quaker Women in the English Left Wing." In *Women of Spirit: Female Leadership in the Jewish and Christian Traditions,* edited by Rosemary Radford Ruether and Eleanor McLaughlin, 154–203. New York: Simon and Schuster, 1979.

Ingle, H. Larry. "A Quaker Woman on Women's Roles: Mary Penington to Friends, 1678." *Signs: Journal of Women in Culture and Society* 16 (Spring 1991): 587–96.

James, Janet Wilson, ed. *Women in American Religion.* Philadelphia: University of Pennsylvania Press, 1980.

King, Anne. "Anne Hutchinson and Anne Bradstreet." *International Journal of Women's Studies* 1 (September/October 1978): 445–67.

Koehler, Lyle. "The Case of the American Jezebels: Anne Hutchinson and Female Agitation During the Years of Antinomian Turmoil, 1636–1640." In *Our Sisters: Women in American Life and Thought,* edited by Jean Friedman and William Shade, 52–75, Boston: Allyn and Bacon, 1976.

Kraditor, Aileen, ed. *Up From the Pedestal: Selected Writings in the History of American Feminism.* Chicago: Quadrangle, 1968.

Kujawa-Holbrook, Sheryl. "The Teacher as Reformer: Sarah Osborn, 1714–1796." *Union Seminary Quarterly Review* 47 (1993): 89–100.

Larson, Rebecca. *Daughters of Light: Quaker Women Preaching and Prophesying in the Colonies and Abroad, 1700–1775.* New York: Knopf, 1999.

Loewenberg, Bert J., and Ruth Bogin, eds. *Black Women in Nineteenth-Century American Life.* University Park, Pa.: Pennsylvania State University Press, 1976.

Lumpkin, William L. "The Role of Women in 18th Century Virginia Baptist Life." *Baptist History and Heritage* 8 (1973): 158–67.

Malmsheimer, Lonna A. "Daughters of Zion: New England Roots of American Feminism." *New England Quarterly* 50 (September 1977): 484–504.

Masson, Margaret. "The Typology of the Female as a Model for the Regenerate: Puritan Preaching 1690–1730." *Signs: Journal of Women in Culture and Society* 2 (Winter 1976): 304–15.

Moore, Susan Hardman. "Sexing the Soul: Gender and the Rhetoric of Puritan Piety." In *Gender and Christian Religion: Papers Read at the 1996 Summer Meeting and the 1997 Winter Meeting of the Ecclesiastical History Society*, edited by R. N. Swanson, 175–86. Woodbridge, England: Boydell, 1998.

Moran, Gerald F. " 'The Hidden Ones': Women and Religion in Puritan New England." In *Triumph over Silence: Women in Protestant History*, edited by Richard L. Greaves, 125–49. Westport, Conn.: Greenwood, 1985.

Norton, Mary Beth. "'My Resting Reaping Times': Sarah Osborn's Defense of Her 'Unfeminine' Activities, 1767," *Signs: Journal of Women in Culture and Society* 2 (Winter 1976): 515–29.

Porterfield, Amanda. *Feminine Spirituality in America*. Philadelphia: Temple University Press, 1970.

———. "Women's Attraction to Puritanism." *Church History* 60 (June 1991): 196–209.

Ruether, Rosemary Radford, and Rosemary Skinner Keller, eds. *Women and Religion in America.* Vol. 2, *The Colonial and Revolutionary Periods.* San Francisco: Harper and Row, 1983.

Ryan, Mary P. *Womanhood in America: From Colonial Times to the Present.* 3rd ed. New York: Franklin Watts, 1983.

Saxton, Martha. "Bearing the Burden? Puritan Wives." *History Today* 44 (October 1994): 28–33.

Smith, Page. *Daughters of the Promised Land: Women in American History.* Boston: Little, Brown, 1970.

Spruill, Julia. *Women's Life and Work in the Southern Colonies.* Chapel Hill, N.C.: University of North Carolina Press, 1938. Reprint. New York: Norton, 1972.

Stein, Stephen. "A Note on Anne Dutton, Eighteenth-Century Evangelical." *Church History* 44 (December 1975): 485–91.

Stuard, Susan Mosher. "Women's Witnessing: A New Departure." In *Witnesses for Change: Quaker Women over Three Centuries*, edited by Elisabeth Potts Brown and Susan Mosher Stuard, 3–24. New Brunswick, N.J.: Rutgers University Press, 1989.

Thomas, Hilah F., and Rosemary Skinner Keller, eds. 2 vols. *Women in New Worlds: Historical Perspectives on the Wesleyan Tradition.* Vol. 1, Nashville: Abingdon, 1981, 1982.

Ulrich, Laurel Thatcher. *Good Wives: Image and Reality in the Lives of Women in Northern New England, 1650–1750.* New York: Knopf, 1982.

———. "Vertuous Women Found: New England Ministerial Literature, 1668–1735." In *Women in American Religion*, edited by Janet Wilson James, 67–87. Philadelphia: University of Pennsylvania Press, 1980.

Washington, Harold C. "'And Your Daughters Shall Prophesy': Gender and Culture in Early Quaker Biblical Interpretation." In *Text and Experience: Towards a Cultural Exegesis of the Bible*, edited by D. Smith-Christopher, 23–42. Sheffield, England: Sheffield Academic Press, 1995.

Watson, JoAnn Ford. "Anne Dutton: An Eighteenth Century British Evangelical Woman Writer." *Ashland Theological Journal* 30 (1998): 51–56.

Westerkamp, Marilyn J. "Anne Hutchinson, Sectarian Mysticism, and the Puritan Order." *Church History* 59 (December 1990): 482–96.

———. *Women and Religion in Early America, 1600–1850: The Puritan and Evangelical Traditions.* New York: Routledge, 1999.

5. Women Organizing for Mission and Reform

Bass, Dorothy. "Their Prodigious Influence: Women, Religion and Reform in Antebellum America." In *Women of Spirit: Female Leadership in the Jewish and Christian Traditions*, edited by Rosemary Radford Ruether and Eleanor McLaughlin, 280–300. New York: Simon and Schuster, 1979.

Beaver, R. Pierce. *American Protestant Women in World Mission: History of the First Feminist Movement in North America.* Rev. ed. Grand Rapids, Mich.: Eerdmans, 1980.

Bendroth, Margaret Lamberts. *Fundamentalism and Gender: 1875 to the Present.* New Haven, Conn.: Yale University Press, 1993.

Berkeley, Kathleen C. " 'Colored Ladies Also Contributed': Black Women's Activities from Benevolence to Social Welfare, 1866–1896." In *Church and Community Among Black Southerners, 1865–1900*, edited by Donald Nieman, 327–49. New York: Garland, 1994.

Bowie, Fiona et al., eds. *Women and Missions: Past and Present: Anthropological and Historical Perceptions.* Providence, R.I.: Berg, 1993.

Boylan, Anne M. "Evangelical Womanhood in Nineteenth-Century America: The Role of Women in Sunday Schools." In *Unspoken Worlds: Women's Religious Lives*, edited by Nancy Auer Falk and Rita M. Gross, 166–78. 2nd ed. Belmont, Calif.: Wadsworth, 1989.

Brackney, William H. "Helen B. Montgomery 1861–1934, Lucy W. Peabody 1861–1949: Jesus Christ, the Great Emancipator of Women." In *Mission Legacies: Biographical Studies of Leaders of the Modern Missionary Movement*, edited by Gerald H. Anderson et al., 62–70. Maryknoll, N.Y.: Orbis, 1994.

Brasher, Brenda E. *Godly Women: Fundamentalism and Female Power*. New Brunswick, N.J.: Rutgers University Press, 1998.

Cott, Nancy. *The Bonds of Womanhood: Woman's Sphere in New England, 1780–1835*. New Haven, Conn.: Yale University Press, 1977.

————. "Young Women in the Second Great Awakening in New England." *Feminist Studies* 3 (1975): 15–29.

DeBerg, Betty A. *Ungodly Women: Gender and the First Wave of American Fundamentalism*. Minneapolis: Fortress Press, 1990.

Deichmann,Wendy J. "Domesticity with a Difference: Woman's Sphere, Women's Leadership, and the Founding of the Baptist Missionary Training School." *American Baptist Quarterly* 9 (September 1990): 141–57.

Douglas, Ann. *The Feminization of American Culture*. New York: Knopf, 1977.

Epstein, Barbara Leslie. *The Politics of Domesticity: Women, Evangelism, and Temperance in Nineteenth-Century America*. Middletown, Conn.: Wesleyan University Press, 1981.

Fishburn, Janet Forsythe. *The Fatherhood of God and the Victorian Family: The Social Gospel in America*. Philadelphia: Fortress Press, 1981.

Flexner, Eleanor. *Century of Struggle: The Woman's Rights Movement in the United States*. Cambridge, Mass.: Belknap, 1975.

Gifford, Carolyn De Swarte. "'For God and Home and Native Land': The W.C.T.U.'s Image of Woman in the Late Nineteenth Century." In *Women in New Worlds: Historical Perspectives on the Wesleyan Tradition*, edited by Hilah F. Thomas and Rosemary Skinner Keller, 310–27. Nashville: Abingdon, 1981.

————. "Sisterhoods of Service and Reform: Organized Methodist Women in the Late 19th Century—an Essay on the State of Research." *Methodist History* 24 (October 1985): 15–30.

Harris, Barbara. *Beyond Her Sphere: Women and the Professions in American History*. Westport, Conn.: Greenwood, 1978.

Harrison, Beverly Wildung. "Early Feminists and the Clergy: A Case Study in the Dynamics of Secularization." *Review and Expositor* 72 (Winter 1975): 41–52.

Haynes, Carolyn. "Women and Protestantism in Nineteenth-Century America." In *Perspectives on American Religion and Culture*, edited by Peter W. Williams, 300–318. Malden, Mass.: Blackwell, 1999.

Hersh, Blanche Glassman. *The Slavery of Sex: Feminist Abolitionists in America*. Urbana, Ill.: University of Illinois Press, 1978.

————. "To Make the World Better: Protestant Women in the Abolitionist Movement." In *Triumph over Silence: Women in Protestant History*, edited by Richard L. Greaves, 173–202. Westport, Conn.: Greenwood, 1985.

Hill, Patricia Ruth. *The World Their Household: The American Woman's Foreign Mission Movement and Cultural Transformation, 1870–1920*. Ann Arbor, Mich.: University of Michigan Press, 1985.

Kirkley, Evelyn A. "'This Work is God's Cause': Religion in the Southern Woman Suffrage Movement, 1880–1920." *Church History* 59 (December 1990): 507–22.

Kirkpatrick, Frank G. "From Shackles to Liberation: Religion, the Grimké Sisters and Dissent." In *Women, Religion and Social Change*, ed. Yvonne Haddad and Ellison Findley, 433–55. Albany, N.Y.: State University Press of New York, 1985.

Lee, Susan Dye. "Evangelical Domesticity: The Women's Temperance Crusade of 1873–1874." In *Women in New Worlds: Historical Perspectives on the Wesleyan Tradition*, edited by Hilah F. Thomas and Rosemary Skinner Keller, 293–309. Nashville: Abingdon, 1981.

McCants, David A. "Evangelicalism and Nineteenth-Century Woman's Rights: A Case Study of Angelina E. Grimké." *Perspectives in Religious Studies* 14 (Spring 1987): 39–57.

McDannell, Colleen. *The Christian Home in Victorian America, 1840–1900*. Bloomington, Ind.: Indiana University Press, 1986.

Meckel, Richard A. "Educating a Ministry of Mothers: Evangelical Maternal Associations, 1815–1860." *Journal of the Early Republic* 2 (1982): 403–23.

Melder, Keith E. *Beginnings of Sisterhood: The American Woman's Rights Movement, 1800–1850*. Studies in the Life of Women, edited by Gerda Lerner. New York: Schocken, 1977.

————. "Ladies Bountiful: Organized Women's Benevolence in Early Nineteenth-Century America." *New York History* 48 (July 1967): 231–54.

Nutt, Rick. "Robert Lewis Dabney, Presbyterians and Women's Suffrage." *Journal of Presbyterian History* 62 (Winter 1984): 339–53.

Reynolds, David S. "The Feminization Controversy: Sexual Stereotypes and the Paradoxes of Piety in Nineteenth-Century America." *New England Quarterly* 53 (1980): 96–106.

Robert, Dana Lee. *American Women in Mission: A Social History of Their Thought and Practice.* Macon, Ga.: Mercer University Press, 1996.

Rossi, Alice S. *The Feminist Papers: From Adams to de Beauvoir.* New York: Bantam, 1974.

Ruether, Rosemary Radford, and Rosemary Skinner Keller, eds. *Women and Religion in America.* Vol. I, *The Nineteenth Century.* San Francisco: Harper and Row, 1981.

Ryan, Mary P. *Womanhood in America from Colonial Times to the Present.* 3rd. ed. New York: Franklin Watts, 1983.

Smith-Rosenberg, Carroll. "Beauty, the Beast and the Militant Woman: A Case Study in Sex Roles and Social Stress in Jacksonian America." *American Quarterly* 23 (October 1971): 562–84.

Sumners, Bill. "Southern Baptists and Women's Right to Vote, 1910–1920." *Baptist History and Heritage* 12 (January 1977): 45–51.

Taves, Ann. "Feminization Revisited: Protestantism and Gender at the Turn of the Century." In *Women and Twentieth-Century Protestantism,* edited by Margaret Lamberts Bendroth and Virginia Lieson Brereton, 304–24. Chicago: University of Illinois Press, 2002.

———. "Women and Gender in American Religion (s)." *Religious Studies Review* 18 (October 1992): 263–70.

Welter, Barbara. "The Cult of True Womanhood, 1820–1860." In *Dimity Convictions: The American Woman in the Nineteenth Century,* 21–41. Athens, Ohio: Ohio University Press, 1976.

———. "The Feminization of American Religion, 1800–1860." In *Dimity Convictions: The American Woman in the Nineteenth Century,* 83–102. Athens, Ohio: Ohio University Press, 1976.

———. "She Hath Done What She Could: Protestant Women's Missionary Careers in Nineteenth-Century America." In *Women in American Religion,* edited by Janet Wilson James, 111–25. Philadelphia: University of Pennsylvania Press, 1980.

Yohn, Susan M. "'Let Christian Women Set the Example in Their Own Gifts': The 'Business' of Protestant Women's Organizations." In *Women and Twentieth-Century Protestantism,* edited by Margaret Lamberts Bendroth and Virginia Lieson Brereton, 213–35. Urbana, Ill.: University of Ilinois Press, 2002.

6. NINETEENTH-CENTURY PREACHERS AND SCHOLARS

Andrews, William L., ed. *Sisters of the Spirit: Three Black Women's Autobiographies of the Nineteenth Century.* Bloomington, Ind.: Indiana University Press, 1986.

Bendroth, Margaret L. "Millennial Themes and Private Visions: The Problem of 'Woman's Place' in Religious History." *Fides et Historia* 20 (June 1988): 24–30.

———. "Religion, Feminism, and the American Family: 1865–1920." In *Religion, Feminism, and the Family,* edited by Anne E. Carr and Mary Stewart Van Leeuwen, 183–96. Louisville: Westminster John Knox, 1996.

Bilhartz, Terry D. "Sex and the Second Great Awakening: The Feminization of American Religion Reconsidered." In *Belief and Behavior: Essays in the New Religious History,* edited by Robert P. Swierenga and Philip R. VanderMeer, 117–35. New Brunswick, N.J.: Rutgers University Press, 1991.

Billington, Lewis. "Female Laborers in the Church: Women Preachers in the Northeastern United States, 1790–1840." *Journal of American Studies* 19 (1985): 369–94.

Blauvelt, Martha Tomhave. "Women and Revivalism." In *Women and Religion in America.* Vol. I, *The Nineteenth Century,* edited by Rosemary Radford Ruether and Rosemary Skinner Keller, 1–45. San Francisco: Harper and Row, 1981.

Blumhofer, Edith. *Aimee Semple McPherson: Everybody's Sister.* Grand Rapids, Mich.: Eerdmans, 1993.

———. "A Confused Legacy: Reflections of Evangelical Attitudes Toward Ministering Women in the Past Century." *Fides et Historia* 22 (Winter/Spring 1990): 49–61.

———. "Women in Evangelicalism and Pentecostalism." In *Women and Church: The Challenge of Ecumenical Solidarity in an Age of Alienation,* edited by Melanie A. May, 3–7. Grand Rapids, Mich.: Eerdmans, 1991.

Bordin, Ruth. *Frances Willard: A Biography.* Chapel Hill, N.C.: University of North Carolina Press, 1986.

Boylan, Anne M. "Evangelical Womanhood in Nineteenth-Century America: The Role of Women in Sunday Schools." In *Unspoken Worlds: Women's Religious Lives,* edited by Nancy Auer Falk and Rita M. Gross, 166–78. Belmont, Calif.: Wadsworth, 1989.

Brekus, Catherine A. *Strangers and Pilgrims: Female Preaching in America, 1740–1845.* Chapel Hill, N.C.: University of North Carolina Press, 1998.

Cazden, Elizabeth. *Antoinette Brown Blackwell.* Old Westbury, N.Y.: Feminist Press, 1983.

Dayton, Donald W. "Evangelical Roots of Feminism." *The Covenant Quarterly* 34 (November 1976): 41–56.

Dayton, Donald W., and Lucille Sider Dayton. "Women as Preachers: Evangelical Precedents." *Christianity Today* 19 (23 May 1975): 4–7.

Dayton, Lucille Sider, and Donald W. Dayton. "'Your Daughters Shall Prophesy': Feminism in the Holiness Movement." *Methodist History* 14 (January 1976): 67–92.

Dougherty, Mary A. "The Methodist Deaconess: A Case of Religious Feminism." *Methodist History* 21 (January 1983): 90–98.

Gifford, Carolyn De Swarte. "'My Own Methodist Hive': Frances Willard's Faith as Disclosed in Her Journal, 1855–1870." In *Spirituality and Social Responsibility: Vocational Vision of Women in the United Methodist Tradition,* edited by Rosemary Skinner Keller, 80–97. Nashville: Abingdon, 1993.

———. "Politicizing the Sacred Texts: Elizabeth Cady Stanton and the *Woman's Bible.*" In vol. 1, *Searching the Scriptures,* edited by Elisabeth Schüssler Fiorenza, 52–63. New York: Crossroad, 1993.

Green, Roger J. *Catherine Booth: A Biography of the Co-Founder of the Salvation Army.* Grand Rapids, Mich.: Baker, 1996.

———. "Settled Views: Catherine Booth and Female Ministry." *Methodist History* 31 (April 1993): 131–47.

Hardesty, Nancy A. "No Rights But Human Rights." *Perkins Journal* 35 (Fall 1981): 58–62.

———. *Women Called to Witness: Evangelical Feminism in the Nineteenth Century.* Nashville: Abingdon, 1984.

———. *Your Daughters Shall Prophesy: Revivalism and Feminism in the Age of Finney.* Brooklyn: Carlson, 1991.

Hardesty, Nancy A., Lucille Sider Dayton, and Donald W. Dayton. "Women in the Holiness Movement: Feminism in the Evangelical Tradition." In *Women of Spirit: Female Leadership in the Jewish and Christian Traditions,* edited by Rosemary Radford Ruether and Eleanor McLaughlin, 226–54. New York: Simon and Schuster, 1979.

Hardesty, Nancy A., and Adrienne Israel. "Amanda Berry Smith: A 'Downright, Outright Christian.'" In *Spirituality and Social Responsibility: Vocational Vision of Women in the United Methodist Tradition,* edited by Rosemary Skinner Keller, 60–79. Nashville: Abingdon, 1993.

Hassey, Janette. *No Time for Silence: Evangelical Women in Public Ministry around the Turn of the Century.* Grand Rapids, Mich.: Academie, 1986.

Hill, Suzan E. "The Woman's Bible: Reformulating Tradition." *Radical Religion* 8 (1977): 23–30.

Huber, Elaine C. "They Weren't Prepared to Hear: A Closer Look at the *Woman's Bible.*" *Andover Newton Quarterly* 16 (March 1976): 271–76.

Hudson, Mary Lin. "'Shall Woman Preach?' Louisa Woosley and the Cumberland Presbyterian Church." *American Presbyterians* 68 (Winter 1990): 221–30.

Humez, Jean M. "'My Spirit Eye': Some Functions of Spiritual and Visionary Experience in the Lives of Five Black Women Preachers, 1810–1880." In *Women and the Structure of Society,* edited by Barbara J. Harris and JoAnn K. McNamara, 129–43. Durham, N.C.: Duke University Press, 1984.

Keefe, Alice A. "When God Says 'Go': Active Mysticism and the Practice of Discernment." *Religious Studies and Theology* 17 (June 1998): 19–32.

Keller, Rosemary Skinner. "The Deaconess: 'New Woman' of Late Nineteenth-Century Methodism." *Explore: A Journal of Theology* 5 (1979): 33–41.

———. "Women and the Nature of Ministry in the United Methodist Tradition." *Methodist History* 22 (January 1984): 99–114.

Kern, Kathi. *Mrs. Stanton's Bible.* Ithaca, N.Y.: Cornell University Press, 2001.

McFadden, Margaret. "The Ironies of Pentecost: Phoebe Palmer, World Evangelism, and Female Networks." *Methodist History* 31 (January 1993): 63–75.

McKay, Nellie Y. "Nineteenth-Century Black Women's Spiritual Autobiographies: Religious Faith and Self-Empowerment." In *Perspectives on American Methodism: Interpretive Essays,* edited by Russell E. Richey et al., 178–91. Nashville: Kingswood, 1993.

Murdoch, Norman H. "Female Ministry in the Thought and Work of Catherine Booth." *Church History* 53 (September 1984): 348–62.

Norwood, Frederick A. "Expanding Horizons: Women in the Methodist Movement." In *Triumph over Silence: Women in Protestant History,* edited by Richard L. Greaves, 151–72. Westport, Conn.: Greenwood, 1985.

Pellauer, Mary D. *Toward a Tradition of Feminist Theology: The Religious Social Thought of Elizabeth Cady Stanton, Susan B. Anthony, and Anna Howard Shaw.* Brooklyn: Carlson, 1991.

Rasche, Ruth W. "The Deaconess Sisters: Pioneer Professional Women." In *Hidden Histories in the United Church of Christ,* edited by Barbara Brown Zikmund, 95–109. New York: United Church Press, 1984.

Raser, Harold E. *Phoebe Palmer: Her Life and Thought.* Lewiston, N.Y.: Edwin Mellen, 1987.

Schmidt, Jean Miller. "Toward a Feminist Theology in the Wesleyan Tradition: Insights from Nineteenth and Early Twentieth-Century American Methodists." In *Wesleyan Theology Today: A Bicentennial Theological Consultation,* edited by Theodore Runyon, 137–42. Nashville: United Methodist Publishing House, 1985.

Schüssler Fiorenza, Elisabeth. "Transforming the Legacy of *The Woman's Bible.*" In vol. I, *Searching the Scriptures,* edited by Elisabeth Schüssler Fiorenza, 1–23. New York: Crossroad, 1993.

Selby, Gary. "'Your Daughters Shall Prophesy': Rhetorical Strategy in the 19th Century Debate over Women's Right to Preach." *Restoration Quarterly* 34 (1992): 151–67.

Smith, Amanda Berry. *An Autobiography: The Story of the Lord's Dealings with Mrs. Amanda Smith, the Colored Evangelist.* Introduction by Jualynne E. Dodson. Schomburg Library of Nineteenth-Century Black Women Writers. New York: Oxford University Press, 1988.

Smith-Rosenberg, Carroll. "Women and Religious Revivals: Anti-Ritualism, Liminality and the Emergence of the American Bourgeosie." In *The Evangelical Tradition in America,* edited by Leonard I. Sweet, 199–231. Macon, Ga.: Mercer University Press, 1984.

Smylie, James. "*The Woman's Bible* and the Spiritual Crisis." *Soundings* 59 (Fall 1976): 305–28.

Spiritual Narratives. Introduction by Sue E. Houchins. Schomburg Library of Nineteenth-Century Black Women Writers. New York: Oxford University Press, 1988

Stevenson-Moessner, Jeanne. "Elizabeth Cady Stanton, Reformer to Revolutionary: A Theological Trajectory." *Journal of the American Academy of Religion* 62 (Fall 1994): 673–97.

Strong, Douglas M. "The Crusade for Women's Rights and the Formative Antecedents of the Holiness Movement." *Wesleyan Theological Journal* 27 (Spring/Fall 1992): 132–60.

Study Guide to The Woman's Bible. Seattle: Coalition Task Force on Women and Religion, 1975.

Tucker, Cynthia Grant. *Prophetic Sisterhood: Liberal Women Ministers of the Frontier, 1880–1930.* Bloomington, Ind.: Indiana University Press, 1994.

Walker, Pamela J. "A Chaste and Fervid Eloquence: Catherine Booth and the Ministry of Women in the Salvation Army." In *Women Preachers and Prophets through Two Millennia of Christianity,* edited by Beverly Mayne Kienzle and Pamela J. Walker, 288–302. Berkeley: University of California Press, 1998.

Weisenfeld, Judith. "We Have Been Believers: Patterns of African American Women's Religiosity." In *This Far By Faith: Readings in African-American Women's Religious Biography,* ed. Judith Weisenfeld and Richard Newman, 1–18. New York: Routledge, 1996.

Weiser, Frederick Sheely. "The Lutheran Deaconess Movement." *Lutheran Forum* 28 (February 1994): 20, 22–24.

White, Charles Edward. "The Beauty of Holiness: The Career of Phoebe Palmer." *Methodist History* 25 (January 1987): 76–90.

———. *The Beauty of Holiness: Phoebe Palmer as Theologian, Revivalist, Feminist, and Humanitarian.* Grand Rapids, Mich.: Asbury, 1986.

The Woman's Bible. Part I, Comments on Genesis, Exodus, Leviticus, Numbers, and Deuteronomy. Part II, Comments on the Old and New Testaments from Joshua to Revelation. New York: European Publishing, 1892, 1895. Reprint. New York: Arno, 1972.

Zikmund, Barbara Brown. "Biblical Arguments and Women's Place in the Church." In *The Bible and Social Reform,* edited by Ernest R. Sandeen, 85–104. Philadelphia: Fortress Press, 1982.

———. "The Struggle for the Right to Preach." In *Women and Religion in America,* Vol. I, *The Nineteenth Century,* edited by Rosemary Radford Ruether and Rosemary Skinner Keller, 193–241. San Francisco: Harper and Row, 1981.

Zink-Sawyer, Beverly A. "From Preachers to Suffragists: Enlisting the Pulpit in the Early Movement for Women's Rights." *ATQ (American Transcendental Quarterly)* 14 (2000): 193–209.

———. *From Preachers to Suffragists: Woman's Rights and Religious Conviction in the Lives of Three Nineteenth-Century American Clergywomen.* Louisville: Westminster John Knox, 2003.

7. American Women in Catholicism and Sectarianism

Baker, Joan. "Women in Utopia: The Nineteenth-Century Experience." In *Utopias: The American Experience,* edited by Gairdner Moment and Otto Kraushaar, 56–71. Metuchen, N.J.: Scarecrow, 1980.

Bednarowski, Mary Farrell. "Outside the Mainstream: Women's Religion and Women Religious Leaders in Nineteenth-Century America." *Journal of the American Academy of Religion* 48 (June 1980): 207–31.

Braude, Ann D. "The Perils of Passivity: Women's Leadership in Spiritualism and Christian Science." In *Women's Leadership in Marginal Religions: Explorations Outside the Mainstream*, edited by Catherine Wessinger, 55–67. Urbana, Ill.: University of Illinois Press, 1993.

———. "Spirits Defend the Rights of Women: Spiritualism and Changing Sex Roles in Nineteenth-Century America." In *Women, Religion, and Social Change*, edited by Yvonne Haddad and Ellison Findly, 419–31. Albany, N.Y.: State University of New York Press, 1985.

Brewer, Priscilla J. "'Tho' of the Weaker Sex': A Reassessment of Gender Equality among the Shakers." *Signs: Journal of Women in Culture and Society* 16 (Spring 1991): 609–35.

Campbell, D'Ann. "Woman's Life in Utopia: The Shaker Experiment in Sexuality Reappraised, 1810–1860." *New England Quarterly* 51 (March 1978): 23–38.

Coburn, Carol K., and Martha Smith. *Spirited Lives: How Nuns Shaped Catholic Culture and American Life, 1836–1920.* Chapel Hill, N.C.: University of North Carolina Press, 1999.

Denig, Stephen. "Catholic Education in the United States: Meeting the Challenge of Immigration." In *Commitment to Diversity: Catholics and Education in a Changing World*, edited by Mary Eaton et al., 210–39. London: Cassell, 2000.

Evans, Vella Neil. "Empowerment and Mormon Women's Publications." In *Women and Authority: Re-Emerging Mormon Feminism*, edited by Maxine Hanks, 49–68. Salt Lake City: Signature, 1992.

Ewens, Mary. "Removing the Veil: The Liberated American Nun." In *Women of Spirit: Female Leadership in the Jewish and Christian Traditions*, edited by Rosemary Radford Ruether and Eleanor McLaughlin, 256–78. New York: Simon and Schuster, 1979.

———. *The Role of the Nun in Nineteenth-Century America.* New York: Arno, 1978.

Foster, Lawrence. *Women, Family, and Utopia: Communal Experiments of the Shakers, the Oneida Community, and the Mormons.* Syracuse: Syracuse University Press, 1991.

Fox, Margery. "Protest in Piety: Christian Science Revisited." *International Journal of Women's Studies* 1 (July/August 1978): 401–16.

Gottlieb, Robert, and Peter Wiley. "The Priesthood and the Black Widow Spider." In *America's Saints: The Rise of Mormon Power*, 187–213. New York: Putnam, 1984.

Humez, Jean M. "'Weary of Petticoat Government': The Specter of Female Rule in Early Nineteenth-Century Shaker Politics." *Communal Societies* 11 (1991): 1–17.

Iadarola, Antoinette. "The American Catholic Bishops and Woman: From the Nineteenth Amendment to ERA." In *Women, Religion, and Social Change*, edited by Yvonne Haddad and Ellison Findly, 457–76. Albany, N.Y.: State University of New York Press, 1985.

Jorgensen, Danny. "Gender-Inclusive Images of God: A Sociological Interpretation of Early Shakerism and Mormonism." *Nova Religio* 4 (October 2000): 66–85.

Kenneally, James J. "Eve, Mary and the Historians: American Catholicism and Women." In *Women in American Religion*, edited by Janet Wilson James, 190–206. Philadelphia: University of Pennsylvania Press, 1980.

———. *The History of American Catholic Women.* New York: Crossroad, 1990.

Kern, Louis J. *An Ordered Love: Sex Roles and Sexuality in Victorian Utopias—the Shakers, the Mormons, and the Oneida Community.* Chapel Hill, N.C.: University of North Carolina Press, 1981.

Klaw, Spencer. *Without Sin: The Life and Death of the Oneida Community.* New York: Penguin, 1993.

Klee-Hartzell, Marlyn. "Family Love, True Womanliness, Motherhood, and the Socialization of Girls in the Oneida Community, 1848–1880." In *Women in Spiritual and Communitarian Societies in the United States*, edited by Wendy Chmielewski et al., 182–200. Syracuse: Syracuse University Press, 1993.

Kolmer, Elizabeth. "Catholic Women Religious and Women's History: A Survey of the Literature." In *Women in American Religion*, edited by Janet Wilson James, 127–39. Philadelphia: University of Pennsylvania Press, 1980.

McDannell, Colleen. "Catholic Domesticity 1860–1960." In *American Catholic Women: A Historical Exploration*, edited by Karen Kennelly, 48–80. New York: Macmillan, 1989.

McDonald, Jean A. "Mary Baker Eddy and the Nineteenth-Century 'Public' Woman: A Feminist Reappraisal." *Journal of Feminist Studies in Religion* 2 (1986): 89–111.

Madsen, Carol Cornwall. "Mormon Women and the Temple: Toward a New Understanding." In *Sisters in Spirit: Mormon Women in Historical and Cultural Perspective*, edited by Lavina Fielding Anderson and Maureen Ursenbach Beecher, 80–110. Urbana, Ill.: University of Illinois Press, 1987.

Marquis, Kathy. "'Diamond Cut Diamond': The Mormon Wife vs. the True Woman, 1840–1890." In *Women in Spiritual and Communitarian Societies in the United States*, edited by Wendy Chmielewski et al., 169–81. Syracuse: Syracuse University Press, 1993.

Mercadante, Linda A. *Gender, Doctrine and God: The Shakers and Contemporary Theology.* Nashville: Abingdon, 1990.

Merrim, Stephanie, ed. *Feminist Perspectives on Sor Juana Inés de la Cruz.* Detroit: Wayne State University, 1991.

Moore, R. Laurence. "Spiritualist Medium: A Study of Female Professionalism in Victorian America." *American Quarterly* 27 (May 1975): 200–221.

Muncy, Raymond Lee. *Sex and Marriage in Utopian Communities.* Bloomington, Ind.: Indiana University Press, 1973.

Newby, Alison M. "Shakers as Feminists? Shakerism as a Vanguard in the Antebellum American Search for Female Autonomy and Independence." In *Locating the Shakers*, edited by Mick Gidley, 96–105. Exeter, England: University of Exeter Press, 1990.

Newell, Linda King. "Gifts of the Spirit: Women's Share." In *Sisters in Spirit: Mormon Women in Historical and Cultural Perspective*, edited by Lavina Fielding Anderson and Maureen Ursenbach Beecher, 111–50. Urbana, Ill.: University of Illinois Press, 1987.

Nickless, Karen, and Pamela Nickless. "Sexual Equality and Economic Authority: The Shaker Experience, 1784–1900." In *Women in Spiritual and Communitarian Societies in the United States*, edited by Wendy Chmielewski et al., 119–32. Syracuse: Syracuse University Press, 1993.

———. "Trustees, Deacons, and Deaconesses: The Temporal Role of the Shaker Sisters, 1820–1890." *Communal Societies* 7 (1987): 16–24.

Orsi, Robert. *Thank You, St. Jude: Women's Devotion to the Patron Saint of Hopeless Causes.* New Haven, Conn.: Yale University Press, 1996.

Owen, Alex. "Women and Nineteenth-Century Spiritualism: Strategies in the Subversion of Femininity." In *Disciplines of Faith: Studies in Religion, Politics, and Patriarchy*, edited by Jim Obelkevich, 130–53. New York: Routledge, 1987.

Procter-Smith, Marjorie. "'In the Line of the Female': Shakerism and Feminism." In *Women's Leadership in Marginal Religions: Explorations Outside the Mainstream*, edited by Catherine Wessinger, 23–40. Urbana, Ill.: University of Illinois Press, 1993.

Setta, Susan M. "When Christ Is a Woman: Theology and Practice in the Shaker Tradition." In *Unspoken Worlds: Women's Religious Lives*, edited by Nancy Auer Falk and Rita M. Gross, 221–32. Belmont, Calif.: Wadsworth, 1989.

Tavard, George H. *Juana Inés de la Cruz and the Theology of Beauty: The First Mexican Theology.* Notre Dame, Ind.: University of Notre Dame Press, 1991.

Thompson, Margaret Susan. "Women and American Catholicism, 1789–1989." In *Perspectives on the American Catholic Church, 1789–1989*, edited by Stephen Vicchio and Virginia Geiger, 123–42. Westminster, Md.: Christian Classics, 1989.

———. "Women, Feminism, and the New Religious History: Catholic Sisters as a Case Study." In *Belief and Behavior: Essays in the New Religious History*, edited by Robert P. Swierenga and Philip R. VanderMeer, 136–63. New Brunswick, N.J.: Rutgers University Press, 1991.

Wayland-Smith, Ellen. "The Status and Self-Perception of Women in the Oneida Community." *Communal Societies* 8 (1988): 18–53.

Wenger, Tisa. "Female Christ and Feminist Foremother: The Many Lives of Ann Lee." *Journal of Feminist Studies in Religion* 18 (Fall 2002): 5–32.

Wilcox, Linda P. "The Mormon Concept of a Mother in Heaven." In *Sisters in Spirit: Mormon Women in Historical and Cultural Perspective*, edited by Lavina Fielding Anderson and Maureen Ursenbach Beecher, 64–77. Urbana, Ill.: University of Illinois Press, 1987.

Zikmund, Barbara Brown. "The Feminist Thrust of Sectarian Christianity." In *Women of Spirit: Female Leadership in the Jewish and Christian Traditions*, edited by Rosemary Radford Ruether and Eleanor McLaughlin, 206–24. New York: Simon and Schuster, 1979.

8. The Move toward Full Participation and
9. Agents of Transformation

Achtemeier, Elizabeth. "The Impossible Possibility: Evaluating the Feminist Approach to Bible and Theology." *Interpretation* 42 (January 1988): 45–57.

Becker, Carol E. "Women in Church Leadership—In But Still Out." *Dialog* 35 (Spring 1996): 144–48.

Behr-Sigel, Elisabeth, and Kallistos Ware. *The Ordination of Women in the Orthodox Church.* Geneva: WCC Publications, 2000.

Bendroth, Margaret Lamberts. *Fundamentalism and Gender, 1875 to the Present.* New Haven, Conn.: Yale University Press, 1993.

Bendroth, Margaret Lamberts, and Virginia Lieson Brereton, eds. *Women and Twentieth-Century Protestantism.* Urbana, Ill.: University of Illinois Press, 2002.

Bennett, Robert A. "The Power of Language in Worship." *Theology Today* 43 (January 1987): 546–51.

Berger, Teresa. *Women's Ways of Worship: Gender Analysis and Liturgical History.* Collegeville, Minn.: Liturgical Press, 1999.

Berry, Wanda Warren. "Images of Sin and Salvation in Feminist Theology." *Anglican Theological Review* 60 (January 1978): 25–54.

Bird, Phyllis A. *Missing Persons and Mistaken Identities: Women and Gender in Ancient Israel.* Minneapolis: Fortress Press, 1997.

Boyd, Lois A., and R. Douglas Brackenridge. *Presbyterian Women in America: Two Centuries of a Quest for Status.* Presbyterian Historical Society Contributions to the Study of Religion 9. Westport, Conn.: Greenwood, 1983.

———. "Presbyterian Women Ministers: A Historical Overview and Study of the Current Status of Women Pastors." In *The Pluralistic Vision: Presbyterians and Mainstream Protestant Education and Leadership,* edited by Milton J. Coalter et al., 289–307. Louisville: Westminster John Knox, 1992.

Brasher, Brenda E. *Godly Women: Fundamentalism and Female Power.* New Brunswick, N.J.: Rutgers University Press, 1998.

Brereton, Virginia, and Christa Klein. "American Women in Ministry: A History of Protestant Beginning Points." In *Women in American Religion,* edited by Janet Wilson James, 171–90. Philadelphia: University of Pennsylvania Press, 1980.

Burrow, Rufus. "Development of Womanist Theology: Some Chief Characteristics." *Asbury Theological Journal* 54 (Spring 1999): 41–57.

Cahill, Lisa Sowle. *Between the Sexes: Foundations for a Christian Ethics of Sexuality.* Philadelphia: Fortress Press, 1985.

Cannon, Katie G. *The Womanist Theology Primer—Remembering What We Never Knew: The Epistemology of Womanist Theology.* Louisville: Women's Ministries Program Area, National Ministries Division, Presbyterian Church (U.S.A.), 2001.

Caron, Gérald. "The Authority of the Bible Challenged by Feminist Hermeneutics." In *Women Also Journeyed with Him,* edited by Jean-Pierre Prévost, translated by Madeleine Beaumont, 153–78. Collegeville, Minn.: Liturgical Press, 2000.

Carroll, Jackson, Barbara Hargrove, and Adair Lummis. *Women of the Cloth: New Opportunity for the Churches.* New York: Harper and Row, 1983.

Carter, Norene, and Rosemary Radford Ruether. "Entering the Sanctuary: The Struggle for Priesthood in Contemporary Episcopalian and Roman Catholic Experience." In *Women of Spirit: Female Leadership in the Jewish and Christian Traditions,* edited by Rosemary Radford Ruether and Eleanor McLaughlin, 356–83. New York: Simon and Schuster, 1979.

Chang, Patricia Mei Yin. "Female Clergy in the Contemporary Protestant Church: A Current Assessment." *Journal for the Scientific Study of Religion* 36 (December 1997): 565–627.

Chaves, Mark. *Ordaining Women: Culture and Conflict in Religious Organizations.* Cambridge, Mass.: Harvard University Press, 1997.

Chaves, Mark, and James C. Cavendish. "Recent Changes in Women's Ordination Conflicts: The Effect of a Social Movement on Intraorganizational Controversy." *Journal for the Scientific Study of Religion* 36 (December 1997): 574–84.

Chittister, Joan. *Women, Ministry, and the Church.* New York: Paulist, 1983.

Christ, Carol P. *Diving Deep and Surfacing: Women Writers on Spiritual Quest.* Boston: Beacon, 1978.

Christ, Carol P., and Judith Plaskow, eds. *Womanspirit Rising: A Feminist Reader in Religion.* San Francisco: Harper and Row, 1979.

Coffman, Sue. "In the Beginning Were the Words: But Not the Same Yesterday, Today, and Forever: Textual Changes in Three Recent Hymnals." *Hymn* 44 (April 1993): 6–11.

Coll, Regina. *Women and Religion: A Reader for the Clergy.* New York: Paulist, 1982.

Collins, Mary. "Principles of Feminist Liturgy." In *Women at Worship: Interpretations of North American Diversity,* edited by Marjorie Procter-Smith and Janet R. Walton, 9–26. Louisville: Westminster John Knox, 1993.

Collins, Sheila. *A Different Heaven and Earth: A Feminist Perspective on Religion.* Valley Forge, Pa.: Judson, 1974.

———. "Toward a Feminist Theology." *Christian Century* 89 (2 August 1972): 796–99.

Cornwall Collective. *Your Daughters Shall Prophesy: Feminist Alternatives in Theological Education.* New York: Pilgrim, 1980.

Daly, Mary. *Beyond God the Father: Toward a Philosophy of Women's Liberation.* Boston: Beacon, 1973.

————. *The Church and the Second Sex*. With a New Feminist Postchristian Introduction by the Author. New York: Harper and Row, 1968; preface and introduction, 1975.

————. *Gyn/Ecology: The Metaethics of Radical Feminism*. Boston: Beacon, 1978.

Darr, Katheryn Pfisterer. *Far More Precious Than Jewels: Perspectives on Biblical Women*. Louisville: Westminster John Knox, 1991.

Dart, John. "Gender and the Bible: Evangelicals Wrangle over New Translations." *Christian Century* 119 (3–10 July 2002): 11–13.

————. "TNIV Bible Braves Gender-Inclusive World." *Christian Century* 119 (13–20 February 2002): 10–11.

DeBerg, Betty A. *Ungodly Women: Gender and the First Wave of American Fundamentalism*. Minneapolis: Fortress Press, 1990.

Dewey, Joanna. "Teaching the New Testament from a Feminist Perspective." *Theological Education* 26 (Autumn 1989): 86–105.

Dowd, Sharyn E. "Reflections on the Inclusive Language Debate." *Lexington Theological Quarterly* 27 (January 1992): 16–25.

Ebaugh, Helen Rose Fuchs. *Women in the Vanishing Cloister: Organizational Decline in Catholic Religious Orders in the United States*. New Brunswick, N.J.: Rutgers University Press, 1993.

Ermath, Margaret Sittler. *Adam's Fractured Rib: Observations on Women in the Church*. Philadelphia: Fortress Press, 1970.

FitzGerald, Kyriaki Karidoyanes. "The Inter-Orthodox Theological Consultation on Women in the Church." *Ecumenical Trends* 18 (March 1989): 33–36.

Gold, Victor, et al., eds. *The New Testament and Psalms: An Inclusive Version*. New York: Oxford University Press, 1995.

Goldenberg, Naomi B. *Changing of the Gods: Feminism and the End of Traditional Religions*. Boston: Beacon, 1979.

Goldstein, Valerie Saiving. "The Human Situation: A Feminine View." *Journal of Religion* 40 (April 1960): 100–112.

Grant, Jacquelyn. "Black Women and the Church." In *All the Women Are White, All the Blacks Are Men, But Some of Us Are Brave*, edited by Gloria T. Hull, et al., 141–52. Old Westbury, N.Y.: Feminist Press, 1982.

Gross, Rita M., ed. *Beyond Androcentrism: New Essays on Women and Religion*. Missoula, Mont.: Scholars, 1977.

Harkness, Georgia. *Women in Church and Society*. Nashville: Abingdon, 1972.

Harrison, Beverly Wildung. "Sexism and the Contemporary Church: When Evasion Becomes Complicity." In *Sexist Religion and Women in the Church: No More Silence!* edited by Alice Hageman, 195–216. New York: Association Press, 1974.

Hoover, Theressa. "Black Women and the Churches: Triple Jeopardy." In *Sexist Religion and Women in the Church: No More Silence!* edited by Alice Hageman, 63–76. New York: Association Press, 1974.

Hopko, Thomas, ed. *Women and the Priesthood*. Crestwood, N.Y.: St. Vladimir's Seminary, 1999.

Hunter, Edwina. "Weaving Life's Experiences into Women's Preaching." *Christian Ministry* 18 (September/October 1987): 14–17.

Ingwersen, Sonja Anne. "Mujerista Theology: A Theology for the Twenty-First Century." *Anglican Theological Review* 80 (Fall 1998): 642–44.

Isasi-Díaz, Ada María. "Mujerista Theology: A Challenge to Traditional Theology." In *Introduction to Christian Theology: Contemporary North American Perspectives*, edited by Roger A. Badham, 237–52. Louisville: Westminster John Knox, 1998.

————. *Mujerista Theology: A Theology for the Twenty-First Century*. Maryknoll, N.Y.: Orbis, 1996.

————. "On the Birthing Stool: Mujerista Liturgy." In *Women at Worship: Interpretations of North American Diversity*, edited by Marjorie Procter-Smith and Janet R. Walton, 191–210. Louisville: Westminster John Knox, 1993.

Jewett, Paul. *The Ordination of Women*. Grand Rapids, Mich.: Eerdmans, 1980.

Joyce, Paul. "Feminist Exegesis of the Old Testament: Some Critical Reflections." In *After Eve*, edited by Janet Martin Soskice, 1–9. Basingstoke, England: Marshal Pickering, 1990.

Keller, Catherine. "Inventing the Goddess: A Study in Ecclesial Backlash." *Christian Century* 111 (6 April 1994): 340–42.

Keller, Rosemary Skinner. "Women and the Nature of Ministry in the United Methodist Tradition." *Methodist History* 22 (January 1984): 99–114.

Klein, Christa Ressmeyer. "Women's Concerns in Theological Education." *Dialog* 24 (Winter 1985): 25–31.

Kraemer, Barbara. "Sisters and Brothers: An Evolved and Evolving Religious Life." In *The Catholic Church in the Twentieth Century: Renewing and Reimaging the City of God*, edited by John G. Deedy, 37–55. Collegeville, Minn.: Liturgical, 2000.

Krugler, John D., and David Weinberg-Kinsey. "Equality of Leadership: The Ordinations of Sarah E. Dickson and Margaret E. Towner in the Presbyterian Church in the U.S.A." *American Presbyterians* 68 (Winter 1990): 245–57.

Kyle, Sharon. "Truly, Madly, Deeply: Women's Experience of Preaching." *Anvil* 14, no. 4 (1997): 254–61.

Lehman, Edward. "Organizational Resistance to Women in Ministry." *Sociological Analysis: A Journal in the Sociology of Religion* 42 (Summer 1981): 101–18.

Limouris, Gennadios. "Women in Orthodoxy." *One World* 150 (November 1989): 5–7.

Maeckelberghe, Els. "Across the Generations in Feminist Theology: From Second to Third Wave Feminisms." *Feminist Theology* 23 (January 2000): 63–69.

McFague, Sallie. *Metaphorical Theology: Models of God in Religious Language*. Philadelphia: Fortress Press, 1982.

Micks, Marianne H. *Our Search for Identity: Humanity in the Image of God*. Philadelphia: Fortress Press, 1982.

Miller-McLemore, Bonnie J. "Feminist Theory in Pastoral Theology." In *Feminist and Womanist Pastoral Theology*, edited by Brita L. Gill-Austern and Bonnie J. Miller-McLemore, 77–94. Nashville: Abingdon, 1999.

Milne, Pamela J. "Feminist Interpretations of the Bible: Then and Now." *Bible Review* 8 (October 1992): 38–43, 52–55.

Mitchell, Norma. "From Social to Radical Feminism: A Survey of Emerging Diversity in Methodist Women's Organizations, 1869–1974." *Methodist History* 13 (April 1975): 21–44.

Morgan, Robert. "Feminist Theological Interpretation of the New Testament." In *After Eve*, edited by Janet Martin Soskice, 10–37. Basingstoke, England: Marshal Pickering, 1990.

Morton, Nelle. *The Journey Is Home*. Boston: Beacon, 1985.

Murray, Pauli. "Black Theology and Feminist Theology: A Comparative View." In *Black Theology: A Documentary History*, edited by Gayraud Wilmore and James H. Cone, 398–417. Maryknoll, N.Y.: Orbis, 1979.

Neal, Marie Augusta. "Ministry of American Catholic Sisters: The Vowed Life in Church Renewal." In *Religious Institutions and Women's Leadership: New Roles Inside the Mainstream*, edited by Catherine Wessinger, 231–43. Columbia, S.C.: University of South Carolina Press, 1996.

Nesbitt, Paula D. "Dual Ordination Tracks: Differential Benefits and Costs for Men and Women Clergy." *Sociology of Religion* 54 (Spring 1993): 13–30.

———. *Feminization of the Clergy in America: Occupational and Organizational Perspectives*. New York: Oxford University Press, 1997.

Neu, Diann. "Women-Church Transforming Liturgy." In *Women at Worship: Interpretations of North American Diversity*, edited by Marjorie Procter-Smith and Janet R. Walton, 163–78. Louisville: Westminster John Knox, 1993.

Orthodox Women: Their Role and Participation in the Orthodox Church. Report on the Consultation of Orthodox Women, 11–17 September 1976. Agapia, Romania: World Council of Churches, Subunit on Women in Church and Society, 1976.

Parvey, Constance F., ed. *The Community of Women and Men in the Church: The Sheffield Report*. Philadelphia: Fortress Press, 1983.

Plaskow, Judith. *Sin, Sex, and Grace: Women's Experience and the Theologies of Reinhold Niebuhr and Paul Tillich*. Washington, D.C.: University Press of America, 1980.

The Power of Language Among the People of God and the Language About God: "Opening the Door": A Resource Document. New York: United Presbyterian Church in the U .S.A., n.d.

Procter-Smith, Marjorie. *In Her Own Rite: Constructing Feminist Liturgical Tradition*. Nashville: Abingdon, 1990.

Reilly, Anne K. "Speaking of God in the Church: Is Inclusive Language a Possibility in Our Worship Life?" *Church and Society* 89 (November–December 1998): 73–83.

"Re-re-imagining in Minnesota." *Christian Century* 112 (20–27 December 1995): 1239–40.

Riley, Maria. "Religious Life and Women's Issues." In *Journey in Faith and Fidelity: Women Shaping Religious Life for a Renewed Church*, edited by Nadine Foley, 242–59. New York: Continuum, 1999.

Ringe, Sharon H. "Women and the Viability of Theological Education." *Ministerial Formation* 70 (July 1995): 19–21.

Rogers, Carole G. *Poverty, Chastity, and Change: Lives of Contemporary American Nuns*. New York: Twayne, 1996.

Ruether, Rosemary Radford. "Crisis in Sex and Race: Black Theology vs. Feminist Theology." *Christianity and Crisis* 34 (15 April 1974): 67–73.

———. "Christianity and Women in the Modern World." In *Today's Woman in World Religions*, edited by Arvind Sharma, 267–301. Albany, N.Y.: State University of New York Press, 1994.

———. *New Woman/New Earth: Sexist Ideologies and Human Liberation*. New York: Seabury, 1975.

———. *Sexism and God-Talk: Toward a Feminist Theology*. Boston: Beacon, 1984.

———. *Womanguides: Readings Toward a Feminist Theology*. Boston: Beacon, 1985.

———. "Women-Church: Emerging Feminist Liturgical Communities." In *Popular Religion*, edited by Norbert Greinacher and Norbert Mette, 52–59. Edinburgh: T. and T. Clark, 1986.

———. "The Women-Church Movement in Contemporary Christianity." In *Women's Leadership in Marginal Religions: Explorations Outside the Mainstream*, edited by Catherine Wessinger, 196–210. Urbana, Ill.: University of Illinois Press, 1993.

Russell, Letty M. "Feminism and the Church: A Quest for New Styles of Ministry." *Ministerial Formation* 55 (October 1991): 28–37.

———. *Human Liberation in a Feminist Perspective: A Theology*. Philadelphia: Westminster, 1974.

———. "Reflections on White Feminist Theology in the United States." In *Women's Visions: Theological Reflection, Celebration, Action*, edited by Ofelia Ortega, 102–11. Geneva: WCC, 1995.

Russell, Letty M. ed. *Changing Contexts of Our Faith*. Philadelphia: Fortress Press, 1985.

Russell, Letty M., and J. Shannon Clarkson, eds. *Dictionary of Feminist Theologies*. Louisville: Westminster John Knox, 1996.

Sakenfeld, Katharine Doob. "Feminist Biblical Interpretation." *Theology Today* 46 (July 1989): 154–68.

Schaper, Donna. "Liturgies Where Women Matter." *Christianity and Crisis* 53 (1 March 1993): 70–72.

Schmidt, Frederick W. *A Still Small Voice. Women, Ordination, and the Church*. Syracuse: Syracuse University Press, 1996.

Schmidt, Lynne. "Feminist Liturgies: Efforts Toward Creative Transformation in the Roman Catholic Church." In *Spiritual Nurture and Congregational Development*, edited by Perry LeFevre and W. Widick Schroeder, 87–104. Chicago: Exploration Press, 1984.

Scholer, David M. "Feminist Hermeneutics and Evangelical Biblical Interpretation." *Journal of the Evangelical Theological Society* 30 (December 1987): 407–20.

Schüssler Fiorenza, Elisabeth. *But SHE Said: Feminist Practices of Biblical Interpretation*. Boston: Beacon, 1992.

———. "Feminist Theology as a Critical Theology of Liberation." *Theological Studies* 36 (December 1975): 605–26.

Small, Joseph D. and John P. Burgess. "Evaluating 'Re-Imagining': Reformed and Reformulating." *Christian Century* 111 (6 April 1994): 342–44.

Smith, Karen S. "Catholic Women: Two Decades of Change." In *Church Polity and American Politics: Issues in Contemporary American Catholicism*, edited by Mary C. Segers, 313–33. New York: Garland, 1990.

Stone, Merlin. *When God Was a Woman*. New York: Harcourt Brace Jovanovich, 1976.

Stratton, Beverly J. *Out of Eden: Reading Rhetoric and Ideology in Genesis 2–3*. Sheffield, England: Sheffield Academic Press, 1995.

Stroup, Karen Leigh. "God Our Mother: A Call to Truly Inclusive God Language." *Lexington Theological Quarterly* 27 (January 1992): 10–15.

Talbert, Charles H. "The Church and Inclusive Language for God." *Perspectives in Religious Studies* 19 (Winter 1992): 421–39.

Thompson, Betty. *A Chance to Change: Women and Men in the Church*. Philadelphia: Fortress Press, 1982.

Thurston, Bonnie. "Language, Gender, and Prayer: The Importance of Naming God." *Lexington Theological Quarterly* 27 (January 1992): 3–9.

Tisdale, Leonora Tubbs. "Women's Ways of Communicating: A New Blessing for Preaching." In *Women, Gender, and Christian Community*, edited by Jane Dempsey Douglass and James F. Kay, 104–16. Louisville: Westminster John Knox, 1997.

Tolbert, Mary Ann. "Protestant Feminists and the Bible: On the Horns of a Dilemma." *Union Seminary Quarterly Review* 43 (1989): 1–17.

Trebbi, Diana. "Women-Church: Catholic Women Produce an Alternative Spirituality." In *In Gods We Trust: New Patterns of Religious Pluralism in America*, edited by Thomas Robbins and Dick Anthony, 347–51, 2nd ed. New Brunswick, N.J.: Transaction, 1990.

Trible, Phyllis. *God and the Rhetoric of Sexuality*. Philadelphia: Fortress Press, 1978.

———. "If the Bible's So Patriarchal, How Come I Love It?" *Bible Review* 8 (October 1992): 44–47, 55.

———. *Texts of Terror: Literary-Feminist Readings of Biblical Narratives*. Philadelphia: Fortress Press, 1984.

Wallace, Ruth A. *They Call Her Pastor: A New Role for Catholic Women*. Albany: State University of New York Press, 1992.

Walsh, Mary-Paula. "Mapping the Literature: 1968–1995." In *Feminism and Christian Tradition: An Annotated Bibliography and Critical Introduction to the Literature*, 15–28. Westport, Conn.: Greenwood, 1999.

Washbourn, Penelope. "Authority or Idolatry? Feminine Theology and the Church." *Christian Century* 92 (29 October 1975): 961–64.

Weidman, Judith, ed. *Women Ministers: How Women Are Redefining Traditional Roles.* San Francisco: Harper and Row, 1981.

Williams, Delores S. "Rituals of Resistance in Womanist Worship." In *Women at Worship: Interpretations of North American Diversity*, edited by Marjorie Procter-Smith and Janet R. Walton, 215–23. Louisville: Westminster John Knox, 1993.

———. "Womanist Theology." In *Women's Visions: Theological Reflection, Celebration, Action*, edited by Ofelia Ortega, 112–26. Geneva: WCC, 1995.

Wilson-Kastner, Patricia. "Christianity and the New Feminist Religions." *Christian Century* 98 (9 September 1981): 864–68.

———. *Faith, Feminism, and the Christ.* Philadelphia: Fortress Press, 1983.

Winter, Miriam Therese, Adair Lumis, and Allison Stokes. *Defecting in Place: Women Claiming Responsibility for Their Own Spiritual Lives.* New York: Crossroad, 1995.

"Women Clergy—How Their Presence Is Changing the Church: A Symposium by Five Women on the Seminary Campus." *Christian Century* 96 (7 February 1979): 122–28.

"Women's Conference and a Theological Crisis." *Christian Century* 111 (23–30 March 1994): 306–7.

Ziel, Catherine A. "Gender and Language: A Question of Authority." *Reformed Liturgy and Music* 28 (Spring 1994): 68–71.

Zikmund, Barbara Brown. "Ministry of Word and Sacrament: Women and Changing Understandings of Ordination." In *The Presbyterian Predicament: Six Perspectives*, edited by Milton J. Coalter et al., 134–58. Louisville: Westminster John Knox, 1990.

———. "Women and Theological Education: North American Reflections." *Ministerial Formation* 38 (June 1987): 7–8.

———. "Women as Preachers: Adding New Dimensions to Worship." *Journal of Women and Religion* 3 (Summer 1984): 12–16.

Zikmund, Barbara Brown, et al. "Women, Men and Styles of Clergy Leadership." *Christian Century* 115 (6 May 1998): 478–80, 482–86.

INDEX OF NAMES AND SUBJECTS

[Page numbers in italics indicate readings.]